MINORITIES AND THE MAKING OF POSTCOLONIAL STATES IN INTERNATIONAL LAW

The ideological function of the postcolonial 'national', 'liberal', and 'developmental' state inflicts various forms of marginalisation on minorities, but simultaneously justifies oppression in the name of national unity, equality and non-discrimination, and economic development. International law plays a central role in the ideological making of the postcolonial state in relation to postcolonial boundaries, the liberal-individualist architecture of rights, and the neoliberal economic vision of development. In this process, international law subjugates minority interests and in turn aggravates the problem of ethno-nationalism. Analysing the geneses of ethno-nationalism in postcolonial states, Mohammad Shahabuddin substantiates these arguments with in-depth case studies on the Rohingya and the hill people of the Chittagong Hill Tracts, against the historical backdrop of the minority question in Indian nationalist and constitutional discourse. Shahabuddin also proposes alternative international law frameworks for minorities.

MOHAMMAD SHAHABUDDIN is Professor of International Law and Human Rights at Birmingham Law School, University of Birmingham. He received a Leverhulme Trust Research Fellowship (2018–20) for completing this monograph. His previous book, *Ethnicity and International Law* (Cambridge, 2016), offered the first ever comprehensive analysis of how ethnicity shaped international law.

CAMBRIDGE STUDIES IN INTERNATIONAL
AND COMPARATIVE LAW: 154

Established in 1946, this series produces high quality, reflective and innovative scholarship in the field of public international law. It publishes works on international law that are of a theoretical, historical, cross-disciplinary or doctrinal nature. The series also welcomes books providing insights from private international law, comparative law and transnational studies which inform international legal thought and practice more generally.

The series seeks to publish views from diverse legal traditions and perspectives, and of any geographical origin. In this respect it invites studies offering regional perspectives on core *problématiques* of international law, and in the same vein, it appreciates contrasts and debates between diverging approaches. Accordingly, books offering new or less orthodox perspectives are very much welcome. Works of a generalist character are greatly valued and the series is also open to studies on specific areas, institutions or problems. Translations of the most outstanding works published in other languages are also considered.

After seventy years, Cambridge Studies in International and Comparative Law sets the standard for international legal scholarship and will continue to define the discipline as it evolves in the years to come.

Series Editors

Larissa van den Herik
Professor of Public International Law,
Grotius Centre for International Legal Studies, Leiden University

Jean d'Aspremont
Professor of International Law, University of Manchester and Sciences Po Law School

A list of books in the series can be found at the end of this volume.

MINORITIES AND THE MAKING OF POSTCOLONIAL STATES IN INTERNATIONAL LAW

MOHAMMAD SHAHABUDDIN

University of Birmingham

CAMBRIDGE
UNIVERSITY PRESS

University Printing House, Cambridge CB2 8BS, United Kingdom

One Liberty Plaza, 20th Floor, New York, NY 10006, USA

477 Williamstown Road, Port Melbourne, VIC 3207, Australia

314–321, 3rd Floor, Plot 3, Splendor Forum, Jasola District Centre, New Delhi – 110025, India

79 Anson Road, #06-04/06, Singapore 079906

Cambridge University Press is part of the University of Cambridge.

It furthers the University's mission by disseminating knowledge in the pursuit of education, learning, and research at the highest international levels of excellence.

www.cambridge.org
Information on this title: www.cambridge.org/9781108483674
DOI: 10.1017/9781108678773

© Mohammad Shahabuddin 2021

This publication is in copyright. Subject to statutory exception and to the provisions of relevant collective licensing agreements, no reproduction of any part may take place without the written permission of Cambridge University Press.

First published 2021

A catalogue record for this publication is available from the British Library.

ISBN 978-1-108-48367-4 Hardback

Cambridge University Press has no responsibility for the persistence or accuracy of URLs for external or third-party internet websites referred to in this publication and does not guarantee that any content on such websites is, or will remain, accurate or appropriate.

For my family

CONTENTS

Foreword page xi
Acknowledgements xv
Table of Cases xvii
List of Abbreviations xxi

Introduction 1

PART I **Ethno-nationalism and the Ideology of the Postcolonial State** 21

1 Geneses of Ethno-nationalism in Postcolonial States 23

   1.1 Introduction 23

   1.2 Nation-Building and Ethnic Accommodation 25

   1.3 Colonialism and Relative Ethnic Entitlements 28

   1.4 Capitalism and Ethnic Polarisation 32

   1.5 The Case of Anticolonial Ethno-nationalism in India 40

   1.6 Conclusion 54

2 Minorities and the 'Ideology' of the Postcolonial State 56

   2.1 Introduction 56

   2.2 'Ideology': What Is It? What Is It For? 57

2.3 The Three Ideologies of the Postcolonial State   64

2.4 Conclusion: International Law and the Postcolonial State   82

PART II   **International Law and the Postcolonial State   87**

3 The Postcolonial 'National' State: Boundaries and International Law   89

3.1 Introduction   89

3.2 International Law and Postcolonial Boundaries   90

3.3 The Case of the Rohingya in Myanmar   105

3.4 The Case of the CHT Hill People in Bangladesh   121

3.5 Conclusion   137

4 The Postcolonial 'Liberal' State: Self-determination, Minorities, and International Law   139

4.1 Introduction   139

4.2 The 'Nation' and Its 'Other' in the European Liberal Tradition   141

4.3 Minorities within the Liberal Framework of International Law   144

4.4 The Case of the Rohingya in Myanmar   175

4.5 The Case of the CHT Hill People in Bangladesh   186

4.6 Conclusion   196

5 The Postcolonial 'Developmental' State: Minority Perspectives and International Law   200

5.1 Introduction   200

5.2 Minorities in the International Law of Economic Development   202

5.3 'Development' in the International Law on Minority Rights   227

5.4 The Case of the Rohingya in Myanmar   240

5.5 The Case of the CHT Hill People in Bangladesh   261

5.6 Conclusion   275

Conclusion   277

Towards an Alternative Future for Minorities   280

Bibliography   305
Index   335

FOREWORD

The strong presence of ethno-nationalism in postcolonial states, and the associated politics, has often translated into the oppression of minorities and the denial to them of the right to self-determination. It has led to internal conflicts and gross violation of human rights, even genocide. Yet few scholars have addressed the matter in depth from an international law perspective. Mohammad Shahabuddin is an honourable exception. He has now written a timely, theoretically informed, and empirically grounded book on the subject of ethno-nationalism, postcolonial states, and international law. It continues the pathbreaking work Shahabuddin began with his previous monograph *Ethnicity and International Law* (2016). His work deserves to be read by anyone interested in the fate of minorities and subaltern groups in postcolonial states.

His theoretical framework is rich, albeit eclectic. He draws insights from liberalism, Marxism, and feminism. He weaves an analysis that relates the problem of ethno-nationalism to continuance of colonial boundaries, particular trajectories of development, the role of ethnic bourgeoisies, the nature and character of the postcolonial state, and the place of minority rights in the constitutional scheme of things. His deconstruction of the 'ideology' of ethno-nationalism and the postcolonial state draws from among others the 'critical hermeneutics' of John Thompson. In so far as the world of international law is concerned he relies on different strands of critical scholarship that include third world approaches to international law (TWAIL), feminist approaches to international law (FtAIL), and new approaches to international law (NAIL). His essential argument, made by all these three approaches in one form or another, is that international law is part of the problem.

The embrace of critical theory allows him to depart from existing work on minorities which essentially adopt a human rights perspective and identify in its matrix the shortcomings in the normative and institutional framework on minority rights. This strand of scholarship usually calls for more effective implementation, and at times a binding treaty to replace the 1992 UN Declaration on Minority Rights. Shahabuddin takes a different track. He argues that international law contributes to the problem of minority oppression by helping construct and promote 'national', 'liberal', and 'developmental' postcolonial states that cannot actualise the accompanying programmatic agenda without coming to clash with minority rights. It results in an over reliance on 'the individualist notion of equality and non-discrimination', as against 'group identity', and stresses a trajectory of capitalist development that excludes marginalised groups from its benefits. The problem of minority rights is in this sense embedded by international law in the very being of the postcolonial state.

Shahabuddin undertakes three case studies to sustain his argument. While these are of countries in South and Southeast Asia, the insights he generates can be productively deployed to analyse the problem of ethno-nationalism across regions. The first case study he undertakes is that of the Indian national movement which serves as backdrop to the two detailed cases of Rohingya Muslims of Myanmar and the hill people of the Chittagong Hill Tracts (CHT) of Bangladesh. The historical literature on the Indian freedom struggle and the partition of British India is substantial and growing. There are multiple readings of its cultural, social, and political dimensions. In other words, there are divergent takes on the history of the period written in and across different nations in the region of South Asia. This is equally the case when it comes to the postcolonial era. In short, the history of the region is multifarious, complex, and contested. Shahabuddin offers from the standpoint of the theme of ethno-nationalism a version of that history that may not always find acceptance but deserves to be engaged with.

In his case study of Rohingya Muslims Shahabuddin shows how individualist notions of citizenship were unable to prevent them being deprived of their citizenship and becoming subjects of genocide. The efforts to secure 'a separate constitutional safeguard' were unsuccessful. Shahabuddin rightly suggests in this regard that taking citizenship seriously should be treated as 'the point of departure and not as the end'. In the case of Bangladesh, the denial of autonomy to the CHT hill people also coexisted with liberal guarantees of equality and non-discrimination and some safeguarding of local cultures. A degree of autonomy was eventually granted through an accord and following it the Hill District Councils Acts and the CHT Regional Council Act of 1998 but only for it to be struck down by the Supreme Court of Bangladesh. It would be imagined that after sufferings in the hands of Pakistan, the makers and interpreters of the constitution of Bangladesh would readily recognise the concerns of the CHT. But it was not to be the case.

An important contribution of the book is to extend the framework dealing with minority rights to 'gender,' arguing that women suffer the same kind of marginalisation as minorities. In Shahabuddin's view feminist approaches to state shed much light on the situation of minorities. His theoretical lens could also be extended to others subaltern groups such as the working class, Dalits, and LGBT communities. To put it differently, the problem of marginalisation in postcolonial states is not simply that of minorities but of all disempowered and dispossessed groups. This does not distract from the fact that postcolonial states oppress ethnic, linguistic, religious, and other minorities in ways that other groups are not.

Unlike much critical work Shahabuddin does not rest with advancing a critique of extant state of affairs. He also offers thoughtful suggestions on how the problem of minority rights can be addressed. Ideally, in his view, a way should be found around the rule of *uti possidetis*. But he recognises that this is not a realistic possibility. He also notes the consensus in the international community against remedial secession. However, he cites the examples of Bangladesh and South Sudan to show that it remains a possible pathway. His support for 'the option of remedial secession of north Rakhine by the Rohingya' may find resonance with even those who are otherwise opposed to the idea. But there is for good reasons a healthy degree of scepticism among scholars and states with regard to the option of remedial secession. The problem of minorities is often recreated by the very act of secession. The condition of other subaltern groups is also unlikely to improve in the new situation. In other words, the fact that the postcolonial state is often actively inconsiderate towards all marginalised groups shows that the option of remedial secession is perhaps not the answer to the problem of ethno-nationalism. It is only inclusive cultural and social development, or of 'development as freedom', that can address the problems that these groups encounter. To be sure, in the instance of minorities it should be accompanied by the grant of cultural and political autonomy. The suggestions that Shahabuddin makes on this count are worthy of serious consideration. The recommendations include ethnic federalism, regional autonomy, and consociational democracy.

At the end of the day these too may not vastly improve the condition of minorities. The argument that international law facilitates the marginalisation of minorities and other subaltern groups in the postcolonial state is a statement about its internal relationship with imperialism. As long as imperialism continues to shape international laws through its cultural and economic policies, the problem of marginalisation and oppression of minorities and other subaltern groups is not going to go away. In fact, imperialism exploits conflicts that arise to further its own agenda. The doctrines of humanitarian intervention or the responsibility to protect are deployed by imperialism to its own ends. Only in a post-imperial world can we expect serious justice for all subaltern groups, including minorities. Meanwhile, as Shahabuddin suggests in this important work, there are a whole range of measures that can help ameliorate the condition of minorities.

B. S. Chimni

ACKNOWLEDGEMENTS

Writing of this book was made possible by a research leave secured under the Leverhulme Trust Research Fellowship. I express my sincerest thanks and gratitude to the Trust for supporting the project. I am also thankful to Birmingham Law School and the College of Arts and Law, University of Birmingham, for necessary research support.

The book also benefitted from generous appreciation and constructive feedback from a number of individuals: Professor Antony Anghie (NUS/Utah), Professor B. S. Chimni (JGLS), Professor Matthew Craven (SOAS), Professor Jean d'Aspremont (Manchester/Sciences Po), Professor Fiona de Londras (Birmingham), Dr. Adil Khan (Melbourne), Professor Ratna Kapur (Queen Mary), Professor Patrick Thornberry (Keele), Professor Michael Whitby (Birmingham), and Professor Karen Yeung (Birmingham). I express my sincerest gratitude to each of them. Needless to say, all errors are solely mine.

Special thanks to Professor B. S. Chimni for writing an insightful foreword to the book. I am also grateful to the General Editors of the Cambridge Studies in International and Comparative Law series – Professor d'Aspremont and Professor Larissa van den Herik (Leiden) – for their confidence in the project. I also thank Cambridge University Press's Commissioning Editor Mr. Tom Randall for his cooperation throughout the process.

During my field visits to Bangladesh, a number of individuals extended their help and support in the most generous way despite challenging circumstances under which they perform their everyday duties. It is not possible to name everyone here, but I must mention Mr. Steven Corliss, UNHCR Country Representative in Bangladesh, and some of his colleagues at the UNHCR Cox's Bazar office: Ms. Tayba Sharif, Mr. Ikteruddin Bayzid, Mr. Istiaque Ahmed, and Mr. Kamrul Hasan Arif. I am also grateful to Bangladesh government's Office of the Refugee Relief and Repatriation Commissioner (RRRC) in Cox's Bazar for facilitating my fieldwork at Rohingya refugee camps. Special thanks to Mr. Md.

Shamsud Douza, Additional Refugee Relief and Repatriation Commissioner, and Ms. Shamima Akter Jahan, Assistant Camp-in-Charge, Kutupalong Rohingya Refugee Camp (Unit 2).

It would have not been possible for me to complete the fieldwork without the efficient assistance of Mr. Shafayat Salam, an Assistant Judge in Bangladesh Judicial Service and a brilliant former student of mine. I am thankful to him for everything he has done with utmost sincerity and care. I also thank three of my students at Birmingham Law School for their excellent research assistance at various stages of the project: Ms. Lilya Belfer, Ms. Kamila Lauer Czerwinski, and Ms. Josephine Gillingwater.

Earlier versions of parts of the book have been published as tweets, blogs, journal articles, or book chapters, and have attracted useful comments from readers. Ideas incorporated in the book have also been enriched through my engagement with colleagues at Birmingham Law School, in Third World Approaches to International Law (TWAIL) network, and in Harvard Law School's Institute for Global Law and Policy (IGLP). I have also benefitted from constructive feedback from participants in a series of invited talks, most notably at Lauterpacht Centre for International Law (Cambridge), Refugee Studies Centre (Oxford), Bangladesh Institute of Law and International Affairs, and law schools at Glasgow, LSE, Melbourne, Queen Mary, Colorado, and Bangladesh University of Professionals (BUP). I am grateful to each of them.

It would be less than fair if I did not thank the production and design teams at Cambridge University Press. Thanks also to Integra Software Services Pvt. Ltd. for managing the production process. I am also thankful to Ms. Allison Turner for her help with editing.

Words are not enough to express my gratitude to my wife Aznin and our three boys (Ehan, Eshan, and Auhon), who have always been there for me with their unfailing support, kindness, and understanding. This book would not have seen the light of day without their sacrifice. My extended family in Bangladesh has also been a source of inspiration for completing this project. Especially, my mother, elder brother, and his family have tried their best to make my frequent visits to Bangladesh pleasant, comfortable, and memorable. I cannot thank them enough.

Memories of my father are my greatest inspirations and the driving force behind all my major works, including this book.

TABLE OF CASES

Aaland Islands case. Commission of Rapporteurs. Report of the Commission of Rapporteurs (1921). League of Nations Council Doc B7 [C] 21/68/106. *Page* 98–99

Aaland Islands case. International Commission of Jurists. Report of the International Commission of Jurists. *League of Nations Official Journal*, Special Supplement No. 3 (1920).   98, 104

Acquisition of Polish Nationality case. Permanent Court of International Justice. PCIJ Reports (1923) Ser. B, No 7.   173

Ángela Poma Poma v. Peru. Human Rights Committee. Communication No. 1457/2006 (26 March 2009). UN Doc CCPR/C/95/D/1457/2006.   232–233

Arbitration Commission Opinion No. 1 (1991) Conference on Yugoslavia. *European Journal of International Law* 3 (1992), 182.   102

Arbitration Commission Opinion No. 2 (1991) Conference on Yugoslavia. *European Journal of International Law* 3 (1992), 184.   104

Arbitration Commission Opinion No. 3 (1991) Conference on Yugoslavia. *European Journal of International Law* 3 (1992), 185.   102–103

Arbitration Commission Opinion No. 8 (1992) Conference on Yugoslavia. *European Journal of International Law* 4 (1993), 87–88.   102

Arrest Warrant of 11 April 2000 (*Democratic Republic of the Congo v. Belgium*) case. International Court of Justice. ICJ Reports (2002).   94

Beagle Channel case (*Case Concerning a Dispute between Argentina and Chile Concerning the Beagle Channel*). International Arbitration. *Reports of International Arbitral Awards* XXI (1977).   101

Bernard Ominayak, Chief of the Lubicon Lake Band v. Canada. Human Rights Committee. Communication No. 167/1984 (26 March 1990). UN Doc Supp No. 40 (A/45/40).   165

Bishna Lal v. The Union of Burma. Supreme Court of Myanmar. BLR 3 (1959) HC.   179

Centre on Housing Rights and Evictions (COHRE) v. Sudan. African Commission on Human and Peoples' Rights. Communication No. 296/2005 (2009).   237

Chagos Islands case (*Legal Consequences of the Separation of the Chagos Archipelago from Mauritius in 1965*). International Court of Justice. ICJ Reports (2019).   96

Chorzow Factory case (*Case Concerning the Factory at Chorzow*). Permanent Court of International Justice. PCIJ Reports (1925) Ser. B, No. 3; PCIJ Reports (1928) Ser. A, No. 17.   146

xviii   TABLE OF CASES

Colombian-Venezuelan Frontier case. International Arbitration. *Reports of International Arbitral Awards* VI (1922).   101
Congrès du Peuple Katangais v. *Zaire.* African Commission on Human and Peoples' Rights. Communication No. 75/92 (1994–1995).   150
East Timor (Portugal v. *Australia)* case. International Court of Justice. ICJ Reports (1995).   149
Endorois case *(Centre for Minority Rights Development and Minority Rights Group International and Centre on Housing Rights and Evictions (on behalf of Endorois Welfare Council)* v. *Kenya).* African Commission on Human and Peoples' Rights. Communication 276/2003 (2009).   231, 235, 238
Frontier Dispute (Benin v. *Niger)* case. International Court of Justice. ICJ Reports (2005).   100
Frontier Dispute (Burkina Faso v. *Mali)* case. International Court of Justice. ICJ Reports (1986).   100–101, 103
German Settlers case. Permanent Court of International Justice. PCIJ Reports (1925) Ser. B, No. 6.   146
Gillot et al. v. *France.* Human Rights Committee. Communication No. 932/2000 (15 July 2002). UN Doc CCPR/C/75/D/932/2000.   166
Guinea Bissau v. *Senegal (Arbitral Award of 31 July 1989)* case. International Court of Justice. ICJ Reports (1991).   100
Hasan Ali and Meher Ali. Supreme Court of Myanmar. Criminal Miscellaneous Applications No. 155 (1959).   179
Hopu and Bessert v. *France.* Human Rights Committee. Communication No. 549/1993 (9 December 1997). UN Doc CCPR/C/60/D/549/1993/Rev. 1.   233
In Re the Thirteenth Amendment to the Constitution. Supreme Court of Sri Lanka. 2 SLR (1987) 319.   195
India/Pakistan Boundary Dispute case *(Boundary Disputes between India and Pakistan Relating to the Interpretation of the Report of the Bengal Boundary Commission).* International Arbitration. *Reports of International Arbitral Awards* XXI (1950).   133
J. G. A. Diergaardt et al. v. *Namibia.* Human Rights Committee. Communication No. 760/1997 (25 July 2000). UN Doc CCPR/C/69/D/760/1997.   166
Karam Singh v. *The Union of Burma.* Supreme Court of Myanmar. BLR 25 (1956) SC.   179
Kasikili/Sedudu Island (Botswana v. *Namibia)* case. International Court of Justice. ICJ Reports (1999).   100
Kitok v. *Sweden.* Human Rights Committee. Communication No. 197/1985 (10 August 1988). UN Doc CCPR/C/33/D/197/1985.   165–166
Kosovo case *(Accordance with International Law of Unilateral Declaration of Independence in Respect of Kosovo).* International Court of Justice. ICJ Reports (2010).   148–150
Land and Maritime Boundary (Cameroon v. *Nigeria)* case. International Court of Justice. ICJ Reports (2002).   100

TABLE OF CASES   xix

Land, Island and Maritime Frontier Dispute (El Salvador/Honduras) case. International Court of Justice. ICJ Reports (1992).   101
Lansman et al. v. Finland. Human Rights Committee. Communication No 511/1992 (8 November 1994). UN Doc CCPR/C/52/D/511/1992.   165, 232–233
Lansman et al. v. Finland (No. 2). Human Rights Committee. Communication No. 671/1995 (22 November 1996). UN Doc CCPR/C/58/D/671/1995.   165, 232–233
Legal Consequences for States of the Continued Presence of South Africa in Namibia (South West Africa) case. International Court of Justice. ICJ Reports (1971).   97, 148
Legal Consequences of the Construction of a Wall in the Occupied Palestinian Territory case. International Court of Justice. ICJ Reports (2004).   149
Letto Law Danga v. The Union of Burma. Supreme Court of Myanmar. BLR 30 (1959) HC.   179
Lovelace v. Canada. Human Rights Committee. Communication No. 24/1977 (30 July 1981). UN Doc CCPR/C/OP/1.   16, 165
Mahuika et al. v. New Zealand. Human Rights Committee. Communication No. 547/1993 (15 November 2000). UN Doc CCPR/C/70/D/547/1993.   232–233
Maya Indigenous Communities of the Toledo District v. Belize. Inter-American Court of Human Rights. Report No. 40/04, Case 12.053 (2004).   231, 235–236
Mayagna (Sumo) Awas Tingni Community v. Nicaragua. Inter-American Court of Human Rights. Series C, No. 79 (2001).   235
Minority Schools in Albania case. Permanent Court of International Justice. PCIJ Reports (1935) Ser. A/B, No. 64.   146
Mohammad Badiuzzaman v. Bangladesh and Others. Supreme Court of Bangladesh. Law Guardian 7 (2010) HCD.   135–136, 186, 189, 193–195
Moiwana Community v. Suriname. Inter-American Court of Human Rights. Series C, No. 124 (2005).   237
Nationality Decrees Issued in Tunis and Morocco (French Zone) case. Permanent Court of International Justice. PCIJ Reports (1923) Ser. B, No. 4.   173
Nicaragua v. Honduras case *(Territorial and Maritime Dispute between Nicaragua and Honduras in the Caribbean Sea).* International Court of Justice. ICJ Reports (2007).   101
O. Sara et al. v. Finland. Human Rights Committee. Communication No. 431/1990 (24 March 1994). UN Doc CCPR/C/50/D/431/1990.   165
Ogiek case *(African Commission on Human and Peoples' Rights v. Republic of Kenya).* African Court of Human and Peoples' Rights. Application No. 006/2012 (2017).   236
Reference re Secession of Quebec. Supreme Court of Canada. 2 SCR (1998) 217.   148
Rights of Minorities in Upper Silesia (Minority Schools) case. Permanent Court of International Justice. PCIJ Reports (1928) Ser. A, No. 15.   146
Saramaka People v. Suriname. Inter-American Court of Human Rights. Series C, No. 185 (2008).   230–231, 235–237
Sawhoyamaxa Indigenous Community v. Paraguay. Inter-American Court of Human Rights. Series C, No. 146 (2006).   235

Social and Economic Rights Action Centre (SERAC) and the Centre for Economic and Social Rights (CESR) v. *Nigeria.* African Commission on Human and Peoples' Rights. Communication No. 370/09 (2008).   237

Tamil Federal Party case. Supreme Court of Sri Lanka. SC SPL 03/2014 (2016).   195

Texaco Overseas Petroleum Co. & California Asiatic Oil Co. v. *The Government of the Libyan Arab Republic.* International Arbitration. *International Law Materials* 17, no. 1 (1978), 1–37.   214

The Gambia v. *Myanmar* case *(Application of the Convention on the Prevention and Punishment of the Crime of Genocide).* International Court of Justice (pending).   1

The Kichwa Peoples of the Sarayaku Community and Its members v. *Ecuador.* Inter-American Court of Human Rights. Series C, No. 245 (2012).   230

Upper Silesia case *(Case Concerning Certain German Interests in Polish Upper Silesia).* Permanent Court of International Justice. PCIJ Reports (1926) Ser. A, No. 7.   146

Western Sahara case. International Court of Justice. ICJ Reports (1975).   149

Yordanova and Others v. *Bulgaria.* European Court of Human Rights. Application No. 25446/06 (2012).   238

ABBREVIATIONS

AA	Arakan Army
ACHPR	African Commission on Human and Peoples' Rights
ACtHPR	African Court on Human and Peoples' Rights
ADB	Asian Development Bank
AFPFL	Anti-Fascist People's Freedom League
ARSA	Arakan Rohingya Salvation Army
ASEAN	Association of Southeast Asian Nations
BIOT	British Indian Ocean Territory
CAD	Constituent Assembly Debates (of India)
CDDH	Steering Committee for Human Rights, Council of Europe
CEDAW	Convention on the Elimination of All Forms of Discrimination Against Women
CERD	Committee on the Elimination of Racial Discrimination
CESR	Centre for Economic and Social Rights
CHT	Chittagong Hill Tracts
CITIC	China International Trust Investment Corporation
CoE	Council of Europe
COHRE	Centre on Housing Rights and Evictions
CSCE	Conference on the Security and Co-operation in Europe
ECE	Eastern and Central Europe
ECHR	European Convention on Human Rights
ECtHR	European Court of Human Rights
ECOSOC	Economic and Social Council
EU	European Union
FAO	Food and Agriculture Organization
FCNM	Framework Convention on National Minorities
FRUS	Foreign Relations of the United States
FtAIL	Feminist approaches to international law
FWAIL	Fourth World Approaches to International Law
GDP	gross domestic product
HCNM	High Commissioner on National Minorities
HR	human rights
HRC	Human Rights Committee

IACtHR	Inter-American Court of Human Rights
ICCPR	International Covenant on Civil and Political Rights
ICESCR	International Covenant on Economic, Social, and Cultural Rights
ICJ	International Court of Justice
IFI	international financial institution
ILO	International Labour Organization
IOR	India Office Records and Private Papers
IMF	International Monetary Fund
KTA	Knappen Tippetts Engineering Co.
MSDP	Myanmar Sustainable Development Plan
NAIL	New approaches to international law
NATO	North Atlantic Treaty Organization
NGO	non-governmental organisation
NIEO	New International Economic Order
OAU	Organisation of African Unity (African Union)
OIC	Organisation of Islamic Cooperation
OSCE	Organization for Security and Co-operation in Europe
PCIJ	Permanent Court of International Justice
PCJS	Parbattyo Chattagram Jana Samiti (The Chittagong Hill Tracts People Association)
PCJSS	Parbattya Chattagram Jana Sanghati Samiti (United People's Party of the Chittagong Hill Tracts)
PSNR	Permanent Sovereignty over Natural Resources
R2P	responsibility to protect
ROB	Royal Orders of Burma
SAP	Structural Adjustment Programme
SERAC	Social and Economic Rights Action Centre
SFRY	Socialist Federal Republic of Yugoslavia
TWAIL	Third World Approaches to International Law
UDHR	Universal Declaration of Human Rights
UEHRD	Union Enterprise for Humanitarian Assistance, Resettlement, and Development in Rakhine
UN	United Nations
UNCT	United Nations Country Team
UNDM	United Nations Declaration on the Rights of Persons Belonging to National or Ethnic, Religious, and Linguistic Minorities
UNDP	United Nations Development Programme
UNDP-CHTDF	United Nations Development Programme Chittagong Hill Tracts Development Facility
UNDRIP	United Nations Declaration on the Rights of Indigenous Peoples
UNESCO	United Nations Educational, Scientific, and Cultural Organization

LIST OF ABBREVIATIONS

UNGA	United Nations General Assembly
UNHCR	United Nations High Commissioner for Refugees (The UN Refugee Agency)
UNHRC	United Nations Human Rights Council
UNICEF	United Nations Children's Fund
UNSC	United Nations Security Council
USAID	United States Agency for International Development
USF	Unclassed State Forest
USSR	Union of Soviet Socialist Republics (The Soviet Union)
WFP	World Food Programme
WGM	Working Group on Minorities, United Nations
WHO	World Health Organization
WWII	World War II (Second World War)

Introduction

The recent persecution of the Rohingya minority in Myanmar has been described by the United Nations Human Rights Council, first, as a 'textbook example of ethnic cleansing'[1] and then, within a few months, as a potential case of 'genocide'.[2] The Independent International Fact-Finding Mission on Myanmar established by the Human Rights Council concluded that the Myanmar army (Tatmadaw) committed war crimes and crimes against humanity in Rakhine State, and also that there was 'sufficient information' to warrant the investigation and prosecution of senior officials in the Tatmadaw chain of command for their liability for genocide in Rakhine State.[3] In December 2019, the Republic of Gambia filed a case against Myanmar before the International Court of Justice (ICJ) under the Genocide Convention (1948).[4] Meanwhile, more than a million Rohingyas who survived and managed to flee to neighbouring Bangladesh are living like packed sardines in makeshift tents in thirty-two refugee camps built on an area of only 26 square kilometres.

While the Rohingya genocide is one of the worst incidents against minorities in recent times, 'ethno-nationalism' and minority oppression

---

[1] Statement made by the UN High Commissioner for Human Rights, Zeid Ra'ad Al-Hussein, before the UN Human Rights Council in Geneva on 11 September 2017, available at www.un.org.
[2] Statement made by the UN High Commissioner for Human Rights, Zeid Ra'ad Al-Hussein, before the UN Human Rights Council in Geneva on 5 December 2017, available at www.ohchr.org.
[3] UN Human Rights Council, *Report of the Detailed Findings of the Independent International Fact-Finding Mission on Myanmar* (17 September 2018), UN Doc A/HRC/39/CRP2.
[4] The Gambia filed the case before the ICJ, allegedly acting on behalf of the Organisation of Islamic Cooperation (OIC). See International Court of Justice, *Application of the Convention on the Prevention and Punishment of the Crime of Genocide (The Gambia v. Myanmar)*, available at www.icj-cij.org/en/case/178.

in various forms and at various intensities are defining features of 'postcolonial states' in general.[5] A global study on peoples under threat in 2019 reveals that of the 115 countries that the study ranked by level of threat, 72 faced conflicts involving claims to self-determination.[6] All but a handful of the countries in the list are postcolonial states. Whereas the majority of states in the world, including Western liberal democracies, are not completely immune from ethno-nationalism, the question remains, why are postcolonial states more vulnerable to this phenomenon? Also, why do postcolonial states respond to ethnic tensions in the manner in which they do? And, what role does international law play in all of this? My motivation for writing this book emanates from these compelling questions.

Every major project has a humble beginning and the present work is not an exception. The writing of this book started with one of my tweets in the wake of the latest wave of the Rohingya massacre and displacement as well as international responses to these horrific events of August 2017. In that tweet, I wrote: 'To see the Rohingya crisis as a failure of international law enforcement is a wrong line of thinking. With *uti possidetis* [continuation of colonial boundaries], ambivalence with minority rights, and "developmentalism", international law has in fact facilitated this crisis.' This conflict-facilitating role of international law is not unique to the Rohingya crisis; the same applies to most ethnic violence in postcolonial states. Norms of international law devised to protect the rights of minorities and to protect individuals from statelessness, together with the recently developed doctrine of 'responsibility to

---

[5] By 'ethno-nationalism', I mean nationalist consciousness based on ethnic identities and ensuing claims towards statehood, regional autonomy, or other political arrangements. Ethnicity is understood here in the broadest sense of the term encompassing race, religion, language, culture, and so on. For the purpose of this book, 'postcolonial states' refer to those states that were under prolonged colonial rule and have subsequently gone through formal decolonisation. Most former colonies in Asia, Africa, and Latin America, which have now emerged as independent states, would come under this broad conventional definition. Although the term 'post' indicates a sense of temporality suggesting the hyphenated notion of 'post-colonial states', in this book I have consciously used the phrase without a hyphen precisely to dismantle that suggestion of temporality. For, postcolonialism as a phenomenon is omnipresent in the subjugation of post-colonial people long after formal decolonisation. It also needs to be noted that although countries, such as Thailand and Nepal, that were not formally colonised or so-called semi-colonial states like China fall outside the scope of the definition, the phenomenon remains relevant for these states too. However, as I make clear later on, my arguments in this book are made with reference to specific contexts and without making any claim of generality.

[6] Minority Rights Group International, 'Peoples Under Threat Data' (2019), available at www.peoplesunderthreat.org/data.

protect', suggest that internatonal law offers a solution to the tragic predicament of minorities. The problem would thus lie in the lack of enforcement. The ironic reality, however, is that international law facilitates ethnic violence in postcolonial states.

In *Minorities and the Making of Postcolonial States in International Law* I articulate the normative argument behind this claim. Offering an analysis of the geneses of ethno-nationalism in postcolonial states, I argue that nationalist elites address the problem of ethno-nationalism in general and minorities in particular by identifying the 'postcolonial state' itself as an 'ideology'. The ideological function of the postcolonial state vis-à-vis minorities takes three different yet interconnected forms: the postcolonial 'national' state, the postcolonial 'liberal' state, and the postcolonial 'developmental' state. As ideologies, the three visions of the postcolonial state inflict various forms of marginalisation on minorities but simultaneously justify the oppression in the name of national unity, liberal principles of equality and non-discrimination, and economic development, respectively. International law, as a core element of the ideology of the postcolonial state, contributes to the marginalisation of minorities. It does so by playing a key role in the ideological making of the postcolonial 'national', 'liberal', and 'developmental' states in relation to: continuation of colonial boundaries in postcolonial states, internal organisation of ethnic relations within the liberal-individualist framework of human rights, and the economic vision of the postcolonial state in the form of 'development' that subjugates minority interests. In other words, the book offers an ideology critique of the postcolonial state and examines the role of international law therein. My arguments in the book are substantiated with case studies. First, to develop a general framework of the ideology of the postcolonial state, I look at Indian nationalist movements and the question of minority protection. I then focus more specifically on the cases of the Rohingya minority in Myanmar and the hill people of the Chittagong Hill Tracts (CHT) in Bangladesh to expose the role of international law in the ideological function of postcolonial states.

Although statehood has always been a central element of international legal studies, the peculiarities of postcolonial states hardly drew any attention in the orthodox narrative of international law. The questions of self-determination and decolonisation, therefore, appear only en passant in the context of creating new states; the assumption is that as soon as these states are created, they will join the ranks of other sovereign states to be governed horizontally by the standard international legal regime. James Crawford's classic work, *The Creation of States in*

International Law, is an archetypical example of how traditional international law scholarship treats the question of postcolonial statehood as a peripheral item.[7] Most such works do not go beyond the law and practice of self-determination and decolonisation. In this way, the 'creation' of a postcolonial state ends as soon as it appears as a 'normal state', a new member of international society. More recent scholarship on self-determination and secession, specifically focused on postcolonial states in Africa, does not break with the trend either.[8]

Likewise, numerous scholars have analysed various aspects of minority rights under international law, including the right to self-determination and democratic participation in decision-making.[9] Following the eruption of ethnic violence in the post–Cold War period, the disciplines of international law, international relations, and security studies have experienced a corresponding eruption of writings on minority protection. A good number of these publications focused on regional studies of minority protection. While the literature on minority rights is thick, most of it adopts doctrinal approaches and makes interventions by re-interpreting existing provisions to expand horizons. As a result, these works fail to fully appreciate the complexities of minority issues in postcolonial states. More importantly, they conceive of international law essentially as a solution to the minority problem rather than as a part of the problem.[10] My previous monograph, *Ethnicity and International Law*, addressed this shortcoming by engaging with the concept of minority protection in a radically different way – by explaining international law's ambivalence towards minority rights within the

---

[7] James Crawford, *The Creation of States in International Law*, 2nd ed. (Oxford: Oxford University Press, 2007). See also Marcelo G. Kohen (ed.), *Secession: International Law Perspectives* (Cambridge: Cambridge University Press, 2006), and Duncan French (ed.), *Statehood and Self-determination: Reconciling Tradition and Modernity in International Law* (Cambridge: Cambridge University Press, 2013).

[8] See, for example, Redie Bereketeab (ed.), *Self-determination and Secession in Africa: The Postcolonial State* (London: Routledge, 2015); Dirdeiry M. Ahmed, *Boundaries and Secession in Africa and International Law: Challenging* Uti Possidetis (Cambridge: Cambridge University Press, 2015).

[9] For example, Kristin Henrard and Robert Dunbar, *Synergies in Minority Protection* (Cambridge: Cambridge University Press, 2009); Gaetano Pentassuglia, *Minority Groups and Judicial Discourse in International Law* (The Hague: Martinus Nijhoff Publishers, 2009); Kristin Henrard, *Devising an Adequate System of Minority Protection* (The Hague: Martinus Nijhoff Publishers, 2000); Patrick Thornberry, *International Law and the Rights of Minorities* (Oxford: Clarendon Press, 1991).

[10] See, for example, Steven Wheatley, *Democracy, Minorities and International Law* (Cambridge: Cambridge University Press, 2005).

historical continuum of the liberal hesitancy vis-à-vis the allegedly 'primitive' concept of ethnicity.[11] Yet, it failed to pay adequate attention to the peculiarities of ethno-nationalism and the minority problem in postcolonial states.

It was Europe that crafted international legal norms, and postcolonial states are to a great extent the creation of these norms via colonisation, decolonisation, and associated rules. Third World Approaches to International Law (TWAIL) scholars have demonstrated how diverse political entities with their own complex characteristics were compelled to adopt a Western concept of 'statehood' – which embodies specific ideas of territory, the nation, and ethnicity – in order to gain recognition. As Antony Anghie notes, 'the embrace and adoption of the Western concept of the nation-state that was a prerequisite for becoming a sovereign state' demanded a transformation of indigenous perceptions of sovereignty and political communities, and 'not all new states were successful in making these changes without experiencing ongoing ethnic tensions and, in some cases, long and devastating civil wars'.[12] Similarly, Obiora Okafor argues that international legal doctrines such as 'peer-review' (as opposed to 'infra-review') in recognising new states and the 'homogenisation' of states have facilitated the process by which many African states have promoted coercive nation-building and legitimised the construction and maintenance of large centralised states in Africa. In this way, international law and institutions have contributed to incidents of ethnic conflicts in Africa.[13]

However, this understanding of international law engagements with postcolonial states, seen from minority rights perspectives, is largely confined to various formal formative aspects of statehood, such as recognition, self-determination, and territory – in line with the limited orthodox understanding of the role of international law in the creation of postcolonial states.[14] On the other hand, TWAIL scholarship on

---

[11] Mohammad Shahabuddin, *Ethnicity and International Law: Histories, Politics and Practices* (Cambridge: Cambridge University Press, 2016).

[12] Antony Anghie, 'Bandung and the Origins of Third World Sovereignty', in *Bandung, Global History, and International Law: Critical Pasts and Pending Futures*, eds. Luis Eslava, Michael Fakhri, and Vasuki Nesiah (Cambridge: Cambridge University Press, 2017), 544.

[13] Obiora Chinedu Okafor, 'After Martyrdom: International Law, Sub-State Groups, and the Construction of Legitimate Statehood in Africa', *Harvard International Law Journal* 41(2000), 503–528.

[14] See also Makau Mutua, 'Why Redraw the Map of Africa: A Moral and Legal Inquiry', *Michigan Journal of International Law* 16, no. 4 (1995), 1113–1176.

other relevant issues, such as developmentalism and economic imperialism, largely focuses on the damaging role of international law in postcolonial states but often without paying adequate attention to the marginalisation of minority groups within those states.[15] In contrast, Hiroshi Fukurai, in his presidential speech at the 2017 Annual Conference of the Asian Law and Society Association, briefly identified the limits of TWAIL approaches in the context of indigenous peoples in Asia. To address such limitations, he proposed the Fourth World Approaches to International Law (FWAIL), but without engaging with the normative issues involved in the making of postcolonial states.[16]

This book addresses these shortcomings in the existing international law literature on statehood and minority rights – both in mainstream and critical genres – by offering a comprehensive analysis that puts both the 'minority' and the 'postcolonial state' at the centre of attention. Explaining the postcolonial state as an ideology, the book demonstrates how international law facilitates the ideological making and functioning of the postcolonial state as 'national', 'liberal', and 'developmental' states and, thereby, legitimises the marginalisation of minorities. Such engagements between international law and postcolonial states do not end with the formal creation of the latter as new subjects of international society. Instead, international law continues to maintain the colonial territorial definition of the state, to shape the internal organisation of ethnic relations through liberal individualism, and to nurture exploitative economic structures in postcolonial states. Thus, through the case studies, this book

---

[15] See B. S. Chimni, *International Law and World Order: A Critique of Contemporary Approaches*, 2nd ed. (Cambridge: Cambridge University Press, 2017); Antony Anghie, *Imperialism, Sovereignty and the Making of International Law* (Cambridge: Cambridge University Press, 2005); Balakrishnan Rajagopal, *International Law from Below: Development, Social Movement and Third World Resistance* (Cambridge: Cambridge University Press, 2003); Sundhya Pahuja, *Decolonising International Law: Development, Economic Growth, and the Politics of Universality* (Cambridge: Cambridge University Press, 2011); Celine Tan, *Governance through Development: Poverty Reduction Strategies, International Law and the Disciplining of Third World States* (London: Routledge, 2011); Sundhya Pahuja and Luis Eslava, 'The State and International Law: A Reading from the Global South?' *Humanity: An International Journal of Human Rights, Humanitarianism and Development* 11, no. 1 (2020), 118–138; Luis Eslava, *Local Space, Global Life: The Everyday Operation of International Law and Development* (Cambridge: Cambridge University Press, 2015).

[16] Hiroshi Fukurai, 'Fourth World Approaches to International Law (FWAIL) and Asia's Indigenous Struggles and Quests for Recognition under International Law', *Asian Journal of Law and Society* 5 (2018), 221–231.

also highlights how international law operates in the material realm by altering the very mode of production and thereby social relations themselves. Each of the international law interventions has important, enduring, and often devastating implications for minorities. International law's involvement with the ideology of the postcolonial state is incessant, as is the anguish of minorities as a result.

The organisation of the book builds on four key questions: (i) Why and how does ethno-nationalism take root in postcolonial states? (ii) How do postcolonial states then respond to this phenomenon? (iii) What role does international law play in the process? (iv) What is the way forward?

The book responds to these questions in two parts. Part I, consisting of Chapters 1 and 2, deals with the first two questions in order to develop the normative framework within which I then respond to the remaining questions in subsequent chapters. Chapter 1 analyses the roots of ethno-nationalism in postcolonial states by highlighting three key elements of ethno-nationalist politics: the modernist response to primordial attachments in the process of nation-building, the active role and passive consequences of colonialism, and the influence of bourgeois and petty bourgeois classes under the material condition of capitalism. My analysis in this chapter underscores that to a great extent ethno-nationalism in postcolonial states is an outcome of a combined force of all three elements.

Against this backdrop of the geneses of ethno-nationalism, Chapter 2 examines how postcolonial states then respond to ethno-nationalism in general and minorities in particular. I argue that nationalist ruling elites conceive of the postcolonial state itself as an 'ideology', claiming that the unified national state, its liberal constitutional structure, and the developmental agenda will solve the trouble of ethnic parochialism and, hence, the problem of minorities. Here, I rely on John Thompson's notion of 'ideology' as a set of ways in which ideas and meanings help create and sustain relations of domination through a series of general modes of operation and strategies of symbolic construction.[17] I elaborate this specific meaning of ideology and then develop my argument that the ideology of the postcolonial state functions in three different forms: the postcolonial 'national' state, the postcolonial 'liberal' state, and the postcolonial 'developmental' state.

In asserting faith in the healing power of the postcolonial state, the nationalist elites conveniently avoid crucial questions as to the continuation of the colonial political order, the class character of the economic

---

[17] See John B. Thompson, *Ideology and Modern Culture: Critical Social Theory in the Era of Mass Communication* (Cambridge: Polity Press, 1990).

organisation, and the hegemony of nation-building projects – factors that lead to ethno-nationalism in the first place. In other words, the idea that the postcolonial state itself will solve the minority problem obscures and glosses over the real reasons for the problem and shifts attention to issues – national unification, liberal individualism, and development – that help maintain asymmetric power relations between the minority and the majority. In this way, the postcolonial state performs the ideological function of suppressing minority group identities, but simultaneously obscures and validates further marginalisation of minorities. Taken together, Chapters 1 and 2 offer a normative framework of the 'ideology of the postcolonial state' for my analysis of the role of international law in the rest of the book.

My arguments in Part I, in relation to the geneses of ethno-nationalism as well as the three ideologies of the postcolonial state, are substantiated with case studies on anticolonial nationalist movements in India and the ensuing minority rights discourse in Indian Constituent Assembly debates between 1946 and 1950. This critical engagement with the broader context of the Indian nationalist movement and the treatment of minorities in the constitutional architecture of the postcolonial Indian state offers a useful backdrop for my more focused case studies on the Rohingya in Myanmar and the hill people of the CHT in Bangladesh in Part II. Given the intertwined colonial experience and history of India, on the one hand, and Myanmar and Bangladesh, on the other, the case studies on the Rohingya and the CHT hill people make better sense once contextualised within the broader narrative of the nationalist movement and the ideology of the postcolonial Indian state at the moment of decolonisation. The prolonged process of Indian decolonisation ultimately vivisected the entire region to beget multiple postcolonial states, including Myanmar and Bangladesh and, thereby, multiplied the problem of minorities.

Part II of the book, consisting of Chapters 3, 4, and 5, engages with the third key question, which constitutes the main focus of the book: what role does international law play in the ideological function of the postcolonial state in marginalising minority groups? By international law, here I mean 'an ensemble of rules, policies, institutions, and practices that directly and indirectly affects the daily lives of millions of people all over the world'.[18] In recent years, a growing network of international institutions has constituted what B. S. Chimni calls a 'global state', which is designed to safeguard

---

[18] 1 *International Law from Below*, 2.

the vested interests of the transnational capitalist class to the disadvantage of subaltern classes globally.[19] Hence, in Part II I put international institutions in the field of human rights, development, and finance – along with various international norms, rules, and principles – under close scrutiny in order to gauge their impacts on minorities.

Chapter 3 deals with the role of international law in the ideology of the postcolonial 'national' state. With its ambition of achieving a homogeneous and unified sovereign entity, the postcolonial state essentially relies on international law principles for the continuity of colonial boundaries (*uti possidetis*), territorial integrity, sovereign equality, and non-interference in internal affairs. Contrary to the conventional wisdom that the *uti possidetis* principle helps in the maintenance of peace and order, I argue that *uti possidetis* is a key problem. Far from being a corrective mechanism halting potential 'disorder' emanating from decolonisation, the continuation of arbitrarily drawn colonial boundaries undermines the legitimate right to self-determination of numerous ethnic minorities in postcolonial states and often results in violent ethnic conflicts. The argument for *uti possidetis* in international law is also normatively inconsistent as it depends upon the capacity of the postcolonial state to efface ethno-nationalism while simultaneously allowing the state to produce its own sustaining nationalist ideology in majoritarian terms. The minority problem is thus embedded in the very ideological making of the postcolonial 'national' state in international law.

Chapter 4 demonstrates how the post–WWII liberal vision of international law feeds into the ideology of the postcolonial 'liberal' state in the form of 'individualism', thereby dominating the discourse on minority protection. One direct implication of the dominance of liberal individualism in the postcolonial constitutional architecture of rights is the denial of protection for minority *groups*. The liberal human rights regime is designed to diffuse cultural groups into individual units, so as to facilitate their assimilation into a homogeneous national (read majoritarian) identity. This chapter explains how international law, with its liberal underpinning, shrinks the scope of the right to self-determination and thereby perpetuates the vulnerability of, or in some cases even leads to the extinction of, minority groups. In this connection, I also highlight the peculiar challenge that postcolonial states face in reconciling the diverging forces of 'liberal individualism' and majoritarian 'ethno-nationalism'. The former

---

[19] B. S. Chimni, 'International Institutions Today: An Imperial Global State in the Making', *European Journal of International Law* 15, no. 1 (2004), 1–37.

emanates from the liberal international legal order, the latter from the nationalist discourse of allegiance, entitlement, and legitimacy. The issue of citizenship and statelessness is also discussed in this context.

And finally, Chapter 5 explains how the ideology of the postcolonial 'developmental' state relies on the language of economic progress and development to undermine the minority question. The idea that economic development is the answer to all social problems is embedded in the very logic of international law's engagement with postcolonial states. I, therefore, offer a critical, in-depth, and multi-layered analysis of the complex interrelationship between minorities, postcolonial states, and dominant international actors with reference to 'development' and international law. The analysis is organised under two major rubrics: I first examine the treatment of minorities in the international law of development and then examine how international law discourse on minority and group rights addresses the issue of economic development. In both cases, critically engaging with central themes in the discourse on both 'development' and 'minority rights' under international law, I argue that international law provides a framework within which international actors and postcolonial states suppress minority interests in the name of economic development and that politically marginalised minorities suffer the most due to such development activities. In this way, international law involvement in the ideological function of the postcolonial 'developmental' state not only results in further marginalisation of already vulnerable minorities but also serves to legitimise and gloss over asymmetric power relations that produce such marginalisation.

In light of the foregoing arguments, the conclusion of the book calls for a renewed international law approach to minority rights and the question of statehood – one that takes into account the unique nature and background of postcolonial states and, at the same time, pays attention to minority perspectives going beyond state-centrism, liberal individualism, and neoliberal developmentalism. It is only through this approach that international law can finally make sense of humanitarian catastrophes in postcolonial states and its involvement therein.

As mentioned earlier, my arguments about the role of international law in the ideological function of postcolonial states are substantiated with in-depth case studies on the Rohingya minority in Myanmar and the CHT hill people in Bangladesh. The states of Myanmar (formerly known as Burma) and Bangladesh (formerly known as East Pakistan), albeit neighbouring countries, are quite different in their geopolitical outlook and culture. While Bangladesh has always had its historic, political, and cultural roots in the Indian sub-continent or South Asia, Myanmar is seen rather as a Southeast Asian nation and belongs to the Association of Southeast Asian Nations (ASEAN). Their common ground is their shared experience of colonialism under British rule, which fundamentally shaped ethnic relations and the attitude towards respective minorities in both countries. Myanmar was colonised and annexed to British India following three Anglo-Burma wars in the nineteenth century. It was separated from British India in 1935 and eventually granted full independence in 1948. On the other hand, Bangladesh was part of Pakistan from 1947 – the time of colonial India's independence from the British and partition into the states of India and Pakistan – until it achieved independence following the liberation war of 1971. Thus, the colonial origin of the minority problem in both Myanmar and Bangladesh can be traced to the same historical sources, as we shall see in Chapter 3.

Apart from the shared colonial experience under the British, what makes the case studies on Myanmar and Bangladesh intriguing is the pre-colonial interactions between the minority groups under scrutiny here. However, as things stand today, the Rohingya are a Muslim minority in a predominantly Buddhist country, while the CHT hill people are traditionally Buddhist in a largely Muslim country.[20] Despite differences in their geopolitical and socio-cultural orientations, both Myanmar and Bangladesh are hostile towards their respective minorities, although the degree and extent of oppression varies. This book takes up the challenge of demonstrating how international law – through its various roles in the ideological function of postcolonial states – facilitates similar types of minority oppression in these otherwise socio-culturally diverse states.

On this score, it is necessary to note the complicated legal status of the Rohingya and the CHT hill people in their respective countries. As we shall see later, the Rohingya in Myanmar are not recognised as one of the 135 official 'national ethnic races'. Instead, they are treated as illegal Bangalee immigrants, whereas Rohingyas have identified themselves as historical inhabitants of the country for centuries. They are not even allowed to describe themselves as the 'Rohingya' lest that legitimise their claim to indigeneity. On the other hand, the hill people of the CHT identify themselves as *pahari* (hill people), who are indigenous to the land. However, to deny the hill people access to the more robust international legal regime for indigenous peoples, Bangladesh has an official

---

[20] Many hill peoples in the CHT have been converted to Christianity in recent years. Also, a small group of the Rohingya follows Hinduism.

12   INTRODUCTION

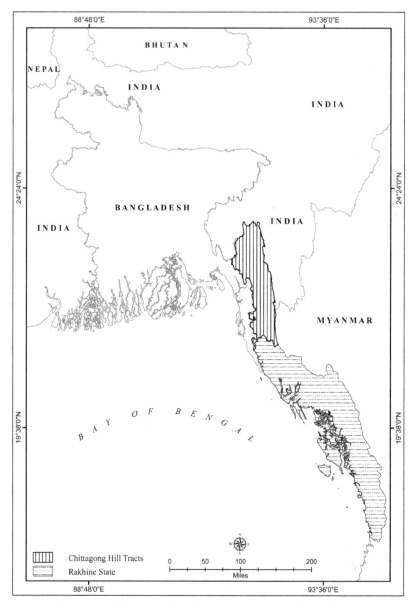

Map 1 Chittagong Hill Tracts and Rakhine State in the regional context
This map was developed specially for this book by Professor Md. Shahedur Rashid and Mr Md. Ashraful Habib of the Department of Geography and Environment at Jahangirnagar University.

policy recognising the CHT hill people as 'ethnic minorities' rather than 'indigenous peoples'. In other words, while the Rohingya are denied the status of an 'ethnic minority' in Myanmar, that status has been imposed on the CHT hill people by Bangladesh.

The issue is further complicated by ambiguity in the legal determination of indigenous peoples and ethnic minorities. Like many other branches of international law, the development of legal regimes for minorities and indigenous peoples is grounded in European experience. The issue of minority rights emerged in international law in relation to the birth of Westphalian nation-states in Europe and subsequently grew in importance following the redrawing of European nation-state boundaries in the aftermath of the Great War. The distinct legal category of indigenous peoples, meanwhile, is primarily informed by European settler colonialists' encounter with native populations in the Americas and the Pacific. The extent to which the distinction between minorities and indigenous peoples, based on uniquely European experience, is globally relevant is open to questions.[21] Especially in Asia and Africa, the boundary between the two groups for the purpose of international law is highly porous. In its advisory opinion, the African Commission on Human and Peoples' Rights concluded that 'any African can legitimately consider him/herself as indigene to the Continent'.[22] As an African international lawyer boldly asserts, '[i]t is next to impossible that any ethnicity in Africa would accept being characterized as a minority or as non-indigenous'.[23] Whether the robust international legal regime of rights for indigenous peoples under the ILO Convention 169 (1989) or the United Nations Declaration on the Rights of Indigenous Peoples (UNDRIP, 2007) applies equally to minority groups is discussed in Chapter 5. However, an analytical focus on the nuanced difference between minorities and indigenous peoples under international law appears less relevant to my general argument than a focus on the commonality of both groups as 'ethnic minorities'.[24] Here, I conceive of

---

[21] Asbjørn Eide, 'An Overview of the UN Declaration and Major Issues Involved', in *The United Nations Declaration on Minorities: An Academic Account on the Occasion of Its 20th Anniversary (1992-2012)*, eds. Ugo Caruso and Rainer Hofmann (Leiden: BRILL, 2015), 76-77, 85.

[22] ACHPR, Advisory Opinion of the African Commission on Human and Peoples' Rights on the United Nations Declaration on the Rights of Indigenous Peoples (41st Session, Accra, 2007), 4.

[23] Ahmed, *Boundaries and Secession in Africa and International Law*, 216.

[24] For a recent discussion on the interrelationship between minority rights and the rights of indigenous peoples, see Eide, 'An Overview of the UN Declaration and Major Issues Involved', 66-86.

a 'minority' in line with the standard definition of the term under international law, discussed in Chapter 4, as a non-dominant group in terms of both number and power, which possesses and intends to preserve a distinct ethnic, religious, and/or linguistic identity within a given polity. In this sense, my treatment of both the Rohingya and the CHT hill people as ethnic minorities is only for the purpose of this book and should not be seen as an attempt to redefine their already-contested identities.

I would also like to make note of the way I have approached the case studies. The stories of the Rohingya and the CHT hill people are stories of historical injustice, dehumanisation, state oppression, and brutality. In the course of conducting this research, especially during my fieldwork in Bangladesh, I have come across reports and victims' testimonies that are nothing short of depressing. Various national and international organisations have meticulously documented graphic accounts of violence, of a genocidal nature in some cases, against both minorities. However, in writing this book, I have consciously attempted to move beyond an exclusive focus on vulnerability per se, and engage more with the *ways* in which such vulnerability is produced and sustained through the ideological operation of the postcolonial state in collaboration with international law. Many of these ways, such as liberal notions of citizenship and development, are also sites of minority resistance against state repression. Therefore, the stories of minority oppression are also stories of heroic resistance and resilience.[25] I have highlighted various forms of minority resistance in my case studies.

In this regard, I also need to acknowledge that while minorities are the focus of this book, they are not the only victims of the hegemonic making of postcolonial states. Minorities, understood as non-dominant groups, are often economically deprived, but the fate of the poorest section of the society is shared beyond ethnic lines. Although there are cases of market-dominant minorities in some societies, such as the ethnic Chinese across Southeast Asia or the Lebanese in West Africa, these 'elites' are rather exceptions. While they also face a certain degree of discrimination, they

---

[25] In an interesting study, Farzana explains how Rohingya refugees in Bangladesh use music and art as non-conventional means of communicating their coherent identity and expressing their resistance to the discrimination and oppression experienced in their country of origin as well as in their exile in Bangladesh. This informal resistance is used to keep their memory alive, to transmit that history through verbal and visual expressions to the new generations, and to communicate information about themselves to outsiders. Kazi Fahmida Farzana, 'Music and Artistic Artefacts: Symbols of Rohingya Identity and Everyday Resistance in Borderlands', *Austrian Journal of South-East Asian Studies* 4, no. 2 (2011), 215–236.

hardly relate to the life experience of their poorer co-ethnics. The capitalist economic structure of the postcolonial state marginalises the poor in general, and the minority's ethnic identity on top of their economic vulnerability creates new avenues for further oppression by the hegemonic state.

The marginalisation of women within the gendered power structure of postcolonial states is also of specific relevance here.[26] Even in the case of minorities, minority women experience marginalisation within both the postcolonial state and their respective minority groups.[27] Minority women are often specific targets of any violence inflicted upon minorities by postcolonial states. The use of rape as a military strategy, as was the case in the Rwandan genocide and Bangladesh's war of independence, is the most prominent example. As is now well documented, violence inflicted upon the Rohingya by the Myanmar army and Rakhine Buddhists had a gendered character. The same pattern is evident, although to a lesser degree, in the treatment of CHT hill women by the Bangladesh army. At the same time, during my field visits to Rohingya refugee camps in Cox's Bazar, a shocking picture of rampant domestic violence against women within the Rohingya community quickly emerged. The marginalisation of minority women is reflected at the

---

[26] For a thorough analysis of the ways that women are marginalised in the making of postcolonial states, see Kumari Jayawardena, *Feminism and Nationalism in the Third World* (1982) (London: Verso Books, 2016); Partha Chatterjee, *The Nation and Its Fragments* (Princeton, NJ: Princeton University Press, 1993), 116–157; and Veena Das, *Life and Words: Violence and the Descent into the Ordinary* (Berkeley, CA: University of California, 2006). See also Nira Yuval-Davis, *Gender and Nation* (London: Sage, 1997), 1–25; Tanika Sarkar, *Hindu Wife and Hindu Nation* (Ranikhet: Permanent Black, 2003); Sikata Banerjee, 'Gender and Nationalism: The Masculinisation of Hinduism and Female Political Participation in India', *Women's Studies International Forum* 26, no. 2 (2003), 167–179; Jyoti Puri, *Encountering Nationalism* (Hoboken, NJ: Wiley, 2004); Mai Taha, 'Reimagining Bandung for Women at Work in Egypt: Law and the Woman between the Factory and the "Social Factory"', in *Bandung, Global History, and International Law*, 337–354.

[27] From intersectional perspectives, the depiction of the marginalisation of women from any single categorial axis of either sex or ethnicity or class is artificial and does not grasp the complexity or the true nature of the discrimination that minority women face. The same is also true about the multiplicity of loci within which women face marginalisation. For details on intersectional approaches, see Kimberlé W. Crenshaw, 'Demarginalizing the Intersection of Race and Sex: A Black Feminist Critique of Antidiscrimination Doctrine, Feminist Theory and Antiracist Politics', *University of Chicago Legal Forum* (1989), 139–167; Adrien K. Wing (ed.), *Critical Race Feminism: A Reader*, 2nd ed. (New York: New York University Press, 2003); Ange-Marie Hancock, *An Intellectual History of Intersectionality* (Oxford: Oxford University Press, 2016); Shreya Atrey, *Intersectional Discrimination* (Oxford: Oxford University Press, 2019).

international level too. States often resist international norms with respect to women, as adopted in the Convention on the Elimination of All Forms of Discrimination Against Women (CEDAW), on the grounds that such norms 'may challenge national culture, traditions, policies, and laws'.[28] However, the protection of the individual human rights of women within minority groups has been a classic theme in the international law discourse on group rights.[29] The 'woman question' has in many ways epitomised inherent tensions between cultural group rights for minorities and individual human rights of minority group members.

The vulnerability of minorities, including this added layer of the vulnerability of minority women, and the protectionist role of international law falls outside the core focus of this book. The limits of the perception of the law in general, either as a tool for protecting women and ensuring gender equality or as a mere instrument of oppression, have long been exposed by critical feminist scholars. Ratna Kapur and Brenda Cossman conceived of law instead 'as a site of discursive struggle, where competing visions of the world are fought out'.[30] Feminist approaches, however, remain relevant for my inquiry into the way the postcolonial

---

[28] Hilary Charlesworth, 'Martha Nussbaum's Feminist Internationalism', *Ethics* 111 (2000), 64. For a critique on feminist approaches to 'culture', see Cyra Akila Choudhury, 'Beyond Culture: Human Rights Universalisms Versus Religious and Cultural Relativism in the Activism for Gender Justice', *Berkeley Journal of Gender, Law & Justice* 30 (2015), 226–266.

[29] See, for example, Radhika Coomaraswamy, 'To Bellow Like a Cow: Women, Ethnicity, and the Discourse of Rights', in *Human Rights of Women: National and International Perspectives*, ed. Rebecca J. Cook (Philadelphia, PA: University of Pennsylvania Press, 1994), 39–57; David S. Berry, 'Conflicts Between Minority Women and Traditional Structures: International Law, Rights and Culture', *Social and Legal Studies* 7, no. 1 (1998), 55–75; Alexi Nicole Wood, 'A Cultural Rite of Passage, or a Form of Torture: Female Genital Mutilation from an International Law Perspective', *Hastings Women's Law Journal* 12, no. 2 (2001), 347–386; Radhika Coomaraswamy, 'Identity Within: Cultural Relativism, Minority Rights, and the Empowerment of Women', *George Washington International Law Review* 34, no. 3 (2002), 483–514; Pratibha Jain, 'Balancing Minority Rights and Gender Justice: The Impact on Protecting Multiculturalism on Women's Rights in India', *Berkeley Journal of International Law* 23, no. 1 (2005), 201–222; Camilla Ida Ravnbøl, 'The Human Rights of Minority Women: Romani Women's Rights from a Perspective on International Human Rights Law and Politics', *International Journal on Minority and Group Rights* 17, no. 1 (2010), 1–45. See also *Lovelace v. Canada*, HRC, Communication No. 24/1977 (30 July 1981), UN Doc CCPR/C/OP/1.

[30] Ratna Kapur and Brenda Cossman, *Subversive Sites: Feminist Engagement with Law in India* (London: Sage Publications, 1996). See also Ratna Kapur and Brenda Cossman, '*Subversive Sites* 20 Years Later: Rethinking Feminist Engagements with Law', *Australian Feminist Law Journal* 44, no. 2 (2018), 265–287.

state operates its ideological tools to justify the marginalisation of minorities. As Vasuki Nesiah argues, 'if feminism was going to be about a politically relevant and engaged analytics, it may not always begin with gender as the starting point of analysis'.[31] She thus calls for a feminist research agenda that is capable of 'mainstreaming and consolidation of feminist insights in other terrains into international legal analysis'.[32] Beyond the framework of the vulnerability of minority women, it is therefore worth examining the extent to which feminist approaches to statehood can offer an alternative future for minorities in general. I will engage with this question in the conclusion as I look at possible ways forward.

So far as my research approach and methodology as a whole is concerned, the mixed historical, normative, and structural nature of the key themes in this book – namely, anticolonial ethno-nationalism, postcolonial boundaries, liberal individualism, and economic development – necessitated multiple research methods. For the most part, the research is informed by critical theoretical analysis. The central argument of the book, that the postcolonial state operates as an ideology vis-à-vis minorities, is informed by Susan Marks's critique of international law as an ideology.[33] My assertion – that despite its conflict-prevention potential, international law also contributes to ethnic conflicts – is influenced by David Kennedy's signature thesis on the 'dark sides of virtue' of international humanitarianism.[34] But I also take seriously Kapur's point about 'taking a walk on the dark side' and Chimni's optimism for reforms in international law, as reflected in the forward-looking aspects of the book.[35]

---

[31] Vasuki Nesiah, 'Priorities of Feminist Legal Research: A Sketch, A Draft Agenda, A Hint of an Outline ...', *feminists@law* 1 (2011), 3.
[32] Ibid., 1.
[33] Susan Marks, *The Riddle of All Constitutions* (Oxford: Oxford University Press, 2000).
[34] David Kennedy, 'International Human Rights Movement: Part of the Problem?' *Harvard Human Rights Journal* 14 (2002), 101–126; David Kennedy, *Dark Sides of Virtue: Reassessing International Humanitarianism* (Princeton, NJ: Princeton University Press, 2004); David Kennedy, *Of War and Law* (Princeton, NJ: Princeton University Press, 2006); David Kennedy, *A World of Struggle: How Power, Law, and Expertise Shape Global Political Economy* (Princeton, NJ: Princeton University Press, 2016). For a thorough critique of Kennedy's approach to international law and institution, see Chimni, *International Law and World Order*, 246–312.
[35] Ratna Kapur, 'Human Rights in the 21st Century: Take a Walk on the Dark Side', *Sydney Law Review* 28, no. 4 (2006), 665–688; Ratna Kapur, *Gender, Alterity and Human Rights: Freedom in a Fishbowl* (Gloucestershire: Edward Elgar Publishing Ltd., 2018); Chimni, *International Law and World Order*, 440–550.

Whenever I needed to tackle literature of relatively wide breadth, I identified the major representative discourse to ensure that the width and the depth of my analysis remained in harmony. To support my analysis throughout the book, I have relied mainly on primary materials and archival sources, whenever possible. The research is also informed by a series of interviews with national and international organisations working in Bangladesh. These interviews, conducted in the course of three field visits to Bangladesh between July 2019 and March 2020, focused on humanitarian actors' encounter with international law on the ground in relation to more than one million Rohingya refugees in Bangladeshi camps.

My critical engagement with the role of international law in the ideological function of the postcolonial state is influenced by postcolonial and TWAIL scholarship. In his recent work, Chimni has described TWAIL as 'a loose network of third world scholars who articulate a critique of the history, structure and process of contemporary international law from the standpoint of third world peoples, in particular its marginal and oppressed groups'.[36] Given the peculiarities of postcolonial states and the centrality of international law therein, conventional doctrinal approaches premised primarily upon European worldviews are bound to fall short of an adequate framework of analysis. Unfortunately, doctrinal approaches premised upon an understanding of international law as a problem-solving tool have hitherto dominated international law discourse on humanitarian crises in the postcolonial world. In contrast, the following chapters offer not only the theoretical framework but also the appropriate approach for a meaningful engagement with similar situations elsewhere. Although the historical context is South Asia and the specific focus is on colonial India and present-day Bangladesh and Myanmar, many of the arguments, observations, and

---

[36] Chimni, *International Law and World Order*, 15. For a general discussion on TWAIL, see Makau Mutua and Antony Anghie, 'What is TWAIL?' *Proceedings of the Annual Meeting (American Society of International Law)* 94 (2000), 31–40; B. S. Chimni, 'The Past, Present and Future of International Law: A Critical Third World Approach', *Melbourne Journal of International Law* 8, no. 2 (2007), 499–515; Karin Mickelson, 'Taking Stock of TWAIL Histories', *International Community Law Review* 10, no. 4 (2008), 355–362; Obiora C. Okafor, 'Critical Third World Approaches to International Law (TWAIL): Theory, Methodology, or Both?' *International Community Law Review* 10, no. 4 (2008), 371–378; Antony Anghie, 'TWAIL: Past and Future', *International Communities Law Review* 10, no. 4 (2008), 479–481; James T. Gathii, 'TWAIL: A Brief History of Its Origins, Its Decentralized Network, and a Tentative Bibliography', *Trade, Law and Development* 3, no. 1 (2011), 26–64; Chimni, *International Law and World Order*, 15–18. See also Upendra Baxi, 'What May the "Third World" Expect from International Law?', *Third World Quarterly* 27, no. 5 (2006), 713–725.

findings of the book should be equally relevant to postcolonial states in Africa and Latin America. The normative and pragmatic significance of the book beyond the Rohingya or the CHT crisis lies in this fact. However, given that specific research on any other region has been outside the scope of this book, I refrain from making any explicit claim as to the universal application of my thesis. Instead, I leave it to relevant experts to test my arguments in other postcolonial contexts.

PART I

Ethno-nationalism and the Ideology
of the Postcolonial State

1

Geneses of Ethno-nationalism in Postcolonial States

1.1 Introduction

Ethno-nationalist politics and, in extreme cases, ethnic violence are defining features of postcolonial states. This is not to say that other states are completely immune from these devastating phenomena. Even in a number of Western democracies, such as Belgium, Canada, France, Spain, and the United Kingdom, minority groups keep challenging the existing state structures in one way or another. However, the prolonged colonial rule that caused the near-complete destruction of indigenous economic and political structures in order to accommodate colonial-capitalist modes of exploitation has shaped ethno-nationalism in postcolonial states in unique ways. Therefore, I begin my examination of international law's engagements with postcolonial states and the consequences of such engagements for minorities – the key focus of the book – with an analysis of some of the peculiar ways in which ethno-nationalism in postcolonial states takes root.

There is a general tendency among liberal scholars to explain destructive forces of nationalism in the non-Western world as a distortion of the otherwise grand liberal connotation and to blame specific 'sociological' conditions in those societies for such forces.[1] For those scholars, therefore, the deviation from the normal version of nationalism to a destructive one needs to be analysed by 'grouping and classifying the various empirical cases and then constructing coherent sets of sociological conditions which may be said to be the cause for each particular type of deviation'.[2] Once established, this sociological understanding of nationalism would then guide the

---

[1] For a detailed account, see Partha Chatterjee, *Nationalist Thought and the Colonial World* (London: Zed Books for the United Nations University, 1986), 1–6.
[2] Ibid., 3–4.

evolutionary process of political development, which has its teleological end in modernity.[3] Similarly, the incursion of ethnic attachments into what the liberal conceives of as civic nationalism is a cause for their concern, for in the liberal political imagination ethnicity is 'backward' and 'primitive'. As I have demonstrated in my earlier work, in the liberal tradition ethnicity symbolises a sense of 'otherness', something that falls outside the domain of liberal Western normalcy: the ethnic is non-Western while the West is post-ethnic. Therefore, by default, ethno-nationalism is generally depicted in international law as a uniquely non-Western phenomenon.[4] The proposed solution to this parochial problem of ethnicity is the same evolutionary progress to civilisation and modernity. The liberal essentialisation of ethno-nationalism as a sociological and cultural problem of non-Western societies – mostly postcolonial states – fails to grasp complexities emanating from colonial rule, its exploitative politico-economic structures, and the way nationalist elites engaged and responded to those structures in the course of anticolonial nationalist movements.

On the other hand, scholars of conflict studies offer useful general frameworks explaining why and how groups are mobilised along ethnic lines and how that leads to ethno-nationalist politics and ethnic violence. Primordialists argue that ethnic attachments that define one's entity in a broader society have enormous emotional value. Hence, any real, perceived, or constructed threat to language, religion, culture, or similar features plays a significant role in mobilising ethnic groups for collective action. By contrast, instrumentalists typically assume that human beings are rational individuals who act primarily for the purposes of optimising their profit in a given situation. They thus conceive of ethnic groups as a collection of profit-maximising individuals and, consequently, see ethnic conflicts as a form of competition over scarce economic resources between or among coalitions identified along ethnic lines.[5] Finally, elite-constructivists, who assert that ethnic conflicts are mere elite constructs, assume that various political, religious, or military elites mobilise individuals by accentuating and inventing individuals' ethnic attachments as well as claims to economic resources.[6] While these schools of thought offer important insights on ethnic

---

[3] Ibid., 5.
[4] See generally Shahabuddin, *Ethnicity and International Law*.
[5] See, for example, Francesco Caselli and Wilbur J. Coleman II, 'On the Theory of Ethnic Conflict', *Journal of the European Economic Association* 11, no. 1 (2013), 161–192.
[6] See, for example, Berch Berberoglu, *Nationalism and Ethnic Conflict: Class, State, and Nation in the Age of Globalization* (Lanham, MD: Rowman and Littlefield, 2004).

mobilisation and conflicts in general, we need to pay closer attention to the unique experience of postcolonial states to make sense of the way primordialism, instrumentalism, and elite-constructivism operate when it comes to ethno-nationalist politics in postcolonial states.

This chapter analyses the geneses of ethno-nationalism in postcolonial states. To this end, the next three sections highlight three key elements of ethno-nationalist politics: the modernist response to primordial attachments in the process of nation-building, the active role and passive consequences of colonialism, and the influence of bourgeois and petty bourgeois classes under capitalism. My analysis underscores that ethno-nationalism in postcolonial states is to a great extent the outcome of a combined force of all three elements. I must note that the three elements highlighted in my analysis of ethno-nationalism, while central to the argument and the framework that the book develops, are not exclusive aspects. Other relevant factors, such as gender, also contribute to this phenomenon. The combined force of these three factors does not operate in isolation of the gendered social structure, for example. However, ethno-nationalism in postcolonial states primarily draws on the elements of nation-building, colonialism, and capitalism.

I substantiate this claim with the case of anticolonial nationalist movements in India. I demonstrate how conditions created by colonialism, capitalism, and the modernist vision of the nascent Indian state gave the nationalist movement an ethno-nationalist character that ultimately led to the partition of the country along religious lines.

1.2 Nation-Building and Ethnic Accommodation

One of the most common themes in the discourse on ethno-nationalism in postcolonial states is the accommodation of ethnic affiliations in the process of modern nation-building. The anthropologist Clifford Geertz, in explicating the challenges of nation-building in postcolonial states, highlights two simultaneous and interconnected yet divergent motives that animate peoples in these states. One is the ego-driven need for the public recognition of their distinct identity and political relevance; the other is the demand for material progress and the pragmatic desire to be part of the modern state in order to benefit from its material values and comforts.[7] The tension between these

---

[7] Clifford Geertz, *The Interpretation of Cultures* (1973) (New York: Basic Books, 2000), 258. See also Isaiah Berlin, *Two Concepts of Liberty* (Oxford: Clarendon Press, 1958), 42; Edward Shils, 'Political Development in the New States', *Comparative Studies in Society and History* 2 (1960), 265–292, 379–411.

forces exists to some extent in all modern states, but Geertz argues that it takes extreme forms in postcolonial states. This is because primordial attachments are so salient in the political imagination of peoples in postcolonial states, even as they are aware of the material well-being they could expect to enjoy within the framework of a modern civil state.[8] In short, the conflict between primordial and civic sentiments strikes at the root of postcolonial statehood.[9]

Contrary to the understanding of primordialism in its classic version as a 'given' or 'natural' phenomenon,[10] Geertz terms ascriptive features as 'assumed given', for culture is inevitably involved in such matters of social existence.[11] Thus, he defines ethnic identity as a 'primordial sentiment' not because it is natural and biologically based, but because 'it is a historically important cultural identity that, in certain parts of the world, has become particularly crucial or salient politically'.[12] Anticolonial nationalist movements often reignited and cemented multiple ethnic consciousnesses, or 'parallel traditionalism' to take Geertz's phrase.[13] Such consciousnesses simultaneously attempted, though not always successfully, to consolidate all these re-energised primordial forces and channel them against colonial rule as a combined force of nationalism. The nationalist campaign had to work through prevalent semi-conscious perceptions of self-identification, often based on primordial attachments among people, and transform those into a notion of

---

[8] Geertz, *The Interpretation of Cultures*, 258-260.
[9] However, Geertz notes that the tension between these two ideologies in postcolonial states does not stem from any natural and irremovable antipathy between them. Instead, their 'clash is an outcome of the contrasting sorts of transformation that traditional political institutions and traditional modes of self-perception undergo as they move along their separate paths toward modernity'. See Geertz, 308.
[10] See, for example, Edward Shils, 'Primordial, Personal, Sacred, and Civil Ties', *British Journal of Sociology* 8 (1957), 130-145; Edward Shils, 'Colour, the Universal Intellectual Community, and the Afro-Asian Intellectual', *Daedalus* 96, no. 2 (Colour and Race) (1967), 279-295. See also John Hope Franklin (ed.), *Colour and Race* (Boston, MA: Houghton Mifflin Co., 1968).
[11] Geertz, *The Interpretation of Cultures*, 259. Although Geertz identifies immediate contiguity and kin connection as the icons of primordial attachment, he recognises that such ascriptive given-ness stems from being born into a particular religious community, speaking a particular language, or even a dialect of a language, and following particular social practices. See Clifford Geertz, *Old Societies and New States* (New York: Free Press, 1963), 108-113; Richard H. Thompson, *Theories of Ethnicity - A Critical Appraisal* (London: Greenwood Press, 1989), 53. For a detailed discussion on various strands of primordialism, see Shahabuddin, *Ethnity and International Law*, 12-19.
[12] Thompson, *Theories of Ethnicity*, 53.
[13] Geertz, *The Interpretation of Cultures*, 245.

collective identity.[14] This campaign reduces nationalism to the popular desire and demand for freedom that is to be enshrined in the to-be sovereign state. Geertz succinctly captures this mood with 'the nationalists would make the state, and the state would make the nation'.[15]

The new civil state, born out of a colonial regime, presents a new ideology of belongingness based on participation in state affairs.[16] At the same time, as primordialism remains for many the only source of legitimate authority, much of this new sense of belongingness translates into renewed concerns with one's relation to the centre of power seen through the optics of old primordial ties: tribe, region, religion, sect, and so on.[17] Anticolonial nationalist movements not only removed alien powers but also 'liberated the nationalisms within nationalisms', posing an immediate threat to 'the new-wrought national identity in whose name the revolution was made'.[18] The superimposition of the newfound civil bond on the century-old primordial alliance (and also opposition) and the reduction of primordial sentiments to a civil order with a view to creating national unity often prove counterproductive and only aggravate the tension between the two forces. 'The move towards national unity intensified group tensions within the society by raising settled cultural forms out of their particular contexts, expanding them into general allegiances, and politicising them.'[19]

Geertz, accordingly, finds the very *process* of the formation of a sovereign civil state primarily responsible for stimulating sentiments of 'parochialism, communalism, and racialism' as it 'introduced into society a valuable new prize over which to fight and a frightening new force with which to contend'.[20] His position contrasts with the dominant view on the origin of ethnic tension in postcolonial states, especially that of nationalist leaders, which attributes the key responsibility to the colonial policy of divide and rule. Instead, he identifies the source of such tensions as 'the replacement of a colonial regime by an independent, domestically anchored, purposeful unitary state', albeit without denying their historical origin and the role of colonialism in accentuating them.[21]

---

[14] Ibid., 239.
[15] Ibid.
[16] Ibid., 269–270.
[17] Ibid., 270.
[18] Ibid., 237.
[19] Ibid., 245.
[20] Ibid., 270. Footnotes omitted.
[21] Ibid.

His conclusion, therefore, follows that though this tension between primordial sentiments and civil politics in postcolonial states can be moderated, it probably cannot be entirely dissolved.[22]

In this sense, Geertz's account of ethno-nationalism in postcolonial states relies to some extent on the specific 'sociological' conditions in these states. He identifies 'the great extent to which their peoples' sense of self remains bound up in the gross actualities of blood, race, language, locality, religion, or tradition' as one of the key reasons behind a strong sense of ethno-nationalism in postcolonial states.[23] This obsession with primordial attachments in postcolonial societies, he argues, appears in contrast with modern societies, where the political relevance of primordialism is kept to the minimum and national unity is maintained by the coercive force – both muscular and ideological – of allegiance to a civil state. In his view, this is why people in postcolonial states often see a potential loss of identity in subordinating their primordial identification to an overarching civil order – through absorption into a 'culturally undifferentiated mass' or, even worse, through domination by some other rival ethnic, racial, or linguistic community.[24]

To break with this essentialised notion of a 'sociological' condition to explain ethno-nationalism, we must clarify how and under what historical and material conditions primordial attachments take the particular political shape that ultimately turns into credible challenges to the legitimacy of the postcolonial state itself. In this regard, the role of colonialism and the influence of bourgeois classes under capitalism require investigation. The next two sections shed light on these core elements of ethno-nationalism.

1.3 Colonialism and Relative Ethnic Entitlements

Unlike Geertz, Donald Horowitz puts colonialism at the heart of the process through which various primordial identities are underscored, sharpened, juxtaposed, and politicised. Geertz is probably right in his

---

[22] Ibid., 276. According to him, these states must not wish primordial attachments out of existence 'by belittling them or even denying their reality'; instead, they must 'reconcile them with the unfolding civil order by divesting them of their legitimizing force with respect to governmental authority, by neutralizing the apparatus of the state in relationship to them, and by channelling discontent arising out of their dislocation into properly political rather than parapolitical forms of expression'. See ibid., 277.
[23] Ibid., 258.
[24] Ibid., 258–260.

assertion that most nationalist writers reduce the role of colonialism to the policy of 'divide and rule'. The story is indeed far more complex; reducing colonialism to a single policy obscures nuances of colonial interventions and their impacts on ethnic relations. Horowitz grasps these nuances in his theory of group entitlement in which 'relative group worth' and 'relative group legitimacy', created and facilitated by colonial interventions, merge into a politics of ethnic entitlement and, ultimately, ethno-nationalism.[25]

In many cases, colonisation was what first led to the juxtaposition of various ethnic groups.[26] Horowitz argues that such juxtaposition paved the way for ethnic group comparison, which essentially produced a sense of relative group worth and relative group legitimacy. First, the dichotomy between 'backward' and 'advanced' groups was facilitated by colonial administrators' differentiated distribution of opportunities. Groups located near the colonial capital, near a rail line or port, or near some centres of colonial commerce were well situated to take up opportunities as they arose.[27] In other cases, different ethnic groups responded differently to new opportunities created by colonialism, thereby engendering relative economic empowerment or backwardness.

However, the relationship between colonialism and group disparity was not always passive. Often, colonial governments more actively promoted differential treatment of ethnic groups as a matter of policy, for example, in the encouragement of immigration, the protection of some groups against others, and the employment of certain groups for colonial administrative purposes.[28] There was also deliberate use of one group against another.[29]

---

[25] Donald Horowitz, *Ethnic Groups in Conflict* (1985) (Berkeley, CA: University of California Press, 2000), 186.

[26] Colonial administrations' engagement with subject populations and attempts to govern them often resulted in the strengthening of ethnic allegiances as against other bonds. For colonial administration, it appeared prudent to adapt preexisting, informal social institutions of kinship and ethnicity, which were not likely to immediately threaten the colonial regime. Also, the combined effect of territorial expansion and centralised government facilitated subgroup amalgamation among previously decentralised groups and sharpened ethnic lines between different groups. In cases, where 'indirect rule' was applied, colonial administrations essentially relied on traditional ethnic leadership and thereby approved the notion that ethnicity was a valid basis for administration and cultural unity. See ibid., 149–151.

[27] Ibid., 151.

[28] Ibid., 157.

[29] Ibid., 158.

Given that the whole colonial structure was based on a civilisational discourse, such premises also had an ambivalent impact on the colonial evaluation of ethnic groups as advanced or backward. The evolutionary science of the nineteenth century that came to be known as 'Darwinism' offered not only a blueprint for a hierarchical mapping of the international society but also an agenda of action for dealing with 'primitive-uncivilised' nations. Depending on underlying monogenic or polygenic perceptions of social Darwinism, responses to these 'backward' nations took different paths.[30] This racially motivated hierarchical mapping worked at the micro level too. Social Darwinism proved to be an extremely handy tool for ordering, according to evolutionary progress, various groups that European colonial powers 'discovered' in the rest of the world. In India, as Meena Radhakrishna notes, the evolutionary theory was applied to 'sort out the loyal from the disloyal, the respectable from the criminal, the malleable from the obstinate'.[31] The colonialists 'set in motion a comparative process by which aptitudes and disabilities imputed on to ethnic groups were to be evaluated. Those evaluations, solidly based in the group disparities that emerged, could not be dismissed as the irrelevant invention of a foreign overlord.'[32] Thus, taken together, the outcomes of various active and passive policy interventions by colonial administrations led to new standards of group evaluation that did not automatically wither away following decolonisation.

For Horowitz, the cutting edge of comparison and conflict is the juxtaposition of backward and advanced groups.[33] To be backward is, first and foremost, to feel weak vis-à-vis advanced groups. He explains how backward groups in general feel at a competitive disadvantage as they compare their imputed personal qualities with those imputed to advanced groups. This results in self-stereotypes and other-stereotypes. When this feeling is manipulated by the in-group elites, there emerge calls for 'catching up', and to this end, '[c]ompensatory measures are demanded to offset the presumed superior ability of advanced groups to compete'.[34] Another aspect of being backward is anxiety about future. This anxiety usually takes the form of apprehension about being

---

[30] See Shahabuddin, *Ethnicity and International Law*, 62–97.
[31] Meena Radhakrishna, 'Of Apes and Ancestors: Evolutionary Science and Colonial Ethnography', in *Adivasis in Colonial India: Survivals, Resistance and Negotiation*, ed. Biswamoy Pati (New Delhi: Orient Blackswan Private Ltd., 2011), 39.
[32] Horowitz, *Ethnic Groups in Conflict*, 164.
[33] Ibid., 166.
[34] Ibid., 174.

dominated by the advanced groups, and in extreme cases, it becomes an issue of survival.[35]

Relative group worth, according to Horowitz, is related to relative group legitimacy in that the need to feel worthy is a fundamental human requirement satisfied in considerable measure by belonging to groups that are regarded as worthy. And collective social recognition of worth is conferred by political affirmation. Hence, struggles over relative group worth are readily transferred to the political system. 'Groups that do suffer from such comparisons tend, therefore, to make stronger claims to priority by virtue of legitimacy, so as to make up on one front what they have lost on the other.'[36] Groups may claim legitimacy on the basis of prior occupation (relating to territory), special mission (often religious in character), traditional rule (earlier domination), or the right to succeed the colonial power (due to close relationship with the coloniser).[37] In many cases, the colonial powers have endorsed these claims of legitimacy for their own expediency. On the basis of such differential claims of legitimacy, the interrelationship between competing groups is often reshaped in postcolonial states.[38] Upon gaining independence from colonial rule, postcolonial states overnight assume the challenging task of mitigating such ethnic tensions.

Thus, the role of colonialism in generating and shaping ethnonationalism in postcolonial states is much more nuanced in nature and more enduring in consequences than a simple policy of divide and rule. The colonial construction of relative group worth and relative group legitimacy through ethnic group comparisons offered necessary conditions by which ethnic relations took political meanings and got translated into material contestations in the political domain of the postcolonial

---

[35] Ibid., 176–181.
[36] Ibid., 186.
[37] See generally ibid., 202–207.
[38] Groups that claim legitimacy on the ground of prior occupation tend to depict other groups as 'immigrants'. If the claims (or pretensions) to legitimacy are acknowledged by other groups, the latter are likely to pursue moderate strategies. Where there is a split between indigenous and immigrants (relative group legitimacy issue), it tends to coincide with the split between backward and advanced groups (relative group worth issue). Backward-indigenous groups feel under siege in their own home, a powerful feeling that often calls up determined and violent political activity, and consequently they typically (i) demand preferential treatment in education, employment, or business; (ii) demand the political exclusion of advanced groups; (iii) behave immoderately; and (iv) sometimes entertain an almost revolutionary bitterness about the past and the hand it dealt them. On the other hand, under such circumstances, the advanced groups make demands for the universal principle of equality. Ibid., 213–215.

state. In this sense, the ethno-nationalism that most postcolonial states inherit is a direct consequence – both intended and unintended – of colonial policy interventions. We are then left with the third element of ethno-nationalism, capitalist conditions, to which we now turn.

1.4 Capitalism and Ethnic Polarisation

While Horowitz sheds lights on how colonial policies trigger ethno-nationalism in a top-down way, Partha Chatterjee adopts a bottom-up approach. He demonstrates how nationalist resistance to colonialism itself, despite its appeal for unity and cohesion, paradoxically took an ethno-nationalist turn that postcolonial states then had to live with following decolonisation. In this narrative, capitalism makes possible the material condition whereby mass mobilisation follows an ethnic alignment, as opposed to a class alignment, which could have been a more natural outcome. Chatterjee thus deviates from the classical Marxist approach to the question of ethno-nationalism, which views nationalism as morally neutral. Horace Davis, for example, values nationalism depending on its class character: 'Considered as a movement against national oppression, it has a positive moral content; considered as the vehicle of aggression, it is morally indefensible.'[39] Therefore, nationalism needs to be looked at in its instrumental aspect: whether or not it furthers the universal movement of historical progress. More recently, Berch Berberoglu has taken the same view, distinguishing the use of nationalist ideology by 'working-class organizations to mobilize the masses, responding to their yearning for national identity and independence under colonial and neocolonial conditions' from the nationalist ideology of 'the bourgeois forces that use nationalism as an extension of their narrow, nationally based class interest, portraying it as the general national interest'.[40]

In contrast, Chatterjee takes a critical Marxist position that relies on the Gramscian notion that the 'passive revolution of capital' is the general form of the transition from colonial to postcolonial nation-states in the twentieth century. With reference to the moment of the 'Resurgence' leading to the unification of the state of Italy (the *Risorgimento*), Gramsci argues in his 'Notes on Italian History' that if new claimants to power – the new

---

[39] Horace B. Davis, *Towards a Marxist Theory of Nationalism* (New York: Monthly Review Press, 1978), 31.
[40] Berberoglu, *Nationalism and Ethnic Conflict*, 113.

bourgeoisie – lack the necessary social and military capacity to subjugate hitherto dominant classes and establish complete hegemony over the new nation, they prefer an alternative mode of operation. They take a toned-down approach in line with the available social and military strength, in which their demands for a new society are 'satisfied by small doses, legally, in a reformist manner – in such a way that it was possible to preserve the political and economic position of the old feudal classes'.[41] In other words, the new bourgeoisie embarks upon a 'passive revolution' by attempting a '"molecular transformation" of the old dominant classes into partners in a new historical bloc and only a partial appropriation of the popular masses, in order first to create a state as the necessary precondition for the establishment of capitalism as the dominant mode of production'.[42]

Gramsci's view here is clearly informed by the Marxist proposition that the social order perishes only after all the productive forces within it have fully developed, and its corollary that no new and higher relations of production are born until the necessary material conditions for their existence have matured within the old society itself.[43] The application of these two Marxist propositions to the case of the Italian Resurgence reveals for Gramsci not only the historical impediments to bourgeois hegemony but also the possibilities of marginal change within those limits.[44] Gramsci examines these limits in terms of three levels of the relation of forces: the objective structure (the lack of an appropriate, fully developed system of capitalist production); political forces (an incomplete and fragmented ideology and organisation of the bourgeoisie, in relation to both the coercive power of the state and the intellectual-moral leadership in society); and technical and politico-military forces (the lack of capacity to either destroy the war potential of the dominant group or compel the dominant military force to 'thin out' and disperse itself over

---

[41] Antonio Gramsci, *Selections from the Prison Notebooks*, trans. Q. Hoare and G. Nowell Smith (New York: International Publishers, 1971), 119.

[42] Chatterjee, *Nationalist Thought and the Colonial World*, 30. For discussions on Gramsci's 'passive revolution' thesis, see Christine Buci-Glucksmann, 'State, Transition and Passive Revolution', in *Gramsci and Social Theory*, ed. Chantal Mouffe (London: Routledge, 1979), 113–167; Christine Buci-Glucksmann, *Gramsci and the State*, trans. David Fernbach (London: Lawrence and Wishart, 1980), 290–324; Anne S. Sassoon, 'Passive Revolution and the Politics of Reform', in *Approaches to Gramsci*, ed. A. Sassoon (London: Writers and Readers, 1982), 127–148.

[43] Karl Marx, 'Preface to *A Contribution to the Critique of Political Economy*', in Karl Marx and Friedrich Engels, *Selected Works*, vol. I (Moscow: Progress Publishers, 1969), 504.

[44] Chatterjee, *Nationalist Thought*, 43.

a large territory).⁴⁵ Taken together, these three limitations of the new bourgeoisie aspiring for hegemony in a new national political order mandate only low-intensity warfare – a 'war of position' – against the old bourgeoisie in which the nascent bourgeoisie can attempt only

> a 'molecular transformation' of the state, neutralizing opponents, converting sections of the former ruling classes into allies in a partially reorganized system of government, undertaking economic reforms on a limited scale so as to appropriate the support of the popular masses but keeping them out of any form of direct participation in the process of governance. This is the 'passive revolution', a historical phase in which the 'war of position' coincides with the revolution of capital.⁴⁶

According to Gramsci, these molecular changes controlled from the top simultaneously face the contrasting tendency of popular initiative and radical challenge – a 'war of movement'. The resulting equilibrium is indeterminate, contingent upon the political-ideological leadership of each tendency.⁴⁷ And there is also a third element besides the relative quality of the leadership on the two sides: the asymmetry arises from certain 'organic tendencies of the modern state' which seem to favour forces that carry out a protracted, many-faceted, and well-coordinated 'war of position' rather than those which think only of an immediate 'war of movement'.⁴⁸

Applying this criterion of 'molecular changes' to anticolonial nationalist campaigns in the third world, Chatterjee argues that at the level of the objective structure, an aspiring bourgeoisie faces a dual problem: the lack of a system of capitalist development at home and the simultaneous dominance of advanced metropolitan capitalism. To mitigate this problem, the bourgeoisie needs to engage in a political struggle with the colonial power and the local forces, both of which obstruct the desired transformation of the domestic economy.⁴⁹ Given that it does not have the military capacity needed to subjugate the colonial power, the default position for the new bourgeoisie therefore is a 'war of position'. Conceiving of the Indian nationalist campaign as a 'war of position', Chatterjee highlights three stages or 'moments' – the moments of departure, manoeuvre, and arrival – as building blocks of the ideological history of the Indian state.

---

[45] Gramsci, *Selections from the Prison Notebooks*, 180–185.
[46] Chatterjee, *Nationalist Thought*, 45.
[47] Gramsci, *Selections from the Prison Notebooks*, 110.
[48] Ibid., 112; Chatterjee, *Nationalist Thought*, 47.
[49] Chatterjee, *Nationalist Thought*, 48.

Here we mainly focus on the three moments as the case of anticolonial ethno-nationalism in India is discussed in the following section.

For Chatterjee, the 'moment of departure' lies in the juxtaposition of the nationalist consciousness with post-Enlightenment rationalist thought. This encounter presented nationalist elites with a dilemma: on the one hand, they denied that the essential cultural difference between Europe and non-Europe represented an inferiority of the colonised people. On the other hand, they had to demonstrate the capacity to 'modernise' the nation while retaining its cultural identity. Long before any organised political movement against the colonial rule, Chatterjee argues, anticolonial nationalism tackled this dilemma by dividing the world of social institutions and practices into two domains. While in the 'external' material domain of the economy, politics, science, and technology, the West had proved its superiority, in the 'inner' spiritual domain the East maintained its superiority.[50] The inner domain was the core of cultural identity, the sovereign domain not to be violated by the colonial power. The proposition that '[t]rue modernity for the non-European nations would lie in combining the superior material qualities of Western cultures with the spiritual greatness of the East', thus, remains a fundamental feature of anticolonial nationalisms in Asia and Africa.[51] In accepting this proposition, the protagonists of anticolonial nationalism accepted the very intellectual premises of 'modernity' on which colonial domination was based.[52]

Chatterjee uses the example of Bankimchandra Chattopadhyay (1838–1894), one of the most influential nationalists of this moment and a prominent Bengali literary figure. He demonstrates how Bankim conceived of the subjection of India in terms of the decay of this cultural superiority – the cultural failure of the Indian people to face up to the realities of power that resulted in 700 years of foreign rule, first by Muslims and subsequently by the British.[53] Bankim therefore argued for a national-cultural project: the creation of a cultural ideal that would retain the spiritual greatness of Eastern culture, with a total regeneration of the national religion, as opposed to the mere religious reforms advocated by many modernists and patronised by the colonial

---

[50] Chatterjee, *The Nation and Its Fragments*, 6.
[51] Chatterjee, *Nationalist Thought*, 51; Chatterjee, *The Nation and Its Fragments*, 6. See also, for example, Okakura Kakuzo, *The Awakening of Japan* (London: John Murray, 1905); Okakura Kakuzo, *The Book of Tea* (1906) (New York: Dover, 1964).
[52] Chatterjee, *Nationalist Thought*, 30.
[53] Ibid., 56.

administration.[54] By definition, this ethno-nationalism was an elitist programme, for 'the act of cultural synthesis can only be performed by the supremely refined intellect'.[55] To enmesh the masses, then, Bankim's imagination of the national religion was rooted exclusively in Hindu ideals, although his home province, Bengal, was heavily populated by Muslims. As Chatterjee notes, 'the national-cultural project was not only to define a distinct cultural identity for the nation and to assert its claim to modernity, it was also to find a viable cultural basis for the convergence of the national and the popular'.[56]

In a large agrarian country like India, it was imperative not only to take nationalist politics to the peasantry but also to establish an intellectual-moral leadership over them, as a precondition to posing a meaningful challenge to the colonial authority. According to Chatterjee, this is where the 'moment of manoeuvre' happens. Here he takes the example of Mahatma Gandhi (1869–1948), exposing how Gandhi intervened in the elite-nationalist politics in India with his non-violent techniques and integrated the agrarian class into the nationalist movement for the first time. Gandhi thus successfully demonstrated that an authentic national movement could only be built upon the organised support of the whole of the peasantry. Yet, with such enthusiastic participation of the masses in nationalist politics, Gandhi did not really ask for any agency for the masses: the politics still had to be conceived and executed by the dominant class. Thus, Gandhism offered 'the conception of a national framework of politics in which the peasants are mobilized but do not participate, of a nation of which they are a part but a national state from which they are for ever distanced'.[57]

Political manoeuvring by the elites to integrate the masses into nationalist politics often relied on primordial attachments. In the case of India specifically, it relied on religious communalism. Largely due to the colonial policy interventions and elite responses to colonialism – as we saw in the previous section on ethnic entitlements – the bourgeois classes in Hindu and Muslim communities emerged at different phases of Indian national movements. As we shall see in the following case study, the competing bourgeois classes mobilised their respective target masses along the line of respective religious revivalism that was packaged as their own version of nationalism. This ethno-nationalism was ultimately

[54] Ibid., 74.
[55] Ibid., 51.
[56] Ibid., 75.
[57] Ibid., 125.

translated into political party form, leading to the partition of India at the moment of decolonisation. There is a direct link between mass mobilisation and ethno-nationalism in most anticolonial movements.

And finally, in Chatterjee's 'moment of arrival', the postcolonial state appears as the final building block of the nationalist thought, one in which 'the central organising principle is the autonomy of state: the legitimising principle is a conception of social justice'.[58] Using the example of Jawaharlal Nehru (1889–1964) Chatterjee demonstrates how at the final stage of the nationalist movement, aspiring statesmen like Nehru conceived of the postcolonial 'state' as the embodiment of the spirit of 'progress' and 'modernity'. Nehru believed that all problems of social injustice would be eradicated within the framework of a modern postcolonial state that would undertake an 'effective reorganisation of the economic structures of production and distribution of the new state by assuming the central planning, coordinating and directing role'.[59] Since such necessary conditions for ensuring social justice were impossible in the colonial state, 'the principal political task before the nation [was] to establish a sovereign national state' that would 'stand above the narrow interests of groups and classes in society, take an overall view of the matter', and with scientific economic planning create enough social wealth to ensure welfare and justice for all.[60] A developmental ethos was central to the imagination of the postcolonial nation-state.[61]

In formulating this economic vision of the nascent state, nationalist leaders at this moment of arrival had to be mindful of the 'backward' counterforces of primordial attachments, communalism, and religious obscurantism that were prevalent in colonial societies. Fortunately, they thought, the modern progressive state had the mitigating power to deal with these backward forces – in the 'public' domain – through liberal constitutionalism, equal rights of citizenship, economic development, and social justice.[62] However, the 'inner' domain, in which nationalism claimed its autonomy and cherished its ties of race, language, and culture, hardly corresponded to the domain of the modern state, which now commenced the task of clearing out these very 'private' ties from the 'public' sphere. Autonomous forms of imagination of the community

---

[58] Ibid., 132.
[59] Ibid., 133.
[60] Ibid.
[61] Chatterjee, *The Nation and Its Fragments*, 203.
[62] Chatterjee, *Nationalist Thought*, 141.

continue to be overwhelmed and swamped by the history of the postcolonial state in this way. Chatterjee, therefore, concludes:

> The presence of populist or communitarian elements in the liberal constitutional order of the postcolonial state ought not to be read as a sign of the inauthenticity or disingenuousness of elite politics; it is rather a recognition in the elite domain of the very real presence of an arena of subaltern politics over which it must dominate and yet which also had to be negotiated on its own terms for the purposes of producing consent.[63]

Thus, taken together, the three accounts of the geneses of ethno-nationalism in postcolonial states – ethnic accommodation in the making of the modern state, the role of colonialism in relative ethnic entitlements, and the capitalist material condition in which nationalism germinates within the framework of passive revolution and consequently cements ethno-nationalism at various phases of its development – reveal the interconnected nature of the building blocks of each approach: modernist nation-building, colonialism, and capitalism. Chatterjee's moments of 'departure' and 'manoeuvre' in the nationalist discourse explain how ethnic elements get political meanings, which are then transformed into a language of polarisation. However, the nationalist elites' confidence at the moment of 'arrival' that progress, modernity, and the science of economic development – in short, the postcolonial state – will suppress elements of communalism and primordial loyalty links to what Geertz identifies as the root cause of the persistent problem of ethno-nationalism in postcolonial states. As we saw, Geertz identifies the unification of modern states – the arbitrary combination of diverse communities within one political unit and dismantling of their primordial attachments – as the key reason for the ethno-nationalist surge in postcolonial states. Unlike Geertz, Chatterjee does not consider communalism a reflection of primordial sentiments; instead, for him, the equation of Hindu nationalism with Indian nationalism – to the exclusion of all other communities – at the moments of 'departure' and 'manoeuvre', can be seen as a 'modernist' phenomenon, in that its appeal is political rather than religious.[64]

Again, with inadequate attention to or only a peripheral treatment of colonialism and its protracted impact on the consolidation and polarisation of ethnic identities, Geertz's analysis remains less than comprehensive. On the other hand, Horowitz's account of the way that relative group

---

[63] Chatterjee, *The Nation and Its Fragments*, 12–13.
[64] Ibid., 110.

worth and relative group legitimacy – initiated, facilitated, or aggravated by colonial policies – ultimately result in some form of politics of ethnic entitlements in postcolonial states does not engage with the vital point of the capitalist material conditions that offer the necessary premise for such polarisation. It, therefore, follows that any meaningful attempt to trace the origin of ethno-nationalism in postcolonial states needs to pay attention to all three elements: the modernist project of nation-building, the influence of colonialism, and the material conditions created by capitalism.

To illustrate the foregoing discussion on the genesis of ethno-nationalism in postcolonial states, in the following section I discuss the specific case of anticolonial nationalist movements in India. It must be noted that I do not intend to offer a comprehensive history of Indian nationalist movements. Instead, my aim is to highlight the manner in which the three key driving forces of ethno-nationalism – the vision of the modern state, colonialism, and capitalism – informed and shaped the anticolonial nationalist movement in India and sowed the seed of communalism. Also, my narrative of the nationalist movement focuses mainly on the religious divide between the Hindus and Muslims, which undoubtedly came to symbolise ethno-nationalism in the Indian context and led ultimately to the partition of the country. However, ethno-nationalism in Indian nationalist movements was far more complex and cannot be fully conveyed with an account of Hindu–Muslim rivalry. Given India's cultural diversity, the connotation of the Hindu–Muslim dichotomy as homogeneous is quite artificial, although this false homogeneity was readily accepted and translated into colonial policies as well as nationalist politics. On the other hand, while the institutional political rivalry between Congress and the Muslim League epitomises my arguments about ethno-nationalism in Indian nationalist movements, anticolonial resistance in India had a far wider reach beyond institutional politics. Subaltern historiographers have demonstrated how other forms of resistance, for example, by peasants or indigenous communities, characterised anticolonial movements in India.[65] There is also rich

---

[65] See, for example, Ranajit Guha, *Elementary Aspects of Peasant Insurgency in Colonial India* (Delhi: Oxford University Press, 1983); Ranajit Guha, *Dominance without Hegemony: History and Power in Colonial India* (Cambridge, MA: Harvard University Press, 1998); Ranajit Guha, *History at the Limit of World-History* (New York: Columbia University Press 2002); Sumit Sarkar, *Modern India 1885–1947* (Delhi: Macmillan, 1983). For a powerful account of how violence in the wake of the Partition shaped everyday lives of women, see Veena Das, *Life and Words: Violence and the Descent into the Ordinary* (Berkeley, CA: University of California Press, 2006).

literature on how feminist movements contributed to all strands of Indian nationalist thought – from bourgeois reformist to communist – in the nineteenth and early twentieth centuries.[66] In this sense, my account in the following section is deliberately narrow. Designed only to substantiate the preceding normative claims regarding the geneses of ethno-nationalism in postcolonial states, it consciously refrains from offering a general framework for explaining ethno-nationalism in the Indian nationalist movement as a whole. However, given the common colonial history of the Indian subcontinent, observations made in the following section will set the backdrop for my analysis of the ideology of the postcolonial state in Chapter 2, and also for my specific case studies on the Rohingya and the hill people of the CHT in subsequent chapters.

1.5 The Case of Anticolonial Ethno-nationalism in India

The protagonists of Indian nationalism bear testimony to Geertz's observation that nationalist leaders of postcolonial states attribute the primary responsibility for ethnic tension to the colonial policy of divide and rule. For example, with reference to minority issues in the future constitution of India, one of the most prominent nationalist leaders, Abul Kalam Azad, in his presidential address at the Ramgarh Conference of the Indian National Congress in December 1940, made the point clear:

> For a hundred and fifty years British imperialism has pursued the policy of divide and rule, and by emphasising internal differences, sought to use various groups for the consolidation of its own power. That was the inevitable result of India's political subjection, and it is folly for us to complain and grow bitter. A foreign government can never encourage internal unity in the subject country, for disunity is the surest guarantee for the continuance of its own domination.[67]

Jawaharlal Nehru too noted the point, albeit in a more subtle way, in his remark that although British policy was initially inclined to be pro-Hindu

---

[66] See, for example, Pratima Asthana, *Women's Movement in India* (New Delhi: Vikas Publishing House, 1974); Vina Mazumdar, 'The Social Reform Movement in India from Ranade to Nehru', in *Indian Women: From Purdah to Modernity*, ed. Bal Ram Nanda (New Delhi: Radiant Publishers, 1976), 41–66; Renu Chakravartty, *Communists in Indian Women's Movement* (New Delhi: People's Publishing House, 1980); Manmohan Kaur, *Women in India's Freedom Struggle* (New Delhi: Sterling Publishers Private Ltd., 1985); Jayawardena, *Feminism and Nationalism in the Third World*, 73–108; Chatterjee, *The Nation and Its Fragments*, 116–157.

[67] A. Moin Zaidi and Shaheda G. Zaidi (eds.), *The Encyclopaedia of the Indian National Congress*, vol. 12 (New Delhi: S. Chand & Co., 1981), 355.

and anti-Muslim, it underwent a gradual change in the 1870s and became more favourable to Muslims. 'This change was essentially due to the policy of balance and counterpoise which the British Government had consistently pursued.'[68] Commenting on the political deadlock caused by Hindu–Muslim rivalry, Nehru identified the crisis primarily as a creation of the British policy. In his words: 'Naturally the British did not favour any real settlement which would strengthen the political movement – now grown to mass proportions – against them. It was a triangle with the Government in a position to play off one side against the other, by giving special privileges.'[69]

As a matter of fact, it would be rather difficult even for an earnest sympathiser of British rule to deny the presence of a conscious colonial policy of divide and rule and the damaging long-term impact it has had and arguably is still having on communal relations in India. Although the initial colonial policy was to work with the ostensibly 'progressive' class of Indian society and advance the religious reform agenda, after the Sepoy Revolt of 1857 (which came to be known as Sepoy 'mutiny' in the official narrative) British policy dramatically changed. The path of social reform was gradually abandoned, and enthusiastic protection was given to every reactionary religious survival and custom instead.[70] The Queen's Proclamation of 1858 formally pledged that the Government would abstain from 'all interference with religious belief or worship' and that 'due regard will be paid to the ancient rights, usages and customs of India'.[71] From this period onwards, the methods of communal division, including playing Hindus and Muslims against one another, were an integral part of British colonial policies in India.[72]

Though honed following the events of 1857, the need for a divisive policy in India was already in the air as early as 1821. In the *Asiatic Review* of May 1821, a British officer writing under the name of 'Carnaticus' declared that '*Divide et impera* should be the motto of our Indian administration, whether political, civil or military'.[73] In the middle of the nineteenth century, the Commandant of Moradabad, Lieutenant-

---

[68] Jawaharlal Nehru, *The Discovery of India* (1946), 3rd ed. (New Delhi: Oxford University Press, 1999), 342–344.
[69] Ibid., 381.
[70] Rajani Palme Dutt, *India To-day* (1940), 10th ed. (New Delhi: People's Publishing House Ltd., 2008), 307.
[71] Ibid.
[72] Ibid., 437. According to Dutt, the other important area is the question of Princely States.
[73] Ibid., 456.

Colonel Coke, argued that '[o]ur endeavour should be to uphold in full force the [...] separation which exists between the different religions and races, not to endeavour to amalgamate them. *Divide et impera* [sic] should be the principle of Indian government.'[74] Similarly, John Strachey, a leading authority on India, wrote in 1888 that '[t]he truth plainly is that the existence side by side of these hostile creeds is one of the strong points in our political position in India'.[75] Although in the 1894 edition of his book Strachey softened this blunt assertion, he nonetheless stood by the divisive policy: 'The better classes of Mohammedans are a source to us of strength and not of weakness. They constitute a comparatively small but energetic minority of the populations, whose political interests are identical with ours, and who, under no conceivable circumstances, would prefer Hindu dominion to our own.'[76] Likewise, the Secretary of State for India, Lord Olivier, wrote in a letter to *The Times* in 1926: 'No one with a close acquaintance with Indian affairs will be prepared to deny that on the whole there is a predominant bias in British officialdom in India in favour of the Muslim community, partly on the ground of closer sympathy, but more largely as a makeweight against Hindu nationalism.'[77] The importance of the Hindu–Muslim divide for the continuation of British rule is expressed in an editorial in *The Times* in 1941, albeit in a more passive form: 'To emphasise the essential importance of Hindu-Muslim agreement does not imply that the British are pursuing a policy of "divide and Rule". *The divisions exist and British rule is certain as long as they do.*'[78]

The colonial policy that had perhaps the deepest influence on cementing the distinct political consciousness between Hindu and Muslim communities that led ultimately to the partition of India was the colonial policy of a separate electorate for Muslims. It was introduced through the legislative council reforms of 1909 under the authority of Viceroy Lord Minto. This system of separate electorates for Muslims and the rest had the longstanding effect of encouraging political organisation and electoral appeal in line with communal affiliations within a given territorial constituency. Under this arrangement, Muslims could only stand for election and be elected by separate Muslim electorates. A political barrier was thus created 'reversing the unifying and amalgamating process which

---

[74] Quoted in Baman Das Basu, *Consolidation of the Christian Power in India* (Calcutta: R. Chatterjee, 1927), 74.
[75] John Strachey, *India* (London: Kegan Paul & Co., 1888), 255.
[76] John Strachey, *India*, rev. ed. (London: Kegan Paul & Co., 1894), 241.
[77] Lord Olivier, letter in *The Times*, 10 July 1926.
[78] Editorial, *The Times*, 21 January 1941. Italic in original.

had been going on for centuries'.[79] Nurtured by official policies, this barrier grew further with every extension of the franchise and thereby affected the whole structure of public and social life. The Government of India Act 1935 extended the provision for separate representation to the Sikhs, the Anglo-Indians, the Indian Christians, and the Depressed Classes, as well as to the Europeans, landholders, commerce, and industry.[80] Instead of actually helping educationally and economically backward minorities, the policy of separate electorates created new vested interest groups and thereby strengthened the ethno-nationalist outlook of the emerging Muslim bourgeois class.

The more politically charged British policy of divide and rule was the partition of Bengal in 1905. The decision to partition Bengal was made by the then Viceroy Lord Curzon, although the need for such a divisive policy was noted as early as 1896 by the commissioner of Chittagong division, W. B. Oldham. Oldham believed the creation of the new Muslim-majority province would 'unite the most important part of the Mohammedan population of Eastern India' and thereby reduce the 'politically threatening' position of the dominant Hindu minority in undivided Bengal.[81] The partition of 1905 enforced the division of Bengal on a communal basis into a Muslim-majority east Bengal and Assam and a Hindu-majority west Bengal. Though the British publicly insisted that the partition was made only for administrative reasons,[82] Curzon's well-known speech in Dhaka (then Dacca) on 18 February 1904 echoes Oldham's point that the partition plan would 'invest the Mohammedans in Eastern Bengal with a unity which they have not enjoyed since the days of the old Mussulman viceroys and kings'.[83] That the separation of the two communities was Curzon's political motive behind the partition appears more vividly in his letter written a day earlier.[84]

---

[79] Nehru, *Discovery of India*, 354.
[80] Dutt, *India To-day*, 461.
[81] W. B. Oldham to Chief Secretary of the Government of Bengal, No. 722 G of 7 February 1896, *Home Public Programmes* A, May 1897, n. 204–234, cited in Kalpana Bishui, 'The Origin and Evolution of the Scheme for the First Partition of Bengal (1905)', *Quarterly Review of Historical Studies* 5, no. 2 (1965–6), 76–96.
[82] Leonard A. Gordon, 'Divided Bengal: Problems of Nationalism and Identity in the 1947 Partition', in *India's Partition: Process, Strategy and Mobilisation* (2001), ed. Mushirul Hasan (New Delhi: Oxford University Press, 2013), 286. See also Z. H. Zaidi, 'The Political Motive in the Partition of Bengal', *Journal of the Pakistan Historical Society* 12 (1964), 113–149.
[83] P. Mukherji, *All About Partition* (Calcutta: 2 Sreenath Das's Lane, 1905), 39.
[84] In that letter, written on board a train from Chittagong to Dhaka, Curzon explains: 'The Bengalis, who like to think themselves a nation, and who dream of a future when the

It is not a coincidence that the All India Muslim League, which ultimately claimed to represent all Indian Muslims, was established in Dhaka in 1906 under the auspices of Nawab Salimullah Khan and with full support from the colonial administration, as we shall see later. The partition helped arouse both Muslim political consciousness and extensive agitation on the part of the economically dominant Hindu minority who feared loss of influence. Heightened communal tension in the aftermath of the partition led to communal riots, in which separatist propaganda by local Muslim leaders managed to bring on board the Muslim agrarian class, which constituted the vast majority of the population of east Bengal.[85] In the face of sustained communal tensions and incessant opposition from nationalists, mainly Hindu elites, the British reversed their decision and the two parts of Bengal were reunited in December 1911 with a transfer of the capital of British India from Calcutta to Delhi. The impact of the short-lived partition and ensuing riots on communal relations in Bengal and the way they shaped politics in the rest of India persisted for a long time after. As Sumit Sarkar notes, 'a national movement which had entered its militant phase with one partition of Bengal would culminate forty-two years later with another, far more permanent and agonising partition [of 1947]'.[86]

However, as discussed in the preceding section in relation to Horowitz's theory of relative group entitlement, the role of colonialism in creating, nurturing, and sustaining ethno-nationalism is much deeper than the mere act of 'divide and rule'. Due to preexisting asymmetrical socio-political conditions and power relations, a series of colonial capitalist interventions, and corresponding responses to new challenges by the respective communities, the growth of the Hindu and Muslim bourgeoisies took divergent paths and followed different timelines. Before the arrival of the British, Muslims were the dominant ruling class in India. Under British rule, the economic position and status of the Muslim upper class drastically declined. The growth of trade, commerce, and

English will have been turned out, and a Bengali Babu will be installed in Government House, Calcutta, of course bitterly resent any disruption that will be likely to interfere with the realisation of this dream. If we are weak enough to yield to their clamour now, we shall be cementing and solidifying, on the eastern flank of India, a force already formidable, and certain to be a source of increasing trouble in future'. Curzon to Brodrick, 17 February 1904, Curzon Collection, MSS Eur, F. 111/163 (vol. 8). See also Sumit Sarkar, *The Swadeshi Movement in Bengal 1903–1908* (1973), 2nd ed. (Ranikhet: Permanent Black, 2010), 17.

[85] Sarkar, *The Swadeshi Movement in Bengal*, 386–390.
[86] Ibid., 394.

education had begun much earlier in the three Presidencies of Bombay, Calcutta, and Madras – all Hindu-majority areas – than in the Muslim areas of the north and the east.[87] With the abolition of all state patronage by the East India Company, the Muslim elites of Bengal were the earliest and the worst affected, for they were more dependent on state patronage than were the strongly entrenched Muslim aristocracy of north India. The combined effect of economic distress and conservative distrust of an alien and secular education system introduced by the British, Sarkar argues, kept Muslims away from the new schools and colleges, at a time when the Hindu elites were eagerly making the switchover from Persian (the official language of the Mughal court) to English education.[88] According to the Hunter Commission Report of 1882, the proportion of Muslims who were in university education was only 3.65 per cent.[89] A list of Calcutta University graduates between 1858 and 1881 reveals that out of a total of 1,720 graduates, only 38 names appear that are indisputably Muslim.[90] Naturally the Muslim backwardness in English education was reflected in the composition of the administrative services: a record from April 1871 indicates that of 2,111 gazetted posts in Bengal, Muslims held only 92 posts compared to 681 posts held by Hindus, while the Europeans (mainly British) held 1,338 posts.[91] The Permanent Settlement of land in favour of the Hindu feudal class and the subsequent Regulations of 1799 and 1812 consolidated the power of the Hindu landlord over a predominantly Muslim peasantry in many parts of east Bengal. Elsewhere, the great landlords, who formed the main basis of the Muslim upper class, experienced the exponential advance of the Hindus in trade and industries in collaboration with the British. While urban Muslim concentrations in Uttar Pradesh towns mainly consisted of artisans, shopkeepers, and petty traders, most big merchants and bankers were Hindus.[92] Thus, it was predominantly out of the Hindu community that the first generation of the Indian bourgeoisie emerged. It was as late as the end of the nineteenth century that the Muslims finally began to take to modern education, and an intelligentsia educated in modern ideas gradually came into being. With this, a commercial and industrial

[87] Dutt, *India To-day*, 458.
[88] Sarkar, *The Swadeshi Movement in Bengal*, 358.
[89] See Dutt, *India To-day*, 458.
[90] Pradip Sinha, *Nineteenth Century Bengal: Aspects of Social History* (Calcutta: Firma K. L. Mukhopadhyay, 1965), 161–199.
[91] William W. Hunter, *The Indian Musalmans* (London: Williams and Norgate, 1871), 126.
[92] Sumit Sarkar, *Modern India 1885–1947* (New Delhi: Macmillan, 1983), 60.

bourgeoisie also began to grow within the Muslim community.[93] This disparity in the development of the respective bourgeois classes constituted a fertile source of ethno-nationalism in India.[94]

As Rajani Dutt asserts, the rise of the Indian bourgeoisie offered necessary conditions of sectional rivalry, which could easily assume a communal character.[95] If the rise of Indian nationalism is an outcome of a conflict between vested interests of the British and of the Indian bourgeoisie,[96] ethno-nationalist politics is primarily a product of the conflict between vested interests of the Hindu bourgeoisie and of the Muslim bourgeoisie. Communal antagonism thus found expression in almost all aspects of political, economic, and social life, where the relative group backwardness of Muslims and their ensuing desire to catch up with their Hindu counterparts resulted in demands for special measures in favour of the former. In Dutt's words, '[t]his was the soil which made it easy for official policy to play on the latent antagonism and build upon them a whole political system'.[97] Jayanti Maitra notes that during the late 1860s and early 1870s, there was a sharp increase in the bureaucratic sympathy for the Muslims, who suffered disproportionately heavily in the aftermath of the 1857 Revolt.[98] For example, in his celebrated book *The Indian Musalmans* (1871), the colonial ethnographer William Hunter concluded that the failure of the Muslim elite in Bengal to secure government education and well-paid jobs contributed to the wider appeal of the radical Islamic movements such as *Wahabi* and *Faraizi* in Bengal.[99]

This new-found sympathy facilitated a series of claims for preferential treatment for Muslims to make up for their relative group backwardness. When a Public Services Commission was appointed in 1886 to review the whole question of public employment, Abdul Latif, the founder of the Muhammadan Literary Society (established in 1863), in his evidence before the Commission argued that although the British government 'recognised the desirability of giving a fair share of public employment

---

[93] A. R. Desai, *Social Background of Indian Nationalism* (1948), 6th ed. (Mumbai: Popular Prakashan, 2000), 281.
[94] Sarkar, *The Swadeshi Movement in Bengal*, 358.
[95] Dutt, *India To-day*, 458–459.
[96] See, for example, Desai, *Social Background*, 288.
[97] Dutt, *India To-day*, 459
[98] Jayanti Maitra, *Muslim Politics in Bengal 1855–1906* (Calcutta: K. P. Bagchi & Company, 1984), 131.
[99] See generally William W. Hunter, *The Indian Musalmans*, 3rd ed. (London: Trubner and Company, 1876), 146–196.

to the Mahommedans, no exclusive system of competition for recruitment' would work for the Muslims. This is because they would 'have no chance of getting a fair share of the appointments'; it would be unlikely 'for the Muslims for many years to come, to compete on equal terms with the Hindus who have taken to English education for the last fifty years'.[100] Similarly, a Muslim deputation met the Viceroy Lord Minto soon after the partition of Bengal in 1905 to demand separate and privileged representation in any electoral system that might be set up. The response from the Viceroy was prompt and unsurprisingly assertive: '[...] you justly claim that your position should be estimated not on your numerical strength, but in respect to the political importance of your community and the service that it has rendered to the Empire, I am entirely in accord with you.'[101] This is the context in which the provisions for separate electorates came into being. As an extension of this policy, by 1935, one-third (82 out of 250) of the Federal Assembly seats were reserved for Muslims, who were less than one-fourth of the population.[102]

Thus, colonial capitalist interventions, the different pace and conditions of the emergence of the Hindu and Muslim bourgeoisies, their juxtaposition within the framework of the colonial policy of divide and rule, the prevalence of a sense of relative group backwardness and the ensuing claims for preferential treatment to redress that backwardness, and more importantly, the incessant enthusiasm on the part of the colonial administration to aggravate this sense of backwardness and entitlements – all of these factors collectively explain the true nature of the role of colonialism in developing and shaping ethno-nationalism in Indian nationalist politics. In other words, such ethno-nationalism grew essentially in the hands of the Hindu and Muslim bourgeois classes and with active patronisation from the colonial administration. As A. R. Desai eloquently writes, Indian communalism 'was the form within which the struggle of the professional classes of different communities over posts and seats was carried on'.[103]

While the central role of the bourgeoisie in sustaining and advancing ethno-nationalism is undeniable, the participation of Hindu and Muslim masses in ethno-national politics and mass violence, despite their shared

---

[100] *Proceedings of the Public Service Commission*, vol. VI (Calcutta, 1887): evidence of Abdul Latif (1 March 1887), 267–268. See also Maitra, *Muslim Politics in Bengal*, 165.
[101] John Buchan, *Lord Minto: A Memoir* (London: Thomas Nelson and Sons Ltd., 1924), 244.
[102] Dutt, *India To-day*, 461.
[103] Desai, *Social Background*, 382–383.

suffering under the colonial rule, deserves some elaboration. The clue remains in the nature and character of anticolonial nationalist movements and mass mobilisation at the 'moment of manoeuvre'.

The first wave of Indian nationalism got its expression in the need for 'modernisation', meaning social and religious reforms. The modernist agenda was a direct outcome of the modern education that the British introduced primarily to turn out an educated class who would staff the subordinate posts in the colonial administration and run the administrative apparatus of the British rule.[104] An inadvertent consequence of the introduction of secular, English-language education was the spread of Western liberal ideas among nationalist elites and the use of those ideas as a political language of modernity, social and religious reform, and ultimately, freedom. The English-educated new intelligentsia, primarily Hindu in faith and Western in cultural outlook, conceived of old social institutions, religious institutions, and ethnical conceptions as obstacles to national progress and launched movements to reform or revolutionise them.[105]

Yet, in its expression, the reform movement adopted a religious tone as opposed to a universal liberal appeal or materialism, as was the case in Western civic nationalism. Invariably the pioneers of Indian nationalism – in the philosophical, political, or cultural field – stood for a revision of traditional religion or of the idea of God on which it is based.[106] According to Desai, the rationale behind this was the perception among the reformists that since liberalism originated in the West and since the Indians were ruled by a Western power, they must rely on something more indigenous and orthodox. It appeared to them that 'in the sphere of philosophy, India must stand on its own legs and must draw from its philosophical legacy from the past which was essentially religio-spiritual'.[107] Thus, they either revived it in its ancient pure shape or tried to remodel it in a liberal spirit to suit the needs of the new Indian society.[108] The claims of India's special 'spiritual genius' proved to be a handy tool in this regard.

---

[104] Ibid., 129–142.
[105] Ibid., 224–225.
[106] Ibid., 276.
[107] Ibid.
[108] As Desai illustrates, 'Raja Ram Mohan Roy (1772–1833), in spite of his rationalist approach, could not overcome his belief in the divinity of the Vedas. His successor, Debendranath Tagore (1817–1905), endeavoured to achieve a synthesis of reason and intuition. Keshub Chandra Sen (1838–1884) proclaimed himself as a prophet entrusted with a message from God to be delivered to humanity'. Ibid., 277–278.

As the nineteenth century progressed, the nationalist sentiment inclined more towards Hindu revivalism in the forms of images of ancient Hindu glory and medieval Hindu resistance to Muslim rule.[109] Much of Bankim's patriotic literature was openly anti-Muslim. Sarkar asserts that even the argument that the Muslims were serving merely as convenient whipping-boys in Bankim's literature – given that as a government official Bankim could hardly attack the British openly – (the notion Bipin Chandra Pal called 'vicarious nationalism'[110]) only reveals the assumption that the sentiments of Muslim contemporaries were not worthy of serious notice.[111] The reformist movement Arya Samaj, based in north India, advanced its Hindu reform agenda in the areas of child marriage, polytheism, widow marriage, and so on essentially within a dominant pan-Hindu revivalist framework and with an extremely aggressive assertion of the superiority of Hinduism over all other faiths.[112] 'Patriotism tended to be identified with Hindu revivalism, "Hindu" and "national" came to be used as almost synonymous terms.'[113] This Hindu revivalism powerfully advanced the anti-Muslim rhetoric that was already embedded in the nationalist consciousness of the early reformers.

Naturally, given that communalism offered an efficient tool for mass mobilisation, the Indian nationalist movement was not free of it in its political organisation, either. Also, communal organisations and campaigns served as disguises for political activities in an environment of strict colonial control.[114] The ethno-nationalist tone in the nationalist movement grew deeper in the hands of so-called militant nationalists, such as Bipin Chandra Pal and Arabinda Ghose in Bengal, Bal Gangadhar Tilak in Maharashtra, and Lajpat Rai in the Punjab, who drew inspiration from India's past, invoked the great episodes in the history of the Indian people, and tried to infuse national pride and self-respect among them.[115] They sought to build the national movement on the basis of the massive forces of social conservatism, orthodox Hinduism, and the affirmation of the ancient Hindu or 'Aryan' civilisation's supposed spiritual superiority to modern 'Western' civilisation.[116] By doing so, they alienated many

---

[109] Sarkar, *The Swadeshi Movement in Bengal*, 349.
[110] See Sarkar, *Modern India*, 84.
[111] Sarkar, *The Swadeshi Movement in Bengal*, 349.
[112] Sarkar, *Modern India*, 74.
[113] Sarkar, *The Swadeshi Movement in Bengal*, 349.
[114] Dutt, *India To-day*, 326.
[115] Desai, *Social Background*, 308.
[116] Dutt, *India To-day*, 325.

Muslim voices from the national movement. Even under Gandhi's leadership, the nationalist movement retained its religious underpinning. Although the programme of the nationalist movement headed by the Indian National Congress was the national democratic transformation of India and not the establishment of any Hindu Raj, Gandhi's declared conception that politics should be spiritualised and be in line with religio-ethical principles, alienated those who wanted the national movement to remain secular.[117] When Gandhi stood as the leader of the national non-cooperation movement of 1920–1922 that temporarily brought both communities together, he was publicly proclaiming himself 'a Sanatanist Hindu'.[118] As Dutt notes, even in his appeals for Hindu–Muslim unity, Gandhi appeared not as 'a national leader appealing to both sections, but as a Hindu leader: the Hindus were "we"; the Muslims were "they"'.[119]

Just as the growth of Muslim bourgeoisie in India was parallel to that of the Hindu bourgeoisie, Islamic revivalism and Muslim mass mobilisation had a parallel existence too, though in essence as a response to its Hindu counterpart. As I have already noted, the arrival of the British hit the Muslim community in India quite hard. A general feeling developed among the Muslims that their political decadence in the eighteenth and nineteenth centuries was due to their deviation from the classical teachings of Islam as enshrined in the Qu'ran and the teaching of the Prophet (*Sunnah*). Hence, religious leaders turned to a revival of the classical Islamic tradition, to the purification of Subcontinental Islamic life from all cultural influences of Hinduism, and also to a complete isolation from all the Western ideas that the British introduced through English-language secular education.[120] The early-nineteenth-century Islamic movement for the rehabilitation of orthodox Islam, started in Delhi in 1818 by Sayyid Ahmad of Rai Bareilly (1786–1831) and Shah Ismail Shahid (1781–1831), soon came to be known in the official circle as *Wahabism*.[121] The

---

[117] Desai, *Social Background*, 279.
[118] Gandhi, in *Young India*, 12 October 1921. Nehru described the essence of the term 'Sanatanist' in the following words: 'The [ultra-conservative] Hindu Mahasabha is left far behind in this backward moving race by the Sanatanists, who combine religious obscurantism of an extreme type with fervent or at any rate loudly expressed loyalty to British rule'. See Jawaharlal Nehru, *An Autobiography* (1936) (New Delhi: Oxford University Press, 2002), 382.
[119] Dutt, *India To-day*, 371. See also Mohandas K. Gandhi, 'Hindu Muslim Unity', in Mahatma Gandhi, *Young India* (1924–1926) (Madras: S. Ganesan, 1927), 73–76.
[120] Maitra, *Muslim Politics in Bengal*, 11.
[121] Ibid. This was based on the Arabian parallel by that name.

movement was driven simultaneously by a consistent anti-British ideology and a call for *Jihad* that helped it exercise a moral influence on the Muslim intelligentsia throughout the country, and also arouse the Muslim masses to free themselves both from the political tyranny of the British and from the economic exploitation of Hindu vested interests.[122] In Bengal, a similar but initially non-violent revivalist movement, generally known as the *Faraizi*, gained immense popularity among the agrarian class given its use of vernacular language and Bangla polemical literature and the propagation of social equality.[123] This movement gradually took the form of a peasant resistance with limited violence against the British and also against local landlords (*zaminders*), the majority of whom happened to be Hindus.[124]

In spite of the popularity of these movements that spread the hope of converting India into a land of Islam after the defeat of the British, the Revolt of 1857 and the ensuing brutal suppression of the Muslim community by the British necessitated new outlets for Muslim political consciousness. One was offered by Sir Syed Ahmad Khan (1817–1898) who was to unite the Muslims and instil in them a desire for Western education and culture with the support of the colonial government. In *The Loyal Muhammadens of India* (1860), he attempted to convince the British that the Indian Muslims were basically loyal and that, therefore, the British government should abandon their hostile attitude towards them. On the other hand, 'the Muslims on their part should participate in the administration and imbibe the progressive new culture which the British had introduced in India'.[125] Perhaps his largest contribution towards the creation of a distinct nationalist sentiment among the middle-class Muslims was the establishment of the Mohammedan Anglo-Oriental College at Aligarh in 1875, which was subsequently transformed into a university. The college aimed at making 'the Mussulmans of India worthy and useful subjects of the British Crown';[126] its founders described the British rule in India as 'the most wonderful phenomenon the world has ever seen'.[127] In Bengal, Abdul Latif initiated a similar

---

[122] K. M. Ashraf, 'Muslim Revivalists and the Revolt of 1857', in *Rebellion, 1857*, ed. Puran C. Joshi (Delhi: People's Publication House, 1957), 72.
[123] The *Faraizis*, however, did not share the radical political ideology of the *Wahabis*; instead, they preached passive non-cooperation. See Maitra, *Muslim Politics in Bengal*, 16.
[124] Ibid., 16–26.
[125] Desai, *Social Background*, 371.
[126] S. G. Wilson, *Modern Movement among Moslems* (New York: Fleming H. Revell, 1916), 188.
[127] G. F. I. Graham, *The Life and Works of Sir Syed Ahmed* (1885) (Calcutta: Thacker, Spink & Co., 1909), 178.

movement in 1863 with the foundation of the Muhammadan Literary Society; Syed Ameer Ali published *The Spirit of Islam* in 1891 to provide a liberal reinterpretation of Islam, and in 1876 together with Syed Amir Hussain organised the Central National Muhammadan Association in Calcutta, which eventually helped proliferate numerous local Muslim community organisations (*Anjumans*).[128] One of the specific objectives of the Association, as formulated in a preparatory meeting as early as 6 May 1855, stipulated that 'no measure should be adopted that might in any measure appear inimical to the British Government'.[129]

Despite the modernist agenda of the Muslim modernisers of the late nineteenth century, there was no clear break with religious orthodoxy. In order to appease the conservative-minded Muslim gentry and obtain funds from them for the Aligarh College, Syed Ahmed had to close down his 'progressive' Urdu monthly *Tahzibul Akhlaq* (Social Reformer).[130] His successor Mohsin-ul-Mulk was even more eager to compromise with the conservative religious leaders.[131] Likewise, the Muslim community organisations in Bengal invested more of their energy in stimulating Muslim solidarity and became strongholds of traditionalist Islamic influence.[132] Collectively they became an important element in the process of 'Islamisation' of rural Muslim society that had been started by the revivalists before 1857.[133] Above all, the greatest irony was that far from contributing to secular nationalism, modern education ignited among the educated Muslims a sense of 'having been left behind in the race for jobs and political influence by the Hindus'.[134]

Although the proportion of Muslims among Congress delegates had risen to about one-sixth of the total between 1888 and 1892, it declined sharply thereafter despite the Aligarh movement. This decline came as a result of various Hindu revivalist campaigns in Maharashtra and large areas of upper India, most notably, the Ganapati festival, the anti-cow-slaughter campaign, and the Urdu-Nagri controversy (over the preferred language of contested communities). Thus, many of the Muslim separatist trends were reactions to Hindu communalism, and Hindu revivalism, as Sarkar concludes, 'supplied fresh wind to the sails of the separatist

---

[128] Sarkar, *The Swadeshi Movement in Bengal*, 351–352.
[129] See *Friend of India*, 17 May 1855, cited in Maitra, *Muslim Politics in Bengal*, 75.
[130] Saiyyad Abid Hussain, *The Destiny of Indian Muslims* (Bombay: Asia, 1965), 31.
[131] G. A. Natesan, *Eminent Mussalmans* (Madras: G. A. Natesan & Co., 1926), 79.
[132] Sarkar, *The Swadeshi Movement in Bengal*, 352.
[133] Ibid.
[134] Ibid., 352.

movement being promoted from Aligarh'.[135] In contrast, a more rigidly orthodox Islamic seminary – Deoband Dar-ul-Ulum – was open about its anti-British sentiments. Founded in 1867 by Muhammad Qasim Nanawtawi and Rashid Ahmed Gangohi – both veterans of the 1857 Revolt – Deoband attracted relatively poor students who could not afford a Western education; it fomented hostility towards Sayyid Ahmed's apparently 'reformist' agenda.[136] The Deoband movement remained influential in the early twentieth century and 'provided fairly consistent support to Congress nationalism'.[137]

The Muslim League was established in 1906 – right after the partition of Bengal – with considerable support from the colonial administration. Its aims were to promote 'among Indian Moslems feelings of loyalty towards the British Government', to protect 'the political and other rights of the Indian Moslems', and to present 'their needs and aspirations before the Government in temperate language'.[138] By no means did the League represent all Muslim political elites. The so-called Congress Muslims, most prominently M. A. Ansari during the 1920s and 1930s and Abual Kalam Azad in the 1940s, extended their wholehearted support to Congress nationalism and remained incessantly committed to the idea of postcolonial India as democratic, secular, and, most importantly, undivided.[139]

However, the Muslim League progressed quickly, taking advantage of the colonial administration's suppression of the Indian Congress.[140] In 1924, at its Lahore session presided over by Muhammad Ali Jinnah, the Muslim League put forward the demand for 'federation with full provincial autonomy to preserve Muslim-majority areas from the danger of "Hindu domination", apart from separate electorates'.[141] This demand soon gained ground and remained 'basic to Muslim communalism till the

---

[135] Sarkar, *Modern India*, 235.
[136] Ibid., 76.
[137] Ibid., 78.
[138] See A. Mehta and A. Patwardhan, *The Communal Triangle in India* (Allahabad: Kitabistan, 1942), 28. The League also included the promotion of friendly feelings between Muslims and other communities without prejudice to objects already mentioned.
[139] See Mushirul Hasan, *Nationalist Conscience: M. A. Ansari, the Congress and the Raj* (New Delhi: Manohar, 1987); Ian Henderson Douglas, *Abul Kalam Azad: An Intellectual and Religious Biography*, eds. Gail Minault and Christian W. Troll (New Delhi: Oxford University Press, 1988). See also Francis Robinson, 'Review: Congress Muslims and Indian Nationalism', *Modern Asian Studies* 23, no. 3 (1989), 609–619.
[140] Sarkar, *Modern India*, 408–409.
[141] Ibid., 235.

1940 demand for Pakistan'.[142] The dream of a separate Muslim homeland, that is, Pakistan, however vague, managed to draw a vast number of politically conscious Muslims of all classes behind the Muslim League.[143] Thus, the growth of communal political organisations, against the background of a sense of loss, helped establish the important link between elite vested interests and popular communalism. The dream of Pakistan was finally materialised with the partition of British India in August 1947 creating the independent states of India and Pakistan.

1.6 Conclusion

As the foregoing discussion highlights, ethno-nationalism in Indian nationalist movements is the outcome of a combination of colonial policy interventions, the divergent growth of Hindu and Muslim bourgeois and petty-bourgeois classes, and primordial reactions to the modernist vision of the postcolonial state. Indeed, colonialism provided the necessary premise for other relevant factors to operate in the way they did by juxtaposing the Hindu and Muslim bourgeoisies within the framework of the colonial policy of divide and rule, thereby engendering a sense of relative group backwardness. The ensuing claims for preferential treatment to redress this backwardness and the colonial administration's incessant aggravation of this sense of backwardness and entitlements only advanced the communal division further. But at the same time, under the prevalent colonial-capitalist material conditions the modernist vision of the postcolonial state, engrained in liberal and reformist nationalism, paradoxically laid a path to revivalist politics along bifurcated ethno-religious lines. This narrative of Indian nationalist movements thus epitomises the complex ways in which colonialism, capitalism, and modernity work together to shape ethno-nationalist politics in postcolonial states.

What remains at the centre of the three catalysts of ethno-nationalism is the very notion of the 'postcolonial state' itself. Horowitz's theory of relative ethnic entitlements is, in a sense, a framework of the process in which the transition from colonial rule to the realisation of postcolonial state takes place in most third world countries. On the other hand, of the four phases of the history of nationalism that Geertz identifies, he finds the first phase 'in which the nationalist movements formed and crystalized'

---

[142] Ibid.
[143] For a detailed discussion on the success of the Muslim League among the peasant class, see ibid., 408–410.

CONCLUSION

and the fourth phase 'in which, organized into states, they find themselves obliged to define and stabilize their relationships both to other states and to the irregular societies out of which they arose' to be the crucial ones. It is during these phases that the more far-reaching changes altering the general shape and direction of social evolution generally occur.[144] In the framework of passive revolution too, the moment of arrival is the celebration of the nascent postcolonial state – a vision nurtured in the womb of history, now ready to materialise its promises of freedom and justice. In other words, if the modernist project of nation-building, the influence of colonialism, and the capitalist material condition collectively offer a plausible explanation of ethno-nationalism, they operate essentially with reference to the making of postcolonial states.

The partition of India in 1947, in line with the so-called two nations theory based on religion, fundamentally shaped the political imagination of India as a postcolonial state and the fate of Muslims and other minorities therein. The bitter and toxic experience of communalism and violent communal riots immediately before and after the Partition – especially in Bengal and the Punjab – made the issue of minorities a top concern for nationalist elites in India. Interestingly but unsurprisingly, in dealing with the problem of ethno-nationalism in general and minorities in particular, the factors that gave the anticolonial movement an ethno-nationalist character – colonial legacies, capitalist material conditions, and modernisation – hardly drew any attention. Instead of reflecting on the perilous consequences of these factors if they were to continue inflicting miseries on the postcolonial Indian state, the solution to the protracted problem of ethno-nationalism was sought in the 'ideology' of the postcolonial state itself – the proposition that the nascent postcolonial state would take care of this problem – within the framework of a passive revolution that maintained colonial-capitalist structures. Broadly outlined, this ideology of the postcolonial state with the mandate of suppressing ethno-nationalism and solving the minority problem found expression in three major ways: in the ideologies of the national state, of the liberal state, and of the developmental state. Chapter 2 elaborates these three ideologies of the postcolonial state with reference to the minority question in Indian Constituent Assembly debates.

---

[144] These four phases are 'that in which the nationalist movements formed and crystalized; that in which they triumphed; that in which they organized themselves into states; that in which, organized into states, they find themselves obliged to define and stabilize their relationships both to other states and to the irregular societies out of which they arose'. Geertz, *The Interpretation of Cultures*, 238.

2

Minorities and the 'Ideology' of the Postcolonial State

2.1 Introduction

In Chapter 1, I explained why and how ethno-nationalism takes root in postcolonial states, illustrating my arguments with the example of anticolonial nationalist movements in India. This chapter examines how postcolonial states then respond to ethno-nationalism in general and minorities in particular. I argue that nationalist ruling elites conceive of the postcolonial state itself as an 'ideology', claiming that the unified national state, its liberal constitutional structure, and the developmental agenda will end the troublesome ethnic parochialism and, therefore, solve the problem of minorities. In asserting their faith in the healing power of the postcolonial state, the elites conveniently avoid crucial questions about the continuation of colonial political order, the class character of the economic structure, and the hegemony of nation-building projects – factors that lead to ethno-nationalism in the first place. Within the framework of the passive revolution, the elites maintain hegemonic power structures and propagate the idea that the postcolonial state itself will solve the minority problem. In the process, they not only obscure and gloss over the real reasons for the problem but also shift attention to issues that help maintain asymmetric power relations. In this way, the postcolonial state performs the ideological function of obscuring and validating further marginalisation of ethnic minorities.

To substantiate this argument, in the following section I first explain John Thompson's notion of 'ideology' as a set of ways in which ideas and meanings help create and sustain relations of domination. I elaborate this specific meaning of ideology for the purpose of this book and then develop my argument that the ideology of the postcolonial state functions in three different forms: the postcolonial 'national' state, the postcolonial 'liberal' state, and the postcolonial 'developmental' state. Working through these three ideologies, the postcolonial state demands the submission of the minority cause to the greater 'national', 'liberal', and 'developmental' interests of the state, thereby legitimising the oppression of minorities. I demonstrate these ideological functions with historical examples: the discourse used in Indian Constituent Assembly debates to discuss minority rights.

Taken together, the previous chapter on the geneses of ethnonationalism and the present chapter on the three ideologies of the postcolonial state offer a normative framework for analysing, in the rest of the book, the role of international law in the ideological function of postcolonial states and implications for minorities.

2.2 'Ideology': What Is It? What Is It For?

The term 'ideology' was first used by the French philosopher Antoine Destutt de Tracy in 1796.[1] By ideology or the 'science of ideas', de Tracy meant the systematic analysis of the ideas and sensations through which we know things. Premised upon systematic analysis, de Tracy believed, ideology would provide a firm basis for all scientific knowledge and cure the moral and political sciences of error and prejudice. It would enable human nature to be understood, and the social and political order to be rearranged in accordance with human needs.[2]

The idea of ideology came under disrepute almost immediate thereafter, following Napoleon's ascent to power. For Napoleon, ideology was an abstract speculative doctrine distant from the realities of political power.[3] The final condemnation of 'ideology' came a decade later with the abdication of Napoleon, when ideologues came to be seen as the reason behind the failure of the Napoleonic regime. Over time, ideology began to refer 'to a body of ideas which are alleged to be erroneous and divorced from the practical realities of political life'.[4] Today, as one author notes, ideology has 'something of a pejorative ring to it, evoking as it does a whole array of negative notions from false consciousness to fanaticism, mental blockage to mystification'.[5]

---

[1] Thompson, *Ideology and Modern Culture*, 29.
[2] Ibid., 30.
[3] Ibid., 31.
[4] Ibid., 32. Emphasis removed.
[5] Terry Eagleton, *Ideology* (Essex: Pearson Education Ltd., 1994), 1.

While for de Tracy, ideology was a part of zoology – of a science of humanity in general, and of a science of intellectual faculties in particular – it is in the writings of Karl Marx that the concept acquired a new status as a critical tool and as an integral part of a new mode of theoretical enquiry.[6] As Susan Marks claims, 'the roots of virtually all notions of ideology can be traced to Marx'.[7] Although Marx never developed a full-fledged theory of 'ideology', in *The German Ideology* (1845–1846) he and Friedrich Engels critically engage with the concept. In contrast to the Young Hegelians, who asserted the salience of ideas as consciousness in history and social life, Marx and Engels argue that the production of ideas, conceptions, or consciousness is rooted in the material condition of life – in 'real' life.[8] Consciousness is nothing but the conscious existence of human beings in their actual life-process. In other words, while the German ideology took consciousness as the point of departure and conceived of life as something determined by consciousness, Marx and Engels understood conceptions, thoughts, ideas, and all products of consciousness as results of one's lived experience. For them, '[m]orality, religion, metaphysics, all the rest of ideology and their corresponding forms of consciousness, thus, no longer retain the semblance of independence. They have no history, no development; but men, developing their material production and their material intercourse, alter, along with this their real existence, their thinking and the products of their thinking.'[9]

This reveals, Nicos Poulantzas notes, that the Hegelian notion of ideology fixes not only a real but also an imaginary relation, which performs a real practical-social function. 'Its social function is not to give agents a true knowledge of the social structure but simply to insert them as it were into their practical activities supporting this structure.' Ideology is, therefore, necessarily false.[10] Thompson calls this understanding of ideology a 'polemical conception', in that an ideology is conceptualised here as a theoretical doctrine that 'erroneously regards ideas as autonomous and efficacious and which fails to grasp the real conditions and characteristics of social-historical life'.[11]

---

[6] Thompson, *Ideology and Modern Culture*, 32.
[7] Marks, *The Riddle of All Constitutions*, 12.
[8] Karl Marx and Friedrich Engels, *The German Ideology* (1846), ed. C. J. Arthur (New York: International Publishers, 1986), 47, 64.
[9] Ibid., 64.
[10] Nicos Poulantzas, *Political Power and Social Classes* (London: New Left Books, 1973), 195–210.
[11] Thompson, *Ideology and Modern Culture*, 35. Emphasis removed.

While refuting the Hegelian notion of ideology, Marx and Engels hint towards a more general role of ideology in the social structures and historical changes to them. Here, ideology is connected to class-consciousness and class-domination. In *The German Ideology*, Marx and Engels write,

> [t]he ideas of the ruling class are in every epoch the ruling ideas, i.e. the class which is the ruling *material* force of society, is at the same time its ruling *intellectual* force. The class which has the means of material production at its disposal has control at the same time over the means of mental production.[12]

This view was later expanded, primarily in Marx's 1859 preface to *A Contribution to the Critique of Political Economy*, where Marx links the relationship between lived life and ideologies to the classic doctrine of base and superstructure. Put briefly, relations of production, which human beings indispensably enter into in their social life, correspond to a definite stage of development of material production forces. The sum total of these relations of production constitutes the economic structure of society – the base upon which a legal and political superstructure develops and to which correspond definite forms of ideas and consciousness.[13] In their words, '[t]he mode of production of Material life conditions the social, political and intellectual life process in general'.[14]

The Marxist thesis is further refined by Poulantzas, who offered a 'structural' analysis of ideology with reference to how in class-divided societies one social class 'lives' its relations to another.[15] In these societies, the specific unity of the ideological, that is, its structure and its relation to the dominant class, is derived fundamentally from the relation between ideology and human experience in a formation, and to the imaginary form which this relation takes on.[16] Here, ideology performs the important function of obscuring the real contradictions and of reconstituting a relatively coherent discourse on an imaginary level. This is a process which Marx calls 'inversion': in the capitalist labour market, labour relationships characterised by inequality and exploitation appear as the outcome of free exchange on

---

[12] Marx and Engels, *The German Ideology*, 47. Emphasis in original.
[13] For a nuanced interpretation of the base-superstructure thesis and the positioning of law therein, see Chimni, *International Law and World Order*, 449–462.
[14] Karl Marx and Friedrich Engels, *Selected Works* (London: Lawrence and Wishart, 1968), 180.
[15] In contrast, for a historicist conception of ideology, see generally Georg Lukacs, *History and Class Consciousness* (1923) (Cambridge, MA: MIT Press, 1971), 46–55, 59–70.
[16] Poulantzas, *Political Power and Social Classes*, 195–210.

a footing of equality and mutuality.[17] In class-divided societies, thus, the correspondence between the dominant ideology and the politically dominant class is achieved by the fact that 'a given ideology is constituted a regional instance within the unity of the structure; and this structure has the domination of a given class as its effect in the field of the class struggle'.[18] By assuring the practical insertion of agents in the social structure, the dominant ideology, in turn, maintains the cohesion of this structure and thereby ensures the continuity of class domination and exploitation. 'It is precisely in this way that within a social formation ideology is dominated by the ensemble of representations, values, notions, beliefs, etc. by means of which class domination is perpetuated: in other words, it is dominated by what can be called the ideology of the dominant class.'[19]

Marx's dominant ideology thesis came under criticism on a number of grounds, though not in any fundamental way. Marks, for example, finds this thesis flawed in that it depicts the dominant ideology as all-pervasive in nature, thereby dismantling the independent agency of subaltern groups and underestimating their capacity for resistance.[20] The thesis simultaneously suffers from what Marks calls its 'overestimation' of the extent to which ruling cultures are themselves determinate and unified and therefore capable of absorbing subordinate classes.[21] On the other hand, Thompson raises concerns about two key elements of Marx's thesis – the class character of ideological domination and the erroneous and illusory nature of ideology – though his criticisms target only the degree of influence, not the relevance of these elements. For him, in the study of ideology, both of these elements are contingent rather than essential. First, he finds the Marxist thesis limited in that it reduces all forms of social domination and subordination into some sort of class relations. While the significance of class relations as a basis of inequality and exploitation cannot be denied, the significance of relations between the sexes, between ethnic groups, and between individuals and the state should not be denied either. 'Class relations are only *one* axis of inequality and exploitation; class relations are by no means the *only* form of domination and subordination.'[22] Secondly, Thompson contends that while the illusory nature of ideology

---

[17] R. Tucker (ed.), *The Marx and Engels Reader*, 2nd ed. (New York: Norton, 1978), 336–337.
[18] Poulantzas, *Political Power and Social Classes*, 208.
[19] Ibid., 210.
[20] Marks, *The Riddle of All Constitutions*, 14.
[21] Ibid.
[22] Thompson, *Ideology and Modern Culture*, 57.

is relevant to the way it operates by concealing or masking social relations, these are contingent possibilities, not necessary characteristics of ideology as such. Therefore, identifying a symbolic phenomenon as ideological does not ipso facto necessitate the 'falsehood' of the phenomenon, in that symbolic forms do not serve to establish and sustain relations of domination only by virtue of being erroneous, illusory, or false.[23]

However, despite its deviation from the Marxist thesis on these points, Thompson's theory of ideology is nonetheless informed by Marxism in a particular way. His central thesis – 'to study ideology is to study the *ways* in which *meaning* serves to establish and sustain *relations of domination*' – draws on the Marxist thesis that ideology sustains relations of domination, but it does so without endorsing the associated elements of 'falsification', 'illusion', and so on.[24] Thompson's notion of 'ideology' is then a series of 'modes of operation' through which ideological meanings or symbolic forms establish and sustain systematically asymmetric relations of power. It is also distinct from so-called neutral conceptions of ideology, as advanced by Clifford Geertz[25] or Karl Mannheim,[26] for example, that tend to characterise ideology as systems of thought, systems of beliefs, or symbolic systems, without attempting to distinguish between the kinds of action or projects different ideologies animate.[27] In contrast, Thompson's version of ideology is 'critical' in nature, in that it is concerned with the *ways* symbolic forms intersect with relations of power. He offers five such general modes of ideological operation, each of which has typical strategies for symbolic constructions (Table 2.1).[28]

By *legitimation*, Thompson means the process by which authority comes to seem to be valid and appropriate. Once the suppressed groups accept the legitimacy of the oppressor's authority, the relations of domination become perpetual. It is for this reason that legitimation is one of the most effective ways of establishing and sustaining relations of

---

[23] Ibid., 56–57.
[24] Ibid., 56. Here 'meaning' stands for 'symbolic forms' – a broad range of actions, utterances, images, and texts – that are produced by subjects and recognised by them and others as meaningful constructs, while 'domination' is understood as established relations of power, which are 'systematically asymmetrical' in nature (57). Emphasis partially removed.
[25] Geertz understands ideology as a cultural system. See Geertz, *The Interpretation of Cultures*, 193–233.
[26] For Mannheim, ideology is a world-view (Weltanschauung) – a framework of belief, values, or concepts about central issues of life that shape the outlook of a social group. See generally Karl Mannheim, *Ideology and Utopia* (London: Routledge, 1936).
[27] Thompson, *Ideology and Modern Culture*, 5, 53
[28] See generally ibid., 60–67.

Table 2.1 *Thompson's framework of ideological modes of operation*

General modes	Some typical strategies of symbolic construction
Legitimation	Rationalisation
	Universalisation
	Narrativisation
Dissimulation	Displacement
	Euphemisation
	Trope (e.g. synecdoche, metonymy, metaphor)
Unification	Standardisation
	Symbolisation of unity
Fragmentation	Differentiation
	Expurgation of the other
Reification	Naturalisation
	Eternalisation
	Nominalisation/passivisation

Thompson, *Ideology and Modern Culture*, 60. Thompson, however, acknowledges that this is not an exhaustive list of modes and strategies through which ideology operates. Also, some of the modes and corresponding strategies are not always clearly demarcated, and they often overlap.

domination.[29] Claims to legitimacy may be based on rational grounds, appealing to the legality of enacted rules; on traditional grounds, appealing to the sanctity of immemorial traditions; or on charismatic grounds, appealing to the exceptional character of an individual person who exercises authority.[30] These claims to legitimacy may be expressed through the strategy of rationalisation, whereby the dominant force constructs a chain of reasoning to defend or justify the asymmetrical social relations and institutions and, thereby, to make any desire for social change look irrational. The second strategy is universalisation, in which institutional arrangements serving the vested interest of the dominant group appear to be operating for the benefit of the society as a whole. Another legitimising strategy is narrativisation, which makes the present social condition part of a long historical tradition.

---

[29] Marks, *The Riddle of All Constitutions*, 19.

[30] Max Weber, *Economy and Society: An Outline of Imperative Sociology*, eds. Guenther Roth and Claus Wittich (Berkeley, CA: University of California Press, 1978), 112–301.

The second general mode of ideological operation is *dissimulation*, by which Thompson means a process whereby relations of domination are established and sustained by being concealed, denied, obscured, or glossed over. This mystification role of ideology must be distinguished from the assumption that ideologies are essentially illusory. While illusion may be involved in some cases, such involvement is not a plain case of error or of ignorance of social reality. To take Marks's example, one might be aware that labour relations involve exploitation and inequality, but still act as if they do not. One may be also unaware of the impact of acting as if labour relations were based on free exchange among equals – unaware of how that pretence itself helps to 'perpetuate asymmetries in the sphere of labour, by keeping alive the idea that those asymmetries do not exist, or are unalterable, or are legitimate'.[31] An important strategy for advancing the mode of dissimulation is what Thompson calls 'displacement': when the positive or negative connotations of one object or individual are attributed to another object or individual. Another relevant strategy is euphemisation, in which actions, institutions, or social relations are described or re-described in a way that elicits a positive valuation. For example, the violent suppression of a protest is described as 'restoration of order'.[32]

Thompson's third mode of ideological operation is *unification* – the process of constructing a form of symbolic unity which embraces individuals in a collective identity, irrespective of the differences and divisions that may separate them. Standardisation, for example in the form of promoting a national language, is an important strategy in this regard. Symbolisation of unity is another relevant strategy; examples are the creation and use of national symbols such as flags and anthems.[33] The fourth mode of ideological operation, in contrast, is *fragmentation*. Here relations of domination are maintained by fragmenting groups who are seen as potential threats to the dominant group. Differentiation (e.g. the colonial policy of divide and rule) and expurgation of the other (constructing a dehumanising 'other' and calling for collective expurgation of the 'other') are relevant strategies in this regard.[34] And finally, Thompson's fifth mode of ideological operation is *reification*: representing a transitory, historical state of affairs as if it were permanent, natural, and timeless. Here the strategies are naturalisation (e.g. explaining division of labour with reference to the difference between sexes), eternalisation (such as of

[31] Marks, *The Riddle of All Constitutions*, 22–23.
[32] See Thompson, *Ideology and Modern Culture*, 62.
[33] Ibid., 63.
[34] Ibid., 64.

customs, traditions, social institutions), and nominalisation/passivisation (hiding the actors and agency and focusing on the listener or the reader, thereby representing 'processes' as 'things' or 'events' which take place in the absence of a subject who produces them).[35]

Marks has persuasively applied Thompson's framework of the modes and techniques of ideological operation in her seminal work *The Riddle of All Constitutions*. By portraying democracy as an 'ideology', she comprehensively explains how the propagation of 'low intensity democracy' – a democratic system that focuses primarily on electoral rituals – is used in international legal processes to legitimise, obscure, deny, reify, naturalise, or otherwise support asymmetrical power relations.[36] I use Thompson's framework in this book to demonstrate how the notion of the 'postcolonial state' operates as an 'ideology' to establish and sustain relations of domination against minority groups. In this process, various forms of marginalisation of the minority are legitimised, glossed over, or obscured by the ruling class in the name of national unity, liberal egalitarianism, and economic development. In what follows, I demonstrate these three different forms of the ideological function of the postcolonial state vis-à-vis minorities with reference to the discourse on minority protection in the Indian Constituent Assembly debates between 1946 and 1950.

2.3 The Three Ideologies of the Postcolonial State

2.3.1 The Postcolonial 'National' State

The fundamental premise of the ideology of the 'national' state is unification. The creation and continuation of the minority problem is intrinsically connected to the formation of the modern sovereign state itself – both in Europe and beyond. This is due to the denial of statehood to aspiring nations, who are then treated as the leftover of the nation-state making process. It is, therefore, a universal phenomenon that minorities are seen as a threat to the political and territorial integrity of the states they live in. The conventional depiction of German minorities in Eastern and Central Europe as a catalyst of European destabilisation and the ensuing German invasion during the interwar period would be an apt example in this context. The nationalist elites in postcolonial states had even more serious reasons for concern. This is because, compared to European political boundaries, which to some extent coincided with linguistic groups, colonial boundaries were drawn arbitrarily,

---

[35] Ibid., 66.
[36] See generally Marks, *The Riddle of All Constitutions*.

with little attention paid to the demographic composition. Since the postcolonial states were set to continue with the colonial boundaries, these elites were well aware of the immediate challenge of unifying the entire nation within the given territorial boundary, however arbitrary. Therefore, the solution to this potential problem was sought in what later came to be popularly known as 'nation-building'.

The ideology of the postcolonial national state is premised upon a homogenous national identity that absorbs all ethno-cultural differences. Given the long-term goal of assimilation and homogenisation, it is expected that the minority problem would wither away. At the same time, the process of diminishing all meaningful ethno-cultural diversity and reducing such diversity to a token showcase element imposes the majoritarian identity on the entire nation. In other words, the majoritarian culture, belief system, and cultural codes come to synonymise the 'national' identity in the name of nation-building and homogenisation. The ideology of the postcolonial national state, presented as a solution to the minority problem, thus in fact acts as a tool to perpetuate the dominance of the majority group over the minority in all political and cultural domains of the new state, leaving the minority at the mercy of the majority on vital political and economic issues.

In the case of India, for example, the Constituent Assembly debates clearly demonstrate this pattern of the depiction of the 'national' state as an ideology to deal with the problem of minorities. The Assembly was created under the Cabinet Mission Plan of 16 May 1946 for the purpose of 'the cession of sovereignty [from Britain] to the Indian people on the basis of a constitution framed by the Assembly'. The plan also stipulated that such cession of power to India would be conditional upon 'adequate provision for the protection of minorities'.[37] While this emphasis on the safeguard of minorities can be seen as a continuation of the divisive colonial policies in India, it needs to be noted that such provisions for minority protection were standard in the creation of new states throughout the interwar period. Although in the aftermath of WWII a dramatic shift from minority rights to human rights began – and the complete abandonment of minority protection in international human rights treaties would ensue – the full effect of the wave of change at the international level was not expected to influence the developments in India immediately. The Indian representative in the Human Rights Commission in 1947 even highlighted the importance of safeguarding Indian (and other) minorities, scattered

---

[37] See Hansard, 'India (Cabinet Mission)', House of Commons Debate (18 July 1946), vol. 425, para. 1423.

around the world, from the danger of cultural assimilation.[38] Also, even though the Congress elites were duty bound to set the framework of the future constitution of India within the remit of the Cabinet Mission Plan (especially in the absence of the Muslim League, which initially boycotted the Assembly), there was a general sense of agreement and acceptance among the Congress elites that the future constitution of India must incorporate provisions for minority protection. For example, the resolution on aims and objectives of the constitution (popularly known as the 'objective resolution'), moved by Jawaharlal Nehru and described by him as the core philosophy behind the constitution of India, proclaims that 'adequate safeguards shall be provided for minorities, backward and tribal areas, and depressed and other backward classes'.[39] An Advisory Committee and afterwards a sub-committee on minorities thereunder were also formed in line with the Cabinet Mission Plan to prepare a report outlining provisions for the protection of minorities.[40]

In its draft report of August 1947, in the same month India was partitioned to create Pakistan, the Advisory Committee outlined a series of special safeguards for minorities in addition to a number of fundamental rights for all citizens. As the Chairman of the Committee and the first Deputy Prime Minister Sardar Vallabhbhai Patel informed the Assembly: '[the fundamental rights] cover a very wide range of the rights of minorities which give them ample protection; and yet there are certain political safeguards which have got to be specifically considered. An attempt has been made in this report to enumerate those safeguards [...] such as representation in legislatures.'[41] As a result, although the heavily criticised British policy of separate electorates for different religious groups was dismantled, the draft report proposed reserving seats in the parliament in proportion to the population of the minorities for a fixed period of ten years.[42] The Committee also mandated that a certain proportion of public service roles be reserved for members of

---

[38] United Nations Commission on Human Rights, 'Drafting Committee Reports on International Bill of Rights', UN Doc E/CN.4/AC.1/3/Add.1 (11 June 1947), 380.

[39] See *Constituent Assembly Debates: Official Report* (hereinafter, *CAD*), vol. I (Delhi, 1946–1950), para. 1.5.10 (13 December 1946). The minority rights provision was also included in the ground rules for the Indian constitution set by a committee under the chairmanship of his father Motilal Nehru as early as 1928. The draft constitution is popularly known as the 'Motilal Nehru Constitutional Draft/Report', 1928. See Neera Chandhoke, *Contested Secessions: Rights, Self-determination, Democracy, and Kashmir* (New Delhi: Oxford University Press, 2012), 56.

[40] *CAD*, vol. II, para. 2.15.13 (24 January 1947).

[41] Ibid., para. 5.43.11 (27 August 1947).

[42] Ibid., para. 5.43.12 (27 August 1947).

certain communities for the same length of time.[43] The draft report also provided for an administrative machinery to ensure that constitutional safeguards for minorities are given effect to at both central and provincial levels.[44] Patel informed the Assembly that these decisions expressed a general consensus of opinion among Committee members, representing minority and majority communities.[45]

However, the Committee's proposed safeguards faced fierce and passionate challenge in the Assembly, based on the ideology of national unity. As a matter of fact, long before the Committee's proposals and as soon as the creation of Pakistan was decided, there was a sharp change in the mood of the Assembly regarding minority rights. As early as December 1946, M. R. Masani, despite his origin in a small minority community, argued before the Assembly for his vision of the national state:

> [T]he conception of a nation does not permit the existence of perpetual or permanent minorities. Either the nation absorbs these minorities or, in course of time, it must break up. Therefore, while welcoming the clause in this Objective Resolution which promises adequate safeguards for the minorities, I would say that it is a good thing that we have these legal and constitutional safeguards, but that ultimately no legal safeguard can protect small minorities from the overwhelming domination of big masses, unless on both sides an effort is made to get closer and *become one corporate nation, a homogeneous nation*.[46]

The minority issue itself was seen as the root cause of India's partition. Therefore, the idea of any continuation of minority protection in postcolonial India was seen as counterproductive and an essential threat to India's territorial and political integrity. For example, responding to the Committee's report on minorities, P. S. Deshmukh commented:

> In my opinion, there is no more monstrous word in the history of Indian politics than the word '*minority*'. Ever since India emerged out of its political infancy, the demon of the interests of minorities and their

---

[43] Ibid., para. 5.43.11 (27 August 1947).
[44] Ibid., para. 5.43.13 (27 August 1947).
[45] Ibid., para. 5.43.10 (27 August 1947). The opinion was, however, divided in the Assembly. A number of Muslim League delegates, especially Pocker Sahib Bahadur, continued to press for the old system of separate electorates for different religious groups, arguing that in a joint electorate system the majority can always get a 'Muslim' of their choice elected to parliament, who will hardly be a 'true' representative of the community s/he will be representing anyway. The argument thus followed that the proposed system of reservation of seats would not ensure political representation of the minority, and, hence, would naturally fall short of democratic norms. See ibid., para. 5.43.70–78 (27 August 1947).
[46] *CAD*, vol. I, para. 1.7.4 (17 December 1946). Emphasis added.

protection stood before us and appeared to bar the progress of the country. It is a matter of history that this was a creation of the British policy, but it succeeded so well that it is, in my view, essentially the work of the Satan of minority that our beloved country united for over a century has been divided into more parts than one. That this monster should at long last have been shorn of its terrors is an achievement worthy of note.[47]

Renuka Ray, likewise, asserted that 'we have stood helplessly while artificially this problem of religious differences – an echo of medieval times, has been fostered and nurtured and enhanced [. . .] Today we see as a result our country divided and provinces like [Bengal] dismembered.'[48] This view was shared by numerous other Assembly members, as the record of the debates reveals.[49] Responding to the Muslim League members of the Assembly who were asking for more robust minority safeguards in the constitution in the form of a separate electorate, the Committee Chairman Patel himself concluded: 'Those who want that kind of thing have a place in Pakistan, not here. Here, we are building a nation and we are laying the foundations of One Nation, and those who choose to divide again and sow the seeds of disruption will have no place, no quarter, here, and I must say that plainly enough.'

The proposals of the Advisory Committee were finally adopted and reflected in the draft constitution. The Chairman of the Drafting Committee, B. R. Ambedkar, himself was a member of the depressed (*dalit*) community. While presenting the draft constitution before the Assembly for discussion, Ambedkar passionately argued that it was wrong for the majority to deny the existence of minorities, but it was equally wrong for the minority to perpetuate their own existence. Therefore, a solution had to be found that would 'enable majorities and minorities to merge someday into one'.[50]

However, even this long-term strategy of offering safeguards to minorities for a limited period of time and simultaneously attempting to absorb them into the body politic of the national state soon appeared unworthy. With the bitter experience of communal violence following the Partition, mass migration, the treatment of Hindu and Sikh minorities in Pakistan, and more importantly, with the consolidation of political power, the nationalist ruling elites in India decided to revisit the whole question of minority protection. Accordingly, in a sudden dramatic move, the

[47] CAD, vol. V, para. 5.43.28 (27 August 1947).
[48] Ibid., para. 5.44.89 (28 August 1947).
[49] See generally ibid., para. 5.43.10–5.46.188 (27–30 August 1947).
[50] CAD, vol. VII, para. 7.48.233 (4 November 1948).

THE THREE IDEOLOGIES OF THE POSTCOLONIAL STATE   69

Advisory Committee reopened the question of minority rights and concluded in its final report of May 1949 that there should be no provision in the constitution for the reservation of seats for any religious minorities. Such protection, however, would remain for various tribal groups and the scheduled caste Hindus[51] – but on the ground of economic and social backwardness; none of these groups was treated as a minority.[52] As the tribal leader Jaipal Singh asserted during Assembly debates, 'a group of people who are the original owners of this country, even if they are only a few, can never be considered a minority'.[53]

As a matter of fact, it is quite clear from the Assembly debates on this issue that with only a handful of exceptions, the representatives of the Muslim and Sikh communities in the Assembly (other, smaller communities never asked for a reservation of seats) by that time preferred to leave the matter to the goodwill of the majority.[54] Begum Aizaz Rasul specifically stated this in the following words: 'To my mind it is very necessary that the Muslims living in this country should throw themselves entirely upon the good-will of the majority community, should give up separatist tendencies and throw their full weight in building up a truly secular state.'[55] Sardar Patel, as the Chairman of the Committee, responded: 'the future of a minority, any minority, is to trust the majority. If the majority misbehaves, it will suffer.'[56] And taking part in the debate on this change of position on minorities, Prime Minister Nehru reminded his audience of the primacy of the national integration that must not be disturbed by any separatist tendency in the name of communalism or provincialism.[57]

Nevertheless, to the surprise of Muslims and Sikhs, all other remaining safeguards in the draft report – including the provisions for reservations of public jobs and the provision for a mechanism for implementing minority protection – were also scrapped for all minorities while the same safeguards remained for the scheduled castes, tribal communities, and in some cases, for Anglo-Indian communities.[58] This, of course, elicited heated debates and fierce criticism from the representatives of the Muslim and Sikh communities, who claimed that no prior consensus

[51] CAD, vol. VIII, para. 8.91.4–8.91.8 (25 May 1949).
[52] See CAD, vol. V, para. 5.43.125 (27 August 1947) and CAD vol. I, para. 1.9.71 (19 December 1946).
[53] See CAD, vol. V, para. 5.43.58 (27 August 1947).
[54] CAD, vol. VIII, para. 8.91.27–8.92.113 (25–26 May 1949).
[55] Ibid., para. 8.91.169 (25 May 1949).
[56] Ibid., para. 8.92.109 (26 May 1949).
[57] Ibid., para. 8.92.41 (26 May 1949).
[58] CAD, vol. X, para. 10.151.4 (14 October 1949).

had been secured on these questions.[59] In an angry response, the Sikh member Hukam Singh commented that 'this nationalism is an argument for vested interests. Even the aggressiveness of the majority would pass off as nationalism, while the helplessness of the minority might be dubbed as communalism. It is very easy for the majority to preach nationalism to the minorities; but it is very difficult to act up to it.'[60] It was, however, confirmed by one of the members of the Committee, K. M. Munshi, that

> at the time when the Advisory Committee met on the last occasion, there was no question of providing safeguards for any religious minority. The negotiations proceeded on the footing that except the backward classes who are economically and socially backward, and the Scheduled Castes and Tribes who have a special claim of their own, no other minority should be recognised in the Constitution.[61]

Despite Ambedkar's strong voice for minority rights previously,[62] on this occasion he was content with the protection of his own community of the scheduled castes. On 16 November 1949, a motion was proposed to remove any mention of 'minorities' even from the titles of relevant parts of the constitution and replace the word 'minorities' with 'certain classes'. The motion was enthusiastically adopted. As the Assembly member Ajit Prasad Jain succinctly put it, while reflecting on the success of the new constitution in dismantling the colonial architecture of minority protection, '[m]ay be that we have not so far succeeded in establishing a fully united and harmonious society, but much of the old rancour has disappeared and we are on the path of achieving a real national unity'.[63]

In this way, the ideology of the postcolonial 'national' state suppressed the issue of minority protection, despite the initial recognition by the ruling elites of the importance of this issue. Through the modes of operation of legitimation, dissimulation, and unification, the ideology of the national state offered necessary justification for adopting a nationalist constitutional mould that had no place for minorities.

---

[59] See ibid., para. 10.151.10–10.151.193 (14 October 1949).
[60] Ibid., para. 10.151.38 (14 October 1949).
[61] Ibid., para. 10.151.256 (14 October 1949).
[62] Cf. *CAD*, vol. III, para. 3.20.260 (1 May 1947). See also B. R. Ambedkar, *States and Minorities: What are Their Rights and How to Secure them in the Constitution of Free India* (1947), Memorandum on the Safeguards for the Scheduled Castes submitted to the Constituent Assembly on behalf of the All India Scheduled Castes Federation, available at www.cadindia.clpr.org.in.
[63] *CAD*, vol. XI, para. 11.162.158 (22 November 1949).

Given the salience of the 'national' state as the dominant international norm for postcolonial statehood, as we shall see in Chapter 3, the ideology of the postcolonial 'national' state also reified such marginalisation of minorities as an obvious historical destiny of minorities in the normal course of nation-building. As a matter of fact, there are plenty of such examples in the pages of world history.

2.3.2 The Postcolonial 'Liberal' State

Even as the vision of the 'national' state – a homogeneous nation within a defined territory – served as an ideology in dealing with minorities, such a national state affirmed the ideological vision of its internal political organisation. After all, when the postcolonial national state dismantles the ethno-religious underpinning of minority groups on grounds of national integration, it needs to find for itself a 'neutral' and apparently 'non-majoritarian' philosophical outlook. The predominance of the liberal worldview of the post–World War II international order provided the necessary ideological foundation for many postcolonial states and their constitutional architecture. This ideology of the postcolonial 'liberal' state also justified the omission of any specific minority group protection in the constitutions of these postcolonial states, thereby reducing minority groups to individual units of citizenry. In other words, the ideology of the postcolonial liberal state worked through the ideological mode of operation of fragmentation.

Within the liberal ideological framework, the constitutional prohibition on discrimination against any citizen on grounds of religion, caste, ethnicity, and so on is generally seen as an adequate protection for minorities. The liberal regime of citizenship and individualist principles of equality and non-discrimination are designed to deal with minority groups without directly engaging with the groups per se. In fact, the idea of protecting minority *groups* is in direct conflict with the liberal ideology itself. As I argued elsewhere, given that the liberal idea of non-discrimination assumes that differential treatment on religious grounds, for example, is fundamentally irrational, this proposition completely undercuts the idea that groups should be protected on the basis of their ethno-religious features and solidarity. Hence, the issue of 'minority protection' is to be addressed through the liberal-individualist principle of 'non-discrimination'.[64]

---

[64] See Shahabuddin, *Ethnicity and International Law*, 152.

The reliance solely on the principles of equality and non-discrimination – within an individualist framework – to offer minority protection is problematic, in that such reliance on non-discrimination often ignores the raison d'être and the nature of discrimination in the first place. When an individual faces discrimination on religious grounds, the discrimination actually arises because of their affiliation with a particular religious community. Therefore, considering the act of discrimination to be directed merely against an individual and perceiving such discrimination as a violation of their individual rights outside the realm of religious group identity would be misguided.[65] Similarly, the liberal notion of the prevention of discrimination is set to ensure 'equality' among individuals of different ethno-cultural affiliations and, therefore, is transitory in nature. Thus, lacking any specific guarantee for minority rights, in the long run the liberal protection against non-discrimination is prone to encourage the minority group's assimilation into the dominant culture.[66] In contrast, as Patrick Thornberry argues, the protection of minorities is supposed to be permanent, provided that the minority remains a minority in need of special protection; that is, unless the composition of a population or the balance of political power fundamentally changes.[67] Thus, the transitory, individualist notions of equality and non-discrimination are not merely inadequate for minority protection but are indeed the modus operandi of assimilation and the extinction of group identity. In other words, the vision of the postcolonial 'liberal' state serves the ideological function of assimilating minorities into the 'national' (read, majoritarian) culture, thereby suppressing minority identity. In addition to fragmentation, thus, legitimation and dissimulation are ideological modes by which the 'liberal' state justifies the denial of any special protection for minorities, and in the name of egalitarianism glosses over the asymmetric power relations in which minorities find themselves vis-à-vis the dominant group in a given polity.

In the Indian context, the ideology of the liberal state is expressed primarily in 'egalitarianism' and 'secularism'. The Indian nation was essentially conceived as a political community united by its commitment to the common political ideals of secularism, democracy, rights, equality, and justice.[68]

---

[65] Ibid., 153.
[66] Ibid.
[67] Thornberry, *International Law and the Rights of Minorities*, 126.
[68] Rochana Bajpai, 'Minority Rights in the Indian Constituent Assembly Debates, 1946–1950', *Queen Elizabeth House Working Paper Series*, University of Oxford 30 (2002), 12–13.

In this political imagination, minority rights naturally appeared as a distraction – something with the potential to undercut the liberal values that the postcolonial Indian state was set to be defined by. Given that citizenship in the postcolonial liberal state was characterised primarily by equal individual rights, the proposition of safeguarding minorities was deemed inappropriate as 'it was thought to compromise its commitment to not discriminate between its citizens on the basis of their caste, creed or community'.[69] The addition of secularism to this liberal egalitarianism made it normatively even more unreasonable to concede special rights to religious minorities.

Pandit Govind Ballabh Pant represented the liberal vision of the postcolonial Indian state most succinctly during the Constituent Assembly debates. Criticising the 'morbid tendency' in Indian politics to highlight communities in political arrangements, Pant reminded the Assembly that the individual citizens constitute the backbone of the state. It is citizens that form communities, and 'the individual as such is essentially the core of all mechanisms and means and devices that are adopted for securing progress and advancement'.[70] Referring to the Atlantic Charter with its Four Freedoms, he concluded that 'the goal and objective of all human activity is a World State in which all citizens would possess the cosmopolitan outlook, would be equal in the eye of the law and would have full and ample opportunity for economic, social and political self-fulfilment'.[71]

Long before the provisions for minority rights were hastily removed from the draft constitution, Damodar Swarup Seth questioned the legitimacy of constitutional protection of religious minorities in a secular state: 'in a secular state minorities based on religion or community should not be recognised. If they are given recognition then I submit that we cannot claim that ours is a secular state. Recognition of minorities based on religion or community is the very negation of secularism.'[72] Sardar Patel echoed the vision of secular India when he informed the Assembly of the removal of all safeguards for religious minorities: 'this Constitution of India, of free India, of a secular India will not hereafter be disfigured by any provision on a communal basis'.[73] When the provisions for reservations for minorities were finally removed from the

[69] Ibid., 13.
[70] *CAD*, vol. II, para. 2.15.24 (24 January 1947).
[71] Ibid., para. 2.15.24 (24 January 1947).
[72] *CAD*, vol. VII, para. 7.69.59 (8 December 1948).
[73] *CAD*, vol. X, para. 10.151.144 (14 October 1949).

constitution, R. K. Sidhva, as a member of the minority Parsee community, described the occasion as a moment of historic victory and national pride, given that Indian constitution has 'kept no room for communalism and that we are in the true sense of the word a secular State'.[74] A number of other members of the Assembly from all religious backgrounds celebrated the secular nature of the constitution, although a handful of speakers did regret the absence of any clear recognition of religious minorities in the constitution.[75] The Assembly member Ajit Prasad Jain summarised the liberal position of the Indian constitution vis-à-vis minorities in the following words:

> The minorities have been guaranteed freedom of religion and freedom to develop their culture, language and script, but in matters of political rights, there is no discrimination either in their favour or against them. The minorities therefore should have nothing to fear or be apprehensive about their future. It is in that sense that we have established what is popularly known as a secular State.[76]

Thus, with this liberal vision of secular India, all references to religious minorities were removed from the constitution. The only groups that were given some protection were the scheduled castes and scheduled tribes. As noted in the preceding section, these two groups were not treated as minorities; the protection was offered on the basis of their socio-economic backwardness. The Anglo-Indian community was also allowed to continue with the privileges they happened to enjoy under the British rule, but it was argued that they were not a religious community and, hence, this exception did not challenge the secular nature of the Indian state.

The constitutional secular ideology of the Indian nation faced a different challenge when it came to the Hindu nationalist demand for cow protection. As we saw in Chapter 1, throughout the nineteenth and early twentieth centuries, cow protection was an issue of grave concern in Hindu nationalist politics and in the communal tension between the Hindu and Muslim communities. Against that backdrop, during the Constituent Assembly debates, demands were made for specific constitutional provisions protecting the cow.[77] As late as 1948, Thakur Das Bhargava demanded a constitutional guarantee that 'the State shall

---

[74] *CAD*, vol. VIII, para. 8.92.3 (26 May 1949).
[75] See generally *CAD*, vol. XI, para. 11.158.3–11.164.44 (17–23 November 1949). Cf. *CAD*, vol. XI, para. 11.164.43 (23 November 1949).
[76] *CAD*, vol. XI, para. 11.162.167 (22 November 1949).
[77] See *CAD*, vol. V, para. 5.46.44 (30 august 1947); *CAD*, vol. VII, para. 7.49.81 (5 November 1948).

endeavour to organise agriculture and animal husbandry on modern and scientific lines and shall in particular take steps for preserving and improving the breeds of cattle and prohibit the slaughter of cow and other useful cattle, specially milch and draught cattle and their young stock'.[78] Although in his demand Bhargava relied mainly on an economic case for prohibiting cow slaughter,[79] in the Assembly discussion on the proposal, a number of members specifically highlighted the religious impetus behind the need for cow protection. Seth Govind Das, for example, added religious and cultural grounds to the economic case and demanded a prohibition on the slaughter of cows of any age and kind. Identifying 'cow protection' as a majoritarian Hindu and therefore Indian cultural issue, along with questions of national language, national script, and national anthem, he argued that 'Swaraj' – self-rule – would have no meaning to people without protection for this culture.[80] Similarly, acknowledging the religious aspect of 'cow protection', Shibban Lal Saxena argued that if thirty crores of the Indian population – that is, three hundred million – feel that this cow protection should be incorporated in the laws of the country, the Assembly should not ignore this simply because it is a religious issue.[81] That view was shared by Raghu Vira Dhulekar, who even claimed:

> our Hindu society, or our Indian society, has included the cow in our fold. It is just like our mother. In fact it is more than our mother. I can declare from this platform that there are thousands of persons who will not run at a man to kill that man for their mother or wife or children, but they will run at a man if that man does not want to protect the cow or wants to kill her.[82]

As ideas of the Hindu society and the Indian nation thus merged, Muslim League representatives in the Assembly took the issue of cow protection as a useful tool for exposing the ambivalence of the liberal secular rhetoric that was flying high in the Assembly to deny concessions to religious minorities. Z. H. Lari, for example, urged the majority make their demand in clear religious terms and asserted that the Muslim minorities would respect that demand, given that Islam did not specifically require the sacrifice of cows.[83] Syed Muhammad Saadulla, too, expressed his sympathy with the Hindu majority demand for cow

---

[78] CAD, vol. VII, para. 7.59.85 (24 November 1948).
[79] Ibid., para. 7.59.92 (24 November 1948).
[80] Ibid., paras. 7.59.102–110 (24 November 1948).
[81] Ibid., para. 7.59.136 (24 November 1948).
[82] Ibid., para. 7.59.148 (24 November 1948).
[83] Ibid., paras. 7.59.151–153 (24 November 1948).

protection as a *religious* matter and advised the majority to 'come out in the open and say directly that "[t]his is part of our religion. The cow should be protected from slaughter and therefore we want its provision either in the Fundamental Rights or in the Directive Principles"', but condemned those, who, in his opinion, put the question on the economic front and thereby attempted to satisfy the ingrained Hindu feeling against cow slaughter by the backdoor.[84]

Bhargava's proposal was finally adopted. The Constitution of India indeed declares, as one of the directive principles of the state, that measures will be taken to prohibit the slaughter of cows.[85] Paradoxically, India is currently the second largest beef-exporting country in the world, next to Brazil – which replaced India in the top spot only in 2018.[86] In contrast, a total of 63 cow vigilante attacks by Hindu fundamentalists occurred in India between 2010 and mid-2017, which saw 28 Indians (24 of them Muslims) killed and 124 injured.[87] Cow vigilante activities increased sharply after Narendra Modi's government, with its Hindutva ideology, came to power in 2014, but as the preceding discussion reveals, even the 'secular' constitution could not avoid some sort of accommodation for cow protection.

Also, in line with liberal egalitarian philosophy, special protection for the scheduled castes and scheduled tribes was explained only as a transitional measure, available for a limited period of time. This is a classic liberal dilemma with any deviation – as, for example, in affirmative action policies – from the principle of equality and non-discrimination. Hence, by definition all such policies have to be temporary and transitional: as soon as the group members in question achieve equality with the rest of the society, such special measures need to end. This solution makes affirmative action policies normatively coherent with the liberal core values of equality and non-discrimination. The time-limited safeguards that the Indian constitution grants to the tribal communities and the scheduled castes follow this logic and simultaneously underscore the liberal underpinning of the internal political organisation of the postcolonial state. When members of the assembly asked for better protection for the tribal communities in India, Sardar Patel expressed his frustration thus:

---

[84] Ibid., paras. 7.59.154–157 (24 November 1948).
[85] See Article 48 of the Constitution of India.
[86] US Department of Agriculture (Economic Research Service), 'Brazil Once Again Becomes the World's Largest Beef Exporter', 2 July 2019, available at www.ers.usda.gov/amber-waves/2019/july/brazil-once-again-becomes-the-world-s-largest-beef-exporter.
[87] 'Protests held across India after attacks against Muslims', *Reuters*, 28 June 2017.

> Is it the intention of people to defend the cause of the tribals to keep the tribes permanently in their present state? [...] I think that it should be our endeavour [...] not keep them as tribes, so that, 10 years hence, when the Fundamental Rights are reconsidered, the word *'tribes'* may be removed altogether, when they would have come up to our level. It is not befitting India's civilization to provide for tribes.

The liberal agenda of 'progress' and assimilation can hardly be ignored here.

2.3.3 The Postcolonial 'Developmental' State

The legitimacy of postcolonial states draws on the ideology of 'development'.[88] As Chatterjee argues, if the postcolonial state had to operate very much within the territorial, political, and administrative frameworks of the colonial regime, the new regime needed a new, distinctive claim to legitimacy. The economic critique of colonial rule did not see the illegitimacy of the colonial regime in its alienness alone. Rather, the focus of the attack was on the 'colonial mode' of exploitation, such as 'the drain of national wealth, the destruction of its productive system, the creation of a backward economy'.[89] The argument, thus, followed that the colonial mode of exploitation must be replaced by new forms of economic development delivered by the independent postcolonial state. Since the very logic of colonial exploitation was dependent upon the deprivation of native development, an independent nation state was essential not only for self-government as an end in itself but also as a means of achieving precisely what it had been historically deprived of.

> The economic critique of colonialism then was the foundation from which a positive content was supplied for the independent national state: the new state represented the only legitimate form of exercise of power because it was a necessary condition for the development of the nation. A developmental ideology then was a constituent part of the self-definition of the postcolonial state.[90]

The developmental ideology also had important implications for the internal organisation of ethnic relations in postcolonial India. If the ideology of the 'liberal' state is put forward as a 'political' solution to

---

[88] Chatterjee, *The Nation and Its Fragments*, 205.
[89] Ibid., 203.
[90] Ibid.

the protracted crisis of ethno-nationalism and the ensuing minority problem in India, the 'economic' solution to these problems comes in the form of the ideology of the 'developmental' state. Here, the ideology of the postcolonial developmental state with its mandate of economic development operates through the general mode of dissimulation. Developmentalism attempts to use dissimulation to gloss over the existing asymmetric power relations that continue to produce socio-economic vulnerability for minority groups.

The perception that economic development advanced by the modern postcolonial state will eradicate communal tensions arises from two legitimate yet inconclusive concerns about the artificiality of ethno-nationalism: instrumentalism and elite-constructivism. As I briefly mentioned in Chapter 1, instrumentalists typically assume that human beings are rational individuals, who act primarily to optimise their economic pay-off. They, thus, conceive ethnic groups as a collection of profit-maximising individuals and, consequently, ethno-nationalism primarily as a form of competition for scarce economic resources between or among coalitions identified along ethnic lines.[91] For example, Francesco Caselli and Wilbur Coleman II's instrumentalist position perceives ethnic conflicts as competitions over economic resources and ethnicity as a mere tool for a rational choice, at the individual level, which will make for peace or conflict.[92]

On the other hand, the assertion that ethno-nationalism is merely an elite construct assumes that various political, religious, or military elites mobilise individuals by accentuating and inventing individuals' ethnic attachments as well as their claims to economic resources.[93] For instance, Berberoglu's socialist theory of ethnic conflict, as we have seen earlier, perceives ethno-nationalism and the ensuing ethnic tension as manifestations of class interests and class forces that invoke national and ethnic symbolism to advance their own narrow class project and do so in the name of the nation or ethnic group they claim to represent.[94] Thus, ethno-national strife is, in fact, the outcome of dominant class forces in society attempting to advance their class interests, both domestically and on a world scale.[95] Given the centrality of considerations of economic competition and resource allocation in both instrumentalist and elite-constructivist approaches to ethno-nationalism, the ideology of a postcolonial 'developmental' state that

[91] Shahabuddin, *Ethnicity and International Law*, 181.
[92] Caselli and Coleman II, 'On the Theory of Ethnic Conflict', 162–192.
[93] Shahabuddin, *Ethnicity and International Law*, 181.
[94] Berberoglu, *Nationalism and Ethnic Conflict*, 107.
[95] Ibid., 107.

has the task of ensuring 'economic progress' appears to be quite a natural response to the problem of ethno-nationalism and minorities.

During the 1940s, a series of commentators addressing the problem of ethno-nationalism in India agreed that the solution to the problem still lay in economic development. Noting that in the trade unions and the peasant unions Hindus and Muslims united without distinction or difference, Dutt hoped that common social and economic needs as well as common bonds of class solidarity would destroy the artificial barriers of communal divisions.[96] He saw a national socialist state – with its mandate of economic development and income redistribution – as a prerequisite for such conditions to prevail. Although he supported the democratic right to self-determination for all nationalities within a free India, Dutt nevertheless believed that Indian unity was essential for advancing the interests of progressive democratic development and especially for 'the most rapid advance of all its parts through common co-operation, and for adequate all-India economic planning and development and the raising of social standards'.[97] This view was shared by Desai, who claimed that only a national state could accomplish the colossal task of implementing the reconstruction of the entire agrarian economy under a comprehensive national economic plan.[98] Therefore, the nationalist movement, he continued, 'desired to retain the political and administrative unification of India, accomplished by the British, which represented a historical advance of Indian society' and surely did not aim to resuscitate the administrative disunity of the pre-British era.[99] For Desai, a unified and independent India, with a socialist economic system and the right to self-determination (to be exercised internally) for various ethno-national groups, would offer a complete solution to the problem of nationalities and minorities.[100]

The vision of the 'developmental' state as a solution to the minority problem was most powerfully expressed in the writings of Nehru. He understood the minority problem as an economic issue *tout court*, and he hoped that the attainment of the political goal of the nationalist movement – that is, the postcolonial national state – would create an environment in which the state would then be able to solve the problems of ethno-nationalism. Written shortly before the partition of India and the complete abandonment of any idea of minority protection in the

---

[96] Dutt, *India To-day*, 463.
[97] Ibid., 477–480.
[98] Desai, *Social Background*, 66–67.
[99] Ibid., 160.
[100] Ibid., 404.

constitution, *The Discovery of India* (1946) conveys Nehru's hope that constitutional guarantees for the fundamental rights of the individual as well as of religious, cultural, and linguistic groups would reassure minorities that those rights would be protected.[101] And then, '[h]aving assured the protection of religion and culture, etc., the major problems that were bound to come up were economic ones which had nothing to do with a person's religion. Class conflicts there might well be, but not religious conflicts, except in so far as religion itself represented some vested interest.'[102]

Since the dominant elements of the postcolonial 'developmental' state were drawn from the ideology of the modern liberal-democratic state, the 'developmental' state, with its modernist agenda of economic progress, was believed to have the mitigating power to deal with backward ethnonationalism through liberal constitutionalism, equal rights of citizenship, economic development, and social justice.[103] To this end, the domain of the public needed to be distinguished from that of the private; in the words of Chatterjee: 'The legitimacy of the state in carrying out this function was to be guaranteed by its indifference to concrete differences between private selves-differences, that is, of race, language, religion, class, caste, and so forth.'[104] It is a state that is based on a consciousness of national solidarity and equality of opportunity. As Nehru urged, '[e]very effort should be made by the state as well as by private agencies to remove all invidious social and customary barriers which came in the way of the full development of the individual as well as any group'.[105] Chatterjee succinctly grasps this 'developmental' vision among the postcolonial elites: 'Once established, this state will stand above the narrow interests of groups and classes in society, take an overall view of the matter and, in accordance with the best scientific procedures plan and direct the economic processes in order to create enough social wealth to ensure welfare and justice for all.'[106]

In other words, science and technology, industrialisation, and agricultural modernisation – all under the rubric of national economic planning – were set to replace everything that was culturally primitive. As early as 1938, a National Planning Committee was established in India under the auspices of the Indian National Congress. It consisted of industrialists,

---

[101] Nehru, *The Discovery of India*, 382.
[102] Ibid., 383.
[103] Chatterjee, *Nationalist Thought*, 141.
[104] Chatterjee, *The Nation and Its Fragments*, 10.
[105] Nehru, *Discovery of India*, 387.
[106] Chatterjee, *Nationalist Thought*, 133.

THE THREE IDEOLOGIES OF THE POSTCOLONIAL STATE 81

financiers, economists, professors, scientists, and representatives of provincial governments, trade unions, and village industry associations.[107] The key motivation for the creation of the Planning Committee was that it would ensure rapid industrialisation; fast and massive industrialisation was considered a prerequisite to addressing the problems of poverty, unemployment, national defence, and economic regeneration.[108] Thus, as Nehru and many like him saw it, the solution to socio-political issues of protracted injustice lay not in politics but in the technical knowledge of planning: 'If *we* could collect the available material, co-ordinate it, and draw up blue-prints, *we* would prepare the ground for the real effective future planning.'[109] Here 'we' represents a select group of experts with necessary technical knowledge: twenty-nine sub-committees, consisting of about 350 specialists or experts, each assigned to investigate and report on specific problems.[110]

Planning was essentially conceived of as a 'scientific' study of the problem of India's underdevelopment. A questionnaire was drawn up at the first session of the Committee and sent to public bodies, universities, chambers of commerce, trade unions, research institutes, and so on, and the sub-committees prepared their interim reports on the basis of the data collected. Having considered all the collected data, the Planning Committee brought out a final report incorporating '*decisions* on that particular subject'.[111] The whole exercise of economic planning was highly technocratic and deliberately kept far from the domain of politics.[112] Nehru himself acknowledges the comfort he enjoyed in this technocratic environment beyond the sphere of political scrutiny: 'To me the spirit of co-operation of the members of the Planning Committee was peculiarly soothing and gratifying, for I found it a pleasant contrast to the squabbles and conflicts of politics.'[113]

Thus, a critical examination of the postcolonial state as an ideology with three strands reveals how it serves to establish and sustain relations of domination by the political majority over vulnerable minority groups

---

[107] Nehru, *Discovery of India*, 395.
[108] Ibid., 396.
[109] Ibid. Emphasis added.
[110] Ibid., 400. The specialists and experts were businessmen, government/state/municipal employees, university professors or lecturers, technicians, scientists, trade unionists, and policemen.
[111] Ibid., 401. Emphasis added.
[112] For a detailed critique of 'economic planning' in the context of postcolonial India, see Chatterjee, *The Nation and Its Fragments*, 200–219.
[113] Nehru, *Discovery of India*, 399.

through a number of modes of ideological operation. In the anticolonial nationalist discourse and the political imagination of the postcolonial order, the vision of the postcolonial state appeared as the natural and obvious choice. This ideological operation of reification by the postcolonial state essentialised the 'state-form' so far as the political emancipation of the colonial state was concerned. Closely related to this phenomenon is the ideological mode of legitimation, and the postcolonial state operated vis-à-vis minorities within that mode too. Once established as the only legitimate outcome of decolonisation, the relations of domination between the majority and the minority become perpetual. Similarly, at the micro level, the ideology of the national state relied on unification as a mode of operation, while the ideology of the liberal state depended on fragmentation – diffusing minority groups into liberal individual citizens of the hostile state. The ideology of the postcolonial developmental state, along with the ideologies of national and liberal states, glossed over the true meanings of these ideas and served to establish and sustain asymmetric power relations within the operative mode of dissimulation. In other words, a critical examination of the postcolonial state as an ideology helps us understand the ways in which the visions of the postcolonial 'national', 'liberal', and 'developmental' state establish and sustain asymmetric power relations to marginalise minorities in these states but at the same time justify and gloss over such marginalisation.

2.4 Conclusion: International Law and the Postcolonial State

So far, Part I has dealt with the first two building blocks of this book: why and how ethno-nationalism takes root in postcolonial states, and how postcolonial states then respond to this phenomenon. I have critically examined dominant thinking on the reasons behind persistent ethno-nationalism in postcolonial states and the roles of colonialism, capitalism, and nation-building in this regard. I have also exposed the way in which the notion of the postcolonial state itself then appears as an ideology ostensibly to mitigate such problems of ethno-nationalism. By elaborating three different forms in which the ideology of the postcolonial states gets expression, I have demonstrated that in reality these ideological expressions of the postcolonial state marginalise minorities through a series of modes of operation and techniques. To substantiate this argument, I have offered an in-depth analysis of the anticolonial nationalist movement in India and also demonstrated how the vision of the postcolonial Indian state as discussed in the Constituent Assembly debates shaped the normative position of minorities in the Indian constitution. Taken together, Chapters 1 and 2 in Part I offer a normative framework for my analysis in Part II to engage with the third building block of the book: what role does international law play in the ideological function of the postcolonial state to marginalise minority groups? Also, my discussion in Part I on the geneses of ethno-nationalism in Indian nationalist movements, along with the minority rights discourse in Indian Constituent Assembly debates, offers a useful backdrop for the case studies on the Rohingya in Myanmar and the hill people of the CHT in Bangladesh in Part II.

International law is central to the making of postcolonial states, and it plays a key role in the ideological function of such states across the three forms discussed here. So far as the postcolonial 'national' state is concerned, international law offers the necessary legal basis for the demarcation of territorial and political boundaries of the national state. With its ambition of achieving a homogenous and unified sovereign entity, the postcolonial state essentially relies on international law principles governing postcolonial boundaries (*uti possidetis*), territorial integrity, sovereign equality, and non-interference in internal affairs. It is within this legal framework that the colonial administrative units, unified for the first time by colonial administrations, transform into postcolonial states. Territorial boundaries, often arbitrarily drawn by colonial administrations without any regard to ethnic composition, come to define the state. In this set-up, where the 'national' often equates to the majoritarian, despite the lofty slogan of nation-building, minority groups remain vulnerable to political and cultural suppression. The minority problem is therefore embedded in the very process of creation of the postcolonial 'national' state through the operation of international law.

Second, the post-WWII liberal vision of international law feeds into the ideology of the postcolonial 'liberal' state in the form of 'individualism', which dominates the discourse on the constitutional architecture of rights. One direct implication of such liberal individualism is the often very weak – or sometimes the total lack of – protection afforded to cultural *groups*. Instead, the whole liberal human rights regime is designed to diffuse groups into liberal individuals, thereby facilitating their assimilation into a homogenous national (read majoritarian) identity. In a way, this complements the vision of the 'national' state. As we have seen in the context of Indian Constituent Assembly debates, a liberal-secular state meant the negation of 'minorities' even as a concept. In general, the 'minority' is seldom a holder of rights in postcolonial constitutional orders.

Another consequence of the liberal underpinning of international law and the ensuing ambivalence towards group rights is the denial to national minorities of the right to self-determination. While the right to self-determination in international law enjoys the status of a peremptory norm (*jus cogens*) in the context of decolonisation, such a right is granted to the colonial peoples – the nascent postcolonial 'national' state – as a whole; minorities in those national states fall outside its operation. In recent years, liberal interpretations of the right to self-determination in the form of democratic entitlements even moved far enough to depict the individual as the holder of this right and, thereby, to establish the primacy of the individual over sovereign states.[114] Liberal international law, however, refrains from extending this right to minorities, except as a remedial measure in cases of extreme violations of human rights. Indeed, international law prefers that minorities slowly disappear through assimilation – a preference that the postcolonial 'liberal' state materialises.

And finally, the ideology of the postcolonial 'developmental' state offers the language of economic progress and development to undermine the minority question as such. The idea that economic development is the answer to all social problems is embedded in the very logic of international law's engagement with postcolonial statehood. As influential international law scholarship in this field persuasively demonstrates, since the creation of the League of Nations, the colonial underpinning of international law has been transformed into a more subtle form of economic imperialism.[115] The free market economy, deregulation, free movement of capital, and so on have become international law and institutions' raison d'être. On the other hand, the Third World resistance, in the form of Permanent Sovereignty over Natural Resources or of the New International Economic Order, almost exclusively operates within the framework of the postcolonial 'national' state and hardly pays any attention to minorities. The more recent proposition of the right to development too suffers from the same limitation of being contextualised

---

[114] See, for example, Thomas Franck, 'The Emerging Right to Democratic Governance', *American Journal of International Law* 86 (1992), 46–91. In making this argument, Franck relied on the writings of Kant. See Immanuel Kant, 'Perpetual Peace: A Philosophical Sketch (1795)', in *Kant: Political Writings*, ed. H. S. Reiss, trans. H. B. Nisbet (New York: Cambridge University Press, 1970), 93–130; See also Immanuel Kant, 'The Metaphysics of Morals (1797)', in *Kant: Political Writings*, 164–173.

[115] See, for example, Chimni, *International Law and World Order*; Anghie, *Imperialism, Sovereignty and the Making of International Law*; Rajagopal, *International Law from Below*; Pahuja, *Decolonising International Law*.

within the individualist framework of human rights. As a result, minorities become the foremost victims of development activities by the state as well as by international development agencies. In the globalised market economy, while the presumably weakening 'national' state was arguably expected to relax its grip on long-oppressed minorities, increasingly powerful national and multinational corporations are disenfranchising already vulnerable communities on an unprecedented scale and pace in the name of economic development.

The following three chapters in Part II critically analyse the role of international law in each of the three forms of the ideology of the postcolonial state with reference to the issues identified earlier. In my analysis, I demonstrate the specific repercussions that international law engagements with postcolonial states have generated for minorities. The case studies on the Rohingya in Myanmar and the CHT hill people in Bangladesh will substantiate my arguments in each chapter.

PART II

International Law and the Postcolonial State

3

The Postcolonial 'National' State:

Boundaries and International Law

3.1 Introduction

The ideology of the postcolonial 'national' state is intrinsically connected to the suppression of minorities in these states. The process of making a homogeneous national state within the confines of colonial boundaries – drawn arbitrarily without any regard to the ethnic makeup of the population – leads to the marginalisation of various minority groups. For, these minorities often find themselves on the wrong side of the state boundaries and under the jurisdiction of hostile new states. The results are often disastrous, and in extreme cases, such as the Rohingya, include genocide. In this chapter, I shed light on the role of international law in the ideological function of the postcolonial 'national' state and its implications for minorities.

By prescribing the continuation of the colonial boundaries in postcolonial states, international law facilitates the ideological function of the postcolonial 'national' state and, thereby, contributes to the oppression of minorities. The problem surrounding colonial boundaries has been widely discussed in relation to conflicts in Africa.[1] Those boundaries have been established in accordance with the international legal principle of *uti possidetis*, which dictates that colonial borders must be respected. Arguably, the reason for adopting this principle in Africa has been to curtail ongoing ethnic conflicts there. By exploring the origins of *uti possidetis* and its extension to Asia, I seek in this chapter to demonstrate the questionable legal status of the *uti*

---

[1] See, for example, Mutua, 'Why Redraw the Map of Africa', 1113–1176; Obiora Chinedu Okafor, '"Righting", Restructuring, and Rejuvenating the Postcolonial African State: The Case for the Establishment of an AU Special Commission on National Minorities', *African Yearbook of International Law* (2006), 43–64.

possidetis principle and the fallacy of its potential for evading conflicts. Conventional wisdom states that *uti possidetis* is essential for settling boundary disputes among postcolonial states and, thus, helps maintain peace and order; I argue that *uti possidetis* itself is a key problem. Far from being a corrective mechanism regulating potential 'disorder' emanating from decolonisation, the continuation of arbitrarily drawn colonial boundaries undermined the legitimate right to self-determination of numerous ethnic minorities at the moment of decolonisation and in many cases resulted in violent ethnic conflicts. Its embrace by postcolonial Asian states, such as Myanmar and Bangladesh, has exacerbated rather than curtailed violence.

In this vein, I also argue that the current violence suffered by the Rohingya and by the hill people of the CHT cannot be fully understood except by studying the complex histories of Rakhine State and the CHT and their relationship with the British Empire. It is this history which created the colonial boundaries that are still enforced in ways that preserve the existence of the insecure postcolonial 'national' states of Myanmar and Bangladesh, which have systematically oppressed their ethnic minorities. In this argument, I also highlight the inherent relationship between colonialism and international law and the way they shape the ideology of the postcolonial 'national' state.

In the following section, I discuss the role of international law in the making of postcolonial boundaries. I start this by explaining how the decolonisation process under international law was restrained by the notion of territorial integrity of the nascent postcolonial state as a whole. As a result, many minority groups were deprived of their legitimate right to self-determination. I follow this discussion on dwarfed decolonisation in international law with an examination of how the international law principle of *uti possidetis*, despite its questionable legal status, continues to maintain the colonial boundaries of postcolonial states. My arguments in this section are then substantiated in subsequent sections with case studies on the Rohingya and the CHT hill people.

3.2 International Law and Postcolonial Boundaries

3.2.1 Decolonisation and the Territorial Integrity of the 'National' State

Following the Great War, when the then US President Woodrow Wilson declared the right to self-determination as one of the governing principles of the Paris Peace Conference of 1919, the Indian Home Rule League submitted a petition to the Great Powers of the Conference arguing for

India's independence under this principle.[2] Itty Abraham argues that the petition was also a response to the Wilsonian idea of self-determination that subjugated peoples need to 'conform to the identity of one people – one land – one state to be accepted as having legitimate claim to political personhood'.[3] Protagonists of anticolonial nationalist movements that lacked these features generally 'sought to redefine the prime criterion for independent statehood as unified political control over a defined piece of land, or territorial sovereignty'.[4] In order to refute the proposition that India's racial and cultural diversity makes it not a 'nation', the petition put forward what it called a 'modern' understanding of the nation. In this regard, the petition relied on Lord Acton's proposition on the subject: a nation is a moral and political being, developed in the course of history by the action of the state and the idea that a nation itself should constitute a state is contrary to modern civilisation.[5] Based on Acton and relying on the promising prospect of the principle of federalism to unify multiple nationalities within the postcolonial Indian state, the petition concluded that 'to require races of India to coalesce into a nation with one religion and one tongue, is midsummer madness'; instead, a territorially defined Indian nation-state was the solution.[6] The petition fell on deaf ears, as we know, but the interwar principle of self-determination solidified the idea of the sovereign, territorially bound nation-state, wherein the majority obtained control of the state apparatus while the minority found itself in a position of perpetual subordination, often under minority protection treaties.

In the aftermath of WWII, the idea of self-determination was primarily expressed through decolonisation. In fact, as Rosalyn Higgins demonstrates, before the claim for decolonisation gained prominence in the discourse on self-determination, the mention of self-determination in the UN Charter simply meant the equal rights of all states to non-interference in their internal affairs.[7] It was through the activism of the

---

[2] Reprinted in India Home Rule League of America, *Self-Determination for India* (New York: India Home Rule League of America, 1919). See also Arnulf Becker Lorca, 'Petitioning the International: A "Pre-history" of Self-determination', *European Journal of International Law* 25, no. 2 (2014), 502.
[3] Itty Abraham, *How India Became Territorial: Foreign Policy, Diaspora, Geopolitics* (Palo Alto, CA: Stanford University Press, 2014), 11.
[4] Ibid., 12.
[5] India Home Rule League of America, *Self-Determination for India*, 9–10.
[6] Ibid., 10.
[7] Rosalyn Higgins, *Problems and Process: International Law and How We Use It* (Oxford: Oxford University Press, 1994), 111–114. See also Shahabuddin, *Ethnicity and International Law*, 136–137.

new states of Asia and Africa in the UN General Assembly (UNGA) that the concept of self-determination turned into the moral and legal force behind decolonisation.[8]

However, at the same time, the nationalist elites who often represented the majority interest in these countries saw themselves as the legitimate and sole successors of the colonial powers, and conceived of the colonial state as a necessary mode of transition to a 'modern' postcolonial state.[9] Abraham notes that as early as 1947, in the Asian Relations Conference in Delhi, all the delegates reached a consensus on the absolute acceptance of the nation-state mould.[10] Consequently, it also emerged that

> [t]he Asian political entities soon to be free were uniformly represented as states composed as national majorities joined by ethnic or cultural minorities. [...] Communities marked by difference from these national majorities were being recast as aliens and outsiders, notwithstanding their long residence in these countries. [...] Under these circumstances, all that could be hoped for was goodwill on the part of majority communities leading to legal and constitutional protections for these 'new' minorities. The Asian Relations Conference made it clear that political independence for Asia would mean a state dominated by a nation defined in terms of an autochthonous majority community.[11]

The same attitude was reinforced during the Bandung Conference of newly independent Asian and African states in 1955. Despite the anti-colonial and anti-imperial theme of the conference, many of these states themselves adopted the 'national state' ethos and ultimately developed

---

[8] See UN General Assembly, *Declaration on the Granting of Independence to the Colonial Countries and Peoples*, Resolution 1514 (XV) of 14 December 1960, UN Doc A/RES/1514 (XV); UN General Assembly, *Principles which should Guide Members in Determining whether or not an Obligation Exists to Transmit the Information Called for under Article 73 e of the Charter*, Resolution 1541 (XV) of 15 December 1960, UN Doc A/RES/1541; UN General Assembly, *Declaration on Principles of International Law concerning Friendly Relations and Cooperation among States in accordance with the Charter of the United Nations*, Resolution 2625 (XXV) of 24 October 1970, UN Doc A/RES/2625 (XXV). See also Thomas D. Musgrave, *Self-Determination and National Minorities* (Oxford: Clarendon Press, 1997), 69–77, 91–96.
[9] See Chatterjee, *Nationalist Thought*, 1–35; Dipesh Chakrabarty, *Provincializing Europe – Postcolonial Thought and Historical Difference* (Princeton, NJ: Princeton University Press, 2000), 27–46.
[10] Abraham, *How India Became Territorial*, 69.
[11] Ibid.

a 'colonial' relationship vis-à-vis their minorities and peoples in annexed territories.[12]

The normative need for continuity from the colonial state to the postcolonial nation-state that was to be governed by nationalist elites and the pragmatic need to avoid letting 'chaos' arise from decolonisation were both addressed by the international law principle of *uti possidetis*, which states that colonial borders are to be maintained for postcolonial states. Thus, the post–WWII application of *uti possidetis* principles cemented the territorial borders that had been arbitrarily drawn by the colonial powers[13] and enforced the multi-ethnic composition of the postcolonial states.[14]

Very much like the core principles of the Bandung Conference, as enshrined in the Final Communiqué,[15] the Colonial Declaration of 1960 proclaimed that '[a]ll peoples have the right to self-determination' and that 'by virtue of that right they freely determine their political status and freely pursue their economic, social and cultural development'.[16] But, at the same time, the Declaration stipulated that all states shall faithfully and strictly respect the sovereign rights of all peoples and their territorial integrity and also made it explicit that '[a]ny attempt aimed at the partial or total disruption of the national unity and the territorial integrity of a country is incompatible with the purposes and principles of the Charter of the United Nations'.[17] As a comment made by the Moroccan delegate during the drafting process of the Declaration revealed, the Asian and African states that drafted the Declaration were concerned about the

---

[12] See, for example, Cyra A. Chowdhury, 'From Bandung 1955 to Bangladesh 1971: Postcolonial Self-determination and Third World Failure in South Asia', in *Bandung, Global History, and International Law*, 322–336; Luwam Dirar, 'Rethinking the Concept of Colonialism in Bandung and Its African Union Aftermath', in *Bandung, Global History, and International Law*, 355–366; Katharine McGregor and Vannessa Hearman, 'Challenging the Lifeline of Imperialism: Reassessing Afro-Asian Solidarity and Related Activism in the Decade 1955–1965', in *Bandung, Global History, and International Law*, 161–176.

[13] However, the option of changing territorial borders by voluntarily joining another state or by remaining in a constitutional relationship with the former colonial Power remained open. See *Principles which should Guide Members in Determining whether or not an Obligation Exists to Transmit the Information Called for under Article 73 e of the Charter*, principles VI–IX.

[14] Thomas M. Franck, *Fairness in International Law and Institutions* (Oxford: Oxford University Press, 1995), 149.

[15] 'Final Communiqué of the Asian-African Conference of Bandung' (24 April 1955), in Ministry of Foreign Affairs, Republic of Indonesia (ed.), *Asia-Africa Speak from Bandung* (Djakarta: Ministry of Foreign Affairs, 1955), 161–169.

[16] *Declaration on the Granting of Independence to the Colonial Countries and Peoples*, Article 2.

[17] Ibid., Articles 6 and 7.

attempts by colonial powers – in line with their longstanding policy of 'divide and rule' – to carve up colonies that were in the process of achieving independence.[18] The emphasis on territorial integrity was a clear attempt to counter such colonial practices. However, it simultaneously restricted the applicability of self-determination to exclude various minority groups and their nationalist aspirations for independent statehood, thereby reinforcing the colonial borders in Asia and Africa.

As a matter of fact, General Assembly debates on the draft Declaration were taking place while the crisis of the Katangese secessionist attempt was unfolding. The Katanga crisis was explicitly referred to in the debate as highlighting the salience of the provisions on territorial integrity in the Declaration.[19] When the Republic of Congo obtained independence from Belgium in 1960, the mineral-rich province of Katanga also declared its independence from Congo with the active support of and protection from the Belgians.[20] Following the outbreak of a civil war, the Congolese government sought assistance from the UN, which asked Belgium to immediately withdraw its troops from Congo.[21] The UN position on the Katanga issue made it very clear that the right to self-determination belonged to Congo as a whole and that no breach of its territorial integrity was permissible under any claim to self-determination by any other group. The Katanga case, in this sense, exemplifies an international consensus regarding the continuity of colonial boundaries and the limits it places on the right to self-determination of other sub-national groups in the new postcolonial 'national' state.

Similarly, in the General Assembly debate on the Declaration, the Indonesian delegate made frequent references to the situation in West Irian (New Guinea) to highlight the importance of territorial integrity in the context of the right to self-determination.[22] Following more than 300 years of Dutch rule, a short period of Japanese occupation between 1942 and 1945, and finally Indonesia's independence in 1949, Indonesia's former colonial power, the Netherlands, disputed the legal status of West Irian on the grounds that the 700,000 inhabitants of the island

---

[18] See the Moroccan delegate's comments at UN Doc A/PV.947 (14 December 1960) 1284, paras. 158–161.
[19] Ibid.
[20] For details, see *Arrest Warrant of 11 April 2000 (Democratic Republic of the Congo v. Belgium)*, ICJ Reports (2002), 3, paras. 6–15, Judge Ad Hoc Bula, separate opinion.
[21] UN Doc S/4382 (13 July 1960) 1; SC Res 143 (14 July 1960); SC Res 161 (21 February 1961).
[22] See UN Doc A/PV.936 (1960) 1153, paras. 53–55.

were racially and culturally distinct from the Indonesians.[23] On the other hand, Indonesia argued that the nation had been founded on a territorial, rather than a racial, basis and that its foundation was rooted in common suffering endured during the Dutch colonial rule.[24] This territorial argument had some relevance, in that, as Anghie notes, given the artificiality of the boundaries of most postcolonial states, relying on race as the legitimate basis of the postcolonial nation-state would dismantle almost all Asian and African states.[25] Indonesia also relied on the colonial ideology of 'civilisation' in arguing that the 'people of West Irian were too "primitive" to exercise the right of self-determination in a conventional way' – a comment that offended many African nations.[26] Although the Dutch position following the adoption of the Colonial Declaration – a position which was also supported by a group of francophone African states – was in favour of granting the people of West Irian the right to self-determination, Indonesia successfully used the General Assembly to press the demand for its territorial integrity under international law,[27] and finally turned to open realism by invading the island in May 1962.[28] Under the US mediation, the people of West Irian obtained the right to express their free choice to decide on their political future. However, the actual expression of this right was limited as it took place under the direct influence of Indonesia – only slightly more than 1% of the total West Irian population were selected by the Indonesian Administration as special delegates, all of whom voted in favour of Indonesian rule. Despite knowledge of these irregularities, the UN refrained from taking any further action in this regard.[29]

---

[23] See Thomas Franck, *Nation against Nation* (New York: Oxford University Press, 1985), 77; see also Anghie, 'Bandung and the Origins of Third World Sovereignty', 544–546.
[24] United Nations, *Revue des Nations Unies* 6, no. 2 (1957), 67. See also Jamie Trinidad, *Self-Determination in Disputed Colonial Territories* (Cambridge: Cambridge University Press, 2018), 26–29.
[25] Anghie, 'Bandung and the Origins of Third World Sovereignty', 545.
[26] Ibid., 546; see also Michla Pomerance, 'Methods of Self-Determination and the Argument of "Primitiveness"', *Canadian Yearbook of International Law* 12 (1974), 51–52, 55. The Dutch vested interest in destabilising the region and thereby perpetuating its control cannot be ignored here. See Kalana Senaratne, 'Internal Self-Determination: A Critical Third World Perspective', *Asian Journal of International Law* 3, no. 2 (2013), 331–332.
[27] The resolution in favour of West Irian self-determination was marginally defeated by 53 votes to 41 votes with nine abstentions. See UN Doc A/L.368 (27 Nov 1961).
[28] Franck, *Nation against Nation*, 78.
[29] *Report of the Secretary General Concerning the Act of Self-Determination in West Irian*. UN Doc A/7723, Agenda item 98 (6 November 1969).

The same principle was applied, albeit in a different context and without involving any minority claim to the right to self-determination, in the more recent ICJ advisory opinion in the *Chagos Island* case.[30] Here the court argued that by detaching the Chagos Archipelago from Mauritius (a non-self-governing territory in the Indian Ocean under British administration) before granting the latter independence, the United Kingdom violated the principle of self-determination under international law, which applied to the entire territory under foreign control. Mauritius had been ceded to the United Kingdom by France under the Treaty of Paris of 1814. Following the Colonial Declaration of 1960, Britain took steps to give independence to Mauritius, at the same time as discussions between the United Kingdom and the United States were beginning about the US military's use of certain British-owned islands in the Indian Ocean. In line with an agreement with the United States and with the ensuing British Indian Ocean Territory Order 1965, the United Kingdom established a new colony – the British Indian Ocean Territory (BIOT) – consisting of the Chagos Archipelago, detached from Mauritius, and the Aldabra, Farquhar, and Desroches islands, detached from Seychelles.[31] Within a few weeks of the detachment of the Chagos Archipelago from Mauritius, the General Assembly adopted a resolution to recall the obligation of the United Kingdom, as the administering Power, to respect the territorial integrity of Mauritius.[32] Mauritius became an independent state in March 1968 without the Chagos Archipelago as its territory, and between 1967 and 1973 the entire population of the Chagos Archipelago was either prevented from returning or forcibly removed and prevented from returning by the United Kingdom.[33] When the matter was finally brought before the ICJ, the court concluded that in accordance with paragraph 6 of the Colonial Declaration, 'the right to self-determination of the people concerned is defined by reference to the entirety of a non-self-governing territory' and

> the peoples of non-self-governing territories are entitled to exercise their right to self-determination in relation to their territory as a whole, the integrity of which must be respected by the administering Power. It follows that any detachment by the administering Power of part of a non-self-governing

---

[30] *Legal Consequences of the Separation of the Chagos Archipelago from Mauritius in 1965* (*Chagos Islands* case), ICJ Reports (2019).
[31] Ibid., paras. 25–53.
[32] UN General Assembly, Resolution 2066 (XX) of 16 December 1965, UN Doc A/RES/2066 (XX).
[33] *Chagos Islands* case, paras. 25–53.

territory, unless based on the freely expressed and genuine will of the people of the territory concerned, is contrary to the right to self-determination.[34]

Likewise, various other UNGA resolutions as well as decisions of the ICJ also unequivocally declared the primacy of territorial integrity of states over ethnic claims for self-determination.[35] As Matthew Craven notes, 'the old opposition between self-determination and *uti possidetis* lost its decisive import by reason of the impossibility of self-determination meaning anything but independence within inherited borders – once the "self" had been identified, any determination could operate only within the parameters of its own existence'.[36] Thomas Franck sees this pattern as a move towards 'reconciliation'; in his words: 'The disintegration of Spanish imperialism in America produced the norm of *uti possidetis*. The end of the German, Austrian, and Ottoman empires [in the interwar period] gave rise to self-determination. In the post-1945 era *uti possidetis* and self-determination were redefined and synthesised into a doctrine of decolonisation.'[37] In this 'reconciliation', however, *uti possidetis* clearly trumped the principle of self-determination so far as minority groups, now entangled in postcolonial states, were concerned.

3.2.2 Uti Possidetis and the Making of the Postcolonial Boundaries

Uti possidetis originated from Roman law, where it arose in cases in which two individuals disagreed as to ownership of property. It was a provisional remedy based on possession, pending a final judicial determination. The principle reappeared in the early eighteenth century together with the concept of the *status quo post bellum* (the state of possession existing at the conclusion of war), though still connected with the fact of possession.[38] The modern formulation of the *uti possidetis* principle is traditionally associated with the decolonisation of Central and South America in the nineteenth century. In some cases, the newly independent Latin American states mutually agreed to adopt former Spanish administrative lines as

---

[34] Para. 160.
[35] See *Declaration on Friendly Relations* (1970). See also *Legal Consequences for States of the Continued Presence of South Africa in Namibia (South West Africa)*, ICJ Reports (1971), para. 52; *Frontier Dispute (Burkina Faso v. Mali)* case, ICJ Reports (1986), para. 25.
[36] Matthew Craven, *The Decolonization of International Law* (Oxford: Oxford University Press, 2007), 205.
[37] Franck, *Fairness in International Law and Institutions*, 147.
[38] See generally Suzanne Lalonde, *Determining Boundaries in a Conflicted World: The Role of* Uti Possidetis (Montreal: McGill-Queen's University Press, 2002), 10–23.

their new international boundaries, a practice that came to be seen as the implementation of the *uti possidetis* principle.[39]

The principle of *uti possidetis* reappeared in the interwar period in relation to the dispute between Finland and Sweden over the Aaland Islands (*Ahuenanmaa* in Finnish). Finland, including the Aaland Islands, was a part of the Swedish administrative region of Åbo (Turku) for more than six centuries starting in 1159. It was only in 1809 that Tsarist Russia under Alexander I seized control of Finland from the Swedish kingdom. Following the Bolshevik Revolution of 1917 and the ensuing disintegration of Tsarist Russia, Finland declared independence from Russia. The Aalanders demanded the recognition of their right to break away from Finland and re-unite with their co-ethnics in Sweden.[40] The League of Nations assigned the task of determining whether the dispute was international in nature, and therefore fell under the jurisdiction of the League, to a Commission of Jurists. This Commission questioned the proposition of an *ipso facto* application of the *uti possidetis* principle:

> The Aaland Islands were undoubtedly part of Finland during the period of Russian rule. Must they, for this reason alone, be considered as definitely incorporated *de jure* in the State of Finland which was formed as a result of the events described above? The Commission finds it impossible to admit this.[41]

However, the Commission of Rapporteurs, appointed subsequently by the League to pave the way for a solution to this dispute, held the opposite view, on the grounds, inter alia, of the *uti possidetis* principle, which was subject to guarantees obtained from the Finnish government for the protection of the Swedish language and culture of the Islanders.[42] In

---

[39] Ibid., 4. For a brief history of *uti possidetis*, see Steven R. Ratner, 'Drawing a Better Line: Uti Possidetis and the Borders of New States', *American Journal of International Law* 90, no. 4 (1996), 592–601.

[40] See generally James Barros, *The Aland Islands Question: Its Settlement by the League of Nations* (New Haven, CT: Yale University Press, 1968).

[41] *Aaland Islands* case, Report of the International Commission of Jurists, *League of Nations Official Journal*, Special Supplement No. 3 (1920), 9.

[42] The Commission of Rapporteurs took into consideration a number of other factors, including the small size of the island community as a claimant of the right to self-determination and also security concerns for both Sweden and Finland. Their report also observed that the sheet of water, the skiftet with its numerous rocks and islets, which separated the islands from the Finnish mainland 'would be a bad frontier between two States, extremely arbitrary from a geographical point of view'. See, *Aaland Islands* case, Report of the Commission of Rapporteurs (1921), League of Nations Council Doc B7 [C] 21/68/106, 3.

the opinion of the Rapporteurs, since the Aaland Islands were part of the Finnish Province of Åbo Björneborg under Tsarist Russia, upon Finnish independence the application of the *uti possidetis* principle should guarantee Finland's pre-independence territory.[43] The League Council adopted the view of the Rapporteurs and finally recommended that the Aaland Islands should belong to Finland.

Against this backdrop, the centrality of the *uti possidetis* principle in the international legal imagination regarding the boundaries of new states soon obtained a stronger foothold in the context of African decolonisation. When the member states of the Organisation of African Unity (OAU, now known as the 'African Union') pledged to respect the colonial boundaries existing at the time of independence in 1964, the ICJ and many commentators viewed the resolution as further evidence of the role of *uti possidetis* in the process of decolonisation.[44] Although prior to independence, many African political parties advocated the readjustment of these artificial boundaries to accord with local realities,[45] such revisionist claims lost traction as African colonies started emerging as independent states and prioritised a peaceful transition to statehood. Article 3(3) of the Charter of the OAU affirmed every member's adherence to 'respect for the sovereignty and territorial integrity of each State and for its inalienable right to independent existence'.[46] At a meeting in Cairo the following year, the OAU adopted a resolution reaffirming the importance of 'the strict respect by all member States of the Organisation for the principles laid down in Article III, paragraph 3 of the Charter' and declared 'that all member States pledge themselves to respect the frontiers existing on their achievement of national independence'.[47] The Katanga experience was surely fresh in the minds of African leaders.

It is widely believed that this acceptance of the continuity of the colonial borders represents the Latin American principle of *uti possidetis* applied in the African context.[48] Thus, through the operation of international law, the

---

[43] Ibid.
[44] Lalonde, *Determining Boundaries in a Conflicted World*, 4.
[45] For example, the resolution proclaimed by the All-African Peoples Conference held in Accra in December 1958, which called for the abolition or readjustment of colonial frontiers at an early date. See ibid., 103.
[46] Adopted in Addis Ababa on 25 May 1963, 479 UNTS 39.
[47] Ian Brownlie (ed.), *Basic Documents on African Affairs* (Oxford: Oxford University Press, 1971), 360. See also Lalonde, *Determining Boundaries in a Conflicted World*, 104.
[48] See, for example, Brownlie, *Basic Documents on African Affairs*, 360; A. O. Chukwurah, 'The Organisation of African Unity and African Territorial and Boundary Problems: 1963–1973', *Indian Journal of International Law* 13, no. 2 (1973), 181; Boutros Boutros-Ghali, *The Addis Ababa Charter* (New York: Carnegie Endowment for International Peace, 1964), 29.

boundaries of colonial Africa, which had been drawn at the Berlin Conference of 1883–1885 on the basis of astronomical or mathematical criteria or prominent physical features and without regard to demographics or culture, came to be the permanent boundaries of postcolonial African states. As Ieuan Griffiths notes,

> [t]he political map of colonial Africa was virtually complete by 1914 and there has been little subsequent change. During the next 50 years, that colonial boundary mesh would become the almost exact basis for territorial division of independent Africa which would then be fossilised by the resolution of the Organisation of African Unity in 1964.[49]

This view that the *uti possidetis* principle should be applied to postcolonial territorial delimitation was shared by the ICJ Chamber in the *Burkina Faso* v. *Mali* case, in which the Chamber declared that *uti possidetis* was a 'general principle' and a 'rule of general scope' for all cases of decolonisation.[50] Although the first use of the principle in the decolonisation of the Latin American colonies involved only a single colonial power, that is, Spain, the Chamber held that the principle of *uti possidetis* 'is not a special rule which pertains solely to one specific system of international law. It is a general principle, which is logically connected with the phenomenon of the obtaining of independence, wherever it occurs.'[51] The Chamber, thus, concluded: 'It was for this reason that, as soon as the phenomenon of decolonisation characteristic of the situation in Spanish America in the 19th century subsequently appeared in Africa in the 20th century, the principle of *uti possidetis* [...] fell to be applied.'[52] This position was later endorsed by the arbitral tribunal in the *Guinea Bissau* v. *Senegal* case,[53] and by the ICJ in the *Kasikili/Sedudu Island (Botswana* v. *Namibia)* case,[54] the *Land and Maritime Boundary (Cameroon* v. *Nigeria)* case,[55] and the *Frontier Dispute (Benin* v. *Niger)* case.[56]

However, this depiction of *uti possidetis* as the general principle of international law to be applied in all decolonisation situations has been challenged by Steven Ratner on a number of grounds: the principle, despite being widely applied in the decolonisation context, lacks *opinio juris*; it does

---

[49] Ieuan Ll. Griffiths, *The Atlas of African Affairs*, 2nd ed. (London: Routledge, 1995), 51.
[50] ICJ Reports (1986), 565.
[51] Ibid.
[52] Ibid.
[53] Arbitral Award of 31 July 1989, *Guinea Bissau* v. *Senegal* case, ICJ Reports (1991), 53.
[54] *Case Concerning Kasikili/Sedudu Island (Botswana* v. *Namibia)*, ICJ Reports (1999), 6.
[55] *The Land and Maritime Boundary* case *(Cameroon* v. *Nigeria)*, ICJ Reports (2002), 303.
[56] *Case Concerning the Frontier Dispute (Benin* v. *Niger)*, ICJ Reports (2005), 90.

not rule out alternative borders during decolonisation, or restrict post-independence changes in borders by consent, or override other legal positions prescribing borders that do not conform to prior administrative units.[57] In a more recent scholarship, Dirdeiry Ahmed argues that even in the Latin American context the key purpose of the *uti possidetis* principle in the nineteenth century was to avoid any possibility of *terra nullius*, thereby ensuring the unification of the entire Latin America in the face of the renewed threat of Spanish imperialism.[58] The argument therefore follows that *uti possidetis* was not a general principle of international law at the time of African decolonisation, and 'did not give rise to the concept of intangibility of inherited frontiers, and was as such inapplicable to Africa on independence'.[59] Hence, by accepting the preexisting frontiers in the absence of any binding international rules, African states created new customary rules – an achievement that the ICJ erroneously undermined in the *Burkina Faso* v. *Mali* case by imposing the *uti possidetis* principle on Africa as a binding general principle of international law.[60]

Similarly, after examining many of the constitutions of and treaties between Latin American states in the period following independence, Suzanne Lalonde challenges the mainstream position that the Latin American states consistently accepted the *uti possidetis* principle in determining their new boundaries.[61] She highlights various conflicting versions of the principle within Latin America, such as *uti possidetis juris* (claimed by most Spanish colonies) and *uti possidetis de facto* (claimed, e.g., by Brazil, which happened to be a Portuguese colony), as evidence of inconsistent state practice.[62] These conflicting claims, together with practical difficulties encountered in the application of the principle and international awards based on alternative principles, led Lalonde to conclude that *uti possidetis* never achieved the status of a general

---

[57] Ratner, 'Drawing a Better Line', 598–601.
[58] Ahmed, *Boundaries and Secession in Africa and International Law*, 20-24. He relies on a number of cases that support this claim: *Colombian-Venezuelan Frontier* case, *Reports of International Arbitral Awards* VI (1922), 223; *Case concerning a Dispute between Argentina and Chile concerning the Beagle Channel* (Beagle Channel case), *Reports of International Arbitral Awards* XXI (1977), 81–82; *Case concerning the Land, Island and Maritime Frontier Dispute* (El Salvador/Honduras case), ICJ Reports (1992), 315, 387; *Territorial and Maritime Dispute between Nicaragua and Honduras in the Caribbean Sea* (Nicaragua/Honduras case), ICJ Reports (2007), 659, 707.
[59] Ahmed, *Boundaries and Secession in Africa and International Law*, 46.
[60] See generally ibid., 11–46.
[61] See generally Lalonde, *Determining Boundaries in a Conflicted World*, 24–60.
[62] Ibid., 31–34.

principle of international law emanating from the Latin American experience of decolonisation.[63] Likewise, she found that the application of *uti possidetis* in the African context was driven by a practical sense of necessity, rather than by the legally binding nature of the principle.[64]

Yet, *uti possidetis* continued to dominate the international legal imagination in relation to boundary-drawing. The principle was applied even in a non-colonial context following the break-up of the Socialist Federal Republic of Yugoslavia (SFRY). Lord Carrington, the President of the Conference on Yugoslavia, asked the Badinter Commission for an opinion on the question of whether the Republics' declaration of independence amounted to secession from the SFRY. The Commission held that 'in the case of a federal-type state, which embraces communities that possess a degree of autonomy and, moreover, participate in the exercise of political power within the framework of institutions common to the Federation, the existence of the state implies that the federal organs represent the components of the Federation and wield effective power'.[65] Given that the Republics had declared their independence and the composition and workings of the essential organs of the Federation ceased to meet the criteria of participation and representation inherent in a federal state, the Commission decided in Opinion No. 1 that the SFRY was in the process of dissolution.[66] This Opinion was accompanied by the recognition of the republics as independent states by the European Community and the United States, subject to the provisions stipulated in the twin declarations on the guidelines for recognition of these states.[67]

The Opinion of the Commission and the recognition policy of the West cemented the statehood of these new states, thereby turning an ostensibly ethnic conflict into an international conflict – an issue of Serbian aggression. As a corollary, the Commission declared in Opinion No. 3 (concerning the question of whether the internal boundaries between Croatia and Serbia and between Bosnia and Herzegovina

---

[63] Ibid., 58–60.
[64] Ibid., 103–137.
[65] Conference on Yugoslavia, Arbitration Commission Opinion No. 1 (1991), *European Journal of International Law* 3 (1992), 182.
[66] Ibid., 183. In its Opinion No. 8 on 8 July 1992, the Commission declared that the process of dissolution of the SFRY was complete. See Arbitration Commission Opinion No. 8 (1992), *European Journal of International Law* 4 (1993), 87–88.
[67] See *Declaration on the Guidelines on the Recognition of New States in Eastern Europe and in the Soviet Union* (16 December 1991), *European Journal of International Law* 3 (1993), 72; *Declaration on Yugoslavia* (Extraordinary EPC Ministerial Meeting, Brussels, 16 December 1991), *European Journal of International Law* 3 (1993), 73.

and Serbia should be regarded as frontiers for the purpose of public international law) that in the circumstances of the emergence of new states following the dissolution of the SFRY, both the external and internal frontiers of the SFRY had to be respected.[68] The Commission categorically stated that this conclusion followed from the principle of respect for the territorial status quo and, in particular, from the principle of *uti possidetis*, which, though initially applied in settling decolonisation issues, was recognised as a general principle, as stated by the ICJ in the *Burkina Faso* v. *Mali* case.[69] In other words, the *internal* boundaries of the SFRY were converted to protected international frontiers, which could only be altered by an agreement. In an approving note, Alain Pallet writes that the application of this principle was indispensable for maintaining peace.[70] This view is also shared by Malcolm Shaw: 'Any attempted ethnic reconfiguration of the Former Yugoslavia on a totally free-for-all basis, without the presumptive *uti possidetis* rule with regard to boundaries, would most likely have produced an even worse situation than that which did occur.'[71]

Thus, the commission moved away from the ethnicity-oriented political organisation of these new states and offered a liberal international legal vision of post-conflict regional order in the Balkans. By viewing the dissolution of the SFRY as a break-up of the federal units and endorsing the existing boundaries of the republics, the Commission envisaged Bosnia and Herzegovina as a non-ethnic unit in which the Bosniac, Croat, and Serb ethnic groups would continue to live together.[72] The Commission's liberal non-ethnic vision of the nation-state was essentially

[68] Arbitration Commission Opinion No. 3 (1991), *European Journal of International Law* 3 (1992), 185. The Commission, in its support, specifically referred to the principles stated in the UN Charter, in the *Declaration on Friendly Relations* (1970) and in the Helsinki Final Act (1975).
[69] Opinion No. 3 (1991), 185. See also *Frontier Dispute (Burkina Faso* v. *Mali)* case, ICJ Reports (1986).
[70] He further asserts that 'the principle is not as rigid as some might feel it ought to be. Stability does not mean intangibility. Although States are prohibited from acquiring a territory by force, they might freely decide, as the Committee made clear, to a modification of their frontiers "by agreement"'. See Alain Pellet, 'The Opinions of the Badinter Arbitration Committee: A Second Breath for the Self-Determination of Peoples', *European Journal of International Law* 3 (1992), 180. For a critical perspective on the 'Badinter Frontiers Principle', see Peter Radan, 'Post-secession International Borders: A Critical Analysis of the Opinions of the Badinter Arbitration Commission', *Melbourne University Law Review* 24 (2000), 50–76.
[71] Malcolm N. Shaw, 'Peoples, Territorialism and Boundaries', *European Journal of International Law* 3 (1997), 502.
[72] See Shahabuddin, *Ethnicity and International Law*, 207.

in conflict with the conservative ethnic notion of the right to self-determination as claimed by Bosnian Serbs and Croats, who were keen to join their co-ethnics in Yugoslavia and Croatia, respectively. The Commission had to address this issue formally when Lord Carrington requested the Commission's opinion on whether the Serbian population in Croatia and Bosnia and Herzegovina, as one of the constituent peoples of Yugoslavia, had the right to self-determination. In conformity with its earlier opinions, the Commission held in Opinion No. 2 that 'whatever the circumstances, the right to self-determination must not involve changes to existing frontiers at the time of independence (*uti possidetis juris*) except where the states concerned agree otherwise'.[73]

In this regard, the Commission did not deviate from the general international legal attitude towards this issue, as we have seen in relation to a number of cases and international instruments, especially in the context of decolonisation. At the European level, the International Commission of Jurists in the *Aaland Island* case declared the right to self-determination, in the conservative sense, legally inapplicable when it challenges state sovereignty and international peace and stability.[74] Similarly, although the Helsinki Final Act (1975) of the Organization for Security and Co-operation in Europe (OSCE) recognised that the right to self-determination goes beyond the colonial context, it nonetheless reiterated the primacy in international law of the norms of territorial integrity and preservation of existing boundaries.[75] Thus, the Badinter Commission endorsed the *uti possidetis* principle as the governing principle of international law in the process of decolonisation and went even further by reinforcing the application of this principle in delimiting international boundaries beyond the colonial context.

In other words, despite the questionable universality of *uti possidetis*, the principle continued to dominate the international legal imagination regarding the making of postcolonial boundaries. The proposition that the continuation of colonial boundaries would prevent territorial conflicts between and among postcolonial states invariably informed all

---

[73] Arbitration Commission Opinion No. 2 (1991), *European Journal of International Law* 3 (1992), 184.

[74] See *Aaland Islands* case, Report of the International Commission of Jurists (1920); cf. *Aaland Islands* case, Report of the Commission of Rapporteurs (1921). However, the commission held that the right to self-determination can be applied when statehood itself was in question.

[75] Cf. Principles IV and VI and Principle VIII of the Helsinki Final Act (1975).

postcolonial and non-colonial boundary settlements for new states. Even those who were sceptical of the universality of the *uti possidetis* principle recognised the pragmatic relevance of the principle. Thus, while Ahmed refuses to accept the application of the Latin American *uti possidetis* principle in the context of African decolonisation as a general principle of international law, he nonetheless does not reject the continuity of colonial boundaries – understood as a unique and novel creation of an African customary international law – due to the pragmatic need to avoid 'chaos' emanating from decolonisation.[76]

This consensus on the pragmatic need for the continuation of the colonial boundaries, along with the normative pull of the doctrine in general, is problematic. This is because far from being a corrective to potential 'chaos', the continuation of arbitrarily drawn colonial boundaries undercuts the possibility of external self-determination for numerous ethnic minorities in postcolonial states. On the other hand, having been premised upon the assumed capacity of the postcolonial 'national' state to efface ethno-nationalism, the application of *uti possidetis* simultaneously allows the postcolonial state to produce its own nationalist ideology in majoritarian terms. Violent ethnic conflicts are often the results. As we shall see in the following case studies, the boundaries of present-day Myanmar and Bangladesh are products of British colonial policies. The continuation of these boundaries in complete defiance of historical realities and the accompanying nation-building projects defined by the colonial territorial limits are at the very heart of the ethnic minority problem in these states. I will demonstrate that the principle of the continuation of colonial borders for postcolonial statehood has deprived the Rohingya and the CHT hill people of their legitimate 'right' to self-determination at the moment of decolonisation and has culminated in present crises in both cases.

3.3 The Case of the Rohingya in Myanmar

Rakhine State, which was known as Arakan during British rule, is one of the poorest states in Myanmar and is fraught with ethnic conflicts between the Buddhist Rakhine and the minority Rohingya communities. It is estimated that approximately 36 per cent of the population in Rakhine are Rohingya Muslims, while 60 per cent are Buddhist

---

[76] For a contrary argument, see Mutua, 'Why Redraw the Map of Africa', 1113–1176. The conclusion of the book closely engages with Mutua's argument.

Rakhines.[77] Most Rohingyas are Muslims; a minority follow Hinduism. Although Rakhine State as a whole faces discriminatory treatment from Myanmar, the Rohingyas in northern Rakhine experience double the discrimination, as they have been historically subjected to oppression by Rakhine Buddhists as well. More than one million Rohingyas are currently refugees in neighbouring Bangladesh, following successive military crackdowns. The worst crackdown, being genocidal in nature, was the one which took place in August 2017. The following discussion reveals how the political boundaries of Arakan evolved over centuries and how the continuation of the colonial boundaries in postcolonial Burma aggravated the plight of the Rohingya.

3.3.1 The Independent Kingdom of Arakan

Arakan, in western Myanmar on the Bay of Bengal and separated from the rest of the country by a chain of mountains, maintained a distinct political identity for most of its history. In the official British narrative of the first Anglo-Burma War of 1824–1826, the century-old fort in Arakan and its defence arrangements receive an admiring mention.[78] Independent Arakan kingdoms can be traced back to antiquity; the last of them was established in 1430, with its capital in Mrauk U.[79] Situated on the border between Buddhist and Muslim Asia, the kingdom had strong economic, trade, and other relations with the Sultanate of Bengal.[80] The relationship between the Arakan kingdom and the Bengal Sultanate deepened when the Arakanese King Min Saw-Mun (also known as 'Narameikha') was temporarily deposed by the Burmese and forced to take refuge in Bengal under the protection of Sultan Ghiasuddin Azam Shah.[81] During his twenty years of exile in Bengal, the Arakanese king was so influenced by the coexistence of Persian, Arabic, and Bengali cultures and traditions in Bengal that when he returned to power in 1426 with the help of the Sultan's army, he took several thousand Muslim courtesans and

---

[77] Mohammed Ashraf Alam, *Marginalization of the Rohingya in Arakan State of Western Burma* (Chittagong: Kaladan Press, 2011), 2.

[78] Horace H. Wilson, *Narrative of the Burmese War, 1824–1826* (London: W. H. Allen and Co,. 1852), 155–156.

[79] The Advisory Commission on Rakhine State, *Towards a Peaceful, Fair and Prosperous Future for the People of Rakhine* (Final Report of the Advisory Commission; also known as the 'Annan Commission Report'), August 2017, 18.

[80] Ibid.

[81] Arthur P. Phayre, *History of Burma* (London: Trubner & Co., 1883), 76.

skilled persons from the Bengal Sultanate with him.[82] According to Arthur Phayre, the restored Arakanese king agreed to be a tributary to the Sultan of Bengal and even adopted an Arabic name and title for himself – Sulaiman Shah or Sawmun Shah – in fulfilment of the promise he made to the Sultan.[83] The practice of taking an Arabic name continued for nearly 200 years.[84] However, the influence of the Bengal Sultanate did not last for long. As Phayre notes, Sawmun Shah's successor, his brother Meng Khari (known as Ali Khan), did not submit to the authority of the Sultan. Instead, taking full advantage of the weakness of the Sultanate, he took possession of territories in Bengal (e.g. Ramu in present-day Cox's Bazar). Later, in 1459, Meng Khari's son Basoahpyu annexed the port city of Chittagong and kept it under Arakanese control until the Mughals took it back.[85]

In his epic *Padmabati* (1652), Alaol described Mrauk U as a truly cosmopolitan city where people of all faiths and races from all places had gathered.[86] Buddhism reached Arakan earlier than the interior parts of Burma. Noting that Arakanese Buddhism served as an inspiration for Buddhism in the rest of Burma, the Swiss Pali scholar and archaeologist Emanuel Forchhammer called Arakan the 'Palestine of the Farther East' in an 1891 publication.[87] Islam was introduced in Arakan at the beginning of the ninth century as Arab merchants arrived and traded in local Arakanese markets. P. B. Smart's *Burma Gazetteer* records that in the early ninth century '[s]everal ships were wrecked on Ramree Island and the crews said to have been Mohammedans were sent to Arakan proper and settled in villages'.[88] It

---

[82] Mofidul Hoque (ed.), *The Rohingya Genocide: Compilation and Analysis of Survivors' Testimonies* (Dhaka: Center for the Study of Genocide and Justice, 2018), 62.
[83] Phayre, *History of Burma*, 78.
[84] Hoque (ed.), *The Rohingya Genocide*, 62. This was also a common practice in the Chakma tribe of the hill tracts of Chittagong under the control of the British East India Company. For example, the eighteenth-century Chakma chief was named Sher Daulat Khan, his son Jan Baksh Khan, and his Deputy Rono Khan. See Mohammad Shahabuddin, 'The Myth of Colonial Protection of Indigenous Peoples: The Case of the Chittagong Hill Tracts under British Rule', *International Journal on Minority and Group Rights* 25, no. 2 (2018), 231.
[85] Phayre, *History of Burma*, 78.
[86] Alaol specifically mentions people from Arabia, Egypt, Syria, Turkey, Abyssinia (Ethiopia), Rome, Khurasan (greater Persia), Uzbekistan, Lahore, Multan, Sindh, Kashmir, Deccan, Hindustan (North India), Bengal, Karnal, Malaya, Kochi, Achi, and Karnataka. See Hoque (ed.), *The Rohingya Genocide*, 64.
[87] Emanuel Forchhammer, *Report on the Antiquities of Arakan* (Rangoon: Government Printing and Stationary, 1891), 3.
[88] R. B. Smart, *Burma Gazetteer* (Rangoon: Government Printing and Stationary, 1917), 19.

should be noted here that settlements of foreign merchants were one of the characteristic features of inter-Asian trade since time immemorial.[89] The Arab merchants gradually connected Arakan to the trade routes with the Middle East and the Far East, thereby paving the way for long-lasting Arab and Islamic influence in Arakan.[90] As Michael Charney notes, these few merchants did not form a well-organised community.[91] However, he argues that large-scale Muslim settlement took place in the sixteenth and seventeenth centuries when the Arakanese and Portuguese communities started to raid southern Bengal and transferred thousands of Bangalees to Arakan as slaves. The Portuguese took approximately 147,000 captives between 1617 and 1666.[92]

François Bernier's *Travels in the Mogul Empire, 1656–1668* indicates that for many years the kingdom of Arakan was the home of several Portuguese settlers, a great number of Christian slaves, and half-caste Portuguese or other Europeans from various parts of the world.[93] Many of them were involved in piracy. The King of Arakan, who lived in perpetual dread of the Mughals, kept these foreigners as advance guards for the protection of his frontier, even permitting them to occupy the Chittagong seaport (in the south-eastern part of Bengal) within the Mughal territory.[94] These pirates also invaded neighbouring seas, entered numerous arms and canals of the Ganges, and ravaged the islands of Lower Bengal.[95] Thus, when the Mughal Emperor Aurungzeb's uncle, Shaista Khan, was sent to Bengal as the General of the Army – and, later, when he was elevated to the rank of the Governor of Bengal – his natural priority was to free Bengal from the cruel and incessant destruction wrought by these pirates. In 1666, Shaista Khan finally managed to free the port city of Chittagong from the control of the pirates with both threats of force and the offer of a better life in Dhaka.[96] However, the defeat of the regime in

---

[89] See Charles H. Alexandrowicz, *The Law of Nations in Global History*, eds. David Armitage and Jennifer Pitts (Oxford: Oxford University Press, 2017), 164.
[90] Hoque (ed.), *The Rohingya Genocide*, 61.
[91] Michael W. Charney, *Where Jambudipa and Islamdom Converged: Religious Change and the Emergence of Buddhist Communalism in Early Modern Arakan (Fifteenth to Nineteenth Centuries)*, PhD dissertation, University of Michigan, 1999, 147.
[92] Ibid., 164–165.
[93] François Bernier, *Travels in the Mogul Empire, 1656–1668* (*Histoire de la dernière révolution des états du Grand Mogol*, 1671), trans. Irving Brock, rev. ed. Archibald Constable (Westminster: Archibald Constable and Company, 1891).
[94] Ibid.
[95] Ibid.
[96] Ibid. See also Philip Gain (ed.), *The Chittagong Hill Tracts: Life and Nature at Risk* (Dhaka: Society for Environment and Human Development, 2000), 107.

Bengal against the British in the Battle of Plassey (1757) paved the way for the British East India Company's rule, first in Bengal and gradually in the rest of India. Meanwhile, the last independent kingdom of Arakan, after thriving for more than 350 years as a prosperous trading hub, came under Burmese control in 1785, as we shall see later.

3.3.2 Burmese Invasion

By the late eighteenth century, the Burmese had developed a sense of proto-nationalism with a common language, a common religion, and a common set of legal and political ideas and institutions; even a shared written history existed throughout the core area of the Ava Kingdom (from Upper Burma to Mandalay).[97] Consolidated and unified, the Ava Kingdom enjoyed unprecedented power internally and externally, and by the turn of the nineteenth century, the court of Ava could claim a series of spectacular successes on the battlefield.[98] It was as part of the expansionist campaign towards the western front that the annexation of Arakan took place.[99] This annexation was indeed a massive operation, conducted under the command of the Crown Prince, with three land forces of 13,706 armed men, 1,103 horsemen, 5,804 gunners, 300 cannons, 8,412 visses[100] of gun powder, and 41,686 cannonballs, as well as a naval force of 1,848 gunners, 4,396 armed men, 165 boats carrying cannons, 633 cannons, 41,400 cannon balls, 769,500 gun shots, and 16,185 flints.[101] Political prisoners and criminals were also sent along with the regular forces.[102] On 20 January 1785, the Arakanese capital city was taken and its king and many of his followers were captured. As soon as the victory was reported to the Burmese King, he ordered a great celebration on 26 January 1785 to mark this triumph over Arakan.[103]

The war against Arakan was officially conceived as a religious war – a mission to re-Buddhicise Arakan.[104] Since the significance of Buddhism

---

[97] Thant Myint-U, *The Making of Modern Burma* (Cambridge: Cambridge University Press, 2001), 88.
[98] Ibid., 94.
[99] Ibid.
[100] A viss is a Burmese unit of measure for weight, equivalent to approximately 1.6 kg.
[101] For details, see Than Tun (ed.), *The Royal Orders of Burma, AD 1598–1885*, part IV (1782–1787) (Kyoto: Kyoto University Centre for Southeast Asian Studies, 1988), 75–83.
[102] See Royal Orders of 28 September 1784 and 2 October 1784.
[103] See Royal Orders of 26 January 1785 in ibid., 54.
[104] See generally Than Tun, 'Paya Lanma – Lord's Highway, over the Yoma – Yakhine Range', *Journal of Asian and African Studies* 25 (1983), 233–241.

was waning in Arakan, the now-powerful Buddhist Kingdom of Ava took on the responsibility of re-establishing Buddhism in the region. Like many imperial powers throughout history who have brought historic artefacts to their centres of power as a physical demonstration of authority and as an illustration of the official narrative of a glorious past and its revival under their leadership, the Burmese King moved Mahamuni (the iconic Great Image of Buddha) from Kyauktaw in North Arakan to Amarapura, the capital of Ava (presently in Mandalay).[105] A Royal Order of Burma dated 16 October 1784 makes the point clear: '[The] Crown Prince shall march as Commander-in-Chief of Arakan Campaign to restore proper conditions in Arakan for the prosperity of the Buddha's Religion.'[106] Although instructions on the conduct of Burmese forces in this campaign prohibited the forcible taking of any young women or taking anything from the local people without payment, the Crown Prince was explicitly instructed to 'clear the place of all bad characters' so that Buddhism might prosper again in Arakan.[107] A series of Buddhist missions were also sent to Arakan following the annexation with the task of re-Buddhicising the area, and local authorities were repeatedly ordered to extend full support to these missions so that they could build Ordination Halls wherever they chose.[108] Various other political changes were also imposed. A Royal Order of 14 October 1787 clarified that since Arakan was now part of the Burmese kingdom, the people of Arakan must not continue using their former seals and coins.[109]

Unsurprisingly, following the Burmese invasion, large numbers of the native population 'fled from the cruelty and oppression of their conquerors, and either found an asylum in the British territory of Chittagong, or secreted themselves amongst the hills and thickets, and alluvial islands along its southern and eastern boundaries'.[110] The Arakanese in Chittagong occasionally launched attacks on the Burmese invaders in Arakan, thereby triggering tension between the Burmese

---

[105] Tun (ed.), *The Royal Orders of Burma, AD 1598–1885*, part IV (1782–1787), xvii. The raft that brought Mahamuni arrived at the Amarapura jetty on 27 April 1785.
[106] Ibid., 75, 83.
[107] Ibid., 83, 84.
[108] See Royal Orders of 25 July 1787 in ibid., 152 and Royal Orders of 3 October 1787 in ibid., 180.
[109] Ibid., 182.
[110] Wilson, *Narrative of the Burmese War*, 3–4; see also A. K. M. Ahsan Ullah, 'Rohingya Refugees to Bangladesh: Historical Exclusions and Contemporary Marginalisation', *Journal of Immigrant & Refugee Studies* 9 (2011), 143.

kingdom and its new neighbour – the British.[111] At the same time, as Thant Myint-U notes, this conquest brought a significant number of ritualists, astronomers, and other learned men from Arakan into the Ava court. The Arakanese had close contact with centres of knowledge in India and the wider Islamic world and introduced important religious and secular texts on science, medicine, and astrology to the Burmese.[112]

With this military, cultural, and intellectual rejuvenation, the Burmese kingdom engaged more assertively, though still cautiously, with the British. Captain T. H. Lewin, the Deputy Commissioner of the Chittagong Hill Tracts under the Government of Bengal from 1866 to 1869 and from 1871 to 1874, recorded two letters dated around 24 June 1787 sent by the King of Burma and the Rajah of Arakan to the British administration in Chittagong (among the earliest written communication between them). The first letter, from the Rajah of Arakan (now a vassal of the Burmese King), stated:

> [Some inhabitants of Arakan] have absconded and taken refuge near the mountains within your border, and exercise depredations on the people belonging to both countries. [...] It is not proper that you should give asylum to them or the other Mughs who have absconded from Arracan, and you will do right to drive them from your country, that our friendship may remain perfect, and that the road of travellers and merchants may be secured. If you do not drive them from your country and give them up, I shall be under the necessity of seeking them out with an army, in whatever part of your territories they may be.[113]

To substantiate his threat to invade, the Rajah mentioned in the same letter that he had taken similar actions previously when the British refused to hand over another Arakanese fugitive, named Keoty.[114] The second letter came from the King of Burma himself:

> As the country of Arracan lies contiguous to Chittagong, if a treaty of commerce were established between me and the English, perfect unity and alliance would ensure from such engagements. I therefore have submitted it to you that the merchants of your country should resort hither for the purpose of purchasing pearls, ivory, wax, and that in return my people

---

[111] Wilson, *Narrative of the Burmese War*, 3–4.
[112] Myint-U, *The Making of Modern Burma*, 96.
[113] See T. H. Lewin, *The Hill Tracts of Chittagong and Dwellers Therein with Comparative Vocabularies of the Hill Dialect* (Calcutta: Bengal Printing Company Ltd., 1869), 29.
[114] Ibid. This Burmese claim can be corroborated by the official British narrative of the first Anglo-Burma War. See Wilson, *Narrative of the Burmese War*, 8.

should be permitted to resort to Chittagong for the purpose of trafficking in such commodities as the country may afford; but as the Mughs [from Arakan] residing at Chittagong have deviated from the principles of religion and morality, they ought to be corrected for their errors and irregularities [...]. I have accordingly sent four elephants' teeth under the charge of 30 persons, who will return with your answer to the above proposals and offers of alliance.[115]

These threats were real – almost immediately after this correspondence a force of armed Burmese entered Chittagong from Arakan. This incursion was reported to the Governor General Lord Cornwallis in the same month, June 1787, by the Chief of Chittagong.[116] Again in 1795, a Burmese Army of 5,000 men invaded Chittagong to pursue some rebellious Chiefs from Arakan.[117] Tension was building up between the Burmese and the British authorities around the emigration of certain Arakanese Chiefs and the ensuing Burmese raids into the British territories. At the macro level, there was a general sense of fear within the Burmese power-circles about the East India Company's incessant expansion in India. During the first two decades of the nineteenth century, the Burmese sent a number of missions to the Mughal court and established contacts with Nepal, the Punjab, and the Marathas, allegedly to suggest forming an anti-British alliance, although no such alliance was eventually formed.[118] The principal aim of the Burmese was to annex the area to the north of Arakan. A Burmese Royal Order of 16 September 1817 revealed their claim to a large area under British control: 'It is not correct [for the East India Company] to take Chittagong, Panwa (Cossimbazar), Dacca and Murshidabad, as English; they are Arakanese and as Burmese has now taken Arakan, these places become Burmese; the English has no right to collect taxes there.'[119] A similar claim had been made in a Royal Order of 18 February 1817, stating that the Company should send back all Arakanese fugitives in Chittagong.[120] A combination of frontier troubles and increasingly belligerent designs by the Burmese on adjacent British territory led to the first Anglo-Burma War of 1824–1826.

[115] See Lewin, *The Hill Tracts of Chittagong and Dwellers Therein*, 30–32.
[116] Ibid., 32.
[117] Charles Macfarlane, *A History of British India, from the Earliest English Intercourse to the Present Time* (London: George Routledge & Co., 1853), 355.
[118] Myint-U, *The Making of Modern Burma*, 99.
[119] Tun (ed.), *The Royal Orders of Burma, AD 1598–1885*, part VII (1811–1819), 136.
[120] Ibid., 103.

3.3.3 British Rule and the Colonial Boundaries of Arakan

The Anglo-Burma War was so significant in opening many new and interesting regions to European access that the Government of Bengal published a series of official documents about the war. The Oxford Professor of Sanskrit, Horace H. Wilson, was entrusted with the task of collecting, editing, and publishing these documents.[121] The British defeated the Burmese and the two sides met on 3 October 1825 to determine the terms of peace.[122] As principal conditions of peace, the British demanded the cession of the four provinces of Arakan, and the payment of two crores[123] of rupees as an indemnification for the expenses of the war. One crore was to be paid immediately, and the Tennasserim provinces (the present-day Tanintharyi Region of Myanmar, bordering Thailand) were to be retained until the payment of the second. 'The court of Ava was also expected to receive a British resident at the capital, and consent to a commercial treaty, upon principles of liberal intercourse and mutual advantage.'[124] The court of Ava's refusal of these demands led to another round of war and another round of defeat for the Burmese.[125] The court of Ava finally submitted to British demands and concluded a treaty on 24 February 1826 allowing the British to annex Arakan and Tennasserim and subsequently incorporate them into British India.[126] As soon as the British got hold of Arakan, Captain John Crawford of the Bombay Marine was ordered to survey the coast of Arakan to ascertain whether there were any easily accessible harbours into which ships in distress might flee in the monsoon.[127]

This was a significant moment in the political future of Burma, for the first-ever precise boundaries of Arakan were drawn up by the British in

---

[121] See Wilson, *Narrative of the Burmese War*, vii-viii.
[122] The British were represented by Major General Sir A. Campbell, Commodore Sir J. Brisbane, Brigadier General Cotton, Captain Alexander, Brigadier McCreagh, Lieutenant Colonel Tidy, and Captain Snodgrass. The chiefs representing the government of Ava were Sada Mengyee Maha Mengom-KyeeWoongyee, Munnoo Rutha Keogong Lamain Woon, Mengyee Maha Menla Rajah Atwenwoon, Maha Sri Senkuyah Woondok, Mengyee Maha Menla Sear Sey Shuagon Mooagoonoon, and Mengyee Attala Maha Sri Soo Asseewoon. See ibid., 204–205.
[123] One crore equals ten million.
[124] Wilson, *Narrative of the Burmese War*, 205.
[125] Ibid., 210–257.
[126] Ibid., 257. See also Myint-U, *The Making of Modern Burma*, 100.
[127] Crawford, however, could not immediately discharge his duty due to logistical limitations. See India Office Records and Private Papers, 'Extract military letter from Bengal dated 31 December 1827', IOR/F/4/1050/28956.

the aftermath of this war. There had been previous attempts at demarcating Arakan's boundaries. The Mughal invasion of 1666 pushed the Arakanese back to the east bank of the Naaf River, demarcating the spheres of respective influence, although the border would be constantly contested. Following the annexation of Arakan by Burma in 1785, the Burmese attempted to demarcate boundaries between Mrauk U and Thandwe on the Arakan side and Salin outside the Arakan Mountain Range in the east. As the Royal Order of 14 October 1787 reveals, the key motivation for this was to revive the land route from Mrauk U to Ba Ai across the Arakan Range. Mrauk U officers were given the responsibility of keeping this road open and well-maintained down to Dalet, and Thandwe (Sandoway) officers had the same responsibilities from Dalet to Ba Ai.[128] Hence, some sort of internal boundary demarcation was necessary. Two more Royal Orders issued on 26 November 1787 and 14 December 1787 indicate further attempts at a more detailed demarcation of boundaries between Mrauk U, Thandwe, and Salin based on pre-war Arakanese records of 1783.[129] Various local headmen lodged complaints against the proposed demarcation, which led to a Royal Order for further investigation into the matter.[130] The Burmese attempts at boundary demarcation were inward looking and different in nature from what the British would achieve. The boundaries drawn by the British following the war of 1825 demarcated the lines between Arakan, the Burmese Kingdom and the Tennasserim, as well as Arakan's administrative boundary with Bengal.[131] In other words, the precise territorial demarcation of Arakan and its external boundaries with both the kingdom of Burma and colonial India were essentially created by the British.

Burmese defeats in two more Anglo-Burma Wars, in 1852 and 1885, resulted in British control over all of Burma. In 1886, Burma formally became a province of British India. Although there was a Rohingya community in Arakan before the Burmese invasion of 1785, its size increased rapidly during colonial times as a result of the British policy of expanding rice cultivation in Arakan.[132] Rice cultivation required intensive labour, and the need for a trained agricultural workforce was

---

[128] Tun (ed.), *The Royal Orders of Burma, AD 1598–1885*, part IV (1782–1787), 182.
[129] See ibid., 196, 203.
[130] Ibid., 203.
[131] Myint-U, *The Making of Modern Burma*, 220.
[132] *Final Report of the Advisory Commission*, 18. This was in line with the general British colonial policy of encouraging settlement cultivation as opposed to the traditional slash and burn cultivation in all hill regions of South Asia. This policy was necessary for the colonial administration to ensure a stable generation of revenue. See Shahabuddin, 'The Myth of Colonial Protection of Hill Peoples', 210–235.

primarily met by Muslim workers from Bengal. While many of these workers came on a seasonal basis, some settled down permanently, thereby altering the demographic composition of the area. As various censuses of British Burma reveal, the size of the Rohingya community in Arakan doubled from the 1880s to the 1930s, from about 13 to 25 per cent of the Arakan population.[133] Around that time, many Rohingyas who had left Arakan following the Burmese conquest of 1785 returned under British protection.[134] The same pattern could be seen during WWII: when the Japanese occupied Burma in 1942 and expelled the British from Arakan, a sizeable proportion of the Rohingya fled Arakan and took refuge in Bengal.[135] In this sense, the political fate of the Rohingya since the first Burmese conquest of 1785 has been linked to the rise and fall of British colonial power.

It is, therefore, no surprise that during the colonial policy discourse of the 1930s on separating Burma from Indian colonial administration and making it a Crown colony, the issue of immigration appeared to be the Burmese nationalist leaders' main concern.[136] In the British Parliamentary Round Table Conference of 1931–1932, the statement of delegates representing the majority interests of Burma highlighted immigration as the root cause of the suffering of the majority.[137] The statement concluded that the 'diseased condition' of Burmese society created by uncontrolled

---

[133] *Report on the Census of British Burma*, Part I: The Enumeration and Compilation of Results, 1881; *Report on the Census of India 1931*, vol. XI: Burma, Part I, 1933.

[134] Ullah, 'Rohingya Refugees to Bangladesh', 143.

[135] E. Pittaway, 'The Rohingya Refugees in Bangladesh: A Failure of the International Protection Regime', in *Protracted Displacement in Asia: No Place to Call Home*, ed. H. Adelman (Surrey: Ashgate, 2008), 83–106.

[136] The British decision was primarily driven by student uprisings for national autonomy triggered by the world depression of the 1930s and the ensuing economic hardship in the country. The decision was also motivated by the need to protect the jewel in the crown of the British Empire – India. Burma was seen as a handy buffer zone in the face of increasing French presence and influence in Southeast Asia. The separation of Burma from India was officially recommended by the authors of the Montagu-Chelmsford Report, by the Statutory Commission, and by the Government of India. The Burma sub-Committee of the Indian Round Table Conference, 1930, endorsed the principle of separation. See House of Commons Parliamentary Papers, *Proceedings of the Burma Round Table Conference*, 27 November 1931 to 12 January 1932 (London: His Majesty's Stationery Office, 1932), 250.

[137] Statement read by U Ba Pe, and signed by U Chit Hlaing, U Ba Pe, U Maung Gyee, U Ohn Ghine, U Tun Aung Gyaw, U Ba Si, Dr. Thein Maung, Miss May Oung, U Tharrawaddy Maung Maung, Tharrawaddy U Pu, and U Ni. See *Proceedings of the Burma Round Table Conference*, 263.

immigration could be cured only by severing ties with the Indian administration and offering the Burmese the right to self-government.[138]

It soon became clear during the Round Table that the delegates representing minority interests were not keen on separating from India.[139] The delegate for the Indian community in Burma demanded

> adequate and effective representation in the Legislative Council and the executive appointments; that it shall have adequate representation in the public services of the country, and that the constitution of Burma shall be such as to prevent any majority community from abusing their legislative power with a view to enacting laws which would create discrimination between one citizen and another.[140]

To justify this position, the spokesperson for the delegation offered a detailed account of the extent to which the Indian community is in charge of many important aspects of Burmese economic life. Ironically, this also served as a substantiation of the frustrations that the majority delegation expressed during the conference.

The British finally separated Burma from British India in 1937 under the Government of Burma Act (1935), making it a Crown colony of Britain, and granted the colony a new constitution calling for a fully elected assembly. With this split between British India and British Burma, the border between the two took on a semi-international status for the first time.[141] The Act, however, maintained the separate status of the frontier areas that included the Arakan Hill Tracts.[142] This 'separate status' was meant to continue until the inhabitants of these areas expressed their desire for some kind of amalgamation into Burma proper.[143]

3.3.4 The Making of Postcolonial Burma

In the aftermath of WWII and following fierce nationalist resistance to British rule, Burma achieved independence in January 1948 under the

---

[138] Ibid., 264.
[139] See generally ibid., 252–257.
[140] Statement read by N. M. Cowasjee. See ibid., 279.
[141] Ullah, 'Rohingya Refugees to Bangladesh', 141.
[142] Government of Burma Act, 1935 (London: King's Printer of Acts of Parliament, 2002), 62.
[143] Clive Christie, *A Modern History of Southeast Asia: Decolonisation, Nationalism, and Separatism* (London: I. B. Tauris, 1998), 66. See also Harrison Akins, 'The Two Faces of Democratisation in Myanmar: A Case Study of the Rohingya and Burmese nationalism', *Journal of Muslim Minority Affairs* 38, no. 2 (2018), 229–245.

Independence Act (1947), a British legislation, 'as a country not within His Majesty's dominions and not entitled to His Majesty's protection'.[144] However, the boundaries of this newly independent nation, crafted by His Majesty's colonial administration, remained as they were. The semi-international boundaries became the fully international borders of Burma. The administrative boundary between Arakan and Bengal, as well as Tennasserim's boundary with Siam (Thailand), became international frontiers of postcolonial Burma. As Myint-U asserts, over the first couple of decades of colonial rule in Upper Burma following the third Anglo-Burma War of 1885,

> the remainder of the new country's frontiers were carefully negotiated and surveyed: in deciding what was Assam, Burma, Tibet and China, the diplomats and cartographers of Fort Williams [in Calcutta] set the Indian–Burmese–Chinese borders of today. Modern Burma thus included the entire heartland of the old kingdom [...] or the land of the "Myanma". But the map also included some, though not all, of her erstwhile tributaries and frontier regions, as well as places never even claimed let alone ruled by the Court of Ava.[145]

Although the Arakan kingdom had remained independent for hundreds of years before the British occupation of Arakan in 1825 and was under Burmese rule for a mere 40 years, the right to self-determination or any other alternative political future for the people of Arakan in general and the Arakanese Muslims (the Rohingya) in particular was never given a serious thought during the decolonisation process. On the eve of Burma's independence, separatist movements demanding at least an autonomous status for Arakan as a whole became stronger and stronger throughout 1947. A mass meeting held on 15 June 1947 in Rangoon specifically highlighted the historical existence of Arakan as an independent kingdom for nearly 4,000 years and its geographical separation by mountains from Burma proper, and concluded that it should be granted the absolute right to determine its own destiny as an Autonomous State.[146] When one of the key figures behind the movement advocating for the Arakan kingdom's independence, a Buddhist monk called U Seinda, was arrested, violence broke out throughout Arakan; the Government of Burma ordered a combined military and police

---

[144] Refer to the full title of the Act. See also Article 1.
[145] Myint-U, *The Making of Modern Burma*, 220.
[146] India Office Records and Private Papers, 'Letter from U Hla Tun Pru, Chairman, All Arakan Representative Working Committee to the Secretary of State for Burma, dated 21 June 1947', IOR/M/4/2503, 18–19.

operation to quell it. However, the Government consistently branded such separatist movements as communist anarchy, robbery, mass looting, or simply lawlessness.[147]

In the British official circle at the Burma Office, there was an awareness of the ongoing separatist movement and the Government of Burma's efforts to obscure it. A Burma Office Minute Paper from 8 July 1947 reveals this fact.[148] The said Paper also indicates a recognition of the relevance and historical basis of the Arakanese demand for self-determination. Nevertheless, the British took the side of the ruling Burmese elites in the Government and discredited the separatist movement as a creation of the main Burmese opposition party for their own vested interest.[149] Burma, crafted by the British colonial administration to include Arakan within its territory, was seen as the only natural makeup of the nascent postcolonial state. Importantly, in his note on the Minute Paper (dated 9 July 1947), the Under-Secretary for Burma Arthur Henderson specifically mentioned that 'the separatist movement in Arakan as a whole must be distinguished from that among the Moslems of North Arakan', but he never deviated from the perception that Arakanese separatism was a menace arising from political opposition in Burma.[150]

The incorporation of Arakan into the independent Burma was unfortunately seen as the default position. As in the case of many other ethnic minorities within new postcolonial states in Africa and Asia, the political future of the Rohingya was thus permanently subordinated to the state of Burma, the latter being the legitimate subject of international law and legally protected against challenges to its territorial integrity.[151] The source of legitimacy of the postcolonial boundaries of present-day Myanmar – unjust outcome of colonial imagination and convenience though they are – is international law. This is a stark reminder of how international law

---

[147] See Government of Burma Press Communique published in *The Times of Burma*, dated 20 November 1947. India Office Records and Private Papers, 'Law and Order: Arakan (12 April–1 December 1947), IOR/M/4/2503.

[148] India Office Records and Private Papers, 'Burma Office Minute Paper (B/C 1235/47)', IOR/M/4/2503, 10–11.

[149] Ibid.

[150] Ibid., 12.

[151] See Article 2 of the UN Charter; *Declaration on Friendly Relations* (1970). Principles of unilateral humanitarian intervention, the responsibility to protect, and remedial self-determination are sometimes argued as 'legitimate' (as opposed to legal) exceptions to the general rule of non-intervention and territorial integrity.

perpetuates colonial legacies, further disempowering already vulnerable groups – such as the Rohingya – and leading to serious humanitarian catastrophes.

However, political resistance to the incorporation of Arakan into Burma followed shortly after. Not long after Myanmar's independence in 1948, a rebellion erupted in Arakan, led by Rohingya Muslims demanding equal rights and an autonomous Muslim area in the north of the state.[152] At the time of Burma's independence, the Rohingya, fearing persecution in the Buddhist state, not only formed their own army but also approached Muhammad Ali Jinnah, the key architect of the Islamic Republic of Pakistan, 'asking him to incorporate Northern Arakan into East Pakistan [present-day Bangladesh]'.[153] Jinnah had little interest in opening a new front of border disputes and thus assured his Burmese counterpart Aung San that he supported integration of the Rohingya into an independent Burma.[154] These events were in turn used by the Burmese ruling elites as excuses for questioning the Rohingyas' political allegiance to Myanmar.

In post-independence Myanmar, the Rohingya have always been referred to as 'Bangalee foreigners' and therefore denied citizenship.[155] It is ironic that Myanmar claimed territorial sovereignty over Arakan without actually accepting a group of people who had been living there long before the state was created in its present form. The Rohingya currently make up the largest community of stateless persons in the world.[156] Myanmar even has an official policy of not using the term 'Rohingya', which might potentially endorse the indigenous origin of the community. During a meeting with the US Ambassador Scot Marciel in October 2017, the Myanmar army chief Senior General Min Aung Hlaing referred to the Rohingya as 'Bangalees' and commented that British colonialists were responsible for the problem.[157] Since independence, various forms of government oppression and the systematic marginalisation of the

---

[152] *Final Report of the Advisory Commission*, 18.
[153] Martin Smith, *Burma: Insurgency and the Politics of Ethnicity* (London: Zed Books, 1991), 41.
[154] Moshe Yegar, *The Muslims of Burma: A Study of a Minority Group* (Wiesbaden: Otto Harrassowitz, 1972), 35.
[155] For a detailed discussion of Myanmar's citizenship laws affecting the Rohingya, see Chapter 4, 177–182.
[156] Rohingya leaders, however, contest the connotation of their statelessness, for Myanmar is their state and they see themselves as the rightful citizens of that country.
[157] Robert Birsel and Thu Thu Aung, 'Myanmar army chief says Rohingya Muslims "not natives", numbers fleeing exaggerated', *Reuters*, 12 October 2017.

Rohingya have met with organised and armed resistance by a fraction of the Rohingya – though the degree and nature of such resistance has varied. The 2017 crackdown in Arakan by the Myanmar army, in collaboration with local Rakhine Buddhist civilians, was a brutal and disproportionate response to one such armed attack by the Arakan Rohingya Salvation Army (ARSA) against Myanmar's security forces.

In the midst of global condemnation of the political and military leadership of Myanmar, albeit in the absence of any concrete action against them, US Congressman Bradley Sherman, Chairman of the Sub-Committee on Asia and the Pacific, called upon the State Department to consider bringing northern Rakhine State under the sovereign jurisdiction of Bangladesh if Myanmar continues to refuse citizenship rights to the Rohingya. The proposal was made on 13 June 2019 during a hearing on the State Department's budget for South Asia.[158] In support of his proposal, Sherman argued that if Myanmar cannot take responsibility for its Rohingya population, then it is only logical to bring North Rakhine under Bangladesh, which took responsibility for the Rohingya refugees. He also referred to the US support for creating the new state of South Sudan, separated from Sudan, and asked why the United States would not do the same to protect the historically oppressed Rohingya community in Myanmar. Sherman raised the issue also in July 2018 by asking

> [H]ow many people does the Myanmar military have to kill before the United States would recognize that North Rakhine state should be independent or join with Bangladesh, rather than continue to be part of the territory of a country that has killed by the many, many thousands?[159]

In itself, this is a radical proposal, for it goes beyond the more conventional liberal prescriptions for Rohingya citizenship and equality and non-discrimination among all citizens, and proposes reorganisation of colonial boundaries. The State Department representative in the 2019 Hearing, acting Assistant Secretary for South and Central Asian Affairs, was quick to respond that the United States follows the traditional approach of respecting territorial integrity. Unsurprisingly, the proposal did not enjoy much support inside or outside the United States

---

[158] United States House of Representatives, Hearing before the Sub-committee on Asia and the Pacific of the Committee on Foreign Affairs, 13 June 2019, available at www.foreignaffairs.house.gov/2019/6/u-s-interests-in-south-asia-and-the-fy-2020-budget (video clip of the hearing; watch from 1:20:10 to 1:22:30).

[159] United States House of Representatives, 'Budget Priorities for South Asia: Hearing before the Sub-committee on Asia and the Pacific of the Committee on Foreign Affairs, 25 July 2018' (Washington, DC: US Government Publishing Office, 2018), 31.

and soon sank into insignificance. Myanmar described the proposal as disrespect for its territorial integrity and sovereignty and called it 'a baseless proposal based on a crazy idea'.[160] Bangladesh too slammed the idea straight away. In a press conference on 8 July 2019, the Bangladesh prime minister unequivocally asserted the importance of the principles of sovereignty and territorial integrity; she even called the proposal extremely wicked, flagitious, and morally wrong.[161] Bangladesh itself came into being following the break-up of Pakistan, but the following section on the CHT in Bangladesh might shed some light on the country's current firm stance on territorial integrity of states.

3.4 The Case of the CHT Hill People in Bangladesh

Historical evidence suggests that the hill people of the CHT were the earliest group to migrate to the CHT from the neighbouring regions of Tripura (in India) and Arakan.[162] In an 1869 publication, the then Deputy Commissioner of the CHT Captain Lewin notes that '[a] greater portion of the hill tribes, at present living in the Chittagong Hills, undoubtedly came about two generations ago from [Arakan]. This is asserted both by their own traditions and by records in the Chittagong Collectorate.'[163] He also refers to a letter of 31 May 1777 from the Chief of Chittagong to the Governor General Warren Hastings stating that some thousands of Arakanese hill men had entered the CHT.[164] Similarly, the Superintendent of the CHT Sneyd Hutchinson's *An Account of the Chittagong Hill Tracts* (1906) records that the CHT were originally inhabited by various Kuki tribes.[165] These tribes were driven to the north-east by the mass migration of the Chakmas from the south when the latter were ousted by the Arakanese Rakhines (known to Bangalees as Maghs or Marma) following the Burmese invasion of

---

[160] Dipanjan Roy Chaudhury, 'US Congressman moves proposal to bring Myanmar's Rakhine state under Bangladesh', *The Economic Times*, 1 Jul 2019, available at www.economictimes.indiatimes.com/news/international/world-news/us-congress man-moves-proposal-to-bring-myanmars-rakhine-state-under-bangladesh.
[161] See *The Prothom-Alo*, 9 July 2019, 1–2.
[162] Nasir Uddin, 'Paradigm of "Better Life": "Development" among the Khumi in the Chittagong Hill Tracts', *Asian Ethnicity* 15, no. 1 (2014), 63.
[163] Lewin, *The Hill Tracts of Chittagong and the Dwellers Therein*, 28.
[164] Ibid., 32.
[165] Bangalees referred to the Kukis as hill people; unlike the joomeahs living close to the border of the district of Chittagong they were unable to speak the vernacular of Bengal. See ibid., 28.

Arakan in 1785. The Chakmas finally settled in the central and northeastern portions of the CHT, 'while their former possessions were absorbed by the Maghs'.[166] Pierre Bessaignet estimates that during the Burmese invasion of Arakan in 1785, nearly two-thirds of the population in Arakan moved to the CHT.[167] Most Marmas in the CHT are descendants of the Buddhist Rakhines from Arakan. However, the Chakma historian Biraj Mohan Dewan in his seminal work, *The Chronicles of the Chakma Nation* (1969), offers a narrative of the Chakma migration to the CHT that corroborates Hutchinson's account but argues that such migration took place following the war between Chakma and Arakan kingdoms in 1418, long before the Burmese invasion of Arakan.[168] Arakanese sources also claim that Rakhine people migrated to the regions of Bengal, CHT, and Tripura in multiple waves beginning in the eighth century, surely long before the conquest of Arakan by the Burmese.[169]

Migration from Arakan to the CHT continued during the rule of the East India Company. A series of letters exchanged between the Commissioner of Chittagong, the Board of Revenue, and the Company Governor General between 14 February 1800 and 26 March 1801 records large-scale migration from Arakan to Chittagong. Initially these emigrants received help and encouragement from the local British administration, primarily from Colonel Cox, to settle in Chittagong, although the Revenue Board and the office of the Governor General wished them to return to Arakan.[170] However, with some persuasion from the local administration, the Company high command gradually changed their mind and approved settling a colony of these emigrants. They had two main reasons: news of brutal oppression by the Burmese of emigrants who had returned and, more importantly, the pragmatic usefulness of this large group of hardworking emigrants for clearing jungles and

---

[166] Sneyd Hutchinson, *An Account of the Chittagong Hill Tracts* (Calcutta: The Bengal Secretariat Book Depot, 1906), 24–25.
[167] Pierre Bessaignet, *Tribesmen of Chittagong Hill Tracts* (1958), trans. Sufia Khan, *Parbottya Chattogramer Upajati* (Dhaka: Bangla Academy, 1997), 7.
[168] Biraj Mohan Dewan, *The Chronicle of the Chakma Nation* (1969) (in Bangla, *Chakma Jatir Itibritto*) (Rangamati: Uday Shangkar Dewan, 2005), 91–95.
[169] Kyaw Mra Than, *The Extraction of Rakhine Divisional Establishment Gazetteers* (Dhaka: Type-script Manuscript, 1993), 3–4; Kyaw Minn Htin, 'The Marma from Bangladesh: A "De-Arakanized" Community in Chittagong Hill Tracts', *Suvannabhumi* 7, no. 2 (2015), 143–148.
[170] See letters of 20 March 1801 and 4 August 1802 in India Office Records and Private Papers, 'Papers regarding the colony of Arakan emigrants in Chittagong District', IOR/F/4/99/2029.

cultivation – and the revenue they would generate.[171] The political fate of the CHT hill people as a whole would dramatically transform with the drawing and re-drawing of colonial boundaries and subsequently of the boundaries of postcolonial states of Pakistan and Bangladesh.

3.4.1 The CHT under British Rule

As I noted in the preceding section, Chittagong was controlled by the Arakanese kings in the sixteenth and seventeenth centuries until it fell to the Mughals in 1666. Even after this period, the people in the CHT still considered themselves to be under the control of the Arakanese kings.[172] The Mughals showed little interest in the interior of the hill tracts of Chittagong, apart from collecting tax in the form of cotton produced in the region. Paying this tax gave the hill tribes access to local markets (*bazars*) under Mughal control. For this reason, the CHT came to be known during the Moghul period as *karpas mohol* – the cotton state. Following the Battle of Plassey of 1757 between the British East India Company and Siraz-ud-Daula, the semi-independent governor under the Mughals, the Company put in power Mir Qasim Ali Khan as a reward for his contributions to the British victory. He returned the favour by ceding the CHT to the Company in 1760.[173] Unlike the Mughals, the British began collecting taxes on joom cultivation,[174] although such taxes continued to be paid in cotton.[175] Bangalee middlemen, serving as agents of the Company (in the absence of a formal administrative structure), collected the cotton, usually exploiting the hill people by collecting more than they paid to the Company.[176]

The Company's incessant attempts to increase its revenue from the hills angered the hill peoples, who ultimately revolted against the Company in

---

[171] Ibid. However, in the face of increasing tension with the Burmese, as noted already, the British refrained from encouraging any further emigration from Arakan to maintain a 'relationship of peace and amity' with the Burmese.
[172] Htin, 'The Marma from Bangladesh', 147.
[173] Mizanur Rahman and Tanim H. Shawon (eds.), *Tying the Knot: Community Law Reform and Confidence Building in the CHT* (Dhaka: ELCOP, 2001), 7.
[174] This is the traditional mode of slash and burn cultivation in the hill; such cultivators were known as 'joomeahs'. The colonial administration found this mode of cultivation problematic, mainly because joomeahs had to move from place to place in search of fresh virgin land necessary for jooming and, therefore, it was difficult to keep trace of them for revenue collection.
[175] Amena Mohsin, *The Politics of Nationalism: The Case of the Chittagong Hill Tracts, Bangladesh* (1997) (Dhaka: University Press Ltd., 2002), 78.
[176] Ibid.

1776 and refused to pay at all.[177] The resistance led by the Chakma chief Sher Daulat Khan, his son Jan Baksh Khan, and Deputy Rono Khan offered the most powerful challenge to the colonial rule in the CHT. Having failed to crush the resistance militarily – largely due to the Chakma guerrilla tactics and the British side's unfamiliarity with the interior terrain of the hills – the British forced an economic embargo upon the hill people, stopping all supplies and not allowing them access to bazars.[178] The Chakma Raja Jan Bux Khan was ultimately compelled to sign a truce with the Company Governor General in 1787, in which the chief not only accepted British sovereignty but also agreed to maintain peace in the areas bordering the hill tracts.[179] With this treaty of 1787, the CHT entered a phase of direct colonisation.[180] The indigenous military capacity was systematically destroyed soon after, and the Company deployed its army in the area to ensure a steady and stable flow of revenue from the CHT.[181]

Around the same time, the colonial administration had to deal with frequent invasions by tribes beyond their immediate control. Hutchinson records a series of military expeditions.[182] These military actions eventually

---

[177] Sneyd Hutchinson, *Eastern Bengal and Assam District Gazetteers: Chittagong Hill Tracts* (Allahabad: Pioneer Press, 1909), 24. Reports of this resistance is found in the earliest record of the colonial administration's dealings with the CHT hill people – a letter dated 10 April 1777 from the Chief of Chittagong to the Governor General, Warren Hastings. See Lewin, *The Hill Tracts of Chittagong and the Dwellers Therein*, 21. A more vivid account of the event was presented by the local Company stakeholders in a petition of 26 June 1778 by Bangalee landlords of the plains and the Company's rent receivers. See S. Islam (ed.), *Bangladesh District Records: Chittagong*, vol. I (1760-1787) (Dhaka: University of Dacca Press, 1978), 83–84.

[178] Lewin, *The Hill Tracts of Chittagong and the Dwellers Therein*, 21. For a detailed account of these expeditions, see R. L. Chakraborty, 'Chakma Resistance to Early British Rule', *Bangladesh Historical Studies* 2 (1977), 148.

[179] A. M. Serajuddin, 'The Chakma Tribe of the Chittagong Hill Tracts in the 18th Century', *Journal of the Royal Asiatic Society of Great Britain and Ireland* 1 (1971), 56.

[180] Raja Devasish Roy, 'The Discordant Accord: Challenges in the Implementation of the Chittagong Hill Tracts Accord of 1997', in *Implementing Negotiated Agreements: The Real Challenge to Intrastate Peace*, ed. M. Boltjes (The Hague: TMC Asser Press, 2007), 115–146. In contrast, Lewin argues that up to 1829, the colonial administration exercised no direct influence or rule over the hill tribes. The near neighbourhood, however, of a powerful and stable government naturally brought the chiefs by degrees under British influence, and by the end of the eighteenth century every leading chief paid to the Chittagong Collector a certain tribute or yearly gift to purchase the privilege of free-trade between the inhabitants of the hills and the men of the plains. The amount of these sums fluctuated at first, but was gradually brought to specified and fixed limits, eventually taking the shape, not of tribute, but of revenue paid to the state. See Lewin, *The Hill Tracts of Chittagong and the Dwellers Therein*, 22–23.

[181] Mohsin, *The Politics of Nationalism*, 144.

[182] Hutchinson, *An Account of the Chittagong Hill Tracts*, 5–7.

consolidated full colonial administrative control in the region but nonetheless came to be depicted by the colonial administration as a necessary response to atrocities committed by some tribal groups against others.[183] It was ostensibly to prevent Kuki invasions that the CHT was created as a separate district by Act XXII of 1860 and withdrawn from the jurisdiction of the civil, criminal, and revenue courts and offices of the Regulation district of Chittagong. This new district served as the buffer district in checking Kuki invasions from the ridge-tops of the CHT as well as the north-eastern borders to the plains of port city Chittagong.[184] The CHT was gradually militarised by the British; it came under the charge of a Superintendent, a military official who in 1867 was re-designated as Deputy Commissioner.[185] Although there were some political activities to pacify tribal chiefs, the control over and administration in the CHT was mainly military.[186]

The Sepoy Revolt of 1857 brought fundamental changes to the administration of India.[187] After 1857, the British administration in general began to fear that 'they could actually be driven out of India, an apprehension that never hereafter left them, and was never dismissed as an impossibility'.[188] As a result, the British took over the direct administration of their Indian colonies from the East India Company. It is in fact against this backdrop that the CHT was created as a separate district in 1860. Following the annexation of the Lushai Hills by the British Government, the CHT was treated as an independent subdivision of Chittagong with a set of special rules for its administration.[189] And finally, the Government

---

[183] Ibid., 5.
[184] S. Mahmud Ali, *The Fearful State: Power, People and Internal War in South Asia* (London: Zed Books, 1993), 170.
[185] A. Mackenzie, *History of the Relations of the Government with the Hill Tribes of the North-East Frontier of Bengal* (Calcutta: Home Office Department Press, 1884), 342. See also M. Ishaq (ed.), *Bangladesh District Gazetteers: Chittagong Hill Tracts* (Dhaka: Ministry of Cabinet Affairs, Government of Bangladesh, 1971), 29.
[186] Mohsin, *The Politics of Nationalism*, 144. This strategy is by no means unique to the CHT. As Piang notes, in the context of colonial policies vis-à-vis hill tribes in north-east India, British officers often capitalised on internal feuds among tribal groups as well as brief raids, and 'on the pretext of pacifying the "savages" and punishing perpetrators of raids, they launched various expeditions into the territorial homelands of tribal people, which resulted in the eventual annexation of these areas'. See L. Lam Khan Piang, 'Overlapping Territorial Claims and Ethnic Conflict in Manipur', *South Asia Research* 35, no. 2 (2015), 161.
[187] T. R. Metcalf, *The Aftermath of Revolt: India 1857–1870* (Princeton, NJ: Princeton University Press, 1965), 298.
[188] Jaswant Singh, *Jinnah: India-Partition-Independence* (New Delhi: Rupa Co., 2009), 26–27.
[189] Hutchinson, *An Account of the Chittagong Hill Tracts*, 4.

of India passed the 1900 Regulation for governing the CHT. The Regulation equipped the Deputy Commissioner with the extensive power necessary for the effective suppression of any indigenous resistance against British rule.[190]

In 1920 the CHT was designated an 'excluded area'. The colonial protectionist attitude appeared most vividly in the 1920s when the British government sent the Indian Statutory Commission (Simon Commission) to India to propose a suitable form of government in India. The Commissioners concluded that the so-called backward tracts, with few exceptions, must be excluded from general constitutional arrangements on the grounds that these people were not yet ready to fully exercise their political rights and that special provision must be made for their administration.[191] Thus, the Government of India Act of 1935 declared the CHT a 'backward tract', formally severing its political links with the province of Bengal. The tribal chiefs themselves shared the views of the Commission in this regard and had petitioned for this special status. For example, the Chakma Crown Prince Nalinakkho Roy pleaded with the Bengal Governor in 1934 not to give the hill people the franchise rights that the rest of India had, citing their backwardness and his wish to 'protect' them.[192]

For the British, this exclusion was an effective way of keeping the CHT out of the nationalist movement then at its height in the rest of India, Bengal being the epicentre. Thus, although the British government allowed limited immigration into the CHT in order to facilitate trade and irrigation-oriented intensive agriculture, it was careful not to allow large-scale immigration, fearing the growth of anti-British sentiment which was more common in the plains of Bengal.[193] By keeping the Hill Tracts segregated from the fervours of the nationalist movement,

---

[190] See Articles XI (i-iv) and XII (i) of the CHT Regulation.

[191] *Report of the Indian Statutory Commission, Presented by the Secretary of State for the Home Department to Parliament by Command of His Majesty*, 17 vols. (London: H. M. Stationery Office, 1930). See also Vinita Damodaran, 'Indigenous Agency: Customary Rights and Tribal Protection in Eastern India, 1830–1930', *History Workshop Journal* 76, no.1 (2013), 106. The grounds for the exclusion of these territories were that 'the stage of development reached by the inhabitants prevented the possibility of applying to them methods of representation adopted elsewhere', and that the people wanted freedom for the 'reasonable exercise of their ancestral customs, freedom in the pursuit of their traditional methods of livelihood and security of land tenure ... Their contentment does not depend so much on rapid political advance as on experienced and sympathetic handling, and on protection from economic subjugation by their neighbours.'

[192] Dewan, *The Chronicle of the Chakma Nation*, 184.

[193] Roy, 'The Discordant Accord', 121–122.

both the colonial administration and the chiefs hoped to safeguard their own mutually dependent powers and privileges.[194]

3.4.2 Partition of India and the CHT Paradox

India was partitioned in August 1947 on the basis of the 'two nations' theory – advocated by the Muslim League and born largely out of Hindu–Muslim political and economic rivalry, as I explained in Chapter 1. At the time of giving its formal consent to the partition in March 1947, the Congress demanded that if the country was to be divided on the basis of religious majority/minority then the provinces of the Punjab and Bengal, where Muslims enjoyed the majority status, must also be divided on the same principle. Following lengthy negotiations with major political parties in India and political manoeuvre, on 3 June 1947 the British Government finally presented the policy framework for the partition in a statement that later came to be popularly known as the 'Partition Plan'.

The Plan stipulated that the Provincial Legislative Assemblies of Bengal and the Punjab (excluding the European members) would meet in two units – one representing the Muslim majority districts and the other the rest of the province – in order to ascertain whether or not the province should be partitioned. The Plan also instructed that for the determination of the religious majority for this purpose, the 1941 census figures would be taken as authoritative. Should a simple majority of *either* part decide in favour of partition, the Plan continued, partition would be given effect in line with the Award of a Boundary Commission to be set up by the Governor General for each province. More importantly, the Plan also dictated the governing principles to be applied by the Boundary Commission: the boundaries of the two parts of the Punjab and Bengal would be demarcated on the basis of the contiguous majority areas of Muslims and non-Muslims. The Commission was also allowed to take into account 'other factors'.[195] Accordingly, the two provisionally partitioned units of the Bengal Provincial National Assembly met on 20 June 1947. While the majority of representatives of the Muslim-majority districts in the East Bengal Assembly voted against partition – precisely due to their majority status – those of the Hindu-majority districts in the West Bengal

---

[194] Mohsin, *The Politics of Nationalism*, 148.
[195] 'Statement by His Majesty's Government, dated the 3rd June 1947', *Partition Proceedings*, vol. I (Alipore: West Bengal Government Press, 1949), 2.

Assembly voted in favour of it.[196] In accordance with the Plan, a Boundary Commission was established on 30 June 1947 under the 'neutral' chairmanship of Sir Cyril John Radcliffe.[197]

In their petitions before the Commission, both the Muslim League and the Hindu Co-ordination Committee[198] used some phrases in the Plan such as 'contiguous areas' and 'other factors' as tools in pressing unreasonable demands for territorial expansion of East Bengal (Pakistan) and West Bengal (India), respectively. In doing so, they went beyond the general framework of the partition premised upon the religious majority of a given population. For example, as Joya Chatterji notes, in order to achieve its objective of extracting for East Pakistan as much territory as possible, the Muslim League wanted the 'contiguity' principle applied only to areas *within* Bengal. This implied that 'if a Hindu-majority area was not contiguous to any other Hindu-majority area in Bengal, it should go to East Bengal, even if it were contiguous to any other Hindu-majority area outside Bengal'.[199]

It was on the ground of this interpretation of the 'contiguity' principle that the Muslim League demanded the inclusion of the CHT, along with Darjeeling and Jalpaiguri, (all outside Bengal at that time) in East Pakistan, despite a very small percentage of Muslim population in these districts. According to the census of 1941 which served as the basis of the Partition Plan, of the total population of 242,000 in the CHT, only 2.8% were Muslims, while 2% were Hindus. Most of the remaining 95.2% were Buddhists or animists.[200] The 'other factors' that the League relied upon to justify their claim for the CHT included the economic, geographic, and historic unity and integrity of the CHT with the district of Chittagong, the importance of

---

[196] Joya Chatterji, 'The Fashioning of a Frontier: The Radcliffe Line and Bengal's Border Landscape, 1947-52', *Modern Asian Studies* 33, no. 1 (1999), 188. For a detailed account of Bengal partition, see Joya Chatterji, *Bengal Divided: Hindu Communalism and Partition, 1932-1947* (Cambridge: Cambridge University Press, 1994).

[197] The Commission was constituted by the announcement of the Governor General, dated 30 June 1947, Reference No. D50/7/47R. There were four other members of the Commission: two nominated by the Congress (namely, Justice Bijan Kumar Mukherjea and Justice C. C. Biswas) and the other two by the Muslim League (namely, Justice Abu Saleh Mohamed Akram and Justice S. A. Rahman).

[198] Composed of twelve representatives from four political parties, namely, the Congress, the Hindu Mahasabha, the Indian Association, and the New Bengal Association.

[199] Chatterji, 'The Fashioning of a Frontier', 198. See also 'Report of the Muslim Bengal Boundary Commission', reproduced in *Partition Proceedings*, vol. VI, *Reports of the Members and Awards of the Chairman of the Boundary Commission* (Alipore: West Bengal Government Press, 1950), 71-82.

[200] P. C. Mahalanobis, 'Distribution of Muslims in the Population of India: 1941', *Sankhyā: The Indian Journal of Statistics (1933-1960)* 7, no. 4 (1946), 430.

the CHT for the security and maintenance of the Chittagong port, and the importance of the Karnaphuli river for a potential hydro-electricity project in the CHT to ensure power supply to the entire region.[201]

Similarly, the Hindu representatives in the Bengal Boundary Commission demanded a sizable territory for the Hindu-majority West Bengal that included two Muslim-majority districts (Malda and Murshidabad) in their entirety and also large parts of the districts of Nadia, Faridpur, Dinajpur, Rangpur, and Rajshahi.[202] However, Hindu representatives did not specifically demand the CHT as part of West Bengal. Rather, they questioned the jurisdiction of the Bengal Boundary Commission on the CHT issue, given that the CHT was an 'excluded area' under the Government of India Act (1935). Also, as I noted earlier, a series of colonial policies kept the CHT aloof from the anticolonial political movements in Bengal. At the time of partition, therefore, non-Muslim Bangalee elites were less enthusiastic about the incorporation of the CHT. Most of all, unlike Darjeeling or Jalpaiguri – the two other districts that the League claimed for East Bengal – the CHT shared no border with the proposed West Bengal. The Congress's indifference to the CHT caused fury and frustration among the CHT elites, as evidenced by Chakma leader Sneha Kumar Chakma's comment:

> Unfortunately while the Muslim League leaders were madly interested in the 5138 [square] miles of resourceful lands of the CHTs in spite of the alien inhabitants therein, the leaders of the Indian National Congress and the Hindu Mahasabha appeared to have been badly prejudiced against these Buddhist Minority Ethnic Groups and their Area.[203]

Various contemporary newspapers also reported on the agitation among hill peoples regarding their betrayal by Congress.[204]

It is to be noted that the CHT's 'excluded area' status meant there was not a single representative from the CHT in either of the Bengal Legislative Assemblies. The CHT had no representation before the Boundary Commission in any other capacity either. Its people's political fate was written in their absence. However, despite the British policy of keeping the CHT aloof from Indian national movements, the region was not

---

[201] See 'Report of the Muslim Bengal Boundary Commission'.
[202] *Memorandum for the Bengal Boundary Commission. Submitted by the Bengal Provincial Hindu Mahasabha and the New Bengal Association*. Dr S. P. Mookerjee Papers, 1st Instalment, Printed Material, File No. 17 (Serial no. 8) (Nehru Memorial Museum and Library).
[203] D. K. Chakma (ed.), *The Partition and the Chakmas and other Writings of Sneha Kumar Chakma* (unknown place, India: published by the author, 2013), 286.
[204] See, for example, *Indian News Chronicle*, 24 August 1947.

untouched by the question of partition and its potential grave consequences for the CHT. The Chittagong Hill Tracts People Association (*Parbattyo Chattagram Jana Samiti*), established in 1916 by a group of Chakma elites, had adopted a clear political character by 1939. The agenda of action for the future of the CHT *within* India, however, was not uniform: while Kamini Mohan Dewan, the founding president of PCJS, preferred a British-style constitutional monarchy in the CHT, the general secretary of the organisation, Sneha Kumar Chakma, demanded a more democratic form of government in the post-independence CHT.[205] Also, being dominated by the Chakmas, PCJS did not attract much sympathy from other circle chiefs of the CHT. Ananda Chakma argues that this might have affected the Congress leadership's attitude to the CHT.[206]

In 1946 the three chiefs (Rajas) of the Chakma, Mong, and Bomong Circles finally made a concerted effort to demand from the Congress the status of 'native states' or 'self-governing states' *within* the Union of India – an effort that failed.[207] The Chittagong Hill Tracts Hillman Association was formed soon after under the auspices of the three circle chiefs, and delegates were sent to the Congress in Delhi to demand that the CHT be constituted into three Buddhist Federated States with the three hereditary tribal chiefs as constitutional heads, one common elected Council, and a common ministry responsible for them. They also demanded that the proposed three states should be grouped with the neighbouring Indian tribal states of Tripura, Manipur, Khasi, and Cooch-Behar, and surely fall outside both Hindu and Muslim Bengal.[208]

The delegation returned with the Congress's assurance that the CHT would be included in India. Nehru and Patel, the two most influential Congress leaders at the time, convinced the hill delegation that there was no question of the CHT being included in Pakistan. However, the Congress never acted forcefully enough to prevent such inclusion. Only when the Boundary Commission Report was leaked out before its formal publication and it appeared that the CHT was going to be part of East Bengal under Pakistan did the All India Congress Committee issue a statement on 13 August 1947 condemning the decision, describing it as lacking 'all

---

[205] Ananda Bikash Chakma, 'Partition of India, Incorporation of Chittagong Hill Tracts into Pakistan and the Politics of Chakmas: A Review', *Journal of the Pakistan Historical Society* 63, no. 2 (2015), 9–12.
[206] Ibid., 12.
[207] Ibid.
[208] K. K. Roy, 'India's Mongolian Fringe', in *The Statesman*, 23 June 1947, and Abani Ranjan Dewan, 'Chittagong Hill Tracts', in *The Statesman*, 24 June 1947, both cited in ibid., 12–13.

sense of justice, equity and propriety'.[209] Patel even wrote a letter on the same day to the Governor General Lord Mountbatten expressing his strong reaction to the decision to award the CHT to Pakistan:

> I feel it is inconceivable that such a blatant and patent breach of the terms of reference should be perpetrated by the Chairman of the Boundary Commission. [...] Any award against the weight of local opinion and of the terms of reference, or without any referendum to ascertain the will of the people concerned must, therefore, be construed as a collusive or partisan award and will have therefore, to be repudiated by us.[210]

In the same letter, Patel also warned the Governor General that he had told the CHT tribes that the proposition of awarding the CHT to Pakistan was so monstrous that if it should happen they would be justified in resisting such a decision to the utmost of their power, and count on the maximum support from the Congress in such resistance.[211]

When the decision of the Boundary Commission finally came into effect and the CHT officially became a part of Pakistan, a group of Chakma leaders did in fact meet Nehru to seek support for their resistance. Nehru was furious about their request for India's support for an armed resistance to Pakistan with a view to redrawing the territorial boundary and redefining the political future of the CHT. A member of the delegation, Sneha Kumar Chakma, offers a first-hand account of that meeting:

> Agitated, he asked us, "Do you want India to come again under foreign yoke?" We were at a loss to understand his reaction. Nehru was opposed to the idea of the CHT joining the Indian dominion, since he thought that reopening this issue would spark off an international controversy and would amount to antagonizing other countries.[212]

Just as his counterpart Jinnah refused to extend similar support to the Rohingya who desired to break away from Myanmar and join East Pakistan, Nehru too accepted the salience of the international boundaries of the postcolonial Indian state crafted by the colonial administration. Even more derogatory and disgraceful in the Chakma

---

[209] See Mukur K. Khisha, *Time and Again* (New Delhi: Macmillan India Ltd., 2004), 181.
[210] India Office Records and Private Papers, 'Viceroys Personal Report No. 17' (Appendix III: Letter to Lord Mountbatten from Vallabhbhai Patel regarding Chittagong Hill Tracts), IOR/L/PO/6/123.
[211] Ibid.
[212] D. K. Chakma (ed.), *The Partition and the Chakmas*, 45.

leaders' opinion was Gandhi's response: 'There are many people like blind, lame and deaf in India but how many people are there in CHT that is necessary for us?'[213]

The CHT – with its negligible population both of Hindus and of Muslims – indeed put a difficult challenge before the Boundary Commission. Although officially Bengal was to be partitioned between Muslim-majority and non-Muslim-majority areas, in reality the work of the Commission came to be seen as dealing with the Hindu–Muslim question. Willem van Schendel finds the root of this popular perception in the religious antagonism of the anticolonial national movements of the twentieth century that, in dominant political interpretations, became narrowed down to the categories of Hindus and Muslims.[214] The geographical position of the CHT and its historic ties with Chittagong was also a factor. As Radcliffe himself noted: 'To which State should the Chittagong Hill Tracts be assigned, an area in which the Muslim population was only 3 per cent, of the whole, but which it was difficult to assign to a State different from that which controlled the district of Chittagong itself?'[215] The complete isolation of the CHT from West Bengal was seen as a major factor.[216] To justify the Commission's decision, Governor General Mountbatten argued that 'the whole economic life of the people of the Hill Tracts depends upon East Bengal. [...] it would be disastrous for the people [of the CHT] themselves to be cut off from East Bengal. [...] In a sense Chittagong, the only port of East Bengal, also depends upon the Hill Tracts.'[217] Some have also argued that the allocation of the CHT to East Bengal was an attempt to compensate Pakistan for its loss on the Punjab front and of course the loss of Calcutta.[218] Some provisions of the Award later became a subject of an Indo-Pak legal dispute, settled in

---

[213] Snehasish Ghosh, *Political Separation in the Chittagong Hill Tracts of Bangladesh with Special Reference to the Chakma Issue* (Unpublished PhD Thesis, Jadavpur University, Calcutta, 1996), 45, cited in A. B. Chakma, 'Partition of India, Incorporation of Chittagong Hill Tracts into Pakistan', 25.

[214] Willem van Schendel, *The Bengal Borderland: Beyond State and Nation in South Asia* (London: Anthem Press, 2004), 47.

[215] See Cyril Radcliffe, *The Report of the Bengal Boundary Commission* (12 August 1947), para. 8 (7).

[216] India Office Records and Private Papers, 'Confidential Report for Secretary of State for Commonwealth Relations on the Events in India and Pakistan', 15–20 August 1947, IOR/L/I/1/42/12.

[217] 'Viceroy's Personal Report', 16 August 1947, IOR/L/PO/6/123.

[218] Tridibsantapa Kundu, 'The Partition (1947) and the Chakmas of Chittagong Hill Tracts', *Partition Studies* (18 June 2006), available at www.bengalpartitionstudies.blogspot.com.

an international arbitration under the UN, but no question was raised about the CHT.[219]

The Indian Independence Act (1947), enacted by the British Parliament, finally created the two independent dominions of India and Pakistan, and specified the territories of the dominions.[220] The province of Bengal as constituted under the Government of India Act (1935) ceased to exist; instead, the provinces of East Bengal and West Bengal were formally constituted as part of Pakistan and India, respectively.[221] Although the Report of the Boundary Commission was ready a few days before independence, Mountbatten decided to delay its publication due to widespread fear of disturbances. He was also worried about being seen as personally responsible for the potential disturbance just before the independence of India and Pakistan.[222] H. M. Seervai even argues that the delay had to do with the awarding of the CHT to East Pakistan, as that news could potentially provoke Indians and spoil the Independence Day celebrations.[223]

The announcement of the Boundary Commission Awards finally came on 17 August 1947 – a couple of days after independence. The Chakma elites of the CHT were so confident of their inclusion in India that on the day of India's independence, they hoisted the Indian flag at Rangamati – only to find a few days later that they were actually part of Pakistan. On the other hand, the Marma hill tribes – of Arakanese origin – hoisted the Burmese flag at Bandarban.[224] At that messy moment of partition of the sub-continent, while the Rohingya Muslims in Arakan desired to be part of the Muslim 'homeland' Pakistan, on the other side of the border, hill communities expressed their preference to escape from Pakistan.

However, despite the shock of finding themselves on the wrong side of the Indo-Pak border, the hill communities continued to hoist Indian and Burmese flags atop all official buildings at Rangamati and Bandarban

---

[219] *Boundary disputes between India and Pakistan relating to the interpretation of the report of the Bengal Boundary Commission* (*India/Pakistan Boundary Dispute* case), *Reports of International Arbitral Awards* XXI (1950), 1–51.

[220] See Section 2 of the Indian Independence Act, 1947 (10 and 11 GEO. 6, chapter 30).

[221] See Section 3 of ibid.

[222] Minutes of Viceroy's Staff Meeting, 9 August 1947, in *Transfer of Power*, eds. Nicholas Mansergh and Penderel Moon, vol. XII, 610–612. See also Hugh Tinker, 'Pressure, Persuasion, Decision: Factors in the Partition of the Punjab, 15 August 1947', *The Journal of Asian Studies* 36 (1977), 699–700.

[223] H. M. Seervai, *Partition of India: Legend and Reality* (Bombay: Emmenem Publications Pvt. Ltd., 1990), 162.

[224] Mohsin, *The Politics of Nationalism*, 37.

until the Baluch Regiment of the Pakistan army was deployed on 21 August 1947 to suppress the protest and pull those flags down. Tridibsantapa Kundu notes that the tribal leaders led by Sneha Kumar Chakma, who fled to India immediately after the military action, continued their efforts to request Indian military intervention in the CHT without much success: 'Though Patel was enthusiastic, Nehru was shaky, unwilling to do anything that might justify the Pakistani inspired effort to take over Kashmir.'[225] The CHT political elites finally decided to accept their political future in Pakistan. But the initial resistance to Pakistani rule remained an important factor in the nationalist discourse of Pakistan. As Van Schendel notes, the events of August 1947 were 'constructed as the core symbol of the district's treason to the state of Pakistan, literally *avant la lettre*. It was the beginning of a historical development that would lead the Chittagong Hill Tracts down the road of marginalisation, repression, armed rebellion, and protracted war.'[226]

3.4.3 The CHT under the Postcolonial States of Pakistan and Bangladesh

It is perhaps due to the fear of further 'disturbance' in the area that as early as 1948 the Pakistan government disbanded the Frontier Police Force composed of hill peoples.[227] To consolidate its power and secure political allegiance from hill communities, the government appointed as the Deputy Commissioner a retired Indian Civil Service officer, Lance Niblett, who was none other than the grandson of Captain Lewin.[228] When the Muslim League leaders of East Bengal attempted to remove the CHT's special status as an 'excluded area' by merging it with the province of East Bengal, Niblett successfully resisted the attempt.[229] It is worth noting here that the First Schedule to the Indian Independence Act (1947), which provisionally included the Bengal districts in the new province of East Pakistan, did not include the CHT. This was due to the status of the CHT as an 'excluded area' in the 1935 Government of India Act, which continued to be the constitution of Pakistan – according

---

[225] See Kundu, 'The Partition (1947) and the Chakmas of Chittagong Hill Tracts'.
[226] Van Schendel, *The Bengal Borderland*, 48–49.
[227] Mohsin, *The Politics of Nationalism*, 148.
[228] Bessaignet, *Tribesmen of Chittagong Hill Tracts*, annexure III (Memoir), 122. Niblett was also the last DC of the CHT of British origin.
[229] Mohsin, *The Politics of Nationalism*, 45.

to Section 8 of the Independence Act – until Pakistan adopted its first constitution in March 1956.[230]

The first Constitution of Pakistan (1956) maintained the status of 'excluded area' and the overall colonial framework of governance in the CHT. However, the next constitution of 1962, under the military rule of Ayub Khan, changed the status of the CHT from an 'excluded area' to a 'tribal area', with the direct implication that the central administrative system was to be gradually imposed on the CHT and all the local administrative staff to be replaced by Bangalees.[231] But all remaining special measures for the CHT under the Pakistani constitution came to an end when in 1963 the Acting President of Pakistan, Fazlul Quader Chowdhury, notoriously amended the constitution to this effect, abusing his sweeping presidential power under the military rule.[232]

The Bangalees of East Pakistan also had serious grievances against Pakistani rule due to deep-rooted discrimination and the dominance of West Pakistan in almost all aspects of political, social, and economic life. Following a successful political movement and the ensuing liberation war, East Pakistan emerged as the independent state of Bangladesh on 16 December 1971. The first constitution of the country, which came into force on the same date the following year, declared Bangladesh to be a *unitary*, independent, and sovereign people's republic comprising the territories which immediately before the declaration of independence on 26 March 1971 constituted East Pakistan.[233] Thus, in line with recognised principles of international law regarding *uti possidetis* and state succession, the CHT now became an integral part of Bangladesh, and the hill people were denied the right to self-determination or any other political future. Any special status for the CHT appeared unrealistic within the unitary framework of the constitution. The CHT ultimately lost the status it had as a 'non-regulated district' under the CHT Regulation of 1900, the 'excluded territories' status it had under the Government of India Act

---

[230] *Mohammad Badiuzzaman* v. *Bangladesh and Others* 7 Law Guardian (2010) High Court Division, para. 8.

[231] See Articles 222 and 223 of the 1962 Constitution of Pakistan. See also M. Mufazzalul Huq, 'Changing Nature of Dominant Social Forces and Interventions in the Chittagong Hill Tracts', *The Journal of Social Studies* 56 (1992), 56; D. E. Sopher, 'The Swidden/Wet Rice Transition in the Chittagong Hill', *Annals of the Association of American Geographers* 54 (1964), 346.

[232] Roy, 'The Erosion of Legal and Constitutional Safeguards of the Hill Peoples of the CHT'. See also Mohsin, *The Politics of Nationalism*, 46.

[233] Article 2 of the Constitution.

(1935) and the 1956 Constitution of Pakistan, and the status of 'tribal area' it had under the 1962 Pakistan constitution.

Ironically, throughout the political movements of the 1970s, the CHT remained aloof. As Amena Mohsin notes, the CHT was one of the two seats in East Pakistan that the main political party Awami League failed to win in the 1970 general election, held immediately before the independence.[234] Soon after the independence, a hill peoples' delegation called on the prime minister, demanding regional autonomy and a separate legislature for the CHT. The prime minister rejected these claims, advising the delegation to relinquish such 'parochial and ethnic aspirations in favour of these being subsumed under a broader notion of nationalism to facilitate national integration'.[235]

Successive military governments pursued even more coercive measures to achieve this goal of national unity. Though started under Pakistani rule, the devastating programme of settlement of tens of thousands of poor Bangalees in the CHT was intensified under successive military regimes in Bangladesh. From 1980 to 1984, as many as 400,000 Bangalees were made to settle in the CHT, and over 50,000 Chakmas were reported to have fled to the Indian state of Tripura.[236] In 1947, the Bangalee population in the CHT was 2.5 per cent; it rose to 10 per cent in 1951 and 35 per cent in 1981.[237] According to the latest Bangladesh census, in 2011, Bangalees constitute the majority in the hill district of Bandarban (56 per cent), while they make up 48 per cent and 40 per cent of the total population in the hill districts of Khagrachari and Rangamati, respectively.[238] Collectively, according to the 2011 census, Bangalees constitute 47 per cent of the total population in the CHT. Various other oppressive measures ultimately resulted in armed conflicts between the Bangladesh army and para-military groups of the CHT lasting nearly

---

[234] Mohsin, *The Politics of Nationalism*, 45.
[235] Quoted in *Mohammad Badiuzzaman v. Bangladesh and Others*, para. 10.
[236] Rahman and Shawon (eds.), *Tying the Knot*, 10.
[237] Willem van Schendal, 'The Invention of "Jumma": State Formation and Ethnicity in Southeastern Bangladesh', *Modern Asian Studies* 26, no. 1 (1992), 95.
[238] Bandarban has a tribal population of 172,401 out of a total population of 388,000; in Khagrachari, the tribal population is 316,987 out of a total of 614,000; and in Rangamati, the total tribal population is 356,153 out of a total population of 596,000. See Bangladesh Bureau of Statistics, *Statistical Pocket Book Bangladesh 2012* (Dhaka: Bangladesh Bureau of Statistics, 2013), 92, 132. The census findings are often questioned, and alternative sources indicate a heavier presence of Bangalee settlers in the CHT. Cf. The CHT Commission, *'Life is Not Ours': Land and Human in the Chittagong Hill Tracts, Bangladesh* (Dhaka: The CHT Commission, 1991).

three decades. The civil war finally ended with the signing of the Chittagong Hill Tracts Peace Accord in 1997. This was largely due to local and international pressure arising from humanitarian concern as well as other economic and geopolitical considerations.

As we shall see in Chapter 4, the Peace Accord offered some regional administrative power to the representatives of hill peoples but denied any constitutional recognition of the distinct identity of the hill communities. Instead, the term 'tribal' (*Upajati* in Bengali, meaning 'sub-nation') was used to describe them. The preamble to the Accord states that the parties to this Accord arrived at an agreement 'under the framework of the constitution of Bangladesh'. That constitution conceives of Bangladesh as a unitary national state, thereby limiting the scope for accommodating ethnic differences.

3.5 Conclusion

The continuation of the colonial boundaries in the politico-legal imagination of postcolonial states is an established norm of international law. Although some international lawyers challenge this general application of the *uti possidetis* principle as a legally binding rule of international law, they nonetheless accept the pragmatic need for this principle, that is, to maintain peace and stability. Ironically, as the examples of the Rohingya and the hill people of the CHT reveal, what seemed at the time of decolonisation or partition or state succession to be a solution turned out to be a recipe for humanitarian catastrophe, as the project of the postcolonial homogenous national state, to be built within the pre-determined territorial boundaries, miserably failed.

In other words, international law unequivocally facilitates the ideological function of the postcolonial 'national' state by prescribing the continuity of the colonial boundaries for postcolonial states, consequently denying minorities the legitimate right to self-determination. Minority oppression in the hands of hostile national states and the ensuing ethnic conflicts are direct results of this. With the reification of the nation-state form to be found at the core of international legal imagination and as the building block of the international order, international law legitimises the marginalisation of minorities as the leftovers of the state-making process. International law, at the same time, dissimulates the vulnerabilities of ethnic minorities with the mantra of national unification. In short, international law advances the ideology of the postcolonial 'national' state through a number of general modes of ideological operation.

Nevertheless, it would be inappropriate to conclude that the boundary-making role of international law is the obvious reason behind minority crises in postcolonial states in general. In the case of the Rohingya and the CHT hill people, various other elements have contributed to the situation, and international law also contributed to many of those. It thus needs to be exposed how, due to its normative reliance on individualism as well as its ambivalence with the right to self-determination and minority protection, international law exacerbates the situation of already vulnerable groups but simultaneously justifies the wrongdoing through the ideology of the postcolonial 'liberal' state. I examine this phenomenon in Chapter 4.

4

The Postcolonial 'Liberal' State

Self-determination, Minorities, and International Law

4.1 Introduction

If provisions in international law regarding boundaries put spatial limits on the nation-building project of the postcolonial state, the normative confines of the project came from the most dominant political philosophy of the post–WWII period – liberalism. Nation-building projects in most postcolonial states faced the challenging task of reconciling two diverging forces: 'nationalism' and 'liberal-universalism'. As we have seen, ethno-nationalism served not only as the vehicle of liberation movements against colonial rule but also as the key to independent statehood. In contrast, post–WWII liberal universalism promised a post-ethnic world order and offered a template for the internal organisation of ethnic relations in postcolonial states. While the force of nationalism saw its fruition in the ideology of the 'national' state, liberal universalism was enshrined in the constitutional architecture of postcolonial states.

As it did in the 'national' state project, international law played a key part in the making of the postcolonial 'liberal' state. Indeed, post–WWII international law was set specifically to reaffirm faith in and promote certain crucial values: fundamental human rights, the dignity and worth of individuals, equal rights of men and women and of nations large and small, among others.[1] In this new era, however, 'progress' equated to liberal values, and universalism simply meant the imposition of these values at a global scale. Thus, since the inception of the UN, individualist notions of human rights and citizenship have become the dominant

---

[1] See the Preamble of the UN Charter (1945).

vocabulary through which the concept of 'minority' is expressed and the discourse on the right to self-determination is shaped.

In Chapter 3, I demonstrated how the international law principle of *uti possidetis* denied many minority groups their legitimate right to self-determination at the moment of decolonisation. This chapter explains how international law, this time with its liberal underpinning, continued to shrink the scope of self-determination, thereby perpetuating the vulnerability, or in some cases even leading to the extinction, of minority groups. I will also show that the international law of minority protection, offered as a fallback position to groups that have been denied the right to self-determination, is rather weak and inadequate. This is because of the liberal-individualist premise of the minority rights regime under international law. Taking these points together, I highlight how international law facilitates the ideology of the postcolonial 'liberal' state – with fragmentation and legitimation as its ideological modes of operation. International law works through these modes to diffuse minority groups into individual subjects of human rights, and to legitimise the denial of minority group protection within the constitutional architecture of the postcolonial 'liberal' state.

In the following section, I first discuss the liberal philosophical tradition behind the understanding of the 'nation' and the treatment of minorities therein in nineteenth-century Europe. Given that this European tradition of understanding the nation served as the foundation of post–WWII international law, my discussion here sets the necessary background for the rest of the chapter on international law and minorities. I then offer an in-depth analysis of how international law responds to minorities along the line of the liberal tradition, specifically focusing, first, on the liberal-individualist connotation of the right to self-determination and, second, on human rights approaches to minority rights discourse. Taken together, my analyses of these issues highlight the fallacy of the notion of 'minority protection' in international law and demonstrate how international law contributes to the marginalisation of minorities in the name of upholding liberal values. The post–WWII liberal-individualist approach to self-determination and minority protection under international law in turn shapes the liberal constitutional architecture of postcolonial states. And in this way, international law advances the ideology of the postcolonial 'liberal' state. I substantiate these arguments with case studies on the Rohingya and the CHT hill people.

4.2 The 'Nation' and Its 'Other' in the European Liberal Tradition

The construction of the national 'self' and its derogatory 'other' in the liberal philosophical tradition is premised upon individualism.[2] The post-Revolution philosophy of the Enlightenment and liberalism relied heavily on individualism and international solidarity to contain the sense of national loyalty. Immanuel Kant's was the most prominent stance, locating the individual within the universal realm. For Kant, a state is a union of an aggregate of 'men', in which *all* individual members sacrifice their freedom, which exists in the state of nature, in order to receive civil rights in return.[3] With the analogy that individuals have to sacrifice their lawless state of nature to join the republic, Kant proposes that states must for the same reason relinquish some of the freedoms they would have in a savage natural condition for the sake of the universal good.[4] The vision of the rights that states ultimately enjoy among themselves is 'cosmopolitan'.[5] Kant's cosmopolitanism is an effort to transcend the natural geographic confinements of ethnicity and nations – a move towards progress in the form of universalism.

The Kantian proposition was criticised by Johann von Herder, who advocates Romantic ideas of ethno-cultural specificity, holding the view that the rights of cultural nations should supersede the natural rights of all.[6] Hegel's opposition to Kant's proposition takes a different approach.

---

[2] In writing this section, I have relied on my earlier works on this subject. Especially, see Shahabuddin, *Ethnicity and International Law*, 22–46; Mohammad Shahabuddin, '"Ethnicity" in the International Law of Minority Protection: The Post–Cold War Context in Perspective', *Leiden Journal of International Law* 25, no. 4 (2012) 885–907; Mohammad Shahabuddin, 'Ethnicity', in *Concepts for International Law: Contributions to Disciplinary Thoughts*, eds. Jean d'Aspremont and Sahib Singh (Gloucestershire: Edward Elgar, 2019), 279–293.

[3] Immanuel Kant, 'The Metaphysics of Morals (1797)', 140. However, women and slaves remained outside the scope of these civil rights as suffrage was denied to them.

[4] Ibid., 165, 171.

[5] Ibid., 172.

[6] Johann Gottfried von Herder, 'Reflections on the Philosophy of the History of Mankind (1791)', in *The Nationalism Reader*, eds. Omar Dahbour and Micheline R. Ishay (Atlantic Highlands, NJ: Humanities Press, 1995), 48–57; Johann Gottfried von Herder, 'Ideas towards a Philosophy of the History of Mankind (1785)', in *Modern Political Doctrines*, ed. Alfred Zimmern (Oxford: Oxford University Press, 1939), 165. A similar Romantic response to the liberal concept of nationalism was offered by Fitche. See Johanne Gottlieb Fichte, 'An Outline of International and Cosmopolitan Law (1796–97)', in *The Political Thought of the German Romantics*, eds. H. S. Reiss and P. Brown (Oxford: Basil Blackwell, 1955), 73–84; Johanne Gottlieb Fichte, 'Addresses to the German Nation – Thirteenth Address (1808)', in *The Political Thought of the German Romantics*, 102–108.

Like Herder, Hegel views the individual as existing within the national consciousness – the substance that underlies the spirit of the nation, that informs all the aims and interests of the nation, and that also determines the nation's rights, customs, and religion.[7] But for Hegel, the spirit of the nation, which is particular in essence, is identical to the universal spirit that is revealed through the human consciousness, corresponding to the divine, hence absolute, spirit.

The spirit of the nation, Hegel continues, is therefore the universal spirit in particular form. The 'particular' is, however, dependent on the 'universal' for its actual being or existence. Although the particular spirit of a particular nation may perish, it disappears as a 'particular moment' of the development of the world spirit, which is absolute, hence omnipresent.[8] What is implied, therefore, is an evolutionary process to reach the absolute universal spirit, wherein particular national spirits fuse to supplement each other; some disappear in the process but an advanced new spirit also appears.[9] The universal spirit that takes a particular national form to come into actual existence as the consciousness within a state is the nation's culture; this is the form to which everything within the state is assimilated.[10] Given that the state has embodied a particular spirit, and the law is the objectivity of the spirit as well as the will in its true expression, Hegel concludes that when the subjective will of men subordinates itself to laws, 'the objective and the subjective will are then reconciled, forming a single, undivided whole'.[11] Unlike German Romantics, Hegel thus reconciles liberalism with the Romantic ethnic appeals by locating national spirits within the framework of the state and its laws.

Yet, in the liberal nation, ethnicity remains on the sidelines, and the liberal discourse on whether the ethnic 'other' – often 'minorities' – should be assimilated or allowed to maintain cultural distinctiveness is informed by an instrumental understanding of ethnicity. For example, although John Stuart Mill argues that for a representative government to

---

Compared to Herder and Fichte, the nineteenth-century scholars of the German Historical School, such as Leopold von Ranke, took a more conservative stance. See Leopold von Ranke, 'The Great Powers (1833)', in *The Nationalism Reader*, 158–159.

[7] George W. F. Hegel, *Lectures on the Philosophy of World History* (1837), ed. D. Forbes, trans. H. B. Nisbet (Cambridge: Cambridge University Press, 1975), 76–77, 80. See also Timothy C. Luther, *Hegel's Critique of Modernity – Reconciling Individual Freedom and the Community* (New York: Lexington Books, 2009).

[8] Hegel, *Lectures on the Philosophy of World History*, 81–83.

[9] Ibid., 83, 147–151.

[10] Ibid., 97.

[11] Ibid.

work efficiently the boundaries of government should coincide with those of nationalities, he nonetheless advocates the assimilation of the lower and backward portion of the human race into that of the higher. For, he believes, such assimilation is necessary for the betterment of the backward as well as the entire human race.[12] He thus proposes that the greater interest of the Breton and the Basque of French Navarre, or the Welshman and the Scottish Highlander, lies in their assimilation into the highly civilised and cultivated French and British nations, respectively.[13]

Acton, by contrast, is of the view that '[t]he combination of different nations in one state is a necessary condition of civilised life'.[14] For him, this diversity not only results from liberty but also maintains liberty by creating a barrier against the intrusion of the government beyond the political sphere, supplying the greatest variety of intellectual resources, and providing perpetual incentives to progress, among other things.[15] Multiculturalism helps the liberal evolutionary process too: 'Inferior races are raised by living in political union with races intellectually superior.'[16] Going against the German ideology of the exclusive ethnic nation, Acton insists that diversity persists under the same state, for as an instrument of civilisation diversity indicates greater advancement and progress than national unity does.[17]

Acton, however, dismantles any claim by the nations within the state of political allegiance over the individuals. In his opinion, it is only to the nationality formed by the state that individuals owe political duties and thereby devolve corresponding political rights.[18] Thus, Acton's proposed diversity is more about a strategic choice to facilitate stability within a multinational state. The pragmatic tone is expressed in the distinctiveness of the approach that he claims: it aims not at an arbitrary change, but at careful respect for the existing conditions of political life; it obeys the laws and results of history, not the aspirations of an ideal future.[19]

---

[12] John Stuart Mill, 'Considerations on Representative Government (1861)', in *Three Essays on Liberty; Representative Government; and the Subjugation of Women* (London: Pelican Classics, 1975), 380–388.
[13] Ibid.
[14] John E. E. Dalberg-Acton, *The History of Freedom and Other Essays*, eds. John N. Figgis and Reginald V. Laurence (London: Macmillan & Co. Ltd., 1907), 290.
[15] Ibid., 289–290.
[16] Ibid., 290.
[17] Ibid.
[18] Ibid., 293.
[19] Ibid., 289–290.

Thus, in both of the liberal approaches to a different ethnic group within the state, ethnicity must either be submerged in the state-imposed national identity or silently remain at the periphery for other instrumental purposes such as socio-political stability. What is common between Mill and Acton is their vision of a nation state that marches towards a progressive, scientific world civilisation – a universal liberal spirit that consistently reflects back on the character of the state. Nevertheless, ethnicity continued to inform the liberal understanding of the minority and minority protection in complex ways, as I shall discuss in the following section.

We have seen in Chapter 2 that the ideology of the postcolonial 'liberal' state offered justification for dismantling the notion of minority protection under the Indian constitution. My case studies on the Rohingya and the CHT hill people in this chapter will more specifically substantiate how the liberal vision of the nation gets translated into the constitutional architecture of postcolonial states and shapes the minority rights discourse. As we shall see, the ideology of the postcolonial 'liberal' state – having recourse to 'fragmentation' and 'legitimation' as its ideological modes of operation – serves to marginalise minorities and deny them group rights by diffusing 'groups' into a collection of individuals. International law – having the same liberal ideology as its premise – facilitates this process. Therefore, before turning to specific examples of the treatment of the Rohingya and the CHT hill people within the liberal constitutional framework in their respective postcolonial states, in the following section I shed light on the way international law deals with minorities within the liberal-individualist framework, and what happens as a result.

4.3 Minorities within the Liberal Framework of International Law

The liberal treatment of minorities as the ethnic 'other' is demonstrated in the interwar international law of minority protection under the League of Nations. The idea of minority rights appeared as a fallback position in cases where Wilson's proposition of the right to self-determination in ethnic terms could not be realised.[20] But both liberal individualism and the assimilationist agenda always co-existed with the concept of minority protection.[21] During the Paris peace negotiations, efforts were made to

---

[20] For the full text of Wilson's address to the Congress, see Gregory R. Suriano (ed.), *Great American Speeches* (New York: Gramercy Books, 1993), 143–146.
[21] See David H. Miller, *The Drafting of the Covenant*, vol. II (New York: G. P. Putnam's Sons, 1928), 70.

reconcile the classical notion of sovereignty with the ethnic notion of self-determination. Since the principle of self-determination could not be generally applied, David Miller asserts, it was suggested that the contrary principle should prevail: 'as the drawing of boundaries according to racial or social conditions is in many cases an impossibility, protection of the rights of minorities and acceptance of such protection by the minorities constitute the only basis of enduring peace'.[22]

However, it was not easy for the liberal West to design a mechanism for the protection of minorities, who were conceived of in ethnic – hence, backward – terms. Thus, Wilson's initial proposal of a general provision for minority protection in the League covenant was replaced with a series of minority treaties that obliged certain Eastern and Central European states to protect minorities within their territories, with the guarantee mechanism being entrusted to the League. By making this change, the liberal West avoided any international obligation for minority protection of its own.

Even then, the intention was not to offer protection to minorities on a permanent basis. During the session of the Supreme Council on 23 June 1919, Wilson had a brief exchange with Headlam-Morley (a member of the British delegation) about the use of minority language as a medium of instruction in schools in Poland, and is reported to have expressed the view that the American model of cultural assimilation should be applicable to Eastern and Central Europe.[23] The British premier Lloyd George adopted the same assimilationist approach towards the Jewish minorities in Poland.[24] He was particularly concerned about the risk of 'the creation of a state within a state' associated with the claim of autonomy for the minorities.[25] Ultimately, while defining the protected minorities in the Polish Minority Treaty, the phrase 'persons belonging to linguistic, racial and religious minorities' rather than 'national minorities' was used in order to avoid recognising them as a separate legal corporation within the state.[26]

---

[22] Ibid., 71. See also Robert Lansing, *The Peace Negotiations: A Personal Narrative* (Boston, MA: Houghton Mifflin Company, 1921).
[23] Paul Mantoux, *Délibérations du Conseil des Quatres. Notes de L'Officier Interprete*, vol. II (Paris: 1955), 489, cited in Christian Raitz von Frenz, *A Lesson Forgotten – Minority Protection under the League of Nations. The Case of the German Minority in Poland, 1920–1934* (New York: St. Martin's Press, 1999), 66.
[24] Foreign Relations of the United States (FRUS), *The Paris Peace Conference*, vol. VI (Washington, DC: Government Printing Press, 1942), 626.
[25] Mantoux, 440, cited in von Frenz, *A Lesson Forgotten*, 59.
[26] See Article 12 of the Polish Minority Treaty.

Thus, to what extent the raison d'être of the minority protection regime was the 'protection' of minorities at all remains an open question. The Report of de Mello-Franco revealed that the architects of the minority protection system in no way envisioned the minorities as groups of inhabitants who would regard themselves as permanently foreign to the general organisation of the country. Rather, they intended for the minorities a certain legal protection which might gradually prepare the way for the conditions necessary for the establishment of a complete 'national unity' within an environment of mutual respect.[27] Joseph Roucek noted that the minority treaties never intended to mitigate the differences of groups within a state. On the contrary, the treaties expressed a desire to promote the consolidation of the states, which would then give the minorities certain rights, thereby protecting them from ultra-nationalism and, in this way, contain ethnic tensions leading to international conflict.[28]

However, far from being completely assimilationist, the interwar minority protection mechanism was reconciliatory in nature. Indeed, efforts were made to reconcile the victors' liberal ideology with the conservative ethno-nationalism of the East, efforts that ultimately gave the minority treaties a hybrid character and the whole regime a transitory nature. The Polish Minority Treaty, which served as a model for other similar minority treaties, is an archetypical example of such an effort of reconciliation and of the resulting hybrid character of the minority protection regime incorporating both liberal individualism and the conservative ethnic group phenomenon.[29] The hybrid nature of the interwar minority protection mechanism was also reflected in a number of cases before the Permanent Court of International Justice.[30]

---

[27] Report of Afranio de Mello-Franco, 'Council Meeting of 9 December 1925', *League of Nations Official Journal* 7, no. 2 (1926), 142.

[28] Joseph S. Roucek, *The Working of the Minorities System under the League of Nations* (Prague: Orbis Publishing, 1929), 74.

[29] See Articles 2, 7, 8, and 9 of the Polish Minority Treaty.

[30] See, for example, *Minority Schools in Albania* case, PCIJ Reports (1935), Ser. A/B, No. 64; *German Settlers* case, PCIJ Reports (1925), Ser. B, No. 6; *Rights of Minorities in Upper Silesia (Minority Schools)* case, PCIJ Reports (1928), Ser. A, No. 15; *Case Concerning Certain German Interests in Polish Upper Silesia*, PCIJ Reports (1926), Ser. A, No. 7; *Case Concerning the Factory at Chorzow*, PCIJ Reports (1925), Ser. B, No. 3 and PCIJ Reports (1928), Ser. A, No. 17. See also Nathaniel Berman, 'A Perilous Ambivalence: Nationalist Desire, Legal Autonomy, and the Limits of the Interwar Framework', *Harvard International Law Journal* 33, no. 2 (1992), 353–380; Nathaniel Berman, '"But the Alternative Is Despair": European Nationalism and the Modernist Renewal of International Law', *Harvard Law Review* 106, no. 8 (1993), 1792–1904; Nathaniel Berman, 'International Law of Nationalism:

The interwar mechanism of minority protection was already in decline some years before WWII broke out, and there was no enthusiasm for maintaining it. Given the discriminatory character of the minority protection regime vis-à-vis Eastern and Central European states as well as the political manoeuvring of the minority issue by Nazi Germany, the League's aim of protecting minorities faced widespread criticism following the war. However, John Humphrey notes that there were deeper reasons for the change in attitude towards minorities: first, the shift in political power and influence from Europe to the United States, which itself was a country of immigration, and, second, the emergence of the new countries in Africa and Asia, which demonstrated a preoccupation with nation-building and consequently with assimilationist projects.[31] Thus, since the inception of the UN, an individualist notion of human rights had become the dominant vocabulary through which the concept of minority was expressed. While the minority protection regime under the League was of a hybrid nature, under the new arrangement the minority protection system was replaced with a human rights regime exclusively centred on the universal protection of individual rights.

It is, therefore, important to expose what happens to the right of self-determination and minority *group* rights when they are understood within the liberal framework of rights. And also, how international law performs the ideological function of 'fragmentation' to diffuse ethnic minorities into rational individuals, who then turn into subjects and holders of individual human rights.

4.3.1 *The Liberal-Individualist Notion of Self-determination*

As we have already seen, the idea of minority protection appeared as the League's pragmatic response to situations where the right to self-determination was not realistically applicable. In Chapter 3, I also examined how international law provisions on territorial integrity and the principle of *uti possidetis* deprived ethnic minorities of their legitimate right to self-determination at the moment of decolonisation. The right to self-determination leading to independent statehood is an obligation *erga omnes* under international law so far as colonial peoples are concerned,

---

Group Identity and Legal History', in *International Law and Ethnic Conflict*, ed. David Wippman (Ithaca, NY: Cornell University Press, 1998), 25–57.

[31] John P. Humphrey, 'The United Nations Sub-Commission on the Prevention of Discrimination and the Protection of Minorities', *American Journal of International Law* 62 (1968), 870.

but no such right is available to minority groups, unless they effect remedial secession, as we shall see later. Although the unilateral secession of East Pakistan is often described by scholars as an application of the right to self-determination in the non-colonial context, those arguments generally rely on the depiction of East Pakistan as a 'neo-colonial' case within Pakistan or simply as a sui generis case. The latter is due to, inter alia, East Pakistan's geographical isolation and ethnic distinctiveness, the massive economic disparity that it suffered, the oppression of the Bangalee 'majority' by the dominant 'minority' of West Pakistan, and genocidal violence inflicted on Bangalee civilians by the Pakistani army in the wake of the full-scale war of independence beginning in March 1971.[32]

In the *Reference* case on the question of the unilateral secession of Québec, the Canadian Supreme Court made the general international law position clear in concluding that a right to secession under the international law principle of (external) self-determination is available only where a 'people' for the purposes of the right is subject to colonial rule or alien subjugation, domination, or exploitation, or (possibly) where the said people is denied any meaningful access to government to pursue its political, economic, social, and cultural development within the state of which it forms a part. In other circumstances, the court asserted, peoples are expected to achieve (internal) self-determination within the framework of their existing state.[33]

The ICJ Advisory Opinion on the legality of the unilateral declaration of independence of post-conflict Kosovo is also pertinent in this context.[34] The court indicated that although in the aftermath of WWII the international law of self-determination developed so as to grant especially peoples of non-self-governing territories and peoples subject to alien rule the right to independence,[35] there were also instances of

---

[32] See, for example, Ved P. Nanda, 'Self-Determination in International Law: The Tragic Tale of Two Cities – Islamabad (West Pakistan) and Dacca (East Pakistan)', *American Journal of International Law* 66, no. 2 (1972), 321–336; M. Rafiqul Islam, 'Secessionist Self-Determination: Some Lessons from Katanga, Biafra and Bangladesh', *Journal of Peace Research* 22, no. 3 (1985), 211–221; Joshua Castellino, 'The Secession of Bangladesh in International Law: Setting New Standards?', *Asian Yearbook of International Law* 7 (1997), 83–104.

[33] *Reference re Secession of Quebec* case (1998) 2 SCR 217, paras. 126–139.

[34] See *Accordance with International Law of Unilateral Declaration of Independence in Respect of Kosovo*, ICJ Reports (2010); Dissenting Opinion of Mohamed Bennouna, paras. 1–16; Dissenting Opinion of Judge Leonid Skotnikov, paras. 1–18; Dissenting Opinion of Judge Abdul G. Koroma.

[35] The court referred to these oft-cited cases: *Legal Consequences for States of the Continued Presence of South Africa in Namibia (South West Africa)*, ICJ Reports (1971), paras. 52–53;

declarations of independence outside this colonial/alien rule context.[36] However, the court carefully refrained from telling us whether such state practice has led to the creation of any positive norm in this regard.[37] The court, thus, bypassed the question of the legality of the right to self-determination altogether in the non-colonial context.[38]

In contrast, in his dissenting opinion, Judge Abdul Koroma held the view that the question put before the court was indeed a legal question (as opposed to a political issue) that required this legal response: the unilateral declaration of independence by the Provisional Institutions of Self-Government of Kosovo amounted to secession and was not in accordance with international law. Given that respect for the sovereignty and territorial integrity of states is the cardinal principle of contemporary international law, '[n]ot even the principles of equal rights and self-determination of peoples as precepts of international law allow for the dismemberment of an existing state without its consent'.[39] Referring to Resolution 1244[40] and the Rambouillet Accords[41] – which reaffirm the sovereignty and territorial integrity of the Federal Republic of Yugoslavia and do not provide for the unilateral secession of Kosovo – Koroma thus concluded that the actual intention

---

East Timor (Portugal v. Australia), ICJ Reports (1995), para. 29; *Legal Consequences of the Construction of a Wall in the Occupied Palestinian Territory*, ICJ Reports (2004), para. 88. Cf. *Western Sahara* case, ICJ Reports (1975).

[36] Advisory Opinion in the *Kosovo* case, para. 79.
[37] Ibid., para. 82.
[38] Ibid., para. 83. While the court in its opinion avoided the problematic question of self-determination, in his dissenting opinion, Judge Mohamed Bennouna wrote that the court should have exercised its discretion to refrain from giving any opinion on a political process that the Security Council initiated but could not finalise. See Dissenting Opinion of Mohamed Bennouna, paras. 1–16; especially, paras. 2, 3, 5. According to him, by doing so, the court 'could have put a stop to any "frivolous" requests which political organs might be tempted to submit to it in future, and indeed thereby protected the integrity of its judicial function'. See ibid., para. 3. The same view is taken by Judge Leonid Skotnikov on the grounds that the court, for the first time in its history, dealt with a question (posed by the General Assembly), the answer to which entirely depended on the interpretation of a decision taken by the Security Council – another United Nations organ. See Dissenting Opinion of Judge Leonid Skotnikov, paras. 1–18.
[39] Dissenting Opinion of Judge Abdul G. Koroma, para. 22.
[40] *Lex specialis* in relation to the political as well as legal matters concerning Kosovo. See United Nations, Official Records of the Security Council (1999), UN Doc S/RES/1244, Annexes 1 and 2. These annexes provide that the political process must take 'full account' of the 'principles of sovereignty and territorial integrity of the Federal Republic of Yugoslavia and the other countries of the region'.
[41] The Interim Agreement for Peace and Self-Government in Kosovo of 1999, drafted by NATO. See United Nations, Official Records of the Security Council (1999), UN Doc S/RES/648.

of the resolution was for Kosovo to enjoy substantial autonomy and self-government but as an integral part of the Federal Republic of Yugoslavia.[42] In other words, the resolution provides for 'substantial autonomy [for the ethnic Albanian people of Kosovo] *within* the Federal Republic of Yugoslavia'.[43] Koroma's account of the 'special rights' of the Albanians in Kosovo, within the general principle of territorial integrity, thus appears to be a fallback position for the right to self-determination leading to secession.

The African Commission had adopted the same approach to the right to self-determination in the very first case on peoples' rights, the *Congrès du Peuple Katangais* v. *Zaire*, in 1995.[44] The case was brought before the Commission under the African Charter on Human and Peoples' Rights (also known as the 'Banjul Charter'), which famously accords rights not only to individuals but also to minority *groups*, especially the right to self-determination to all peoples under Article 20 (1) of the Charter.[45] Accordingly, the president of the Katangese Peoples' Congress requested that the Commission recognise the independence of Katanga under the African Charter.[46] In its response to the question of the legality of a subnational group's right to self-determination within a sovereign state, the Commission underscored the existence of two different sets of the right to self-determination: one that belongs to all *Zaireoise* as a people, and the other for a section of the population of a state, that is, the Katangese. Having recognised the legitimacy of the Katangese right to self-determination, however, the Commission turned to the limited scope of this right: it must be in full conformity with other recognised principles of international law, such as sovereignty and territorial integrity.[47] In doing so, the Commission also highlighted the exceptional circumstances under which the minority could potentially claim a right to external self-determination:

> In the absence of concrete evidence of violations of human rights to the point that the territorial integrity of Zaire should be called to question *and* in the absence of evidence that the people of Katanga are denied the right

[42] Dissenting Opinion of Judge Abdul G. Koroma, para. 13.
[43] Ibid. Emphasis added.
[44] *Congrès du Peuple Katangais* v. *Zaire* (*Katanga* case), Communication 75/92, 8th Annual Activity Report (1994–1995).
[45] The Clause reads: 'All peoples shall have the right to existence. They shall have the unquestionable and inalienable right to self-determination. They shall freely determine their political status and shall pursue their economic and social development according to the policy they have freely chosen'.
[46] *Katanga* case (1995), para. 1.
[47] Ibid., para. 4.

to participate in government as guaranteed by Article 13 of the African Charter, the Commission holds the view that Katanga is obliged to exercise a variant of self-determination that is compatible with the sovereignty and territorial integrity of Zaire.[48]

The Commission's decision in the *Katanga* case, thus, falls in line with standard international law norms and practices. Solomon Dersso, however, notes that with the inclusion of the conjunction 'and' in the aforementioned quote, the Commission has in fact heightened the threshold for any remedial secession – by requiring *both* human rights violations and the absence of democratic participation – compared to relevant provisions in the UN Declaration on Principles of International Law concerning Friendly Relations and Cooperation among States (1970) or the Vienna Declaration and Programme of Action adopted by the World Conference on Human Rights in 1993.[49] Having denied the external right to self-determination to the Katangese people, who do not meet these two requirements, the Commission directs the Katangese people to alternative forms of self-determination, including 'self-government, local government, federalism, confederalism, unitarism, or any other form of relations' as long as they respect the sovereignty and territorial integrity of the state.[50]

Undoubtedly, securing independent statehood is not the only way of exercising the right to self-determination; this right can be enjoyed by minorities in a variety of ways, including regional autonomy, power-sharing, and other consociational arrangements.[51] However, the fact remains that with its ideological premise in liberalism, international law often shies away from any regime of rights that is not shaped by the primacy of liberal individualism. Since the collapse of the Soviet Union and the apparent landslide of liberalism, international law's faith in the liberal ideology has been renewed; its zeal is unprecedented. The eighteenth-century Kantian idea of individual freedom as the core of global ordering has claimed prominence once again. The re-emergence

---

[48] Ibid., para. 6. Emphasis added.
[49] Solomon A. Dersoo, 'The 1992 UN Declaration on Minorities and the African Human Rights System', in *The United Nations Declaration on Minorities: An Academic Account on the Occasion of Its 20th Anniversary (1992–2012)*, eds. Ugo Caruso and Rainer Hofmann (Leiden: BRILL, 2015), 275–279.
[50] *Katanga* case (1995), para. 4.
[51] See, for example, Arend Lijphart, *Democracy in Plural Societies* (New Haven, CT: Yale University Press, 1977); Sid Noel (ed.), *From Power Sharing to Democracy* (Montreal: McGill-Queen's University Press, 2005); Christine Bell, 'Power-Sharing, Conflict Resolution, and Women: A Global Reappraisal', *Nationalism and Ethnic Politics* 24, no. 1 (2018), 13–32.

of individual primacy in the legal domain of rights has significantly transformed the right to self-determination, as discussed later.

In Perpetual Peace, Kant offers a vision of permanent world peace that has its root in the freedom of each citizen in a polity. Thus, the first definitive article of his perpetual peace thesis claims that republicanism will lead to perpetual peace. This is because under a republican constitution the unlikely consent of the citizens would be required before war is declared.[52] Having linked the exercise of state power to the primacy of individual freedom, in the second definitive article Kant then envisages a constitution at the global level, to be drawn up in the light of a republican constitution within which each nation would guarantee each other's rights. This would mean establishing a federation of peoples, but not an international state of hegemonic character, with the aim of preventing war and expanding the zone of peace.[53] Fernando Tesón claims that by 'republican' Kant is referring to 'what we would call today a liberal democracy, a form of political organisation that provides full respect for human rights'.[54]

The Kantian vision of global peace, which linked peace to the idea of democracy and individual human rights,[55] is translated into Thomas Franck's 'theory of democratic entitlement' that a new norm was emerging in international law that required democracy to legitimise the governance of the state. While governance has always fallen within the internal affairs of a state and been protected under its sovereign veil, Franck argues that this emerging law is becoming 'a requirement of international law, applicable to all and implemented through global standards, with the help of regional and international organisations'.[56] Having traced the pedigree of the individual's right to democratic entitlement to the early twentieth-century idea of self-determination, which was initially meant for communities, Franck diffuses the 'collective' entitlement of self-determination and reconceptualises it as a collection of the individuals' rights to political participation, which flourished in post–WWII international law.[57] Nonetheless, as Gaetano Pentassuglia

---

[52] Immanuel Kant, 'Perpetual Peace', 100. See also Kant, 'The Metaphysics of Morals', 164–173.
[53] Kant, 'Perpetual Peace', 102.
[54] Fernando Tesón, 'The Kantian Theory of International Law', *Columbia Law Review* 92 (1992), 61.
[55] See ibid.
[56] Franck, 'The Emerging Right to Democratic Governance', 47.
[57] Ibid., 52–56.

notes, the proposition of equating self-determination to a distinct 'right to democracy' under international law – meaning the right of a people to engage in meaningful decision-making within the state – remains ambiguous due to its elusive empirical foundations and the lack of a monolithic perception of democracy.[58]

It is worth noting here that in the *Reference* case, the Canadian Supreme Court interpreted 'democracy' in a way that paradoxically denied Québec the constitutional right to unilateral secession that is to be exercised subject to a democratic mandate secured in a referendum. In its opinion, the court asserted that far from being a system based on a simple majority rule, democracy exists in the larger context of other constitutional values, such as federalism, constitutionalism, rule of law, and respect for minorities. As a Confederation, the people of the provinces and territories in Canada as a whole have created close ties of interdependence based on these values. Arguing that a 'democratic' decision by the Québécois people in favour of secession 'under the constitution' would put those relationships at risk, the court concluded that such a decision could not be achieved unilaterally, that is, without principled negotiation with other participants in Confederation within the existing constitutional framework.[59] In particular, the use of the language of minority protection – in favour of minorities within a minority, that is, aboriginal peoples and linguistic minorities (Anglophones) within Québec – to deny a minority their right to external self-determination exposes the court's ambivalence to the notion of self-determination. In this context, it can also be argued that what seemed to be a minority rights protection regime was in fact quite a deliberate means of limiting the nation-building efforts of a particular minority group (the Québécois).[60]

Yet, elsewhere, Franck locates peoples' (collective) right to self-determination in the concept of fairness: instead of being a general

---

[58] Gaetano Pentassuglia, 'Do Human Rights Have Anything to Say about Group Autonomy?', in *Ethno-Cultural Diversity and Human Rights*, ed. Gaetano Pentassuglia (Leiden: Brill-Nijhoff, 2018), 157.
[59] *Reference* case (1998), paras. 32–108, especially paras. 61–69.
[60] See D. Salée, 'Quebec Sovereignty and the Challenge of Linguistic and Ethno-cultural Minorities: Identity, Difference, and the Politics of Ressentiment', in *Contemporary Quebec: Selected Readings and Commentaries*, eds. M. D. Behiels and M. Hayday (Montreal: McGill-Queen's University Press, 2011), 472; Dwight Newman, 'Why Majority Rights Matter in the Context of Ethno-Cultural Diversity: The Interlinkage of Minority Rights, Indigenous Rights, and Majority Rights', in *Ethno-Cultural Diversity and Human Rights*, 74.

principle, he argues, self-determination of peoples is a principle that should be applied on a case-by-case basis using the fairness paradigm. Thus, the right to self-determination can prevail over territorial integrity in limited cases, such as the disintegration of existing states or where there would be economically maldistributive side effects.[61] In this liberal fairness discourse, ethnic claims to self-determination and ensuing conflicts are thus essentially perceived as 'post-modern neo-tribalism'. They are post-modern because ethnic tribalism is a direct challenge to modernism, tending to reverse the modernist process of globalising commerce, homogenising culture, and creating a global village, among other reasons.[62] They are neo-tribalist because ethnicity is no longer the monopoly of backward peoples, in that minority elites in modern societies also present their claims along ethnic lines.[63]

Like Franck, Tesón borrows directly from the Kantian framework to claim that the rights of states under international law derive their legitimacy from the rights and interests of individuals who reside within them.[64] Criticising traditional international legal scholarship for not acknowledging this normative structure and for thus perceiving international law as a matter between and among states, Tesón contends that 'the sovereignty of the state is dependent upon the state's domestic legitimacy; and therefore, the principles of international justice must be congruent with the principles of internal justice'.[65] Against this backdrop of the Kantian conception of the individual as the building block of international law, Tesón argues that liberal theory commits itself to 'normative individualism' – the idea that individuals constitute the primary units of a state.[66] Thus, for him, as a matter of general principle,

---

[61] See generally Franck, *Fairness in International Law and Institutions*, 140–169.
[62] Ibid., 140–141. See also Thomas Franck, 'Postmodern Tribalism and the Right to Secession', in *Peoples and Minorities in International Law*, eds. Catherine Brölmann, René Lefeber, and Marjoleine Zieck (Dordrecht: Martinus Nijhoff, 1993), 3–27; Rosalyn Higgins, 'Postmodern Tribalism and the Right to Secession: Comments', in *Peoples and Minorities in International Law*, 29–35. Koskenniemi notes that the Romantic ethnic challenge to statehood in the form of self-determination is 'post- (not pre-) modern precisely because of the urgent sense that these emerging identifications are not capable of being carried out by the creation of new States to represent them, with the unified, formal political structure of the modern State'. See Martti Koskenniemi, 'National Self-determination Today: Problems of Legal Theory and Practice', *International and Comparative Law Quarterly* 43, no. 1 (1994), 259.
[63] Franck, *Fairness*, 143–144.
[64] Tesón, 'The Kantian Theory of International Law', 53.
[65] Ibid., 54.
[66] Ibid.

groups defined by ethnic characteristics should not enjoy any special privilege '*merely by virtue of the fact that they possess some common ethnic trait*'.[67] His key criticism of the proposition that 'groups' have the right to self-determination therefore follows: such a position perceives the encompassing group as entitled to the right to self-determination on the basis of non-voluntary ethnic traits. This, according to Tesón, violates the fundamental liberal notion of consent and individual preference as the basis of political institutions.[68]

On the other hand, if the culture decays spontaneously as a result of 'market failure' – because individual members rationally prefer another culture to their own or because their ignorance or free-riding keeps them from contributing to the survival of their culture – Tesón argues, 'it is hard to see how that fact would justify special group rights or secession from a liberal state'.[69] Similarly, regarding the territorial claims thesis of the right to self-determination, Tesón endorses Lea Brilmayer's position that the role of ethnicity is limited to identifying the people making the territorial claim and that claims to territory do not follow ipso facto from ethnic distinctiveness.[70] Thus, a claim to a separate territory on the grounds of the oppression of a people within a territory can be addressed by simply eliminating such oppression.[71]

Tesón, however, offers specific exceptional conditions under which special group rights can be granted to minority groups. First, if any despotic government flagrantly violates human rights, then members of a group have the right to take necessary steps, even secession in relevant cases, to free themselves from that oppression, provided that no other means of redress is available.[72] Secondly, if injustice to groups takes the form of discriminatory redistribution of resources, groups with a territorial claim attain a moral right to greater autonomy or even to break up the existing state. However, if the group with territorial title does not intend to observe the human rights of its individual members, then its title to territory does not suffice to engender any right to self-

---

[67] Fernando Tesón, 'Ethnicity, Human Rights, and Self-Determination', in *International Law and Ethnic Conflict*, 86. Italics in original.
[68] Ibid., 88–89.
[69] Ibid.
[70] Ibid., 95.
[71] Ibid.
[72] Ibid., 99. Allan Buchanan calls this the 'remedial right to secession', which, according to him, can be rightfully exercised only in exceptional circumstances. See Allan Buchanan, 'Democracy and Secession', in *National-Self-determination and Secession*, ed. M. Moor (Oxford: Oxford University Press, 1998), 14–33.

determination.[73] And finally and most significantly, Tesón addresses the notion of ethnic 'group rights' by deconstructing the concept itself and claiming that group rights or collective rights are not distinct categories in the liberal theory. Philosophically, rights are individualised, non-aggregative, and distributive, in contrast to social policies, which are non-individualised, aggregative, and non-distributive.[74] In the classical liberal understanding of 'right', Tesón continues, collective rights in the conservative sense are not rights but aggregative social policies lacking 'deontological bite', and the word 'right' in 'collective right' is used only for rhetorical purposes.[75] He thus concludes that various conservative claims framed in the rhetorical language of collective or group rights cannot be called rights in the same sense that liberal theory defines rights.[76]

Thus, within this liberal-individualist framework of international law, other forms of self-determination short of outright secession are inconsistent with norms. Although David Wippman highlights the success of ethnicity-based power-sharing mechanisms in securing ethnic peace, he is nonetheless aware that such measures encounter the problem of compatibility with the existing liberal architecture of international human rights law. In general, power-sharing mechanisms tend to favour collective rights over individual rights. As Christine Bell notes, a global data set of peace agreements indicate three main functions for political power-sharing: permanent group accommodation, equitable representation of minorities in autonomy regimes, and transition management.[77] Many such practices appear discriminatory when viewed from a liberal-individualist perspective.[78] From an individual-rights standpoint, Wippman identifies at least three specific human rights norms that are infringed by power-sharing practices: first, decisions about these practices depend on characteristics such as race, religion, and language rather

[73] Tesón, 'Ethnicity, Human Rights, and Self-Determination', 107.
[74] Ibid., 103.
[75] Ibid., 105. Cf. Peter Jones, 'Human Rights, Group Rights and Peoples' Rights', *Human Rights Quarterly* 21 (1999), 82–83.
[76] Tesón, 'Ethnicity, Human Rights, and Self-Determination', 106. Tesón, nevertheless, mentions that 'nothing in [his argument] precludes the establishment of legal group rights or other forms of group autonomy for weighty pragmatic or prudential reasons, such as the need to avert ethnic conflict'. Ibid., 111.
[77] Bell, 'Power-Sharing, Conflict Resolution, and Women', 13–32.
[78] David Wippman, 'Practical and Legal Constraints on Internal Power Sharing', in *International Law and Ethnic Conflict*, 240. Cf. Christine Bell, *Peace Agreements and Human Rights* (Oxford: Oxford University Press, 2004); Christine Bell, 'Peace Settlements and Human Rights: A Post–Cold War Circular History', *Journal of Human Rights Practice* 9, no. 3 (2017), 358–378.

than on neutral merit-based criteria, thereby violating the fundamental liberal principle of non-discrimination on these grounds. Secondly, ethnic power-sharing practices may violate the participatory rights of individuals who are not members of a protected ethnic group. And, finally, some of the autonomy schemes place restrictions on individuals' efforts to settle in areas controlled by members of another ethnic group and, therefore, violate the right to freedom of movement and residence.[79]

Indeed, using power-sharing devices to confer power on particular groups in excess of what is reasonably necessary to protect their interests and in ways that are designed to deny other groups meaningful participation in the governance of the state may be taken as a violation of international human rights obligations. For example, the power-sharing aspects of consociationalism are challenged by established norms of equal rights to political participation for all, including the right to take part in the conduct of public affairs, the right to vote and to be elected, and the right to have access, on general terms of equality, to public services.[80] Consociational arrangements violate these rights of the members of the majority community by allowing minority ethnic groups political power disproportionate to their number, through reserved seats and offices, minority veto rights, or similar devices.[81] And finally, territorial autonomy for a particular ethnic group prevents the rest of the citizens from full enjoyment of the freedom of movement and residence stipulated in Article 12(1) of the International Covenant on Civil and Political Rights (ICCPR), which reads: 'Everyone lawfully within the territory of a State shall, within that territory, have the right to liberty of movement and freedom to choose his residence.' Similar provisions can also be found in Article 13 of the Universal declaration of human rights (UDHR) and Protocol No. 4, Article 2(1) of the European Convention for the Protection of Human Rights and Fundamental Freedoms.

In a reconciliatory move, Wippman therefore seeks refuge in interpretative techniques to expand the relevant human rights provisions in a way that would open up space, albeit limited space, to incorporate ethnicity-defined power-sharing measures. He argues that despite being violations of the international human rights instruments from an individualist perspective, power-sharing arrangements are not ipso facto violations of established human rights norms from a group perspective, and hence, they are compatible with international human rights law. Consociational

---

[79] Wippman, 'Practical and Legal Constraints', 231.
[80] Such rights are incorporated in Article 21 of the UDHR and Article 25 of the ICCPR.
[81] Wippman, 'Practical and Legal Constraints', 234.

practices, he continues, should be viewed not as creating separate or discriminatory rights for ethnic minorities but as enabling ethnic minorities to exercise their rights on a level as close as possible to parity with the dominant groups and thereby as ensuring equality among groups.[82]

Although he extends this analogy to the ICCPR, Wippman concedes that while it is possible to interpret general 'terms of equality' broadly enough to encompass the equality of groups rather than of individuals, 'such an interpretation seems inconsistent with the predominantly individual rights focus of the Covenant itself'.[83] Thus, in order to develop a legal justification for power-sharing, Wippman ultimately takes a 'purely pragmatic standpoint' and concludes that even if power-sharing mechanisms compromise some human rights norms, they can potentially 'help avoid the even greater injustices associated with other possible solutions'.[84]

A more recent edited volume, however, offers a more optimistic view on this question.[85] Its editor Pentassuglia highlights the increasingly multi-layered and hybrid role of ethno-cultural diversity in human rights discourse. He notes that while in some cases human rights practice enables vitally important group activity, in other cases it protects distinctive collective interests in a targeted way. Additionally, human rights discourse has the potential to create a framework for institutional and policy action to be worked out at the local level.[86]

Within this framework of hybridity, Peter Jones's piece in the volume draws a distinction between 'corporate' and 'collective' connotations of group rights to put forward the argument that group rights can be accommodated within the liberal framework of rights, which is premised upon the individual as the only right-bearer. Jones argues that while in the corporate conception of group rights, the group itself is the rightholder and therefore falls outside the liberal domain of rights, in the collective conception of group rights it is the individual members of such groups that hold the right. It is a group right nonetheless, for the group members hold the rights 'collectively rather than separately, jointly rather than severally'.[87] Seen through the optic of collective yet liberal 'group'

---

[82] Ibid., 233.
[83] Ibid., 237.
[84] Ibid., 241.
[85] See generally Pentassuglia (ed.), *Ethno-Cultural Diversity and Human Rights*.
[86] Gaetano Pentassuglia, 'Introduction: The Unpacking of Ethno-Cultural Diversity', in *Ethno-Cultural Diversity and Human Rights*, 1–24.
[87] Peter Jones, 'Collective and Group-Specific: Can the Rights of Ethno-Cultural Minorities Be Human Rights?' in *Ethno-Cultural Diversity and Human Rights*, 27–35. See also Jones, 'Human Rights, Group Rights and Peoples' Rights'.

rights, the right to self-determination belongs to the 'flesh-and-blood individuals' who constitute the relevant 'people' for the purpose of the right but who hold their right only collectively.[88] The essentialisation of individual right-holders and the omnipresence of 'fragmentation' as a tool for diffusing groups into individuals are hard to ignore in this liberal ideological construction of self-determination.

4.3.2 The Human Rights Approach to Minority 'Protection'

In 1950 the UN Sub-Commission on Prevention of Discrimination and Protection of Minorities formulated guidelines for a definition of the minority, one of which conceives the minority as those non-dominant groups in a given population that 'possess and wish to preserve stable ethnic, religious or linguistic traditions or characteristics markedly different from those of the rest of the population'.[89] The minority was defined accordingly in 1954.[90] A similar approach was adopted by Capotorti and Deschenes, the special rapporteurs on minorities, in their seminal works.[91] This trend is also unmistakably reflected in the post–Cold War international and European instruments. The text of the UN Declaration on the Rights of Persons Belonging to National or Ethnic, Religious and Linguistic Minorities (UNDM, 1992) and the document issued by the CSCE Meeting of Experts on National Minorities (1991) both perceive minorities as bearers of 'ethnic, cultural, linguistic and religious identity'.[92]

What is common to all definitions of the term 'minority' is the image of a group in a subordinate position, which has at its core certain ethnic features that the members of the group not only share but also intend to preserve as an insignia of their identity. In this sense, the minority is not only the 'other' of the majority within a given polity because of its

---

[88] Ibid.
[89] UN Commission on Human Rights, *Report of the Third Session of the Sub-Commission on the Prevention of Discrimination and the Protection of Minorities to the Commission on Human Rights* (30 January 1950), UN Doc E/CN.4/358; see also Kristin Henrard, *Devising an Adequate System of Minority Protection* (The Hague: Martinus Nijhoff, 2000), 20.
[90] UN Commission on Human Rights, *Report of the 10th Session, 23 February–16 April 1954*, Supplement No. 7 (April 1954), UN Doc E/2573, 48–49.
[91] For a detail discussion on the definition of 'minority', see Francesco Capotorti, *Study on the Rights of Persons Belonging to Ethnic, Religious or Linguistic Minorities* (20 May 1977), UN Doc E/CN.4/Sub.2/384/Rev.1, 5–15; see also Natan Lerner, *Group Rights and Discrimination in International Law*, 2nd ed. (The Hague: Martinus Nijhoff, 2003), 9.
[92] See Lerner, *Group Rights and Discrimination in International Law*, 22.

distinctive ethnic features, but also the 'other' of liberal universalism due to its tendency to portray its self-image in ethnic terms. In other words, this process of defining a minority can be seen as an ambiguous pronouncement: in one direction it speaks of the 'otherness' of the minority understood in terms of its ethnic differentiation from the majority, the converse of its 'otherness' being an affirmation of the ethnic homogeneity of the majority. In another direction it may speak to the liberal tradition by emphasising the contrast between those who are committed to speaking the language of ethnicity in their self-identification and the majority who have dispensed with such a tendency. Therefore, instead of being understood as an isolated object with certain distinctive features, the minority needs to be perceived in relational terms – it is in this uneven relationship with the majority (in the realm of power and in terms of demographic composition) and with liberalism (at the ideological level) that the 'minority' is consistently defined and understood as 'distinct' as well as primitive.

Having identified the minority as the backward ethnic 'other', international law within the liberal-individualist framework then attempts to suppress this very ethnic element when it comes to the 'protection' of minorities. The liberal disavowal of the protection of minorities in the conservative sense was explicit from the outset of the post–WWII world order. The issue of the protection of the constitutive features of minorities as well as their sense of solidarity (hereinafter minority protection) was carefully avoided during the San Francisco Conference, where few references to minorities were actually made.[93] In the UN Charter, discrimination on the basis of sex, race, language, religion, and birthplace is explicitly prohibited in a number of places,[94] and for the framers of the Charter, the reliance on non-discrimination was adequate to address the issue of minority rights.[95] Although the Sub-Commission on Prevention of Discrimination and the Protection of Minorities was created as a compensatory measure, its work towards the protection of minorities

---

[93] See Thornberry, *International Law and the Rights of Minorities*, 118; for a chronological account of minority protection in international law, see also Jennifer Preece, 'Minority Rights in Europe: From Westphalia to Helsinki', *Review of International Studies* 23 (1997), 75–92. Different historical approaches to minorities are briefly discussed in Jennifer Preece, 'National Minorities and International System', *Politics* 18 (1998), 17–23.

[94] Articles 1(3), 13, 55, and 76 of the UN Charter.

[95] Thornberry is of the opinion that 'the Charter *does* have a view on minorities to be read by necessary implication, that the issue is now part of human rights'. See Thornberry, *International Law and the Rights of Minorities*, 119.

made little progress due to its constant prioritisation of the prevention of discrimination.[96]

In the UDHR too, the principle of non-discrimination prevailed without any reference to minorities, although some efforts to accommodate minority rights provisions were initially made.[97] During the drafting process, it was generally agreed that provisions to secure the general rights of minorities should be included in the Declaration. The Commission on Human Rights during its first session and the Drafting Committee set up during the second session proposed texts to that effect.[98] The Sub-Commission put forward a similar proposal.[99] However, at the third session of the Commission, most delegates resisted any idea of minority protection in the Declaration on the grounds that it deals with groups rather than individuals, the latter being the subject of the Declaration.[100] Although during the first session of the Drafting Committee, the French delegate proposed a minority protection article to be incorporated in the UDHR,[101] he subsequently changed his position and noted that '[t]he Charter had shifted the centre of gravity by putting the emphasis on the universal aspect of human rights, and that had to be taken into consideration'.[102] He ultimately proclaimed that 'in France there were no minorities' while acknowledging that they existed in its colonial possessions and Non-Self-Governing Territories.[103]

The Latin American countries spoke strongly against incorporating any minority rights provision in the Declaration, primarily due to their concern that such provisions would disturb their 'national unity'. The Brazilian delegate was quite explicit on this point:

> If groups of foreigners living within a State remained too closely attached to the country of their origin, their assimilation into the country that had received them would be jeopardised. That country would be pursuing

---

[96] Joseph L. Kunz, 'The Present Status of the International Law for the Protection of Minorities', *American Journal of International Law* 48 (1954), 285–286.

[97] However, the Draft Outline of International Bill of Rights, prepared by the Division of Human Rights under the UN Secretariat, included a draft provision on minority protection. See UN Doc E/CN.4/AC.1/3 (4 June 1947), 16.

[98] See, respectively, W/CN.4/21, Annex F, Article 36, and E/CN.4/95, Annex A, Article 31.

[99] See E/CN.4/52, Section 1, Article 36.

[100] E/CN.4/SR.73–74. The Soviet Delegation's proposal for an effectively individualist cultural rights provision was also rejected in the third session. See UN Doc E/88 (28 June 1948), 44, Article 25.

[101] See UN Commission on Human Rights, *Report of the Drafting Committee (1st session) on an International Bill of Rights* (1 July 1947), UN Doc E/CN.4/21, Annex D, 65.

[102] *Draft Declaration of Human Rights (continued)*, UN Doc A/C.3/SR.147, 587.

[103] Ibid., UN Doc A/C.3/SR.161, 723.

a policy of national suicide if it were to harbour groups of foreign agents who might prove to be extremely dangerous.[104]

These countries also argued that the minority issue was a uniquely European problem. As countries of immigration, they did not think the same was relevant for them. Thus, given the universal nature of the UDHR, no minority rights issue should be included therein.[105] Australia adopted the same line of argument.[106] It appeared that a number of states adopted the French attitude of 'not our problem' in dealing with the minority question. As we shall see later, this attitude was also reflected in the wording of Article 27 of the ICCPR (1966), which starts with the phrase 'In those States in which [...] minorities exist'.

Speaking against the minority provision in the declaration, the Syrian delegate argued that the notion of minority protection had often been used as a political excuse to interfere with the domestic affairs of other nations. If it were to be incorporated in the Declaration, he was afraid that some nations would again feel justified in abusing that principle.[107] Going beyond realism, he also offered a normative argument against minority protection provisions: given that discrimination against any minority member could be the only possible rationale behind the minority protection principle, the provision was redundant as the Declaration proclaimed the equality of rights among all individuals without any distinction.[108]

The only serious demand for a minority rights provision came from the representatives of the USSR and Yugoslavia.[109] The Yugoslav delegate passionately argued for the protection of minority 'groups': in order to ensure the protection of the individuals who formed a community, that community must first of all be recognised and protected so that collective efforts can be made to create the necessary conditions for the enjoyment of those rights.[110] Thus, 'equality of individuals was impossible without the equality of the national groups to which they belonged'.[111] Refuting the argument that the Declaration with its focus on individual rights should not accommodate minority group rights, the USSR delegate argued that individuals could not

---

[104] Ibid., UN Doc A/C.3/SR.161, 721.
[105] Ibid., 721.
[106] Ibid., 724. See also UNGA, *Draft International Covenants on Human Rights: Report of the Third Committee* (5 December 1951), UN Doc A/5000, para. 120.
[107] *Draft Declaration of Human Rights (continued)*, UN Doc A/C.3/SR.162, 729.
[108] Ibid., UN Doc A/C.3/SR.163, 738.
[109] Denmark and Belgium also argued for minority protection in some cases.
[110] *Draft Declaration of Human Rights (continued)*, UN Doc A/C.3/SR.161, 720.
[111] Ibid., UN Doc A/C.3/SR.163, 736.

be considered apart from the community in which they lived and, therefore, there was no reason why the Declaration should not guarantee the rights of that community, since by so doing it would advance individual rights.[112]

Such views stood no chance of getting incorporated in the Declaration against the dominance of the liberal-individualist ideology in the UN. The dominant argument remained that the individual human rights would, in themselves, provide necessary protections to minorities through the principle of non-discrimination. The US delegate explicitly declared that there should be no minority provision in the Declaration, and asserted that 'the best solution of the problem of minorities was to encourage respect for human rights'.[113] This view was unsurprisingly endorsed by the British delegate, who held the view that the Declaration already fully protected the rights of all minorities, such as freedom of religion, freedom of the press and opinion, freedom of assembly, choice in education, and the right to participate in the cultural life of the communities; there was consequently no need for any separate minority rights provision.[114] A liberal-individualist human rights approach was thus considered adequate for dealing with minorities.

Later, in the context of the draft international human rights covenant, the British delegate made clear his expectation of the ultimate future of minorities: 'With the march of civilisation certain backward groups would in the course of time become assimilated, and it would be undesirable to insert a [minority protection] provision in the draft covenant which would oblige States to delay that inevitable historical process.'[115] The Australian delegate also found assimilation to be the 'only possible solution' to the cultural problem posed by Aborigines.[116] The Egyptian representative took the same stance and asked whether it was in the interest of 'progress' to encourage the perpetuation of minorities by granting them rights and privileges. He also warned off the correlation between the protection of minorities, on the one hand, and the proportionate persecution of them due to their very minority status, on the other.[117] The Chilean delegate was prepared to concede the principle of non-discrimination but firmly opposed the idea of granting any special rights, 'super rights' to take his

---

[112] Ibid., 738–739.
[113] Ibid., UN Doc A/C.3/SR.161, 726.
[114] Ibid., UN Doc A/C.3/SR.162, 731.
[115] UN Commission on Human Rights, *Summary Record of the 369th Meeting* (30 April 1953), UN Doc E/CN.4/SR369, 5.
[116] Ibid., 11.
[117] Ibid., 8.

terms, that might eventually culminate in an autonomous regime within a state. He found that prospect 'very dangerous'.[118] The same view was taken by Uruguay.[119] The Indian delegate too agreed with the Chilean delegation's apprehension that once a linguistic group felt itself to be a cultural entity it began to insist upon its rights and became reluctant to play its part in the common national life.[120] By that time, the notions of the unified national state, the sanctity of territorial integrity, and the liberal-individualist framework of rights had all merged together to offer a monolithic vision of statehood in international law, in which the minority was conceived as a backward, parochial connotation; hence, a constant threat to the liberal state.

Similarly, Article 27 of the ICCPR addressed the issue of minorities within the individualist framework of the Covenant.[121] The phrase 'in community with the other members of their group' surely envisages the right-bearer in the context of a group. Nevertheless, the right-bearers are definitely the individual members of the group, not the group as such.[122] This formulation was necessary, according to Capotorti, for three reasons: historical continuity; coherence with the overall individualist tone of the covenant; and, lastly and perhaps most importantly, mitigation of the threat to the territorial integrity and political independence of existing states while still upholding the individual freedom of voluntary assimilation.[123] The individualism in this article is substantiated when read with Article 5(1) of the Covenant, which stipulates that nothing in the Covenant will be interpreted in a way

---

[118] UN Commission on Human Rights, *Summary Record of the 368th Meeting* (30 April 1953), UN Doc E/CN.4/SR371, 4.
[119] UN Commission on Human Rights, *Summary Record of the 371st Meeting* (4 May 1953), UN Doc E/CN.4/SR368,
[120] UN Commission on Human Rights, *Summary Record of the 369th Meeting* (30 April 1953), UN Doc E/CN.4/SR369, 7.
[121] Article 27 stipulates: 'In those States in which ethnic, religious or linguistic minorities exist, persons belonging to such minorities shall not be denied the right, in community with the other members of their group, to enjoy their own culture, to profess and practice their religion, or to use their own language.' The Sub-Commission's proposed original text was amended to limit its scope and was finally adopted by twelve votes to one with three abstentions. The Pakistan delegate, Sir Abdur Rahman, voted against as he found the scope of the article quite limited due to amendments. See UN Doc E/CN.4/SR371, 7.
[122] As Jones explains, when individual members of a group hold rights as separate individuals, their several individual rights, though they lead to a collectivity, do not add up to a group right. A right is a group right only if it is borne by the group qua group; '[w]hat distinguishes a right as a group right is its subject rather than its object – who it is that holds the right rather than what the right is a right to'. See Jones, 'Human Rights, Group Rights and Peoples' Rights', 82–83.
[123] Capotorti Report, 35.

that would jeopardise the individual rights and freedoms guaranteed in other provisions of the Covenant. It is also reinforced in the Optional Protocol to the ICCPR, which recognises the competence of the Human Rights Committee to receive and consider communications only from individual victims.[124] As Rein Mullerson notes, Article 27 'does not grant minorities any privilege in comparison with the majority'; it is simply another aspect of the requirement of non-discrimination.[125]

A recent survey of the Human Rights Committee's engagement with Article 27 concludes that in cases where the Committee finds violations of Article 27, the Committee often finds such violations in conjunction with another article of the ICCPR; Article 27 itself does not receive much attention. And whatever attention is given to Article 27, it refers to 'the established quasi-jurisprudence of older communications or General Comment No. 23'.[126] More importantly, no claims on the violation of the right to self-determination have been admitted; the 'Human Rights Committee continues its sharp rejection of meddling with Article 1 of the ICCPR'.[127] As the former Chairperson-Rapporteur of the UN Forum on Minorities, Asbjørn Eide, approvingly notes, 'the rights of persons belonging to minorities are different from the rights of peoples to self-determination, and minority rights cannot serve as a basis for claims of secession or dismemberment of a State', although I noted earlier that the right to self-determination within the liberal framework is far away from generating any such secessionist possibility.[128] Thus, in *Kitok* v. *Sweden*

---

[124] Optional Protocol to the International Covenant on Civil and Political Rights (1966), Article 1. Thus, in the cases of *Lansman et al.* v. *Finland I and II* as well as *O. Sara et al.* v. *Finland*, although the group rights of the Sami indigenous communities of Finland were threatened by mining, logging, road construction, and related activities, the complainants brought the issue under Article 27 and not under Article 1 of the same covenant, which guarantees peoples' right to self-determination. See *Lansman et al.* v. *Finland*, HRC, Communication No. 511/1992 (8 November 1994), UN Doc CCPR/C/52/D/511/1992 and *O. Sara et al.* v. *Finland*, HRC, Communication No. 431/1990 (24 March 1994), UN Doc CCPR/C/50/D/431/1990. See also *Bernard Ominayak, Chief of the Lubicon Lake Band* v. *Canada*, HRC, Communication No. 167/1984 (26 March 1990), UN Doc Supp No. 40 (A/45/40). Cf. *Kitok* v. *Sweden*, HRC, Communication No. 197/1985 (10 August 1988), UN Doc CCPR/C/33/D/197/1985; *Lovelace* v. *Canada*, HRC, Communication No. 24/1977 (30 July 1981), UN Doc CCPR/C/OP/1.

[125] Rein Mullerson, 'Minorities in Eastern Europe and the Former USSR: Problems, Tendencies and Protection', *Modern Law Review* 56 (1993), 805.

[126] Ulrike Barten, 'Article 27 of ICCPR: A First Point of Reference', in *The United Nations Declaration on Minorities*, 62.

[127] Ibid.

[128] Asbjørn Eide, *Final Text of the Commentary to the Declaration on the Rights of National or Ethnic, Religious and Linguistic Minorities*, Sub-Commission on Promotion and Protection

case,[129] the Committee decided that the claim under Article 1 was inadmissible under the Optional Protocol, although subsequently in *J. G. A. Diergaardt et al. v. Namibia* case[130] and *Gillot et al. v. France* case[131] the Committee held that Article 1 is nevertheless relevant in the interpretation of other rights protected by the Covenant, in particular Articles 25, 26, and 27.[132] The issue of minority protection appeared in a number of other international human rights instruments and, necessarily, non-discrimination was the guiding principle in approaching the issue.[133]

From a liberal standpoint, this is nothing short of desired, in that within the liberal-individualist framework it is not even considered necessary to 'protect' any culture per se.[134] The protection of minorities in a liberal sense can at best be perceived as the protection of minorities from the very constitutive element of their identity – ethnicity. Given that ethnicity not only turns the minority into the victim of oppression by the majority but also undermines the individual rights of the minority group members, the liberal method of minority protection would thus logically mean the suppression of ethnicity through the individualist principles of equality and non-discrimination. In other words, the liberal version of minority protection appears as an emancipatory project: the liberal not only constructs minorities as a symbol of conservative backward traditions but also protects them from the curse of ethnicity – the very constitutive element of minorities. The conservative notion of minority protection, meaning the

---

of Human Rights (2 April 2001), UN Doc E/CN4/Sub2/AC5/2001/2, para. 84. *Travaux préparatoires* on Article 1 also confirm this. See UNGA, *Draft International Covenants on Human Rights: Report of the Third Committee* (8 December 1955), UN Doc A/3077, para. 39.

[129] *Kitok v. Sweden*, HRC, Communication No. 197/1985 (10 August 1988), UN Doc CCPR/C/33/D/197/1985.

[130] *J. G. A. Diergaardt et al. v. Namibia* case, HRC, Communication No. 760/1997 (25 July 2000), CCPR/C/69/D/760/1997, para. 10.3.

[131] *Gillot et al. v. France*, HRC, Communication No. 932/2000 (26 July 2002), UN Doc CCPR/C/75/D/932/2000, para. 13.4.

[132] Alexander H. E. Morawa, 'The United Nations Treaty Monitoring Bodies and Minority Rights, with Particular Emphasis on the Human Rights Committee', in *Mechanisms for the Implementation of Minority Rights*, eds. M. Weller and A. H. E. Morawa (Strasbourg: Council of Europe Publishing, 2004), 39.

[133] Such as the International Convention on the Elimination of All Forms of Racial Discrimination (1965) or the UNESCO Convention on the Elimination of Discrimination in Education (1980).

[134] See generally John Packer, 'Problems in Defining Minorities', in *Minority and Group Rights in the New Millennium*, eds. Deirdre Fottrell and Bill Bowring (Leiden: Brill, 1999), 223–273; Brian Barry, *Culture and Equality* (Cambridge: Polity Press, 2001); Chandran Kukathas, *The Liberal Archipelago* (Oxford: Oxford University Press, 2003).

promotion of ethnic features and solidarity, is therefore considered incompatible with liberalism.

Such a liberal regime of minority protection, from the perspective of ethnic minorities, readily permits the subordination of minorities to the majority culture under the veil of principles of non-discrimination, equality, and so on.[135] As Lucía Payero-López and Ephraim Nimni succinctly note, the conflation of equality with 'sameness', in the name of liberalism, leads to egalitarian citizenship laws in which citizens enjoy equal rights through a common culture. But in reality, it is usually the culture of the dominant group that equates to the national culture: the dominant group's language becomes the official language of the state; the religion and culture of the dominant group are privileged in state symbols such as the flag and national anthem; broadcasting and educational outlets emphasise the culture of the dominant group.

> Yet this is done while democratic policies in the state-making process highlight a broad and inclusive citizenship that provides equal individual rights to all. All individuals are equal under the culture of the dominant [group], but minority [groups] tend not to have collective representation. Here the minorities' accusations of hypocrisy are difficult to refute.[136]

In the aftermath of the Cold War, the protection of minorities in ethnic terms once again gained attention as a viable pragmatic response to ethnic tension. The UNDM (1992) is the iconic document in this context, accommodating the post–Cold War consciousness about the ethnic dimension of minority protection.[137] The impetus for adopting the Declaration surely came from security concerns within Europe due to emerging ethnic tensions, for in the decade from 1978 to 1988 only four articles of the Declaration had been agreed and significant parts of the draft were left open for further renegotiation.[138] It is also noted that the drafting group's

---

[135] See Antony Anghie, 'Human Rights and Cultural Identity: New Hope for Ethnic Peace', *Harvard International Law Journal* 33 (1992), 345.

[136] Lucía Payero-López and Ephraim Nimni, 'The Liberal Democratic Deficit in Minority Representation: The Case of Spain', in *Ethno-Cultural Diversity and Human Rights*, ed. Gaetano Pentassuglia (Leiden: Brill-Nijhoff, 2018), 99. Footnotes omitted. Although they made this argument in the context of various 'nations' within the state of Spain, the argument has relevance for all modern states in general and postcolonial states in particular.

[137] UN General Assembly, *Declaration on the Rights of Persons Belonging to National or Ethnic, Religious and Linguistic Minorities*, Resolution 47/135 of 18 December 1992, UN Doc A/RES/47/135.

[138] See Alan Phillips, 'Historical Background on the Declaration', in *The United Nations Declaration on Minorities*, 7.

sessions were not well attended and did not attract much interest.[139] When the declaration was finally adopted by consensus under Resolution 47/135 of 18 December 1992, it was without the customary applause, as excitement for the Declaration had already declined with the eruption of ethnic violence in the Balkans.[140] The Declaration remains the sole UN document dedicated to minority rights. Although designed to address the rights of individuals, the Declaration formulates state responsibilities towards the minority groups. Unlike Article 27, the Declaration makes it clear that these rights often require action, including protective measures and the encouragement of conditions that promote minority identity,[141] and specifies active measures by the state.[142]

However, the process was far from being straightforward. It was not an easy task to break with the dominant liberal-individualist approach to minority protection; a consistent balance had to be struck. Thus, in the first place, the Declaration advocated rights for individuals in line with Article 27, and not for any group. In his oft-cited Commentary on the Declaration, Eide confirms: 'The rights of persons belonging to minorities are individual rights, even if they in most cases can only be enjoyed in community with others.'[143] Therefore, the right to self-determination, which is a collective right of peoples, is outside the purview of the Declaration. The issue of autonomy shares the same fate.

This view is shared by Gudmundur Alfredsson, who asserts that the Declaration 'even falls below the standards' that were already set forth, for example, in the ICCPR, the International Convention on the Elimination of All Forms of Racial Discrimination, and the Convention against Discrimination in Education, and remains 'disappointingly incomplete' in the breadth and depth of the issues involved.[144] He finds the Declaration too much focused on individual rights and weak in tone, with qualifications such as 'where appropriate', 'wherever possible', and 'in a manner not incompatible with national legislation'.[145] Moreover, as Kristin Henrard claims, the Declaration has little or no concrete content in relation to the right to enjoy one's own culture, the right to profess and practise one's own

---

[139] Gudmundur Alfredsson, 'Minority Rights and the United Nations', in *The United Nations Declaration on Minorities*, 38.
[140] Phillips, 'Historical Background on the Declaration', 10.
[141] Ibid., Article 1.
[142] Ibid., Article 4.
[143] Eide, *Final Text of the Commentary*, para. 15.
[144] Alfredsson, 'Minority Rights and the United Nations', 38.
[145] Ibid.

MINORITIES WITHIN THE LIBERAL INTERNATIONAL LAW   169

religion, or the right to participate in the religious life of the state.[146] In the final evaluation, Henrard depicts the provisions of the Declaration as merely some open 'guidelines' for states with positive attitudes towards minority protection.[147]

The ambivalence of international law towards minority protection is reflected in the recent South Asian regional attempt to come up with a legal framework for minority protection, namely, the South Asian Regional Charter on Minority and Group Rights. The Charter, initiated by five regional human rights organisations, was finalised by the Sri Lanka-based International Centre for Ethnic Studies in 2008.[148] The Charter was designed to enhance regional responses to minority issues by addressing constitutional and other legislative drawbacks and also to serve as a reference tool for various governmental and non-governmental policymaking and advocacy organisations.[149] As discussed in previous chapters, the notion of 'minority' is a contested idea in the region, given the bitter histories of colonial divide-and-rule policy, the ethno-religious nature of the nationalist movement, postcolonial nation-building, and so on. In that context, any regional attempt to develop a legal framework for minority protection in South Asia is commendable. And the specific mention of 'group rights' in the title is difficult to ignore.

However, in actually dealing with the issue, the Charter hardly deviated from the established human rights approaches to minority protection. The Charter was essentially imagined within the already fragile and toothless international framework.[150] For example, in affirming the right to identity and characteristics, the Charter adopted the formulation of the UNDM (1992).[151] More importantly, in the provision dealing with implementation of these rights, the Charter does not move beyond the weak formulations of obligations in the UNDM and the European Framework Convention, such as that state parties 'should ensure', 'should cooperate',

---

[146] Henrard, *Devising an Adequate System of Minority Protection*, 192.
[147] Ibid., 193.
[148] The five regional organisations are: International Centre for Ethnic Studies (Sri Lanka), Centre for Policy Alternatives (Sri Lanka), Human and Democratic Forum (Nepal), Mahanirban Calcutta Research Group (India), and the Human Rights Commission of Pakistan (Pakistan). The full text of the Charter is available at www.eurac.edu/Org/Minorities/eurasia-net/index.htm.
[149] See the Preamble of the Charter in ibid.
[150] See Article 6 of the Charter in ibid.
[151] See also Thomas Benedikter, 'The South Asian Regional Charter on Minority and Group Rights: A Proposal for Soft Law at Its Softest', in *European Yearbook on Minority Issues* (special issue on South Asia), eds. Arie Bloed, et al. (Bolzano: EURAC, 2010), 121.

and 'should promote'.[152] Thus, the provision on the use of minority language reads:

> In areas traditionally inhabited by substantial numbers of persons belonging to a minority, if there is sufficient demand, the State Parties to the present Charter shall endeavour to ensure, where resources permit, and within the framework of their education systems, that persons belonging to those minorities have adequate opportunities for being taught the minority language or for receiving instruction in this language.

Thomas Benedikter finds it surprising and regrettable that such a vague formulation was chosen by a group of human rights activists and not by diplomats and politicians.[153] Unsurprisingly, as the institutional mechanism for the promotion of minority and group rights too, the Charter recommends a South Asian Human Rights Commission, rather than a minority rights commission.[154]

So far as the general situation of minority protection in South Asia is concerned, Joshua Castellino and Elvira Domínguez-Redondo note that while postcolonial states in the region demonstrate a clear awareness of minority issues – especially in the context of constitutional debates – paranoia of the Partition (1947) or simple pragmatism have resulted in a state architecture that is heavily majoritarian and aimed at consolidating state power. As a result, the region's track record shows minority protection that is considerably weaker than international practice.[155]

Minority protection in the Southeast Asian region is no better. A recent work on the Association of Southeast Asian Nations (ASEAN) demonstrates that even the general idea of human rights, let alone minority rights, is peripheral to the functioning of ASEAN.[156] Although some initiatives have recently been taken to promote the human rights of women, children, and migrant workers, ASEAN members continue to prioritise the non-

---

[152] Ibid., 122.
[153] His frustration on this point appears in three different places in a relatively short piece. See ibid., 122, 123, and 124.
[154] This point is noted by David Keane, 'Draft South Asian Regional Charter on Minority and Group Rights: Comparative Regional Analysis', in *European Yearbook on Minority Issues*, 153–157.
[155] Joshua Castellino and Elvira Domínguez-Redondo, 'The Declaration and Its Guidance: A View from South Asia', *The United Nations Declaration on Minorities*, 294, 304. For a general discussion on the state of minority protection in South Asia, see Borhan Uddin Khan and Mahbubur Rahman, *Protection of Minorities: Regimes, Norms, and Issues in South Asia* (Newcastle: Cambridge Scholars Publishing, 2012).
[156] Arie Bloed and Nicole Girard, 'ASEAN: Background and Human Rights Mechanisms', in *The United Nations Declaration on Minorities*, 306.

interference principle. As a result, serious human rights violations in member states are often labelled as 'internal affairs' not to be discussed at ASEAN meetings.[157] The evasive nature of the ASEAN Chairman's statement on the Rohingya situation epitomises this point:

> The Foreign Ministers of ASEAN expressed concern over the *recent developments* in Northern Rakhine State of Myanmar and extended their deepest condolences to all the victims and affected communities of the conflict. They condemned the attacks *against* Myanmar security forces on 25 August 2017 and all acts of violence which resulted in loss of civilian lives, destruction of homes and displacement of large numbers of people.[158]

By the time this farcical statement was released on 24 September 2017, describing Rohingya persecution as 'recent developments', the UN Human Rights Council had already described the situation as a 'textbook example of ethnic cleansing' and a 'potential case of genocide' against the Rohingya – committed 'by' Myanmar security forces.

Thus, this account of the liberal notion of minority protection demonstrates international law's rigorous efforts to eliminate ethnicity from the idea of minority protection. While such efforts were premised upon the liberal-individualist philosophy and marked the dawn of a new universal regime of human rights in the aftermath of WWII, the de facto existence of minorities in the ethnic form and the ensuing pragmatic needs gradually made accommodating minorities necessary. However, the overall individualist tone of the existing regime of rights – the celebrated universal norm that has been advocated to the postcolonial world as a policy prescription for ethnic peace – remained an obstacle to the effective accommodation of minorities. What appears as a result is the rhetoric of minority protection, without the actual creation of any legal norm to this effect that would undercut liberalism itself.

The liberal vision of the state and its individualist treatment of minorities are essentially premised upon the notions of equality and non-discrimination among individual citizens. As the liberals argue, it is precisely this idea of equal citizenship within a state that refutes the proposition of protecting any group simply because of its ethnicity or religion. The liberal human rights regime is arguably designed to ensure that individual citizens enjoy their rights without any discrimination on the grounds of sex, religion, colour, place of birth, and so on. Citizenship

---

[157] Ibid., 307.
[158] Available at www.asean.org. Emphasis added.

is, therefore, what Arendt called 'the right to have rights'.[159] As we shall see later, the issue of citizenship within the liberal framework of rights is relevant to both the case studies. Therefore, the international legal regime on citizenship rights deserves some elaboration here.

Arendt's now-famous framework of understanding citizenship as the core of human rights has been used in subsequent scholarship in multiple ways. Alison Kesby, for example, explains 'the right to have rights', first, as an expression of a 'place in the world in the sense of a place of lawful residence'.[160] Due to the legal and political configuration of the global space and the way international law has developed, she argues, our physical presence is characterised through our legal status, which depends upon our nationality.[161] Under customary international law, the state's duty to admit its nationals to reside within its borders is the product of the system of 'territorially sovereign states'[162] and is the essence of nationality.[163] In international human rights, this mere inter-state duty becomes the right of the individual; the individual is at the centre.[164] In Kesby's second formulation of 'the right to have rights', the phrase offers a framework for the right to nationality in line with the incorporation of the said right in the UDHR. Of the different meanings of the right to nationality within this strand, what is of particular significance for our purpose is the understanding of nationality as the essence of democratic governance, where the relevant sphere of belonging and inclusion 'is the national political community with nationality as the status which provides the individual with voice within it'.[165] In this approach, democratic principles form the justificatory basis for the conferral of nationality, and nationality serves as the bridge for political participation within the state of residence.[166] And, finally, Kesby conceptualises the 'right to have rights' as citizenship, where membership in a political community is essential and a prerequisite for the enjoyment of all rights[167] and where both de jure and de facto membership in a community is vital for the exercise of political

---

[159] Hannah Arendt, *The Origins of Totalitarianism* (London: Allen and Unwin, 1967), 296.
[160] Alison Kesby, *The Right to Have Rights: Citizenship, Humanity, and International Law* (Oxford: Oxford University Press, 2012), 13.
[161] Ibid., 13–16.
[162] Haro van Panhuys, *The Role of Nationality in International Law: An Outline* (Leyden: A. W. Sythoff, 1959), 56.
[163] Kesby, *The Right to Have Rights*, 16.
[164] Ibid.
[165] Ibid., 57.
[166] Ibid., 58.
[167] Ibid., 67.

and civil rights.[168] Whichever framework one chooses, the concept of 'the right to have rights' constitutes the core of what citizenship is all about, a key consequence of statelessness being the 'loss of the very right to have rights'.[169]

Conventionally, international law left the issue of citizenship in the hands of sovereign states and offered them broad discretionary power to decide on it. In the *Tunis-Morocco Nationality Decrees* case, the PCIJ held the opinion that nationality fell within a domain of legal competence reserved for internal law, although it may be limited by treaty obligations.[170] However, the court's argument that in the absence of treaty obligations customary international law did not limit state authority to ascribe nationality was reversed in the *Polish Nationality* case.[171] The Harvard Convention of Nationality (1929) in its commentary also supported the court's view that custom and general principles of international law also restricted the state's internal competence to confer nationality.[172] However, the commentary did not specify the nature or content of those limits.[173]

To address the ambiguity on the extent of states' discretion when they lack any clear legal obligation, human rights jurisprudence stepped in. Under the UDHR, everyone has the right to a nationality and the right not to be arbitrarily deprived of their nationality,[174] although there is no corresponding legal obligation on states to grant nationality.[175] The obligation was incorporated in the ICCPR but only with reference to children.[176]

---

[168] Ibid., 86.
[169] Matthew Gibney, 'Statelessness and Citizenship in Ethical and Political Perspectives', in *Nationality and Statelessness under International Law*, eds. Alice Edwards and Laura van Waas (Cambridge: Cambridge University Press, 2014), 52. Arendt and other international law scholars attempted to address this problem by including the right to nationality in the UDHR. Paradoxically, the principles of human rights would maintain that 'being human is the right to have human rights' irrespective of nationality status. See David Weissbrodt and Clay Collins, 'The Human Rights of Stateless Persons', *Human Rights Quarterly* 28 (2006), 248–259.
[170] *Nationality Decrees Issued in Tunis and Morocco (French Zone* case), PCIJ Reports (1923), Ser. B, No. 4, para. 24.
[171] *Acquisition of Polish Nationality* case, PCIJ Reports (1923), Ser. B, No. 7.
[172] Research in International Law of the Harvard Law School, 'The Law of Nationality', *American Journal of International Law* 23 no. 1 (1929), 25.
[173] Robert Sloane, 'Breaking the Genuine Link: The Contemporary International Legal Regulation of Nationality', *Harvard International Law Review* 50, no. 1 (2009), 7.
[174] Article 15 of the UDHR.
[175] Alice Edwards, 'The Meaning of Nationality in International Law in an Era of Human Rights: Procedural and Substantive Aspects', in *Nationality and Statelessness under International Law*, 14.
[176] Article 24(3) of the ICCPR.

Even then, there is no obligation on state parties to grant nationality to every child born in a state or to protect every child against arbitrary deprivation of nationality.[177] The Human Rights Council, nevertheless, asserts that the article requires states to adopt appropriate measures 'both internally and in cooperation with other States, to ensure that every child has a nationality'.[178] The UN Secretary General held in 2009 that the right to a nationality implies both the right of each individual to acquire, change, and retain their nationality and protection against arbitrary removal of nationality.[179] International conventions on statelessness, despite low ratification rates for them, are also important instruments in this regard.[180] Paradoxically, in practice, the enjoyment and protection of many human rights are dependent upon citizenship rights that require legal nationality.[181] Such a lack of voice makes the stateless particularly vulnerable.[182] The statelessness of the Rohingya illustrates the case here.

While individual right to citizenship on the basis of equality and non-discrimination is the very basic premise upon which the liberal state is organised, as I demonstrated in the preceding discussion, mere citizenship protected by the individualist canon of equality and non-discrimination is not adequate for the meaningful protection of minority groups. I have also argued that the very language of equality often serves as an ideology to perpetuate inequality among groups. As the case study on the hill people of the CHT will highlight, the guarantee of equal citizenship under the liberal constitutional framework failed to protect the hill people from political, economic, and cultural aggression by the majority.

The foregoing discussion on the liberal treatment of self-determination and minority rights reveals how international law fragments the group identity of minorities and reduces them to individual subjects of human rights. In cases where group-oriented measures are accommodated for pragmatic reasons, such as to prevent ethnic conflicts, those measures often face compatibility crises when accommodated within the dominant liberal-individualist framework of rights. The liberal-universalist ideology

---

[177] For this argument, see Edwards, 'The Meaning of Nationality', 14.
[178] HRC CCPR, *General Comment 17 on Rights of the Child* (7 April 1989), para 8.
[179] Report of the Secretary General to the General Assembly, *Human Rights and Arbitrary Deprivation of Nationality* (14 December 2009), UN Doc A/HRC/13/34, para 21.
[180] Convention Relating to the Status of Stateless Persons (1954) and Convention on the Reduction of Statelessness (1961). Article 7 of the Convention on the Rights of the Child (CRC) also imposes the duty on states to prevent statelessness with respect to children.
[181] See Lindsey Kingston, 'A Forgotten Human Rights Crisis: Statelessness and Issue (Non) Emergence', *Human Rights Review* 14, no. 2 (2013), 76.
[182] See Gibney, 'Statelessness and Citizenship in Ethical and Political Perspectives', 52.

offers postcolonial states the template for a constitutional architecture of rights that naturally refrains from conceding any special rights to minorities beyond the human rights norms of equality and non-discrimination. In this way, international law facilitates the ideology of the postcolonial 'liberal' state, thereby denying minority groups adequate protection against the majoritarian hegemony and dominance. Such a policy of dismantling the notion of minorities in the postcolonial legal structure also advances the ideology of the 'national' state. It is against this background of the liberal-individualist response to self-determination and minority protection under international law that in the following two sections I critically engage with the cases of the Rohingya and the CHT hill people to substantiate my argument.

4.4 The Case of the Rohingya in Myanmar

International responses to the Rohingya humanitarian crisis are an archetypal example of the individualist human rights approach to the persecution of a people due to their distinct religious and cultural identity. For example, the August 2017 Final Report of the Advisory Commission on Rakhine State, established at the behest of Myanmar's State Counsellor and Nobel Peace Laureate Aung San Suu Kyi, adopted the human rights approach to the Rohingya minority crisis in its recommendations. Although the Commission was conceived of as a national entity and the majority of its members were from Myanmar, Suu Kyi chose the former UN Secretary General Kofi Annan to chair it, thereby securing an international profile for the Commission. Under the Commission's terms of reference, agreed by the Government of Myanmar and the Kofi Annan Foundation, the Commission's mandate was to analyse the situation of all communities in Rakhine State and identify the factors that have resulted in violence, displacement, and underdevelopment.[183] In its Final Report, the Commission predictably recommended measures such as increased investment and economic development in Rakhine State and a series of civil and political rights – including citizenship, freedom of movement, and communal participation and representation – for the Rohingya. Although there are mentions in the report of inter-communal cohesion and protection of cultural sites, there is no mention of any protection for Rohingya group identity. As a matter of fact, the report makes it clear at the outset that at Suu Kyi's

---

[183] *Final Report of the Advisory Commission*, 12.

request, the Commission refrained from even using the word 'Rohingya', instead referring to 'Muslims' or 'the Muslim community in Rakhine'.[184]

A close reading of the reports of UN Special Rapporteurs on Myanmar over a number of years reveals the same human rights approach of equality and non-discrimination to minority problems in Myanmar in general and the Rohingya in particular. The 2016 report, for example, states that

> In order to combat discrimination against minorities, the Government of Myanmar should:
>
> (a) Implement a comprehensive set of measures to combat and prevent acts of incitement to discrimination, hostility and violence against minorities, including an anti-discrimination law or policy, while upholding internationally recognized human rights standards;
> (b) Lift the curfew order and restrictions on freedom of movement in Rakhine State;
> (c) Remove all discriminatory local orders, instructions and other policies and practices.[185]

So far as the Rohingya minority is concerned, these reports rightly expressed concerns about the discriminatory citizenship laws against the Rohingya but did not go beyond the framework of individualist citizenship rights. Similarly, in its recommendation, the 2018 report specifically asks the Myanmar government to implement the recommendation of the Annan Commission Report (2017), which simply involves a series of individual human rights measures, as we have just seen.[186]

The recent report of the Independent International Fact-Finding Mission on Myanmar established by the Human Rights Council under Resolution 34/22 offered a detailed and horrific account of atrocities of genocidal nature committed primarily by the Myanmar Army (the Tatmadaw) against the country's minorities, especially the Rohingya.[187] However, the recommendations of the report follow the long tradition of full reliance on the individualist notion of equality and non-discrimination. The report of the Independent Commission thus asks the Myanmar government to implement the prior recommendations of

---

[184] Ibid., 12.
[185] UN General Assembly, *Report of the Special Rapporteur on the Situation of Human Rights in Myanmar 2016* (29 August 2016), UN Doc A/71/361, para. 100.
[186] UN General Assembly, *Report of the Special Rapporteur on the Situation of Human Rights in Myanmar 2018* (20 August 2018), UN Doc A/73/332, para. 77.
[187] *Report of the Detailed Findings of the Independent International Fact-Finding Mission on Myanmar*, UN Doc A/HRC/39/CRP2.

the UN Special Rapporteur as well as the Annan Commission.[188] The report also recommends that the government ensure full enjoyment of human rights for all citizens on the basis of full equality regardless of citizenship or 'national race' status and, to that end, that it 'replace the concept of citizenship based on "national race" with a citizenship regime based on objective, non-discriminatory criteria'.[189]

The individual right to citizenship on the basis of equality and non-discrimination is the very basic premise upon which the liberal state is organised. Yet, as I demonstrated earlier, mere citizenship protected by the individualist canon of equality and non-discrimination is not adequate for the meaningful protection of minority groups. In the case of the Rohingya, however, they have been denied even this basic citizenship right. It is only appropriate that international law responses to the Rohingya humanitarian crisis take up the issue of citizenship seriously – but as the point of departure and not as the end.

4.4.1 The Issue of Rohingya Citizenship

Citizenship and allegiance to the state are the most contentious issues in Myanmar so far as the Rohingya are concerned. During WWII, while the Burmese nationalist leaders under the leadership of General Aung San and his Anti-Fascist People's Freedom League (AFPFL) made an alliance with the Japanese to expedite national independence from the British, most ethnic minorities sided with the British. The Rohingya supported the underground V Force that was established by the British during the Burma Campaign to gather intelligence.[190] The only exception was the Rakhine Buddhist minority in Arakan, who continued to attack British military forces even after the war had ended.[191] The fact that the Rohingya Muslims helped the British during the war was used to question Rohingya allegiance to the state since then.

During British rule, no attempt was made to define citizenship of Burma, but the term 'foreigner' was spelled out as applying to subjects of foreign states in the Foreigners Act (1864). The Act was designed to prevent foreigners from residing or sojourning in Burma, and from passing through or travelling therein without prior

---

[188] Ibid., para. 1674.
[189] Ibid., para. 1681 (a).
[190] Yegar, *The Muslims of Burma*, 34.
[191] Martin Smith, *Burma: Insurgency and the Politics of Ethnicity* (London: Zed Books, 1991), 71.

permission.[192] The British also enacted the Registration of Foreigners Act in 1940; it required foreigners to report and register themselves with the relevant authority.[193] Under this law, all registered foreigners were issued Foreigner Registration Certificates, which in some cases were later used to assign foreigner status to members of unrecognised minority groups.[194] A 'Burma national' was, however, defined in the Aung San-Atlee Agreement of 27 January 1947, which paved the way for Myanmar's independence and set the framework for the Constituent Assembly of the nascent state. Under Annex A of the Agreement, for the purpose of eligibility to vote and to stand as a candidate at the election of the Constituent Assembly, a Burma national was defined as a 'British subject or the subject of an Indian State who was born in Burma and resided there for a total period not less than eight years in the ten years immediately preceding either 1st January, 1942 or 1st January, 1947'.[195]

After independence, Aung San's government in power demonstrated a genuine interest in national unity in line with most newly independent postcolonial states and their vision of the 'national' state. As a matter of fact, the Burmese Constituent Assembly had close cooperation from its Indian counterpart in translating the common vision of a strong and unified national state into the future constitution.[196] Given the ethnic diversity of Burma, the constitution of 1947 went far beyond that of most postcolonial states – granting constituent states even a right to secession, though not to be exercised within the first ten years of independence.[197] In line with the dominant liberal ideology of the time, the constitution largely avoided classifications between and among citizens. The preamble of the constitution declared equal rights for all and included guarantees of equality of status and social, economic, and political justice for all citizens. The constitution extended citizenship to anyone who belonged to an 'indigenous race' of Burma, had a grandparent from an 'indigenous race', was a child of citizens, or was born in and lived in British Burma

---

[192] The Foreigners Act, India Act III, 1864.
[193] The Registration of Foreigners Act, Burma Act VII, 1940.
[194] Mehmet Şükrü Güzel, *Solving Statelessness in Myanmar* (Ankara: Sonçağ Matbaacilik Ltd., 2018), 109.
[195] Nicholas Mansergh, *Documents and Speeches on British Commonwealth Affairs 1931–1952*, vol. II (Oxford: Oxford University Press, 1953), 770.
[196] CAD, vol. IV, para. 4.22.46 (14 July 1947).
[197] See Chapter X of the Constitution of the Union of Burma, 1947.

prior to 1942.[198] The Union Citizenship Act of 1948 specified the 'indigenous races' as the Arakanese, Burmese, Chin, Kachin, Karen, Kayah, Mon, and Shan, and also racial groups that settled in any of the territories included within the Union as their permanent home from a period prior to 1823.[199] All these provisions, along with the mention of the broad category of Arakanese (as opposed to Rakhine, which specifically refers to the Arakanese Buddhists) as an indigenous race, allowed no doubt about the Rohingya's citizenship status, and many Rohingyas did not even bother to apply for a citizenship certificate under the Union Citizenship (Election) Act of 1948.[200]

Following the assassination of Aung San along with six of his council members in July 1947, only a few months before the country's independence, U Nu came to power and became the first Prime Minister of the independent Burma. He had a different vision of unity for the nation – Buddhist nationalism, which was naturally inclined to exclude non-Buddhists from the national self-image. Thus, under the new regime, the Rohingya were driven from the civil service as well as all other official positions in Arakan and replaced with Buddhist administrators of the AFPFL.[201] With direct patronage of the government, the Rakhine Buddhist community emerged as the dominant force in the region; they forced many Rohingya off their land and allowed the Buddhist refugees to return to re-build their homes destroyed during the war.[202] Restrictions were imposed on Rohingya movements outside north Arakan, thereby limiting their employment opportunities.[203] Despite the harsh treatment of the Rohingya, their citizenship was not denied. U Nu reportedly accepted Rohingyas as citizens in a speech: 'the people living in Maungdaw and Buthidaung regions are our nationals, our brethren. They are called Rohingyas. They are one of the same par in status of

---

[198] See Article 11, ibid.
[199] See Section 3 of the Union Citizenship Act, 1948.
[200] For a detailed analysis of the citizenship status of the Rohingya, see Archana Parashar and Jobair Alam, 'The National Laws of Myanmar: Making of Statelessness for the Rohingya', *International Migration* 57, no. 1 (2019), 94–108. See also *Letto Law Danga v. The Union of Burma*, BLR 30 (1959) HC; *Hasan Ali and Meher Ali*, Criminal Miscellaneous Applications No. 155 (1959); *Karam Singh v. The Union of Burma*, BLR 25 (1956) SC; *Bishna Lal v. The Union of Burma*, BLR 3 (1959) HC.
[201] Harrison Akins, 'The Two Faces of Democratization in Myanmar: A Case Study of the Rohingya and Burmese Nationalism', *Journal of Muslim Minority Affairs* 38, no. 2 (2018), 235.
[202] Ibid.
[203] J. A. Berlie, *The Burmanization of Myanmar's Muslims* (Bangkok: White Lotus Press, 2008), 56.

nationality with Kachin, Kyah, Karen, Mon, Rakhine and Shan. They are one of the ethnic races of Burma.'[204] So far as U Nu's approach to minorities in general is concerned, he saw them as a threat to national unity and integration; thus, he opposed the idea of any special minority rights:

> The term "Minority Rights" is a clever invention of the Imperialists to enable them to divide-and-rule over us for as long as they please. With this spectre they have succeeded in dividing us further and further apart [...] So long as we allow this spectre of Minority Rights to continue in our midst, so long shall our efforts to achieve Unity and national solidarity be of no avail.[205]

By that time, India too had come to the same conclusion.

Notwithstanding, ethnic minorities continued to intensify demands for regional autonomy, demands that ultimately served as an excuse for the armed forces to take power in a coup d'etat in 1962.[206] As the new Prime Minister, General Ne Win opted for a unitary state with centralised power. The very justification for the military takeover – restoring order and maintaining national unity – meant suppressing ethnic minorities across the country in a brutal fashion. The already marginalised Rohingya minority was hit disproportionately as the new government recognised the Buddhist Rakhine as the only indigenous race in Arakan under the new constitution of 1974. The constitution also toughened provisions regarding acquiring citizenship by requiring that a citizen must be a person born of parents who were both nationals of Myanmar or have been vested with citizenship according to existing laws.[207]

It was under the initiative of Ne Win that in 1976 preparations began for the drafting of the notorious Citizenship Law (1982) that ultimately stripped the Rohingya of their citizenship right. This new citizenship law offers three categories of citizenship with corresponding colour-coded

---

[204] Radio speech by Prime Minister U Nu on 25 September 1954 at 8 pm and public speeches by Prime Minister and Defense Minister U Ba Swe at Maungdaw and Buthidaung, respectively, on 3 and 4 November 1959. Cited in Md. Mahbubul Haque, 'Rohingya Ethnic Muslim Minority and the 1982 Citizenship Law in Burma', *Journal of Muslim Minority Affairs* 37, no. 4 (2017), 466.

[205] U Nu, *Burma Looks Ahead. Translation of selected speeches by the Honorable PM of the Union of Burma, delivered on various occasions from 19th July 1951 to 4th August 1952* (Rangoon: The Ministry of Information, Government of Burma, 1952), 15.

[206] It needs to be noted that U Nu invited the armed forces earlier to run the country as a caretaker government during 1958–1960.

[207] See Article 145 of the Constitution of the Union of Burma, 1974. Cf. corresponding provision in the 1947 Constitution that required one to have lived in Burma prior to 1942 or to have a grandparent of the recognised indigenous race.

Citizen Scrutiny Cards. Full Citizenship (pink cards) belongs to '*Nationals* such as the Kachin, Kayah, Karen, Chin, Burman, Mon, *Rakhine* or Shan and ethnic groups as have settled in any of the territories included within the State as their permanent home from a period anterior to 1185 B.E., 1823 AD'.[208] Unlike the Rakhine Buddhists, the Rohingya are not included in this list. These eight major 'national ethnic races' are sub-divided into 135 groups that the Myanmar government officially recognises as distinct ethnic groups. The Rohingya do not appear in this long list either; rather, they are depicted as illegal Bangalee migrants. The second category, Associate Citizenship (blue cards), was offered to those who had applied for citizenship under the 1948 law and their children and to those whose application was ongoing at the time of promulgation.[209] As noted earlier, only a few Rohingya applied for citizenship certificates under 1948 laws and, thus, most were deemed ineligible for this category of citizenship. And finally, the category of Naturalised Citizenship (green cards) can be granted to members of ethnic groups which are not one of 135 officially recognised ethnic groups of Myanmar, to any holder of foreign registration card, or to stateless persons as long as they 'speak well one of the national languages' and are of 'good character' and of 'sound mind'.[210] While theoretically the Rohingya are allowed to apply for citizenship following this route, giving up their status as historic inhabitants of the land is clearly a precondition. As Md. Haque notes, the Rohingya leaders therefore logically argued that there was no reason for them to apply for naturalised citizenship, for they enjoyed full citizenship rights in the Union before the 1982 Citizenship Law.[211]

The foregoing narrative of the Rohingyas' ordeal with citizenship rights highlights that their very identity as the Rohingya is at stake here. Successive regimes in Myanmar adopted arbitrary measures to wipe out the Rohingya identity, the 1982 Citizenship Law being the most effective tool to achieve that goal. The transition to so-called democracy hardly changed the situation. The 2008 Constitution requires that to be a citizen one has to already be a citizen according to law on the day this constitution came into force, or one has to be born of parents both of whom are nationals of Myanmar.[212] This provision has drastically narrowed down the grounds for the Rohingya to acquire citizenship,

---

[208] Chapter II, Section 3 of the Citizenship Law, 1982. Emphasis added.
[209] Chapter III, Sections 23 and 24 of the Citizenship Law, 1982.
[210] Chapter IV, Sections 42–61 of the Citizenship Law, 1982.
[211] For a detailed discussion, see Haque, 'Rohingya Ethnic Muslim Minority', 456–460.
[212] Article 345 of the Constitution of the Republic of the Union of Myanmar, 2008.

as they are now required to prove either that their parents are citizens or that they themselves are already citizens. Most Rohingyas are not able to meet these requirements, for the majority of parents of the Rohingya do not hold any document to show that they are citizens of the country.[213]

At the political level, there is an almost absolute embargo on the very use of the term 'Rohingya'. The Ministry of Foreign Affairs, headed by none other than Suu Kyi, advised embassies in Myanmar to stop using the term 'Rohingya' to describe the country's 'stateless Muslim minority'.[214] In Myanmar's Population and Housing Census of 2014, with technical support from the UN Population Fund and nearly USD 60 million in donor funding, the question on race–ethnicity–nationality was framed along the line of the country's eight major national races and 135 officially recognised ethnic minority groups.[215] Although initially there was an option for writing in a group name, the government finally conceded to the Rakhine Buddhist pressure and took that option out. This meant that the Rohingya minority could no longer be identified as the Rohingya.[216] Many protested by not participating in the census. It is precisely this Rohingya identity that the Rohingya are fighting for in their battle for regaining citizenship rights.

In this sense, while the Myanmar government is using citizenship and census as tools of governmentality at its disposal to supress minorities, the Rohingya in turn are using the same tools as sites of resistance to maintain their distinct ethnic group identity against the very reality of statelessness. It is in this spirit that a Rohingya community leader, in his oral statement before the UN Human Rights Council in March 2019, refuted the notion of statelessness that is often associated with the Rohingya, and claimed: 'We are citizens of Myanmar. We are Rohingya. We are not stateless. Stop calling us that. We have a state. It is Myanmar. So, we want to go home to Myanmar with our rights, our citizenship, and international security on the ground.'[217]

---

[213] Parashar and Alam, 'The National Laws of Myanmar', 102.
[214] Shibani Mahtani and Myo Myo, 'Suu Kyi's Ministry Sides with Hard-line Buddhists', *Wall Street Journal*, 5 May 2016.
[215] Roman David and Ian Holliday, *Liberalism and Democracy in Myanmar* (Oxford: Oxford University Press, 2018), 124.
[216] Ibid.
[217] UN Human Rights Council, Oral Statement for the Interactive Dialogue with the Special Rapporteur on the Situation of Human Rights in Myanmar, 11 March 2019. Statement made by Muhib Ullah, representing Arakan Rohingya Society for Peace and Human Rights. Available at www.fidh.org.

4.4.2 The Limits of Liberal Individualism

At the same time, mere assurance of citizenship under the protective shield of the liberal-individualist notion of equality and non-discrimination, albeit essential for a short-term redress of the current brutality, is unlikely to protect the Rohingya minority groups from state-sponsored assimilationist projects. After all, even the 2008 Constitution declares that '[e]very citizen is entitled to equal rights to freedom of religion or belief, as well as to establish a religion, subject to public order, morality, health, and other provisions of the Constitution'.[218] This provision on equality is then juxtaposed with the provision on the country's recognition of the 'special position of Buddhism as the faith professed by the great majority of the citizens', although the constitution also 'recognizes Christianity, Islam, Hinduism and Animism as the religions existing in the Union at the day of the coming into operation of this Constitution'.[219] In this sense, despite all of Myanmar's brutal and 'illiberal' policies towards its minorities, the case of the Rohingya is a useful reminder of how the ideology of the postcolonial 'liberal' state is capable of marginalising minorities. This also demonstrates the inherent difficulty of postcolonial nation-building projects in reconciling the diverging forces of 'nationalism' as a reflection of the ethno-religious 'self', on the one hand, and 'liberal universalism' as the expression of a post-ethnic liberal world order, on the other.

What is lost in this liberal campaign for citizenship and human rights is any active engagement with the need for self-determination for the Rohingya. It is hardly the case that in dealing with the appalling crisis the international community put self-determination on their agenda of action for a long-term solution. Ironically, not even the discourse on remedial self-determination that has the potential to survive the liberal scrutiny – given its individualist foundation in the democratic entitlement thesis – is considered an option in existing policy prescriptions regarding the Rohingya extermination. The UN Independent International Fact Finding Mission, as well as other local and international human rights organisations, has documented graphic accounts of the most brutal persecution of the Rohingya, which can potentially build a strong case for remedial self-determination in the form of the secession of north Rakhine, where the Rohingya have been living for centuries.[220] Despite

---

[218] Article 34 of the 2008 Constitution.
[219] Articles 361 and 362, ibid.
[220] UN Human Rights Council, *Report of the Detailed Findings of the Independent International Fact-Finding Mission on Myanmar* (17 September 2018), UN Doc A/

the ample evidence available, not even the neighbouring country Bangladesh – which is sympathetic to the Rohingya cause and is currently hosting more than a million Rohingya refugees within its territory – has ever made any demand for Rohingya self-determination. Most postcolonial states have their own minority 'problem'; solutions that stay within the limits of the 'national', 'liberal' state are therefore preferred. This is where the visions of postcolonial states and liberal international law merge.

The liberal-individualist premise of self-determination and sovereign legitimacy is, instead, translated into an argument for humanitarian intervention under the rubric of the 'responsibility to protect (R2P)'. The concept emanates from three inter-connected foundational formulations of the relationship between states (the 'savage'), their citizens (the 'victim'), and the international community (the 'saviour').[221] First, it is the primary responsibility of all states to protect their own citizens. This must, however, be reconciled with the sovereign privilege of territorial and political integrity and non-interference. Second, sovereignty is conceived as 'responsibility' and, therefore, the legitimacy of sovereign privilege is contingent upon the state's protection of citizens. And finally, in cases where the national authorities themselves commit gross crimes against humanity or manifestly fail to protect citizens from similar gross violations of human rights, the international community has a collective responsibility to take necessary actions to protect the vulnerable population.[222] The proposition of the R2P got its first normative articulation in the International Commission on Intervention and State Responsibility (ICISS) report entitled 'The Responsibility to Protect' in 2001.[223] The concept gained momentum with its unanimous adoption by the General Assembly in the World

---

HRC/39/CRP2; Amnesty International, *'My World is Finished': Rohingya Targeted in Crimes against Humanity in Myanmar* (London: Amnesty International, 2017); Hoque (ed.), *The Rohingya Genocide*.

[221] I have borrowed these terms from Mutua. See Makau Mutua, 'Savages, Victims, and Saviors: The Metaphor of Human Rights', *Harvard International Law Journal* 42, no. 1 (2001), 201–245.

[222] See generally UN General Assembly, Resolution 60/1, Provisional Agenda Items 46 and 120, Supp. No. 49 (24 October 2005), UN Doc A/RES/60/1, paras. 138–139. See also Roberta Cohen and Francis M. Deng, *Masses in Flight: The Global Crisis of Internal Displacement* (Washington, DC: Brookings Institution Press, 1998), 275–276; Gareth Evans, *The Responsibility to Protect: Ending Mass Atrocity Crimes Once and For All* (Washington, DC: Brookings Institution Press, 2008); Roberta Cohen, 'Humanitarian Imperatives are Transforming Sovereignty', *Northwestern Journal of International Affairs* 9 (Winter 2008), 2–13.

[223] International Commission on Intervention and State Responsibility, *The Responsibility to Protect* (Ottawa: International Development Research Centre, 2001).

Summit Outcome of 2005,[224] and appeared at the top of the UN agenda when the UN Secretary General Ban Ki-moon put the weight of his good office behind the concept and declared that the UN was committed to the project of 'implementing the responsibility to protect'.[225]

In response to the Rohingya crisis specifically, although no such argument for international intervention has yet been made at the UN level – primarily due to the Security Council deadlock and also the vested interests of powerful states that are expected to be the first to take action – the R2P argument is prominent in academic scholarship.[226] On this score, it is also worth referring to Anne Orford's argument that the proposition of the 'responsibility to protect' operates in the shadow of empire: by grounding authority on the capacity to protect, it paves the way for international executive action in managing governance of postcolonial states. In doing so, it even shifts the basis of legitimate authority from democratic entitlement to the de facto capacity to maintain control.[227] This can potentially lead to hegemony, authoritarianism, and imperialism in the name of discharging the international collective 'moral-turned-legal' responsibility to protect.

It is worth remembering the messy situation that the NATO intervention in Libya in the name of R2P – based on a controversial interpretation of the UN Security Council Resolution 1973 of 2011 – engendered in that region. This experience prompted Brazil to put forward a new initiative – 'Responsibility While Protecting' (RWP).[228] The initiative sought to promote the R2P principle but simultaneously proposed to contain its arbitrariness and damaging effect in three ways: first, by focusing on preventive measures rather than military actions; second, by tightening

---

[224] General Assembly Resolution 60/1, para. 138–139.
[225] UN Secretary-General, *Implementing the Responsibility to Protect: Report of the Secretary-General*, Agenda Items 44 and 107 (12 January 2009), UN Doc A/63/677.
[226] See, for example, Katherine Southwick, 'Preventing Mass Atrocities against the Stateless Rohingya in Myanmar: A Call for Solutions', *Journal of International Affairs* 68, no. 2 (2015), 137–156; Lindsey N. Kingston, 'Protecting the World's Most Persecuted: The Responsibility to Protect and Burma's Rohingya Minority', *The International Journal of Human Rights* 19, no. 8 (2015), 1163–1175; Mohammad Tanzimuddin Khan and Saima Ahmed, 'Dealing with the Rohingya Crisis: The Relevance of the General Assembly and R2P', *Asian Journal of Comparative Politics* 20 (2019), 1–23.
[227] Orford finds the origin of the R2P principle in the writings of Thomas Hobbes and Carl Schmidt. See generally Anne Orford, *International Authority and the Responsibility to Protect* (Cambridge: Cambridge University Press, 2011).
[228] The Letter dated 9 November 2011 from the Permanent Representative of Brazil to the United Nations addressed to the Secretary-General, *Integrated and Coordinated Implementation of and Follow-up to the Outcomes of the Major United Nations Conferences and Summits in the Economic, Social and Related Fields* (11 November 2011), UN Doc A/66/551–S/2011/701.

the criteria for implementing the UN authorisation; and third, by monitoring and assessing the criteria for the UNSC's implementation from the date that the resolution was adopted to the end of the mandate.[229] As the experience of post-conflict Bosnia–Herzegovina also illustrates, interventions of this kind, however useful as an immediate recourse to brutality, are a far cry from any sustainable solution.[230] The experience of the Rohingya is unlikely to be any different. Third World countries are therefore less supportive of the idea.[231]

4.5 The Case of the CHT Hill People in Bangladesh

The treatment of the CHT hill people within the constitutional architecture of Bangladesh best illustrates how the interplay of the 'national' and 'liberal' ideologies of the postcolonial state marginalises ethnic minorities in the name of national unity, on the one hand, and equality and non-discrimination, on the other. This also reinforces my argument that reliance only on individualist citizenship rights within the liberal-individualist framework of rights falls short of adequate protection for minorities. While the Rohingyas in Myanmar have been denied their 'Rohingya' ethnic identity as the hegemonic state *excluded* them from the domain of the nation, thereby turning them stateless, the hill people of the CHT have been denied their distinct ethnic identity as the making of the homogenous Bangladeshi nation-state aimed to forcefully *include* all different ethnic groups within a monolithic and dominant Bangalee identity using the liberal language of citizenship.

4.5.1 *The CHT Hill People within the Liberal Constitutional Architecture*

As briefly noted in Chapter 3, soon after Bangladesh's independence from Pakistan in December 1971, a delegation of the hill people led by Charu Bikash Chakma met the then president, prime minister, and minister for law and parliamentary affairs to press – unsuccessfully – for a separate constitutional safeguard for the hill people.[232] Another

---

[229] Ibid., 11.
[230] See Sumantra Bose, *Bosnia after Dayton: Nationalist Partition and International Intervention* (London: Hurst and Company, 2002); Shahabuddin, *Ethnicity and International Law*, 203–216.
[231] Chimni, *International Law and World Order*, 347.
[232] *Mohammad Badiuzzaman v. Bangladesh and Others*, para. 10.

delegation, this time led by the Independent Chakma Constituent Assembly member from the CHT, Manabendra Narayan Larma, met the prime minister and the key architect of independent Bangladesh Sheikh Mujibur Rahman on 15 February 1972 and demanded: autonomy for the CHT, establishment of a special legislative body, retention of the CHT Regulation 1900 in the new Constitution of Bangladesh, continuation of the offices of the tribal chiefs, a constitutional provision restricting the amendment of the CHT Regulation 1900, and a ban on Bangalee settlements in the CHT.[233] The prime minister rejected these claims, advising the delegation to relinquish such 'parochial and ethnic aspirations in favour of these being subsumed under a broader notion of nationalism to facilitate national integration'.[234] In his memoir, former Chakma Raja Tridiv Roy notes that at a rally in the hill district of Rangamati, the prime minister even declared that 'all tribal people would be known as Bangalee and would have no other identity'.[235]

This attitude towards the hill people and their demand for constitutional recognition also appeared conspicuously in Bangladesh Constituent Assembly debates. Participating in an assembly debate on 25 October 1972, Manabendra Larma expressed his regret that the draft constitution of the country did not recognise the existence of ethnic minorities in Bangladesh. Drawing the attention of the Assembly to the fact that even the colonial and oppressive Pakistani regimes recognised the distinct identity of the hill people and provided special constitutional status and safeguards to the CHT, he exclaimed: now that the country is going to be a socialist democracy, how can it ignore its ethnic minorities?[236] During the debate, when Larma referred to the demand for autonomy presented to the prime minister, a member of the Assembly arose on a point of order and claimed that by demanding an autonomous region, Larma was in fact 'attacking' the independence of the country.[237] Sajeda Chowdhury, who later held senior cabinet positions in a number of governments, sarcastically commented that with the inclusion of hill tribes *as* Bangalees, the constitution had

---

[233] Ibid.
[234] Quoted in ibid.
[235] Raja Tridiv Roy, *The Departed Melody* (Islamabad: PPA Publications, 2003), 330–331.
[236] Government of Bangladesh, *Debates of the Constituent Assembly of Bangladesh*, vol. II (12 October 1972–15 December 1972) (Dhaka: Parliament Secretariat, 1973), (debates on 25 October 1972), 292. All translations of Assembly debates are mine.
[237] Ibid., 294.

indeed recognised the hill people. She then asked: 'isn't it more dignified to get recognition as a nation rather than a sub-nation'?[238]

Tension intensified when the prime minister's initial pronouncement of the homogenous national identity at a political rally made its way into the citizenship clause in the constitution, which read: the citizens of Bangladesh will be known as Bangalees.[239] In an assembly debate on the citizenship clause on 31 October 1972, Larma forcefully resisted this hegemonic imposition of Bangalee identity on the hill peoples and asked why fellow assembly members wanted the hill people to adopt Bangalee identity.[240] The speaker of the house responded: 'Don't you want to be a Bangalee?' Larma argued that if the constitution finally adopted this definition of citizenship, it would lead to the extinction of distinct identities of hill peoples. He continued that as citizens of Bangladesh, they see themselves as Bangladeshis but not as Bangalees, as they have a distinct ethnic identity.[241] In response this time, the speaker simply asked Larma to retake his seat.[242] Upon the adoption of the citizenship clause on the same day, Larma boycotted the assembly debates and refused to put his signature on the original handwritten version of the constitution.[243] On this score, Dina Siddique succinctly asserts that the speaker's call to become Bangalee even goes beyond the liberal expectation of citizens that they transcend cultures in private spheres; it aims to 'recast subjectivity altogether'.[244]

The Constitution of Bangladesh was finally adopted and enforced without any recognition of the existence of any ethnic minorities in the country, and the citizenship clause in Article 6 maintained that citizens of Bangladesh are all known as Bangalees. Although the military regime that followed propagated an alternative territorial model of 'Bangladeshi' nationalism for its own Islamic-nationalist political ends, the hegemonic idea that the dominant Bangalee majority alone constitutes the nation

---

[238] Ibid., 293.
[239] Article 6 of the Constitution of Bangladesh 1972. Siddiqi, however, notes that the original Draft did not contain language that specifically tied citizenship to Bangalee ethnicity; it was a private member's bill that called for redefining the principle of nationalism as Bangalee nationalism. See Dina M. Siddiqi, 'Secular Quests, National Others: Revisiting Bangladesh's Constituent Assembly Debates', *Asian Affairs* 49, no. 2 (2018), 248.
[240] *Debates of the Constituent Assembly of Bangladesh* (31 October 1972), 452.
[241] Although he specifically mentioned the Chakma identity.
[242] Ibid.
[243] *Debates of the Constituent Assembly of Bangladesh* (31 October 1972), 453.
[244] Siddiqi, 'Secular Quest, National Others', 247. See also Aamir Mufti, *Enlightenment in the Colony: The Jewish Question and the Crisis of Postcolonial Culture* (Princeton, NJ: Princeton University Press, 2007).

was brought back in the fifteenth amendment of the constitution in an attempt to reinstate the original constitution of 1972. Accordingly, the current constitution stipulates that '[t]he people of Bangladesh shall be known as Bangalees as a nation and citizens of Bangladesh shall be known as Bangladeshis'.[245] Likewise, Article 3 names Bangla as the official language and Article 9 refers to '[t]he unity and solidarity of the Bangalee nation which, deriving its identity from its language and culture [...] shall be the basis of Bangalee nationalism'.[246] It is in Article 23A that the constitution imposes an obligation on the state to 'take steps to protect and develop the unique local culture and tradition of the tribes, minor races, ethnic sects and communities'.[247] While this provision finally acknowledges the existence of communities other than Bangalees, it nonetheless underscores that unique cultures of these communities fall outside the 'national culture' (defined in line with Bangalee nationalism) that the state is obliged to promote under Article 23.[248] In this way, as Tridiv Roy notes, with the dominance and hegemony of Bangalee nationalism as translated into the Constitution of Bangladesh, the hill people of the CHT have become constitutional outcasts.[249]

Simultaneously, the fifteenth amendment retained an earlier amendment declaring Islam as the state religion of Bangladesh and, like in the corresponding provision of the Constitution of Myanmar, the Article guarantees 'equal status and equal right in the practice of the Hindu, Buddhist, Christian and other religions'.[250] Within the liberal architecture of international human rights law, the constitution also unsurprisingly guarantees that 'the State shall not discriminate against any citizen on grounds only of religion, race, caste, sex or place of birth',[251] and also that on these grounds no citizen shall be ineligible for, or discriminated against in respect of, any employment or office in the service of the Republic.[252] There are also constitutional guarantees of equality before law and equality of

---

[245] Constitution of the People's Republic of Bangladesh amended by the Constitution (Fifteenth Amendment) Act, 2011 (Act XIV of 2011), Article 6.
[246] Ibid., Article 9.
[247] Ibid., Article 14.
[248] Ibid., Article 23.
[249] Roy, *The Departed Melody*, 330-331. See also *Mohammad Badiuzzaman v. Bangladesh and Others*, para. 24.
[250] Article 2A of the Constitution. For an account of the interplay of religion and ethnicity in constituting the minority as the 'other' in the making of the constitution, see Siddiqi, 'Secular Quests, National Others', 238-258.
[251] Article 28 (1) of the Constitution.
[252] Article 29 (2) of the Constitution.

opportunities.[253] Thus, the 'liberal' ideology of equality and non-discrimination is seen as appropriate and effective not only for addressing concerns of minorities but also, and primarily, for materialising the ideology of the postcolonial 'national' state. Although the constitution permits affirmative measures for backward sections of the society,[254] it is quite difficult to make use of such measures for meaningful cultural protection for minorities, such as regional autonomy, within the individualist framework of rights, as I discussed earlier and as we shall see soon in the specific context of the CHT. In this sense, like the Constitution of Myanmar and, for that matter, those of most postcolonial states, the Constitution of Bangladesh too reveals an inherent tension between the diverging forces of 'nationalism' and 'liberal universalism' in its nation-building roadmap.

Like in Myanmar, the situation of the CHT hill people only worsened under successive military regimes following the assassination of Sheikh Mujib in August 1975. In 1976, during the regime of Ziaur Rahman, the CHT Development Board headed by military personnel was formed. The board undertook a devastating programme of settling tens of thousands of poor Bangalees in the CHT to change the demography of the region.[255] Bangla, the state language of the country, was the only official language and the medium of instructions in all schools in the CHT. The nation-building process ultimately led to the extinction of a number of indigenous languages. The massacre of hill peoples, burning of their houses, arbitrary arrests, torture, rape, extra-judicial executions, and 'disappearances' reportedly perpetrated by or with the connivance of the military and law enforcement agencies depict the human rights situation in the region during the years of armed conflict.[256] These were 'planned actions as a part of macro objective of nation building through forced assimilation and forced expulsion'.[257]

In resistance, *Parbattya Chattagram Jana Sanghati Samiti* (PCJSS: United People's Party of the Chittagong Hill Tracts) – the major political representative of the indigenous communities in the CHT – undertook to

---

[253] Articles 29 (1) and 27 of the Constitution, respectively.
[254] See Articles 28 (4) and 29 (3) of the Constitution.
[255] See Willem van Schendal, 'The Invention of "Jumma": State Formation and Ethnicity in Southeastern Bangladesh', *Modern Asian Studies* 26, part. 1 (1992), 65; The CHT Commission, *"Life is Not Ours": Land and Human in the Chittagong Hill Tracts, Bangladesh* (Dhaka: The CHT Commission, 1991), 8.
[256] See generally The CHT Commission, *"Life is Not Ours"*.
[257] Meghna Guhathakurta, 'Overcoming Otherness and Building Trust: The Kalpana Chakma Case', in *Living on the Edge: Essays on the Chittagong Hill Tracts*, ed. Subir Bhaumik, et al. (Kathmandu: SAFHR, 1997), 182–184.

organise the hill people on a micro-nationalist agenda. The persecution in the CHT led to a demand by the PCJSS for a separate nationhood for the hill people. This party, formed in the wake of government refusal in 1972 to recognise the distinct identity of hill peoples in the constitution, had since the mid-1980s been referring to the hill people as the 'Jumma nation'.[258] During the period of insurgency the PCJSS set out a number of power-sharing demands, including regional autonomy, with a view to realising Jumma nationalism by way of autonomy for the hill people.[259] The military and political elites perceived these PCJSS power-sharing demands as a threat to national security. In 1993 the political government rejected the demands, holding that 'Bangladesh is an integrated and homogenous society bound by common language and rich cultural heritage. [...] Bangladesh is a unitary state with a democratic Constitution that extends to the entire territory without exception'.[260] Following three decades of armed conflicts and loss of lives and resources, the CHT Peace Accord between the PCJSS and the National Committee on CHT Affairs formed by the government was finally concluded on 2 December 1997, although a section of hill peoples rejected the Accord as a compromise and formed a political party – United Peoples Democratic Front (UPDF) – to carry on the struggle for the 'full autonomy' of the CHT. The Peace Accord accommodated a number of power-sharing provisions, which in turn led to normative inconsistency with the liberal-individualist premise of the constitution, as discussed in the following section.

4.5.2 *Liberal Constitutionalism and Accommodation of Group Rights*

Like most peace treaties, the CHT Peace Accord goes beyond liberal constitutional safeguards of equality and non-discrimination and accommodates a series of group rights for the hill peoples of the CHT in line with their long-standing demands, although, to the dissatisfaction of the hill people, the Accord remained silent apropos their constitutional recognition. Instead, the term 'tribal' (*upajati* in Bangla, literally meaning

---

[258] Van Schendal, 'The Invention of "Jumma"', 121.
[259] *Dabeenama* (Charter of Demands of the PCJSS to the Government of Bangladesh), JSS Publications, 1992 and 1996.
[260] Special Affairs Division, *A Report on the Problems of Chittagong Hill Tracts and Bangladesh: Responses for their Solution* (Dhaka: Government of Bangladesh, 1993), cited in Amena Mohsin, *Politics of Nationalism* (Dhaka: The University Press Limited, 1997), 201.

sub-nation) was used to describe the hill people. It is worth noting here that when Bangladesh ratified and acceded to the International Covenant on Economic, Social and Cultural Rights shortly after the Peace Accord – on 5 October 1998, to be precise – it added a declaration to Article 1 on the right to self-determination that read: 'It is the understanding of the Government of the People's Republic of Bangladesh that the words "the right of self-determination of Peoples" appearing in this article apply in the historical context of colonial rule, administration, foreign domination, occupation and similar situations.'[261] It was for the same reason that following the independence referendum in the Catalonia region of Spain in 2017, the Ministry of Foreign Affairs of Bangladesh issued a press release on 2 November 2017. The press release expressed Bangladesh's support for the 'measures undertaken by the Spanish government to uphold national unity and territorial integrity' in line with 'the principle of mutual respect for each other's sovereignty and territorial integrity'.[262]

Nevertheless, the Accord provides for three Hill District Councils, of which only the permanent residents of the CHT will be members.[263] The Accord also provides for a Regional Council with the mandate to coordinate among the three Hill District Councils. The Chairman of this Council shall be elected indirectly by the elected members of the District Councils. The Regional Council shall have 22 members, of whom two-thirds will be elected from among the 'tribals'. The Regional Council is given the responsibility of supervising and coordinating the subjects vested under the Hill District Councils. However, some major subjects that directly relate to autonomy and to the preservation of indigenous cultures – general administration and law and order, education, cultural affairs, information and statistics, population control, and family

---

[261] See www.indicators.ohchr.org. The position, as we have seen earlier in this chapter, falls very much in line with the current international law position on external self-determination for minority groups. However, the Bangladesh declaration in this regard drew objection and criticism from delegates of Finland, France, Germany, Sweden, and the Netherlands, who argued that the declaration imposes conditions on the right to self-determination that are not included in international law and that by doing so the declaration limits the scope of the right to self-determination, undermines the concept itself, and seriously weakens its universally acceptable character.

[262] Ministry of Foreign Affairs of Bangladesh, 'Bangladesh Position on Catalonia', press release issued on 2 November 2017, available at www.mofa.gov.bd/site/press_release/dd69996e-a4c8-488a-98d4-b8e6b61df05c.

[263] According to the Peace Accord, Bangalees who legally possess land in the Hill District and generally live at a certain address in the Hill District are also permanent residents of the CHT.

planning – are not vested under the Hill Districts. But it is provided that the government and elected representatives shall make efforts to maintain the separate cultures and traditions of the 'tribals', and that in order to develop the 'tribal' cultural activities at the national level the government shall offer the necessary patronisation and assistance. Regarding pending land issues, the Accord stipulates that no land within the boundaries of the Hill Districts shall be given in settlement, purchased, sold, or transferred, including giving lease without prior approval of the Council. Some government establishments are kept outside this restriction. The Accord also prohibits any acquisition and transfer of land within the boundaries of the Hill Districts by the government without consultation and prior consent of the respective Hill District Council.

However, the legality of the Accord's group-oriented measures within the 'unitary' character of the state and the liberal-individualist framework of rights in the constitution was quickly challenged in the case of *Mohammad Badiuzzaman v. Bangladesh and Others*.[264] In this case, the petitioner argued that the three Hill District Regional Acts of 1989, as amended in 1998 in line with the Peace Accord, violated fundamental rights to equality and non-discrimination as enshrined in the constitution by stipulating that: (i) a non-tribal person shall not be able to contest the election of a District Council,[265] (ii) a person who is not a permanent resident of a district cannot be a voter,[266] (iii) preference will be given to tribal people in the Police Service,[267] and (iv) no land in the CHT will be transferred without prior permission from the Council.[268] The petitioner also argued that the CHT Regional Council Act of 1998, enacted in line with the Accord, negates the unitary character of the state and, therefore, is incompatible and inconsistent with the Constitution of Bangladesh.[269] The petitioner, therefore, concluded that

> the cumulative effect of the various clauses of the impugned acts and the creation of the Regional Council is not only that of violating various provisions of the Constitution as mentioned hereinabove, but also of

---

[264] Writ Petition No. 2669 (2000) before the High Court Division of the Supreme Court of Bangladesh. See also Writ Petition No. 6451 (2007), which challenged the legality of the CHT Peace Accord itself.
[265] Section 6 (Uo) of the impugned Acts, 1998.
[266] Section 11 of the impugned Acts, 1998.
[267] Section 15 (Kha) of Rangamati and Khagrachari Hill District Acts, 1998 and Section 27 of the Bandarban Hill District Acts, 1998.
[268] Under the new Section 64 of the impugned Acts. See *Mohammad Badiuzzaman v. Bangladesh and Others*, para. 17.
[269] According to Articles 1, 7, and 59 of the Constitution. See ibid., para. 18.

destroying one of the basic structures of the Constitution, namely, the unitary character of the state by supporting to create a territorial unit which eventually may claim the status of a federating unit. In other words, the enactments impugned are seen as a collective device at establishing regionalism and paving the way for the ultimate dismantlement of the very unitary fabric of the Republic.

Taking up the question of the unitary character of the state, the court in its judgment accepted the view of the petitioner. To reach its decision, the court relied on an earlier decision by the Appellate Division of the Supreme Court in the *Anwar Hossain* v. *Bangladesh* case (also known as the '*Eighth Amendment* case').[270] In the latter, the Supreme Court nullified a constitutional amendment attempting to establish permanent benches of the High Court Division in different regions of the country, ostensibly to facilitate peoples' access to justice. In his judgment in the *Eighth Amendment* case, Badrul Haider Chowdhury described the decentralisation attempt as 'sowing the seeds of regionalism' from which 'the next step can be dismantling the fabric of the Republic'.[271] Similarly, Shahabuddin Ahmed in his judgment argued that 'the State has been [...] organised as a Unitary State by its founding fathers leaving no scope for devolution of executive, legislative and judicial powers on different regions to turn into Province ultimately' and, therefore, the sanctity of the unitary character of the state must be retained.[272] Building on these judgments, the court in *Mohammad Badiuzzaman* v. *Bangladesh and Others* was satisfied that the CHT Regional Council, focusing 'wholly on promoting the interests of people living in a particular territory and in that process inherently permitting of a carving out of a specific territory of the Republic' is an endorsement of the notion of autonomy or devolution that the Constitution of Bangladesh does not provide for – hence, ultra vires the constitution and void ab initio.[273] This perception of a unitary state is not

---

[270] BLD (special issues) 9 (A) 1989.
[271] Ibid., para. 238.
[272] Ibid., para. 362.
[273] *Mohammad Badiuzzaman* v. *Bangladesh and Others*, para. 41. Responding to the Respondent's argument that unitary states, such as Italy, Spain, and China, allow autonomy of regions and provinces, the court asserted that 'unlike the constitution of Bangladesh the constitutions of these countries specifically allow for autonomous regions to be established within the framework of a unitary state, and therefore, there is no question of the creation of autonomous regions in these countries as being in violation of their respective constitutions.' The court also noted that the United Kingdom, which has devolved extensive power to constituent parts despite officially retaining the unitary character of its state, does not have a comparable written constitution.

unique in the broader South Asian context. The Supreme Court of Sri Lanka similarly ruled in *Re the Thirteenth Amendment to the Constitution* case that 'the essence of a Unitary State is that the sovereignty is undivided – in other words, that the powers of the central government are unrestricted'.[274]

Regarding the question of group rights allegedly in violation of the constitutional guarantee of equality and non-discrimination among individual citizens, the court heavily relied on David Held's 'democratic autonomy' thesis that in a pluralistic democracy

> persons should enjoy equal rights and, accordingly, equal obligations in the specification of the political framework which generates and limits the opportunities available to them, that is, they should be free and equal in the determination of the conditions of their own lives, *so long as they do not deploy this framework to negate the rights of others*.[275]

Conceiving of the CHT Peace Accord as political formulae for 'negotiating difference' within Held's framework of equal rights, the court found that in the absence of any objective criteria in the constitution for such preferential treatment of one section of the citizenry, special affirmative measures for the hill people in various provisions of the three Hill District Council Acts of 1998 are violations of the relevant provisions of the constitution. This is because the constitution guarantees equality and non-discrimination for individual citizens of the entire country.[276] Having thus been confined by the liberal-individualist architecture of rights and the unitary character of the state as embodied in the constitution, the court failed to offer legal approval to measures that parties to the Accord accepted as crucial elements of peacebuilding in the region. The court, instead, called upon political actors for progressive and innovative engagement with and revision of the relevant constitutional provisions.[277] The case is currently pending before the Appellate Division for final determination. In the meantime, the progress on the implementation of the Accord

---

[274] The court, however, noted that the unitary nature does not mean 'the absence of subsidiary law-making bodies, but it does mean that they may exist and can be abolished at the discretion of the central authority'. *In Re the Thirteenth Amendment to the Constitution*, Supreme Court of Sri Lanka, 2 SLR (1987) 319. See also *Tamil Federal Party* case, Supreme Court of Sri Lanka, SC SPL 03/2014 (2016).

[275] David Held, *Models of Democracy*, 2nd ed. (Stanford, CA: Stanford University Press, 1996), 301. Emphasis added.

[276] *Mohammad Badiuzzaman v. Bangladesh and Others*, para. 45–46. See also Articles 27–31 of the Constitution.

[277] Ibid., para. 49 (f).

has been very slow, and that in turn means continued marginalisation of the hill people in new ways, as we shall see in Chapter 5.[278] This brief account of the interaction between the dominant Bangalee majority and the CHT hill people, against the backdrop of constitutional provisions on equality among citizens and non-discrimination on the grounds of religion, race, place of birth, and so on, highlights the inherent complexities that postcolonial states face in reconciling nationalism with liberalism and the role international law plays in the process. This narrative also brings forth the issue of the normative compatibility of current liberal legal norms with an effective response to ethnic conflicts that requires that group rights be accommodated in one form or the other. This gap between the normative stance and pragmatic needs implies that postcolonial states deal with ethnic conflicts in a 'quasi-legal' realm. The CHT story also indicates what complications any future peace settlement – in the case of the Rohingya or other similar situations – will face within the liberal-individualist framework of international law as well as postcolonial 'liberal' constitutionalism.

4.6 Conclusion

The foregoing analysis reveals the way liberal individualism in international law feeds into the vision of the postcolonial 'liberal' state and how this vision is then translated into an 'ideology' to marginalise minorities within the liberal framework of equality and non-discrimination. Of the various ideological modes of operation, fragmentation appears to be the most apt to this end, given its immense capacity to diffuse a minority group into a collection of individuals, who then become subjects and holders of human rights in individual capacities in line with the dominant liberal philosophy. Similarly, legitimation – another mode of ideological operation – serves to justify a regime of rights for individual citizens, as opposed to rights for national or sub-national groups within a state, to maintain the sanctity and integrity of the postcolonial 'national' state. In this sense, the diffusion of minority groups into individual citizens, followed by their subjection to a human rights regime that maintains formal

---

[278] In a press conference on the eve of the twenty-second anniversary of the Accord in December 2019, Jyotirindra Bodhipriya Larma (Santu Larma), the Chairman of the PCJSS and also the Chairman of the CHT Regional Council, rejected the government's claim that out of 72 provisions of the Accord 48 had been fully implemented. Larma, in contrast, claimed that despite being in power for more than eleven years in a row, the government left crucial aspects of the Accord unimplemented. See *The Prothom-Alo*, 2 December 2019, 4.

equality among citizens, is seen as the very precondition of the 'national' state that is always nervous about the legitimacy of its sovereign claims over arbitrarily drawn territorial boundaries and an ethnically heterogeneous population.

As we have seen, international law plays a key role in this ideological function of the postcolonial state. With its inherent structural bias in favour of maintaining the status quo of international order and by denying ethnic minorities the right to self-determination, the current international legal regime fails to offer adequate remedies for vulnerable minority groups. To make the case even worse, minority groups, thus deprived of the right to self-determination and left within a political unit they do not recognise as a legitimate authority to exercise sovereignty over them, enjoy rather limited protection under international law beyond individualist human rights norms. As I have explained in great detail, such a human rights approach to minority protection is inadequate and incapable of protecting minorities from state-sponsored assimilation in the name of nation-building. As my historical analysis of the evolution of minority rights under the League and UN regimes demonstrates, such notions of assimilation of minorities was nothing short of desired. International law in fact facilitates, or at least offers legitimacy to, postcolonial states' nation-building projects and the ensuing assimilation of ethnic minorities into the dominant majority culture. In this connection, I have also noted the peculiar challenge that postcolonial states face in reconciling the diverging forces of, on the one hand, 'liberal individualism' emanating from the liberal international legal order, and on the other, majoritarian 'nationalism' emanating from the nationalist discourse of allegiance, entitlement, and legitimacy.

The issue of citizenship and statelessness was also discussed in this context. The liberal human rights regime is designed to ensure that individual citizens within a given polity enjoy rights without discrimination on grounds of sex, race, religion, colour, place of birth, and so on. Citizenship is, therefore, a prior condition for having rights. Given ambiguities in traditional international law on the limits of state power in dealing with citizenship, international human rights law stepped in and formulated the right to nationality as universal human rights. Paradoxically, in practice, the enjoyment and protection of many human rights are dependent upon citizenship status. Authoritarian regimes often deprive minorities of citizenship rights as a technique of marginalisation. The case of the Rohingya in Myanmar illustrates this fact. On the other hand, while the individual right to citizenship is the very basic premise upon which the liberal state is organised, mere citizenship under the protective shields of individual equality and non-discrimination is not always adequate for meaningful protection of minority groups. To some extent, the very language of equality serves as an ideology to perpetuate inequality among groups, as the case of the CHT highlights. Taken together, the cases demonstrate the contrasting use of citizenship as an oppressive tool: in the case of the Rohingya, it operated through forced exclusion, while in the case of the CHT hill people, it took the form of forced inclusion.

At the political level, when minorities somehow manage to organise themselves into political and/or armed forces – strong enough to challenge the hegemony of states and force the latter to concede to the minority demands of autonomy and similar group-oriented measures – the liberal architecture of international law as well as postcolonial constitutional norms appear to be rather a hindrance to the political compromise between the majority and the minority. The fate of the CHT Peace Accord illustrates the fact. The same is, however, true in other postcolonial contexts too. To explain the limitation of the liberal-individualist approach to ethnic conflicts, Ninan Koshy describes the proceedings involving the Sri Lankan ethnic conflict before the Human Rights Commission and the Sub-Commission in which attention was given almost exclusively to the violations of core individual rights rather than to the ethnic and political structures giving rise to the conflict as such or to the related claims of some Tamil groups for an autonomy scheme.[279] Similarly, in the context of Nigeria, Eghosa Osaghae registers his distrust of individualist human rights as the sole system for addressing ethnic tension and argues that although individual rights are necessary, group rights which 'regard ethnic groups as deserving of protection of justice in competition with others are also needed' for ethnic conflict management.[280] Absent these rights, he concludes, the continued existence of ethnic groups cannot be guaranteed, nor can their subjugation by other groups be prevented, in that the entrenchment of individual rights alone cannot serve the purposes which group rights are meant to serve.[281]

---

[279] See Ninan Koshy, 'Ethnic Conflicts in Sri Lanka and the UN Human Rights System', in *Ethnic Conflicts and the UN Human Rights System*, ed. Henry J. Steiner, cited in Henry J. Steiner, 'Ideals and Counter-Ideals in the Struggle over Autonomy Regimes for Minorities', *Notre Dame Law Review* 66 (1991), footnote 33.

[280] See Eghosa E. Osaghae, 'Human Rights and Ethnic Conflict Management: The Case of Nigeria', *Journal of Peace Research* 33, no. 2 (1996), 171.

[281] Ibid., 178–186.

Despite occasional accommodation of this view for pragmatic reasons, international legal norms – far away from acknowledging this reality – continue to push for the liberal human rights agenda in dealing with minority groups. In the process, international law continues to facilitate the ideology of the postcolonial 'liberal' state, aggravating and simultaneously glossing over minority sufferings.

5

The Postcolonial 'Developmental' State

Minority Perspectives and International Law

5.1 Introduction

While the ideology of the postcolonial 'liberal' state offered a template for the internal organisation of ethnic relations and the constitutional architecture of rights, the ideology of the postcolonial 'developmental' state – operating along the line of the same liberal ideological vision – puts forward the agenda for the postcolonial state's internal and external organisation of economic affairs. As I have demonstrated so far, the ideological functions of the postcolonial state not only result in the marginalisation of minorities but also serve to legitimise and gloss over the asymmetric power relations that produce such marginalisation. International law plays key roles in the ideological function of the postcolonial state, especially in the case of the 'developmental' ideology. This chapter explains the roles that international law plays in the ideology of the postcolonial 'developmental' state and the consequences for minorities.

I discussed in Chapter 2 how the developmental ideology was put in place as a nation-building technology to address minority issues in the context of Indian nationalist discourse. However, the perception of 'development' as a body of technical knowledge and an exclusive domain of expertise in the postcolonial context cannot be fully appreciated without a close scrutiny of corresponding developments in international law since WWII. The post-WWII discourse on development in international law offers the necessary backdrop against which the ideology of the postcolonial 'developmental' state acquired meanings that helped create, continue, and sustain various forms of new and old asymmetric power relations – not only between newly independent postcolonial states and their former colonial powers but also between the dominant majority and marginalised minorities *within* postcolonial states.

In the following sections, I offer an in-depth and multi-layered analysis of the complex interrelationship between minorities, postcolonial states, and dominant international actors with reference to 'development', minority rights, and international law. My analysis is organised under two major rubrics. I first analyse the treatment of minorities in the international law of development. Here, I closely examine various aspects of power-asymmetries produced and maintained by international laws concerning development. In this regard, I specifically focus on the way the postcolonial state, on the one hand, and liberal individuals, on the other, remain at the centre of the developmental ideology and what implications such an approach to developmentalism has for minorities. This analysis is then followed by an examination of how international law discourse on minority and group rights addresses the issue of economic development. In both cases, critically engaging with central themes in the discourse on both 'development' and 'minority rights' under international law, I argue that international law provides a framework within which international actors and postcolonial states suppress minority interests in the name of economic development, whereas politically marginalised minorities suffer the most from such development activities. As we shall see, development projects often target minority lands and forests, with long-term devastating effects on minority cultures or even threats to their very existence.

In this way, as we shall see, international law advances the ideology of the postcolonial 'developmental' state, with legitimation as its ideological mode of operation. Given that such legitimation of minority oppression in the name of economic development glosses over the existing structural power imbalance in both the political and the socio-economic domain between the minority and the dominant majority, dissimulation is another mode of ideological operation that comes into play. And, finally, since the very notion of development is conceived as an integral part of the transition narrative of modernity, international law at the same time reifies the centrality of 'development' in the making of the postcolonial state undermining minority rights concerns. This chapter again substantiates these arguments with case studies on the Rohingya in Myanmar and the CHT hill people in Bangladesh.

5.2 Minorities in the International Law of Economic Development

5.2.1 Development and Culture

By the end of WWII, it was more or less certain that an international order keeping the vast majority of nations outside Europe under colonial rule was no longer sustainable. International lawyers, therefore, had to seriously engage with decolonisation and the ensuing question of how to deal with nascent postcolonial states. As Sundhya Pahuja argues, international law responded to this problem within its general framework of duality vis-à-vis decolonisation. In the political domain, international law proclaimed the principle of sovereign equality among all nations; in the economic domain, it had the parallel task of addressing the problem of economic 'backwardness' that many postcolonial states themselves identified as a challenge to their progressive march towards modernity.[1] In other words, international law offered postcolonial states sovereign equality at the political level but simultaneously maintained a system of hierarchy at the economic level whereby the postcolonial state remained in constant need of expert interventions to mitigate the problem of backwardness.

These interventions came in the form of 'economic development'. Development quickly came to be seen as 'the only way to understand questions of material inequality and global distribution because of its ability to maintain a hierarchy between the West and the Rest'.[2] Thus, in its political role the ideology of development, despite the proclamation of formal equality, could manage to prevent substantive equality between the coloniser and the colonised through the creation and maintenance of 'a scalar, or graduated, organisation of states secured by positing an ostensibly universally attainable end point in the status of "developed"' as well as 'an institutional location which created the possibility for ongoing surveillance and interventions to transform "developing" states'.[3]

The essential venue in which this 'development' was to be performed by both postcolonial states and international institutions was the nation-state. The postcolonial 'developmental' state was, thus, naturally imagined within the confines of the postcolonial 'national' state, which international law took pride in having created as its new subject in the first place. At the same time, within the framework of the postcolonial

---

[1] See generally Pahuja, *Decolonising International Law*, 44–94.
[2] Ibid., 115.
[3] Ibid., 46.

'liberal' state, shaped by liberal international legal norms, the focus of development remained on the individual citizens of the state. With the centrality of the state and the individual in the development discourse, minority groups and their interests have often been ignored. As a result, minorities have traditionally been easy victims of postcolonial states' developmental agenda, actively endorsed and supported by international law and institutions.

Although the move towards 'development' was an international effort to find a new culture-neutral ideology of dominance, the developmental discourse was not separated from the old ideas of colonialism and its cultural categories of civilised and uncivilised, advanced and backward. The nineteenth-century concept of world civilisation was translated into the theory of modernisation in the early twentieth century, and then into the notion of globalisation in the era that followed.[4] Antony Anghie persuasively demonstrates how the development agenda of international financial institutions (IFIs), along with modes of economic surveillance and governance technologies, has its origin in the Mandate System of the League of Nations.[5] The official 'mandate' was to ensure the welfare and development of the mandate territories, thereby promoting global trade and commerce.[6] In reality, as Anghie demonstrates, the Mandate System was far from a mechanism for mutual benefit, for the terms of exploitation were set by mandatory powers that never worked to the benefit of the natives.[7] Development thus justified the maltreatment and suffering of native populations, who were simply expected to pay the price for civilisation. In this sense, the Mandate System was hardly different from the colonial idea of the civilising mission.

In this new era of 'economic development' as a civilising mission, the question of native cultures was unavoidable. The question of what to do

---

[4] Adam Kuper, *Culture: The Anthropologists' Account* (Cambridge, MA: Harvard University Press, 1999), 10.
[5] Anghie, *Imperialism, Sovereignty and the Making of International Law*, 115–195. See also Antony Anghie, 'Colonialism and the Birth of International Institutions: Sovereignty, Economy, and the Mandate System of the League of Nations', *New York University Journal of International Law and Politics* 34 (2001–2002), 513–633.
[6] Lord Lugard, *The Dual Mandate in British Tropical Africa* (1922) (Hamden, CT: Archon Books, 1965), 618. Lugard was surely more concerned about the need to maintain easy access to raw materials in colonies under the new realities on the international plane, wherein formal colonialism increasingly came to be seen as economically burdensome and morally unjustifiable. In his words, '[t]he democracies of to-day claim the right to work, and the satisfaction of that claim is impossible without the raw materials of the tropics on the one hand and their markets on the other' (61).
[7] Anghie, *Imperialism, Sovereignty and the Making of International Law*, 160.

with these cultures was, however, normatively less complicated. For, seen through the optic of the nineteenth-century evolutionary science of social Darwinism, 'development' appeared to be part of the progressive narrative of modernity and, hence, set to transcend primitive cultures. As Peter Dickens notes, the social Darwinists' description of social evolution included 'progress occurring through evolution, direction to social change, and teleology, an end which is built into social change itself'.[8] Given that this monogenic understanding of evolution was informed by Enlightenment philosophy, it is not surprising that all these concepts – progress, direction, and teleology – are in fact related to the realisation of a civilised society in the Western European sense.[9] Thus, 'progress' is exemplified by modernisation; a modern society is a fully developed one that relies on modern political, educational, and legal systems and also values economic growth. In contrast, traditional societies largely depend on clan-based or autocratic systems of government and pre-Newtonian science and technology.[10] Modernisation also exemplifies the concepts of 'direction' and 'end'.[11] In other words, in the liberal account of evolution, progress is portrayed as cultural attributes which are not 'fixed' but instead are in constant fusion. At the same time, culture is perceived as an efficient way of reaching the ultimate destination of progress.[12] Given that the 'high culture' that would lead to the liberal 'progress' comprises the selected cultural traits in the social evolutionary process, everything else is arguably destined to submit to this high culture.

Accordingly, the Mandate System was premised on the conviction that the promotion of economic progress in mandate territories would solve

---

[8] Peter Dickens, *Social Darwinism* (Buckingham: Open University Press, 2000), 31–44.

[9] Monogenists conceived human races as emanating from a common origin; despite possessing different ranks in the civilisational process, they would ultimately survive as the superior whole through the evolutionary continuum. In contrast, polygenists perceived human races as fundamentally distinct species, whose hierarchical positions are fixed in the evolutionary process so that the superior is preserved from any intermixing with the inferior.

[10] Dickens, *Social Darwinism*, 32.

[11] For example, Fukuyama famously claimed that liberal capitalism indicates 'the end of the history' by giving every individual a sense of recognition and worth, while simultaneously providing high levels of material well-being. See generally Francis Fukuyama, 'The End of History?' *The National Interest* 16 (1989), 3–18. Other writers, such as Kerr and Aron, saw the end in the convergence of different forms of industrialisation. See Dickens, *Social Darwinism*, 35–41.

[12] Talcott Parsons, *Societies: Evolutionary and Comparative Perspectives* (New York: Prentice Hall, 1966), 26. For the background of Parsons' social science account of culture, see Kuper, *Culture*, 47–72. See also Dickens, *Social Darwinism*, 36.

problems emanating from native cultural traits. Economic progress was seen as a neutral universal category – as opposed to the racial criteria of the old regime – and thus a neutral test that would decide objectively and effectively what traits of native cultures would survive, or whether they should survive at all.[13] In line with this liberal evolutionary logic, economic development under the Mandate System was also expected to develop individualism by breaking with the curse of tribalism, seen as an obstacle to the advancement of mandate territories.[14] Thus, within the Mandate System, Anghie concludes, 'the market is associated with modernity, progress, individualism and the universal. Culture, on the other hand, is connected with backwardness, tribal community and the particular.'[15]

With its origin in the Mandate System, the present mainstream development thinking continues to advance the old civilisational discourse. International law and institutions after WWII found in 'economic development' a new language of civilising mission that not only undermines the sovereignty of postcolonial states but also shapes the internal political and cultural reconfiguration of these states within the liberal ideological framework. 'Development' has come to mean not only economic growth but also modernity symbolised by individualism and post-ethnic social organisation. As Walt Rostow famously argued, the evolutionary process of development and economic growth of a nation is comparable to the emergence of 'modern' man as the ultimate destination of human development. While the primitive stage of human existence is characterised by illiteracy, tribalism, kinship ties, and irrationality, modernity is associated with the superior values of rationality, literacy, secularism, individualism, and industry.[16]

Within this liberal framework, the lack of development in postcolonial states is attributable to 'backwardness' in the political, economic, social, and cultural systems in those states. Culture, as the shorthand for all these variants of backwardness, is invoked to explain apparently irrational behaviour and self-destructive strategies directed towards the attributes of advanced societies, such as development and democracy.[17] The developmental state represented 'universal' interests that would prevail against

---

[13] Anghie, *Imperialism, Sovereignty and the Making of International Law*, 161.
[14] Ibid., 162.
[15] Ibid.
[16] See Walt W. Rostow, *The Stages of Economic Growth: A Non-Communist Manifesto* (Cambridge: Cambridge University Press, 1960).
[17] Kuper, *Culture*, 10.

the 'particular' interests of minorities that 'were absorbed and assessed by criteria which were often externally determined and which purported, with formidable force, to be universal'.[18] In the words of Ashis Nandy, 'when after decolonisation, the indigenous elites acquired control over the state apparatus, they quickly learnt to seek legitimacy in a native version of the civilising mission and sought to establish a similar colonial relationship between state and society'.[19]

In this sense, what the liberal language of human rights has done to minorities in the field of politics, 'development' has done in the field of economics. Working together, this is a recipe for both political and economic marginalisation of ethnic minorities in postcolonial states. While the human rights-based approach to development is a more recent attempt to contain some of the disastrous consequences of a more traditional understanding of development focused solely on economic growth, as we shall see later, such an approach did not mean much from the perspective of minorities. Thus, the development discourse in international law reinforced the old notion of civilising mission vis-à-vis postcolonial states as well as minorities therein.

While this line of argumentation follows a top-down reasoning, it is also necessary to examine how postcolonial states resisted and responded to the ideological hegemony of development, what consequences such engagements engendered for minorities, and what role international law played in the process. The following section addresses these issues.

5.2.2 Third World Resistance and the Minority Question

Being part of the evolutionary narrative of modernity, the ideology of the postcolonial 'developmental' state, with 'reification' as its mode of operation, came to be seen as historically inevitable in the aftermath of WWII. Postcolonial states wholeheartedly accepted the teleological end that development promised – progress and civilisation.[20] The Bandung Conference (1955) is a perfect illustration of this attitude. This anti-colonial, anti-imperial conference of newly independent states of Asia and Africa recognised in its Final Communiqué the 'urgency of promoting economic development in the Asian-African region' and expressed

---

[18] Anghie, *Imperialism, Sovereignty and the Making of International Law*, 206.
[19] Ashis Nandy, 'State', in *The Development Dictionary: A Guide to Knowledge as Power*, ed. Wolfgang Sachs (London: Zed Books, 1992), 269.
[20] Rajagopal, *International Law from Below*, 33; Pahuja, *Decolonising International Law*, 116.

a desire for global economic cooperation, including the investment of foreign capital.[21] So far as Third World international lawyers are concerned, Balakrishnan Rajagopal argues, in the post-WWII era most of them shared an 'essential belief' in the emancipatory potential of modernity and progress offered by the ideology of development, and expected international institutions to advance their respective projects. This convergence of pragmatism and institutionalism played a major role in consolidating international institutions as 'apparatuses of management of social reality' in postcolonial states.[22]

A difference of views arose, however, regarding the role that international law and institutions should play to advance divergent economic interests of postcolonial states and their former rulers. On the one hand, powerful industrialised countries wished to benefit from this new moment of international order in their favour by using existing international law norms, for example, regarding foreign investment and treaty enforcement. On the other hand, postcolonial 'underdeveloped' countries argued that as former colonies they had not participated in international law making; they wished to use the 'new' international legal order to prevent and reverse the hegemonic use of international law, albeit within the framework of economic development and human rights.[23]

Unlike the Bretton Woods Institutions, where voting rights were tied to financial contributions, or the UN Security Council, where the five permanent members enjoyed veto powers, the UN General Assembly's more democratic set-up was thus the primary as well as natural choice of venue for postcolonial states to fight their battle in international law. In

---

[21] 'Final Communiqué of the Asian-African Conference of Bandung', 161–169. See also Priya S. Gupta, 'From Statesmen to Technocrats to Financiers: Development Agents in the Third World', in *Bandung, Global History, and International Law*, 481–497.

[22] Rajagopal, *International Law from Below*, 26. To substantiate his argument, Rajagopal offers a critical reading of Mohammed Bedjaoui's *Towards a New International Economic Order* (Paris: UNESCO, 1979). See Rajagopal, 89–94. Cf. Umut Özsu, '"In the Interests of Mankind as a Whole": Mohammed Bedjaoui's New International Economic Order', *Humanity: An International Journal of Human Rights, Humanitarianism, and Development* 6, no. 1 (2015), 129–143. For a relevant account of Bedjaoui's contemporary Bangladeshi international lawyer Kamal Hossain, see Cynthia Farid, 'Legal Scholactivists in the Third World: Between Ambition, Altruism and Access', *Winsor Yearbook of Access to Justice* 33 (2016), 57–86.

[23] See Ram P. Anand, 'Attitude of the Asian-African States Towards Certain Problems of International Law' (1962), in *Third World Attitudes Toward International Law: An Introduction*, eds. F. Snyder and Surakiart Sathirathai (Boston, MA: Martinus Nijhoff, 1987), 5–22; S. N. Guha-Roy, 'Is the Law of Responsibility of States for Injuries to Aliens a Part of Universal International Law?' *American Journal of International Law* 55, no. 4 (1961), 863–891.

the story of Third World resistance to the hegemonic economic structure of international law, the oft-cited milestones are therefore a series of UNGA resolutions, including the Resolution on Permanent Sovereignty over Natural Resources (PSNR, 1962),[24] the Declaration on the Establishment of a New International Economic Order (NIEO, 1974),[25] the Programme of Action on the Establishment of a New International Economic Order (1974),[26] and the Charter of Economic Rights and Duties of States (1974).[27] Ironically, as a critical analysis of these instruments reveals later, in their resistance to global injustice postcolonial states readily sacrificed minority interests and focused almost exclusively on the 'national' state and its sovereignty, which included the right to economic self-determination.

The principle of PSNR developed against the backdrop of colonial exploitation of natural resources in former colonies, many of which had already emerged or were in the process of emerging as independent states by the 1960s. It is now an established fact that colonial rule permitted trading and mining corporations from the metropolis to secure special concessions – often by exercising coercive measures – for the exploitation of valuable minerals within the colony. It was therefore imperative for the newly independent postcolonial states to assert their right to control and exploit their own resources as part of their sovereignty. With faith in the international legal system, postcolonial states saw the importance of establishing a legal regime guaranteeing their permanent sovereignty over their natural resources. As the prominent Bangladeshi international lawyer of the time Kamal Hossain asserts, the principle of PSNR was 'originally articulated in response to the perception that during the colonial period inequitable and onerous agreements, mainly in the form of "concessions", had been imposed upon unwary and vulnerable governments'.[28] Once in place, Hossain argues, the PSNR principle had engendered far-reaching consequences for the protection of natural resources of capital-importing developing states, even allowing the repudiation or alteration of legal arrangements for the development of

---

[24] UN General Assembly, Resolution 1803 (XVII), UN Doc A/5217.
[25] UN General Assembly, Resolution 3201 (S-VI), UN Doc A/9559.
[26] UN General Assembly, Resolution 3202 (S-VI), UN Doc A/9559.
[27] UN General Assembly, Resolution 3281 (XXIX), UN Doc A/Res/29/3281.
[28] Kamal Hossain, 'Introduction', in *Permanent Sovereignty over Natural Resources in International Law: Principle and Practice*, eds. Kamal Hossain and Subrata Roy Chowdhury (London: Frances Pinter, 1984), ix–xx, ix. For a detailed account of the development of the principle of PSNR, see generally Nico Schrijver, *Permanent Sovereignty over Natural Resources* (Cambridge: Cambridge University Press, 1997).

minerals or other natural resources at the instance of the host state, if it could demonstrate that such arrangements were incompatible with the PSNR principle.[29]

Hossain's contemporary, the Egyptian international lawyer Georges Abi-Saab, explains the PSNR principle as an extension of the conventional principle of sovereignty that had been traditionally understood within the political context to bear on the use and disposal of natural resources. In this way, Abi-Saab argues, the PSNR principle was premised upon the 'continuous and unseverable link' between sovereignty and self-determination: 'sovereignty serving not only as the protective legal shield of the political outcome of self-determination, namely independence, but also as the permanent guarantee of its effective exercise in the economic field beyond accession to formal independence', that is, economic self-determination.[30] Drawing a distinction between the conceptions of *imperium* (jurisdiction of the state over persons and properties within its territory) and *dominium* (the state's power inherent in the institution of property in private law, including the right to disposal), he argues further that under the principle of PSNR, the state exercises not only *imperium* in general but also *dominium* over its wealth and natural resources.[31] Therefore, unlike the claim propagated under the Mandate System that the international community owns natural resources, the PSNR principle in essence meant that natural resources by their very nature fall under the public domain of the state.[32]

The procedural history of the General Assembly resolution on PSNR reveals that at the UN level the principle was initially raised in the context of the promotion and financing of economic development in underdeveloped countries. Under the title of 'Integrated Economic Development and Commercial Agreements', a UNGA resolution of January 1952 acknowledges that underdeveloped countries have the right to freely decide on the use of their natural resources.[33] The same resolution also urged that the underdeveloped countries must utilise such resources not only in realising their plans for economic development but also in

---

[29] Kamal Hossain, 'Introduction', in *Legal Aspects of the New International Economic Order*, ed. Kamal Hossain (London: Frances Pinter Publishers Ltd., 1980), 39.
[30] Georges Abi-Saab, 'Permanent Sovereignty over Natural Resources and Economic Activities', in *International Law: Achievements and Prospects*, ed. Mohammed Bedjaoui (Paris: UNESCO, 1991), 597.
[31] Ibid., 602.
[32] Ibid.
[33] See UN General Assembly, *Integrated Economic Development and Commercial Agreements*, Resolution 523 (VI) of 12 January 1952, UN Doc A/RES/523 (VI).

furthering the expansion of the world economy.[34] Another UNGA resolution later that year reiterated the sovereignty of underdeveloped countries over their natural resources and renewed the call for the exploitation of their natural resources for economic development.[35] Importantly, the resolution recommended that in exercising sovereignty over natural resources, states should have due regard for the need to maintain the flow of capital in conditions of security, mutual confidence, and economic cooperation among nations.[36]

However, a parallel development of the principle of PSNR took place in the context of the draft international human rights covenants with special reference to the right to self-determination.[37] It was Chile that first linked the principle of PSNR with the human rights provision on self-determination, in the course of a debate at the Human Rights Commission in April 1952.[38] The principle of PSNR as a human rights issue gradually gained prominence and finally made its way to the twin international human rights covenants of 1966 as part of their proclamation of the right to self-determination.[39] As we shall see soon, the human rights dimension of the PSNR principle had specific implications for minorities.

At the same time, some postcolonial states conceived of the principle of PSNR as a legal tool for nationalising mining and other exploitation industries, thereby preventing foreign corporations from exploiting natural resources under preferential terms. In November 1952, Uruguay placed before the General Assembly a draft resolution – 'Economic Development of Under-developed Countries' – that recommended that member states 'should recognize the right of each country to nationalize and freely exploit its natural wealth, as an essential factor of complete independence'.[40] This proposition was premised upon the argument that it

---

[34] Ibid.
[35] UN General Assembly, *Right to Exploit Freely Natural Wealth and Resources*, Resolution 626 (VIII) of 21 December 1952, UN Doc A/RES/626 (VIII).
[36] Ibid.
[37] Commission on Human Rights, *Report of the Eighth Session*, UN Doc E/2256 (1952). See also UN General Assembly, Resolution 421 D (V) of 4 December 1950, UN Doc A/RES/421D(V).
[38] UN Doc E/CN.4/L.24 (16 April 1952). The draft resolution proposed that 'the right of peoples to self-determination shall also include permanent sovereignty over their natural wealth and resources'.
[39] The common Article 1(2) of the International Covenant on Civil and Political Rights (1966) and the International Covenant on Economic, Social and Cultural Rights (1966).
[40] UN Doc A/C.2/L.165 (5 November 1962).

is in the general interest of economically weak nations that they should have direct possession of their natural wealth, and that the nationalisation of this wealth is in keeping with the principles of sovereign equality and peoples' right to self-determination as enshrined in the UN Charter.[41]

Thus, the eight governing principles of the finished product, that is, the UNGA Resolution on Permanent Sovereignty over Natural Resources (1962), adopted a reconciliatory tone and aimed at safeguarding competing interests. The resolution guarantees permanent sovereignty of states over their natural resources, allows regulatory control over foreign capital investments in exploiting such resources, and stipulates that such resources shall be used only for the national development and well-being of the people of the concerned state.[42] However, it also extends protection under international standards (read, standards set by the developed nations) to foreign investment in case of nationalisation.[43] And finally, the resolution underscores the importance of mutual cooperation between developed and underdeveloped states – in the form of 'public and private capital investments, exchange of goods and services, technical assistance, or exchange of scientific information' – in exploiting natural resources to ultimately advance the universalist agenda of economic development, peace, and security.[44] Under the UN, economic development of the underdeveloped countries was seen as one of the fundamental requisites for the strengthening of universal peace.[45]

Especially, the combination of two sources of legitimacy – control over natural resources as a matter of sovereignty and the exercise of this sovereign right as a matter of human rights (the right to self-determination) – had important repercussions for minorities. Both of these ideas were designed to respond externally to the dominance of the developed nations but in the process offered effective tools to postcolonial states to dominate their own minorities. The sovereign control over natural resources under the principle of PSNR was indeed meant for *national* development against the backdrop of the nation-building project in most of these states.[46] Similarly, the preamble to the resolution acknowledges 'the inalienable right of all States freely to dispose of their natural

---

[41] Ibid.
[42] Clauses 1, 2, 5, and 8 of the Resolution.
[43] Clauses 3 and 5 of the Resolution.
[44] Clauses 6 and 7 of the Resolution.
[45] UN General Assembly, *Right to Exploit Freely Natural Wealth and Resources*, Resolution 626 (VII) of 21 December 1952, UN Doc A/RES/626 (VII).
[46] Clause 1.

wealth and resources in accordance with their *national* interest'.[47] As we saw in Chapter 3, the notion of 'national' interest or security or development as part of the ideology of the postcolonial 'national' state – with unification, legitimation, and reification as ideological modes of operation – often results in the complete denial of minority rights and gross marginalisation of minority groups.

On the other hand, the human rights dimension of the principle of PSNR with reference to the right to self-determination of peoples and nations needs to be contextualised within the discourse on minority rights that I analysed in detail in Chapter 4. While the phrase 'nation' in the resolution refers to already independent states, the inclusion of the term 'people' raised problems in interpretation. Building on his ideas of *imperium* and the restriction on *dominium* to the disposal of natural resources as such except granting permission to foreign entities for limited exploitation, Abi-Saab argues that the rationale behind the PSNR principle is to protect the 'human component' of the state, that is, the population, from the weakness or failures of its 'institutional component', that is, the government. It is for this reason, he concludes, that despite the principle of PSNR's formulation in terms of state sovereignty, it is essentially a people's right; hence, it is a component of self-determination in the twin international human rights covenants.[48] The inclusion of PSNR in the human rights provision of self-determination is designed to preserve the people's rights to their natural wealth and resources before self-determination is achieved and to protect natural resources once independence is attained.[49]

Similarly, Anghie notes that in line with the interpretation of the 'people's right to self-determination' in the context of decolonisation and the common Article 1 of the human rights covenants, the use of the term 'people' in the PSNR resolution refers to 'people' under colonial rule and suggests that 'these peoples possess a latent sovereignty over resources and, therefore, an accompanying right to their natural resources'. In other words, even those colonised peoples, who had not as yet become independent, were granted certain rights that could protect their resources, and the violation of such a right to natural resources by colonial powers could arguably give rise to claims of compensation for colonial exploitation.[50]

---

[47] See paragraph 3 of the preamble. Emphasis added.
[48] Abi-Saab, 'Permanent Sovereignty over National Resources and Economic Activity', 603.
[49] Ibid.
[50] Anghie, *Imperialism, Sovereignty and the Making of International Law*, 217–218. He refers to the Nauru's action against Australia as an illustration of this argument. See

While an emancipatory potential of international law can be inferred from these arguments on the meaning of 'people' in the PSNR resolution so far as nascent postcolonial states are concerned, this understanding of 'people' also implicitly acknowledges the limits of that potential so far as minorities are concerned. As we have seen in Chapter 4, there is no generally recognised right to self-determination for minorities under current international law.[51] Therefore, the human rights reading of the PSNR principle can hardly be extended to minorities; nor was that anyone's intention during the drafting process. It was later made clear by the Human Rights Commission in relation to the international dimension of the right to development that '[a] people should not be confused with ethnic, religious or linguistic minorities, whose existence and rights are recognised in Article 27 of the [ICCPR]'.[52] Thus, seen from the minority point of view, the PSNR principle gives postcolonial national states rather a free hand over natural resources, often concentrated in minority and indigenous areas where these cultural communities preserved such resources over millennia as part of their cultural being.

As we have already seen, the PSNR and other UNGA resolutions also actively encouraged national states to exploit these natural resources for economic development defined by growth. I have also demonstrated in the preceding discussion how the post–WWII notion of development – with liberalism as its guiding principle, individuals as stake holders, and the nation-state as the political site for developmental experiments – kept minorities outside the remit of developmental discourse. Thus, UNGA resolutions as a venue for Third World resistance to the hegemonic aspects of international law also facilitated the ideological convergence of liberal individualism and the nation-state vis-à-vis minorities and advanced the cause of the postcolonial 'developmental' state.

Despite various other limitations, such as the acceptance of 'international standards' when it comes to the question of compensation for the nationalisation of natural resources or offering corporations an equal footing with sovereign states, the PSNR resolution represents the first call

also Antony Anghie, 'The Heart of My Home: Colonialism, Environmental Damage, and the Nauru Case', *Harvard International Law Journal* 34, no. 2 (1993), 445–506.

[51] For a contrary view on the meaning of 'people' in the postcolonial Indonesian context, see Muhammad Y. Aiyub Kadir and Alexander Murray, 'Resource Nationalism in the Law and Policies of Indonesia: A Contest of State, Foreign Investors, and Indigenous Peoples', *Asian Journal of International Law* 9, no. 2 (2019), 27–31.

[52] UN ECOSOC, *Report of the Secretary-General on the International Dimensions of the Right to Development as a Human Right* (2 January 1979), UN Doc E/CN. 4/1334, para. 89.

for a new international economic order.[53] By the 1970s, in the face of a sharp increase in the price of crude oil and the ensuing push back from big oil companies, the General Assembly had to address the issue of sovereignty over natural resources in a more organised fashion within the framework of development.[54] The Declaration on the Establishment of a New International Economic Order (NIEO, 1974), the Programme of Action on the Establishment of a New International Economic Order (1974), and the Charter of Economic Rights and Duties of States (1974) were all concerted efforts by developing countries – as new members of the UNGA – to clarify ambiguities in the PSNR resolution. The goal was to assert in more concrete terms developing countries' permanent sovereignty over their natural resources on the basis of sovereign equality and the right to nationalise these resources, subject to compensation, in line with *national* laws and regulations.[55]

However, as Rajagopal notes, despite its radical potential, the NIEO did not really deviate from the teleological end of 'development' and was firmly premised upon the need to accelerate the modernisation process.[56] To substantiate his argument, Rajagopal offers a critical reading of Mohammed Bedjaoui's *Towards a New International Economic Order*,[57] arguing that though Bedjaoui knew that alternative cultural organisations of nations beyond the Western template of modern state are possible, he nonetheless concluded that the gap between the West and the developing states needed to be eradicated through economic development.[58]

---

[53] Hasan S. Zakariya, 'Sovereignty over Natural Resources and the Search for a New International Economic Order', in *Legal Aspects of the New International Economic Order*, 216.

[54] In April 1974, the UNGA convened the sixth special session on raw materials and development.

[55] The Charter, adopted by a vote of 120 in favour to 6 against with 10 abstentions, introduced certain norms or rules which some developed nations considered a fundamental departure from the traditional rules of international law. See, for example, the arbitral decision in *Texaco Overseas Petroleum Co. & California Asiatic Oil Co. v. The Government of the Libyan Arab Republic* (1977), *International Law Materials* 17, no. 1 (1978), 1–37. For an analysis of the legal status of the Charter, see Subrata Roy Chowdhury, 'Legal Status of the Charter of Economic Rights and Duties of States', in *Legal Aspects of the New International Economic Order*, 79–94.

[56] Rajagopal, *International Law from Below*, 73–76.

[57] Bedjaoui, *Towards a New International Economic Order*.

[58] Rajagopal, *International Law from Below*, 89–94. Rajagopal explains this phenomenon as a 'double identity' of Third World international lawyers: 'On the one hand, he/she is a political activist who is interested in social transformation and in that capacity he/she develops a radical critique of the entire edifice of the "old" law and the economic system

More importantly, none of these instruments had anything to say for minorities and their right to land and natural resources, or their protection from invasive development activities by the postcolonial state and its private agents. The NIEO radicalism fell short of attending to minority groups and concerned itself only with the *national* state and the supremacy of sovereignty vis-à-vis its oppressive counterparts in the developed world. Thus, the key principles on which the NIEO was founded include '[s]overeign equality of States, self-determination of all peoples, inadmissibility of the acquisition of territories by force, and territorial integrity and non-interference in the internal affairs of other states'.[59] Similarly, the Charter of Economic Rights and Duties of States declares '[s]overeignty, territorial integrity and political independence of States' as among the fundamentals of international economic relations.[60] At the same time, frequent references to the need for mutual international cooperation for development, along with the link between development and peace and security, highlight the underlying assumption that since economic development is destined to ensure peace and harmony at the international level, there is no reason why it cannot achieve the same at the national level. The ideology of the postcolonial 'developmental' state was indeed an effective way of silencing any minority concern.

5.2.3 Minorities and the Right to Development

By the mid-1970s, Third World resistance to the hegemonic international economic order under the rubric of NIEO started showing signs of success failing.[61] Demands for a new economic order designed to redistribute global wealth and redress historical injustice then met with the rise of neoliberal economic agenda, for example, in the hands of

---

that it sustains. On the other hand, he/she is also a postcolonial lawyer who identifies himself/herself with building his/her 'nation', and in this capacity he/she needs to use law to achieve the best possible conditions for the emergence of his/her 'nation' as a respected power'. See Rajagopal, 92.

[59] Article 4 (a) of the Declaration on the Establishment of NIEO.
[60] Chapter 1 of the Charter.
[61] While the state-oriented resistance of the Third World falls short of any radical response to 'developmentalism' that ultimately led to its failure, Rajagopal argues that it is various grassroots non-state actors such as peasants, women, environmentalists, human-rights activities, and indigenous peoples who mounted more meaningful resistance to traditional development activities, thereby forcing changes in the development policies of international financial institutions. Ironically, such grassroots resistances are not often acknowledged in the standard narrative of international law making. See generally Rajagopal, *International Law from Below*.

Ronald Reagan in the United States and Margaret Thatcher in the United Kingdom, which celebrated the free market economy.[62] Having lost the battle on the NIEO front, Third World states then looked to human rights as a new venue to advance their cause.

Before development became a human rights issue proper, the concept of the 'right to development' was conceived of as a right of the *state* to development. As Bedjaoui notes, the right to development was proclaimed in the 1960s by Algerian Christians for 'underdeveloped peoples' and the 'Third World'.[63] He himself understands the right as belonging to peoples, states, and the proletarian nations. Accordingly, in a speech given in 1969, he associates the right to development with a 'new international law' – 'a law of solidarity and co-operation between States at different levels of development, a law which contained the seeds of a "new international economic order"'.[64]

Having identified the right to self-determination and international solidarity as the basis of the right of development of peoples and states, Bedjaoui unsurprisingly finds its contents in two component parts. First, 'the right to develop claimed *erga omnes* by the State which is "master in its own house" and *opposable* by the State against all parties', and second, 'the right to develop claimed by the States as "an active agent in international relations" and constituting *a right over others*, in other words a right which is *due* to the State from the international community of States'.[65] While the first component emanates from Third World claims to permanent sovereignty over natural resources and reparations for past injustices, the second component relies on the equitable redistribution of global wealth under the socialist principles of 'from each his due' and 'to each according to his needs' to be applied at the international level.[66] Bedjaoui regrets that the subsequent association of the right to development with human rights has shifted the attention away from states and unwisely confined the right to the domain of individual rights recognised as belonging to individual human beings in relation to national communities of which they were part.[67]

---

[62] Ibid., 209.
[63] Mohammed Bedjaoui, 'The Right to Development', in *International Law: Achievements and Prospects*, 1178.
[64] Ibid., 1179.
[65] Ibid., 1188.
[66] See ibid., 1188–1193.
[67] Ibid., 1179. It is generally believed that the Senegalese judge at the IOC and the ICJ, Kéba Mbaye, was the first to depict the right to development as a human right, in his 1972 lecture delivered to the International Institute of Human Rights in Strasbourg. See

Once it has been depicted as a human right, the treatment of the right to development as an individual right is far from unusual. As discussed in Chapter 4, within the post–WWII liberal ideological framework of human rights it is the individual that is seen as the sole legitimate right-bearer. Thus, in the human rights discourse on the right to development too, the individual and their treatment within the sovereign state had to be the centre of attention.

This domestication of the right was not what Third World states hoped to bring out of the right to development. They also had the apprehension that the focus on the individual could bring Third World sovereignty under additional international scrutiny while they wished to remain the 'master of their own house'. Such an approach could also conceal the real international power-political factors behind underdevelopment. 'International law would, in such a case, unjustly and ineffectually point the finger at a "scapegoat" in a situation for which the State being called to account is not responsible.'[68] On the other hand, former colonial powers found in the individualist notion of the right to development an effective way of undermining everything the Third World sovereigns demanded as part of this very right. As a result, the concept of the right to development itself became a new site of contestation between postcolonial states and imperial powers on the divergent meanings of the right as an individual or a collective one. It needs to be noted here that the term 'collective' essentially referred only to states or non-self-governing peoples under foreign rule and not to any sub-state group such as minorities, as explained later.

Kéba Mbaye, 'Le droit au développment comme un droit de l'homme', *Revue internationale des droits de l'homme* 5 (1972), 505–534, cited in ibid., 1179. Bedjaoui, however, notes that Mbaye never ceased to undermine the international dimension of the right granting this to states. The integration of development and human rights serves other important and equally devastating agendas too. Pahuja, for example, argues that the integration facilitates the transformation of rights into a regulatory regime; 'human rights becomes a means by which society is subordinated to the imperative of economic growth through markets.' See generally Sundhya Pahuja, 'Rights as Regulation: The Integration of Development and Human Rights', in *The Intersection of Rights and Regulation: New Directions in Socio-Legal Scholarship*, ed. B. Moran (Surrey: Ashgate, 2007), 167–191. Anghie persuasively demonstrates how the 'good governance' agenda of the international financial institutions linked itself with the already integrated notions of human rights and development to complete the nexus of governance, development, and human rights, and thereby allowed IFIs to take control of vast areas of decision-making, traditionally under national jurisdiction, in the name of promoting human rights and development. See Anghie, *Imperialism, Sovereignty and the Making of International Law*, 258–263.

[68] Bedjaoui, 'The Right to Development', 1180.

The individual and collective aspects of the right to development are given full consideration in the UN Secretary General's report on the international dimensions of the right to development as a human right, presented before the Human Rights Commission in 1979.[69] Under the section on the subjects and beneficiaries of the right to development, the report adopts a reconciliatory tone and finds it unnecessary to think of individual and collective dimensions of the right to development as mutually exclusive. Instead, the report asserts, 'the enjoyment of the right to development necessarily involves a careful balancing between the interests of the collectivity on the one hand, and those of the individual on the other'.[70] Thus, while the self-realisation of the individual contributes to the efforts of the collectivity to pursue its right to development, individual development and fulfilment can be achieved only through the satisfaction of collective prerequisites.[71] It is in this context that the right to self-determination, independence from alien rule, and free exercise of sovereignty are seen as the precondition for any right to development in both individual and collective senses.

Having thus established the interconnection between the individual and the collective, the report then specifies the subjects of the right to development as individuals, on the one hand, and states, peoples, and minorities, on the other. When it comes to the 'people' as a subject of the right to development, the report defines the term within the context of the right to self-determination and specifically mentions that '[a] people should not be confused with ethnic, religious or linguistic minorities, whose existence and rights are recognised in Article 27 of the [ICCPR]'.[72] As I have already discussed at great length in Chapter 4, the minority rights provision in Article 27 of the ICCPR operates within the liberal-individualist as well as assimilationist framework of the human rights jurisprudence and the right is afforded to individual persons belonging to minority groups rather than minorities themselves. It is within this individualistic understanding that minorities appear as a subject of the right to development in the report of the Secretary General. Although the report acknowledges the importance of preserving minority identities, cultures, and traditions and the right of minorities to share in the development of the whole community, its framework remains the liberal

---

[69] UN ECOSOC, *Report of the Secretary-General on the International Dimensions of the Right to Development as a Human Right* (2 January 1979), UN Doc E/CN. 4/1334.
[70] Ibid., para. 85.
[71] Ibid.
[72] Ibid., para. 89.

notion of non-discrimination and the territorial integrity of states in which minorities live.[73]

Similarly, the Working Group of Governmental Experts on the Right to Development, in its report submitted to the Human Rights Commission in 1982, unanimously concluded that the collective and individual dimensions of the right to development are interdependent because they have the same ultimate goal, namely, the integral development of the individual.[74] However, in its understanding of the collective dimension, the Working Group adopted a more restrictive approach compared to the report of the Secretary General, and specifically mentioned that 'the holders of the right to development in its collective dimension are peoples and States'.[75] The Working Group paid particular attention to the enjoyment of the right to development by developing *states*. Although a member of the Working Group highlighted the over-emphasis on states and even referred to other collectivities such as village bodies and co-operatives, there was no mention of minority groups as a holder of the right to development in the collective sense. Such an omission appears less ambiguous when read with the Working Group's identification of self-determination, sovereignty, territorial integrity, and political independence of states as the basis of the right to development in its collective dimension.[76]

It is also interesting to see how both reports adopted the human rights language of equality and non-discrimination among individuals and translated this into inter-state relations.[77] Indeed, the right to development – as an independent, separate human right and also an umbrella term comprising a series of other human rights such as the right to life – squarely fitted into the individualist human rights lexicon.[78] It is quite ironic too that it was the US expert member of the Working Group who highlighted that 'collectivity' must not be confined to states alone and that the role of various non-state groups including ethnic minorities in

---

[73] Ibid., paras. 91, 102. In this context, the report specifically refers to the findings of a seminar on the Promotion and Protection of the Human Rights of National, Ethnic and Other Minorities held in Ohrid, Yugoslavia on 25 June–8 July 1974. UN Doc ST/TAO/HR/49, para. 130.

[74] UN ECOSOC, *Report of the Working Group of Governmental Experts on the Right to Development* (11 February 1982), UN Doc E/CN. 4/1489.

[75] Ibid., para. 17.

[76] Ibid., para. 21.

[77] Ibid., paras. 21, 24; *Report of the Secretary-General*, UN Doc E/CN. 4/1334, para. 84; *Strategy for the Second UN Development Decade*, UN Doc E/CN. 4/SR. 1397, para. 42.

[78] *Report of the Secretary-General*, paras. 55–78.

the development process should be recognised and their cultural traditions must be respected.[79] His comments, however, came in the context of the US conviction of the superiority of a free market economy over the state-managed economy of the socialist order and the important role that various ethno-cultural groups can play in advancing economic development in socialist developing countries where private enterprise by individuals is not permitted.[80]

The Declaration on the Right to Development, which was ultimately adopted as a UNGA resolution in 1986, maintains the reconciliatory tone between the collective and the individual by declaring that equality of opportunity for development is a prerogative both of nations (read states) and of individuals who make up nations.[81] However, the Declaration simultaneously confirms that 'the human person is the central subject of the development process and that development policy should therefore make the human being the main participant and beneficiary of development'.[82] Although there is enough emphasis on the need for ensuring popular participation in all spheres of development, such participation by minority groups, as we shall see later, is not likely to offer them any meaningful bargaining power within the individualist framework of rights under the Declaration.[83]

Thus, the whole discourse on the right to development evolved around individuals, on the one hand, and states or peoples (in the sense of nascent states), on the other, with no attention paid to minorities. The very adoption of human rights language to promote development made this omission only too obvious. Being part of the liberal human rights discourse, the right to development then performs the ideological function of fragmentation too, in that like in the traditional human rights approach to minorities, here also minority groups are diffused into individual stakeholders of economic development. It is the individual

---

[79] UN ECOSOC, *General United States Approach: Contribution by Professor Peter L. Berger, United States Expert* (26 November 1981), UN Doc E/CN. 4/ AC. 34/ WP. 13, para. 4 (III).
[80] Ibid.
[81] The sixteenth preambular paragraph of the Declaration. See UN General Assembly, *Declaration on the Right to Development*, Resolution 41/128 of 4 December 1986, UN Doc A/RES/41/128.
[82] The thirteenth preambular paragraph and Article 2 of the Declaration. See ibid.
[83] See, for example, Article 8 of the Declaration. Rajagopal sees the whole notion of democratic participation in a more critical way and argues that the rhetoric of participatory development is rather a mechanism for the expansion and consolidation of international institutions that takes democratisation as its point of entry. See Rajagopal, *International Law from Below*, 146–155.

that is at the centre of the development discourse even though such development is expected to be materialised through the mediation of the state. The Declaration on the Right to Development perfectly epitomises such a developmental philosophy.

The association with human rights also advances the ideology of the 'developmental' state by dissimulating and glossing over violence inflicted on minorities and indigenous peoples. Rajagopal notes that since development itself is the raison d'état of the postcolonial state, any resistance to state-imposed development activities is necessarily seen as 'anti-national' and hence a moral justification for state repression.[84] This convergence of the ideologies of national liberation, state-building, and development ultimately excludes economic violence carried out under the banner of modernisation and development from the human-rights discourse.[85] Rajagopal argues further that since the rational individual as the subject of human rights has the state and the global market as the ultimate domain for the realisation of their full potential, 'certain forms of resistance to the dominance of the modern market or the state are inherently incapable of being subsumed under the banner of human rights'.[86] As a result, various forms of developmental violence incessantly inflicted on minorities and also on individuals 'remain out of the bounds of the human rights discourse, which treats those forms of violence as "normal" and "necessary" to the task of governance'.[87]

This is also a useful reminder of the inherent relationship between violence and international law, including human rights.[88] On the other hand, development-induced human rights violations against minorities often work as a catalyst for protracted ethnic conflicts in postcolonial states. Interestingly, it is again a combination of the liberal notions of human rights, democracy, and development that dominates the international response to such conflicts. The following section briefly touches upon this phenomenon.

5.2.4 Development and Peacebuilding

Invariably all UN instruments on development connect the notion of economic development with the idea of peace and security in international law. This merger of development with the core UN mandate

---

[84] Ibid., 198.
[85] Ibid., 199.
[86] Ibid.
[87] Ibid.
[88] Ibid., 197.

of maintaining global peace and security was indeed quite useful in internationalising the idea of 'development', thereby bringing developmental interventions under the rubric of international law. For example, Chapter IX of the UN Charter deals with international economic and social cooperation with a view to the 'creation of conditions of stability and well-being which are necessary for ensuring peaceful and friendly relations among nations'.[89] To achieve this goal the Charter mandates assuming responsibilities at both national and international levels and, thereby, eliminates potential sources of tension and conflict.[90] Various specialised agencies of the UN, vested with international legal personalities, are mandated to play a key role in advancing the agenda of peace through economic development.[91] Similarly, the UNGA resolution on the Right to Exploit Freely Natural Wealth and Resources (1952) states that 'the economic development of the under-developed countries is one of the fundamental requisites for the strengthening of universal peace'.[92] The relationship between development and peace was also reiterated in a number of subsequent UNGA resolutions with reference to PSNR and the NIEO.[93] And finally, the Declaration on the Right to Development, too, re-emphasised the intrinsic connection between development, human rights, and peace.[94]

All these instruments conceived of development as necessary means of maintaining global peace and security, but since the collapse of the Soviet Union, the free-market economic version of development along with democracy – primarily identified with mere electoral rituals – has gained popularity in international response to ethnic violence and post-conflict peacebuilding. However, such imposition of free-market democracy as a peacebuilding prescription is often counter-productive, especially in postcolonial states. Examining post-conflict peacebuilding efforts by international organisations – including NGOs and financial institutions

---

[89] Article 55 of the UN Charter.
[90] Article 56 of the UN Charter.
[91] Articles 57–59 of the UN Charter. See also Mohamed Bennouna, 'International Law and Development', in *International Law: Achievements and Prospects*, 620, 625–629.
[92] UN General Assembly, *Right to Exploit Freely Natural Wealth and Resources*, Resolution 626 (VII) of 21 December 1952, UN Doc A/RES/626 (VII).
[93] See UN General Assembly, Resolution 1803 (XVII), UN Doc A/RES/1803 (XVII); UN General Assembly, Resolution 3201 (S-VI), UN Doc A/RES/3201 (S-VI); UN General Assembly, Resolution 3202 (S-VI), UN Doc A/RES/3202 (S-VI); UN General Assembly, Resolution 3281 (XXIX), UN Doc A/RES/3281 (XXIX).
[94] See generally UN General Assembly, *Declaration on the Right to Development*, Resolution 41/128 of 4 December 1986, UN Doc A/RES/41/128.

such as the World Bank and IMF – in Cambodia, El Salvador, Nicaragua, Mozambique, Angola, Rwanda, Namibia, and Bosnia, Roland Paris demonstrates that most international agencies in their peacebuilding projects followed the agenda of what he calls 'market democracy', that is, a liberal democratic polity and a market-oriented economy. In all cases except Namibia the market democracy formula failed to secure sustainable peace; in some cases the introduction of democracy and market economy in fact caused further instability and sparked renewed violence.[95]

This is because, Paris explains, both democracy and capitalism do not merely encourage conflict and competition but thrive on them. Democracy encourages the public expression of conflicting interests in order to limit the intensity of such conflicts by channelling them through peaceful political institutions before they turn violent. However, problems arise when those conflicting demands cannot be channelled through existing institutions. Especially in ethnically divided societies, encouraging political activity can give rise to demagogues and polarise the populace into a number of separated, potentially hostile communities. In such circumstances, holding democratic elections often reinforces societal differences and works against the goal of establishing a stable democratic system.[96] Similarly, Paris continues, capitalism encourages conflict not only by encouraging fierce competition for a larger share of the national wealth but also by creating economic inequalities, leading to resentment and confrontation. Advanced industrialised states – which are also leading market economies – respond to this problem by implementing welfare policies. In contrast, developing countries' attempts to create market economies through economic liberalisation frequently

---

[95] See generally Roland Paris, 'Peacebuilding and the Limits of Liberal Internationalism', *International Security* 22, no. 2 (1997), 54–89. According to Paris, the Namibia exception mainly comes down to the fact that one of the principal belligerents in Namibia's civil war was a foreign party, South Africa, which withdrew its forces from the country as part of the peace process (64). See also Roland Paris, *At War's End: Building Peace after Civil Conflict* (Cambridge: Cambridge University Press, 2004); Edward Newman, Roland Paris, and Oliver P. Richmond, *New Perspectives on Liberal Peacebuilding* (Tokyo: United Nations University Press, 2009).

[96] Ibid., 73–75. See also Robert A. Dahl, *Democracy, Liberty, and Equality* (Oslo: Norwegian University Press, 1986); Richard Sandbrook, 'Transitions Without Consolidation: Democratization in Six African Cases', *Third World Quarterly* 17, no. 1 (1996), 76; Samuel P. Huntington, 'Democracy for the Long Haul', *Journal of Democracy* 7, no. 2 (1996), 6; Alvin Rabushka and Kenneth A. Shepsle, *Politics in Plural Societies: A Theory of Democratic Instability* (Columbus, OH: Charles E. Merrill, 1972); Dennis Austin, *Democracy and Violence in India and Sri Lanka* (London: Royal Institute of International Affairs, 1994).

cause further distributional inequalities – 'largely because such policies often entail reductions in government subsidies, social expenditures, and public-sector employment, which tend to have disproportionately detrimental effects on the poor and the urban working class'.[97] The Structural Adjustment Programmes (SAP) of the World Bank, which promote economic liberalisation as a new model of economic growth and development, are pertinent examples here.[98] SAP-induced economic deprivation and hardship then create the perfect breeding-ground for political mobilisation, often along ethnic lines, within the liberal-democratic framework of political expression, that is, electoral politics.

Thus, by imposing the Western model of market democracy in the non-Western context, international agencies not only cause harm but also advance what Paris calls a benign form of 'civilising mission'.[99] One fundamental drawback of this liberal internationalist venture is that it expects the 'beneficiaries' of this venture 'to become democracies and market economies in the space of a few years – effectively completing a transformation that took several centuries in the oldest European states' and, most importantly, within fragile political structures.[100] This leads to an interesting causal relationship – not between the existence of market democracy and ethnic peace but, ironically, between market democracy and ethnic conflict, at least under some circumstances. As Paris concludes, given the inherently mutually conflictual character of democracy and capitalism, their implantation by international design can further destabilise the weak, unstable, and damaged social and political framework of post-conflict societies.[101]

Similarly, Chimni also argues that in post-conflict societies IFIs prescribe conditions that 'tend to reproduce the general environment that is vulnerable to conflict'.[102] Especially, neoliberal structural adjustment programmes and policies of greater integration with the world economy – as part of the conditionality package imposed by these IFIs – aggravate the legitimacy crisis of the state and generate social protest that can potentially take an ethnic turn against the backdrop of already prevalent

[97] Paris, 'Peacebuilding and the Limits of Liberal Internationalism', 76.
[98] Ibid., 77–78.
[99] Roland Paris, 'International Peacebuilding and the "*Mission Civilisatrice*"', *Review of International Studies* 28, no. 4 (2002), 637–656. Cf. Roland Paris, 'Saving Liberal Peacebuilding', *Review of International Studies* 36 (2010), 337–365.
[100] Paris, 'Peacebuilding and the Limits of Liberal Internationalism', 78.
[101] Ibid.
[102] B. S. Chimni, 'Refugees, Return and Reconstruction of "Post-conflict" Societies: A Critical Perspective', *International Peacekeeping* 9, no. 2 (2002), 166.

ethnic tensions. Given that contesting political parties in post-conflict societies seldom have the desire or means to deviate from the neoliberal agenda of the IFIs, Chimni asserts, 'the state continues to manipulate divisions within society, making the renewal of conflict a distinct possibility'.[103] Orford notes that while 'ancient hatreds, ethnic tensions, post-modern tribalism or emerging nationalisms' are regularly treated as the prime causes of ethnic violence, most international legal literature fails to critically assess these events as consequences of the post–Cold War ruthless divisions of labour and resources. As a result, the nature of the economic order that is put forward in the process of post-conflict reconstruction is seldom scrutinised.[104]

Likewise, Amy Chua provides a persuasive argument about how the globalisation of democracy and the market economy has created ethnic hatred and ultimately conflicts in many parts of the non-Western world. She argues that in many countries outside the West, the economic impact of the free market economy has created market-dominant ethnic minority groups, but the simultaneous exporting of democracy to these countries has politically empowered the economically impoverished majority. Ethnic hatred and backlash have been the obvious results of this process.[105] Although these ethnic minorities were dominant long before the market economy phase, Chua argues that globalisation gave them an enormous opportunity to accumulate a prodigious amount of resources, making their dominance more visible.[106] Simultaneously, the political impact of globalisation in the form of a global campaign for democracy has politically empowered impoverished majorities in these countries. The competition for votes fosters the emergence of demagogues who scapegoat the resented minorities and foment active ethno-nationalist movements demanding that the country's wealth and identity be reclaimed by the 'true owners of the nation'. Under such circumstances, backlash against the ethnic minority in the form of expulsion or even genocide is quite predictable.[107]

---

[103] Ibid., 167.
[104] Anne Orford, 'Feminism, Imperialism and the Mission of International Law', *Nordic Journal of International Law* 71 (2002), 288.
[105] Amy Chua, *World on Fire: How Exporting Free Market Democracy Breeds Ethnic Hatred and Global Instability* (New York: Doubleday, 2003), 9–12. See also Zlatko Isakovic, 'Democracy, Human Rights and Ethnic Conflicts in the Globalised World', *East European Human Rights Review* 8, no. 2 (2002), 199–236.
[106] Chua, *World on Fire*, 35.
[107] To substantiate her argument, Chua discusses backlashes against market-dominant ethnic minorities in all regions of the world although the scale of such incidents is limited in some cases.

In this sense, Chua's thesis not only refutes the universal claim that the liberal ideology of market democracy prevents ethnic conflicts but also highlights the poverty of such an ideology by identifying it as a cause of ethnic conflicts, at least in the non-Western world. In a more recent empirical study, Jason Sorens and William Ruger examined the influence of economic globalisation, especially aspects of foreign direct investment, on intrastate conflicts in Uganda, Kenya, Tanzania, Thailand, Vietnam, Malaysia, and China. The study found that there was no evidence of a universal ameliorative effect of foreign investment on conflict; a few results indicated rather an adverse effect of foreign direct investments on existing ethnic tensions.[108] While some degree of ameliorative effects of foreign investments in some range of circumstances cannot be ruled out, they argue, 'the state will not compromise fundamental security interests in order to appeal to foreign investors and generate economic gains for society as a whole'.[109] The challenges of formulating coherent policies reconciling the often-diverging priorities of peace, security, human rights, and economic growth in other conflict-prone societies, such as Afghanistan, Sri Lanka, Guatemala, and sub-Saharan African states, are now well documented.[110]

Yet, the imposition of the free-market-economy model of development along with a model of democracy that solely focuses on free and fair elections continues to be the centrepiece of any international engagement with post-conflict peacebuilding in many postcolonial states. In this way, the developmental ideology serves to 'dissimulate' aspects of existing asymmetric power relations that provide the premise for the eruption of ethnic tensions in the first place.

In this section on 'minorities in the international law of economic development', we have seen that the development discourse in

---

[108] Jason Sorens and William Ruger, 'Globalisation and Intrastate Conflict: An Empirical Analysis', *Civil Wars* 14, no. 4 (2015), 381–401.

[109] Ibid., 394, 396.

[110] See Vasuki Nesiah, 'Uncomfortable Alliances: Women, Peace, and Security in Sri Lanka', in *South Asian Feminisms*, eds. Ania Loomba and Ritty A. Lukose (Durham, NC: Duke University Press, 2012), 139–161; Shahrbanou Tadjbaksh, 'Conflicted Outcomes and Values: (Neo)Liberal Peace in Central Asia and Afghanistan', *International Peacekeeping* 16, no. 5 (2009), 635–651; Gilles Carbonnier, 'The Competing Agendas of Economic Reform and Peace Process: A Politico-Economic Model Applied to Guatemala', *World Development* 30, no. 8 (2002), 1323–1339; Margit Bussmann, Gerald Schneider, and Nina Wiesehomeier, 'Foreign Economic Liberalization & Peace: The Case of Sub-Saharan Africa', *European Journal of International Relations* 11, no. 4 (2005), 551–579; Daria Davitti, *Investment and Human Rights in Armed Conflicts: Charting an Elusive Intersection* (Oxford: Hart Publishing, 2019).

international law revolves almost exclusively around individuals, on the one hand, and states, on the other. This is evident in the approach to development by both international institutions and states, most notably by postcolonial states. In this process, minorities, who suffer disproportionately from developmental atrocities due to their weak political standing and bargaining power, are almost completely ignored in development discourse. The ideology of the postcolonial 'developmental' state thus offers legitimacy to the further marginalisation of minorities, and international law plays a key role in this process of dissimulation of developmental violence. In the following section, I explore the reverse: to what extent the international law of minority protection engages with development discourse and offers specific protection to minorities vis-à-vis harmful development activities.

5.3 'Development' in the International Law on Minority Rights

Developmental interventions often come in the form of extractive industry, hydroelectric dams, infrastructure development, tourism, and reserve forests. Industrial agriculture is also added to the list as a relatively new phenomenon due to the hike and volatility in food prices following the 2007–2008 crisis.[111] The communities residing on the land that is required for these development projects are subjected to forced eviction and 'land grabbing' by the state, military, and private business actors as a result.[112] It is estimated that each year approximately '15 million people are forced to leave their homes and land to make

---

[111] Lucy Claridge, *Moving towards a Right to Land: The Committee on Economic, Social and Cultural Rights' Treatment of Land Rights as Human Rights* (London: Minority Rights Group International, 2015); Evande Grant and Onita Das, 'Land Grabbing, Sustainable Development and Human Rights', *Transnational Environmental Law* 4, no. 2 (2015), 289–291; Jérémie Gilbert, 'Land Grabbing, Investors, and Indigenous Peoples: New Legal Strategies for an Old Practice?' *Community Development Journal* 51, no. 3 (2015), 350–366.

[112] Olivier De Schutter, former UN Special Rapporteur on the right to food, defined 'land grabbing' as '[a] global enclosure movement in which large areas of arable land change hands through deals often negotiated between host governments and foreign investors with little or no participation from the local communities who depend on access to those lands for their livelihoods'. See Olivier De Schutter, 'The Green Rush: The Global Race for Farmland and the Rights of Land Users', *Harvard International Law Journal* 52, no. 2 (2011), 504. See also Ntina Tzouvala, 'A False-Promise? Regulating Land-grabbing and the Post-colonial State', *Leiden Journal of International Law* 32, no. 2 (2019), 235–253; Umut Özsu, 'Grabbing Land Legally: A Marxist Analysis', *Leiden Journal of International Law* 32, no. 2 (2019), 215–233.

way for large development and business projects'.[113] This means that over the past 20 years, around 300 million people have been affected by 'development-related displacement' globally. David Harvey calls this phenomenon a capitalist 'accumulation by dispossession' characterised by the global misappropriation of natural resources, including land, mineral, water, and biological resources by transnational corporations. He thus rightly identifies this phenomenon as a mode of 'new imperialism' on a global scale.[114]

The supposed benefits of these development projects that are routinely propagated from a neoliberal economic standpoint – such as greater employment, better infrastructure, and growth in GDP, consumption, expenditure, or income – are often factitious. Typically, the goods and services produced, such as energy or food, are primarily meant for export[115] and are rarely affordable by the affected communities even if accessible to them.[116] Employment opportunities for the local community are also minimal compared to the size of the investment and the disruption it brings forth. They hardly compensate for the loss in lifestyle, identity, and culture of affected communities. The people most affected by such developmental interventions are often those who are already the most vulnerable in the society, such as minorities, indigenous peoples, tribal groups, small-scale farmers, and pastoralists.[117] Alexandra Hughes describes how in some cases governments have taken 'explicit measures to prevent minority political participation and/or erode their distinct identities through forced assimilation', thereby rendering them less powerful against their oppressor.[118] The constrained capacity of these groups to protest is part of what makes the expropriation of their land so attractive. In this section, I explore to what extent the international legal regime on minority rights offers minorities protection from such

---

[113] UNCHR, *Report of the United Nations High Commissioner for Human Rights, Economic and Social Council* (2014), UN Doc E/2014/86, para. 5; UNCHR, *Report of the Special Rapporteur on the Right to Food: 'Large-scale Acquisitions and Leases: A Set of Minimum Principles and Measures to Address the Human Rights Challenge'* (2009), UN Doc A/HRC/13/33/Add.2, p. 1.

[114] See generally David Harvey, *The New Imperialism* (New York: Oxford University Press, 2003).

[115] Das and Grant, 'Land Grabbing, Sustainable Development and Human Rights', 293.

[116] The Burma Environmental Working Group (BEWG), *Burma's Environment: People, Problem, Policies* (June 2011), 53–56.

[117] Claridge, *Moving towards a Right to Land*.

[118] Alexandra Hughes, *PRSPs, Minorities and Indigenous Peoples – An Issue Paper* (London: Minority Rights Group International, 2005), 10.

developmental atrocities. I specifically look into the issues of land rights, protection against development-led displacements, and the right to participate in development decision-making.

As discussed in Chapter 4, since the creation of the UN, a general reluctance about the promotion of minority rights is evident in international law, despite occasional rises in enthusiasm for minority protection, especially in the face of ethnic tensions in Europe. As a result, compared to the international legal regime for indigenous peoples, legal protections for minorities from devastations caused by large development projects are rather minimal. Even the most progressive instrument – the UN Declaration on Minority Rights (1992) – despite its non-binding legal status, does not specifically address the issue of land rights or protection against development-led displacements. However, the Declaration, albeit half-heartedly, mentions the right of minorities to participate fully in the economic progress and development of their countries.[119] In his interpretation of 'full participation', Eide suggests that such a participation calls for the integration of everyone in the overall economic development of the society as a whole but in ways which make it possible for persons belonging to minorities to preserve their own identity and traditional resources.[120]

Also, Article 5(1) of the Declaration stipulates that the planning and implementation of national policies and programmes will take into account the 'legitimate' interests of persons belonging to minorities. Ironically, 'legitimate' interests of minorities are frequently quashed by 'more legitimate' national interests. Developmental burdens are often imposed on politically marginalised communities and legitimised in the name of national economic growth and prosperity. This is precisely the ideological function that the postcolonial 'developmental' state performs through 'legitimation' as its ideological mode of operation.

On the other hand, Article 5(2) calls upon development agencies, financial institutions, and others involved in international cooperation to plan and implement their programmes of cooperation and assistance in a way that pays attention to legitimate interests of persons belonging to minorities. As noted earlier and as we shall see in the case studies, the neoliberal economic agenda of these development actors along with their colonial modus operandi generally acts as an important catalyst for land grabbing, forced displacement, and overall economic marginalisation of

---

[119] Article 4 (5) of the Declaration.
[120] Eide, *Final Text of the Commentary*, paras. 71–72.

minorities in many postcolonial states. It is hardly surprising now that the most devastating development projects, such as hydroelectricity-producing dams, are regularly funded by IFIs. While Article 5(2) of the Declaration makes sense in this context, to what extent the toothless provision is likely to have any deterrence on powerful financial institutions and their neoliberal economic agenda in postcolonial states is a different question.

One area where the Declaration is quite explicit is the right to effective participation, within the limits of existing laws, in national- and regional-level decision-making on issues concerning minorities.[121] The need for effective participation of minorities was also enumerated in a Meeting of Experts on National Minorities organised by the Conference on Security and Cooperation in Europe in Geneva in 1991, and also in a meeting of a group of independent experts in Lund, Sweden, in 1999.[122] The Working Group on Minorities adopted a set of recommendations on the same issue at its fifth session in May 1999.[123] As the Commentary on the Declaration notes, minority representation should be ensured beginning at the initial stages of decision-making, for it is of little use to involve minorities only at the final stages, when there is very little room for compromise.

The Inter-American Court of Human Rights (IACtHR) has comprehensively outlined the elements that ought to be fulfilled for the right to participation to be held as satisfied. First, the consultation must be continuous, that is, from the initial stages of planning and preparation to the eventual implementation of the project and notably 'not only when the need arises to obtain approval from the community'.[124] Second, considering the secrecy that typically surrounds large-scale land deals and leases,[125] not only should access to information be assured but also the state must take proactive steps to share information freely so that the affected groups

---

[121] Article 2(3) of the Declaration.
[122] See Eide, *Final Text*, paras. 39–40.
[123] *Report of the Working Group on Minorities on its fifth session*, UN Doc E/CN.4/Sub.2/1999/21, paras. 81–88.
[124] *Saramaka People v. Suriname*, Inter-American Court of Human Rights, Series C, No. 185 (2008), para. 133; *The Kichwa Peoples of the Sarayaku Community and Its Members v. Ecuador*, Inter-American Court of Human Rights, Series C, No. 245 (2012), para. 167. See also UNCHR, *Recommendations of the Forum on Minority Issues at its seventh session: Preventing and addressing violence and atrocity crimes targeted against minorities* (January 2014), UN Doc A/HRC/28/77, para 34. It stipulates: 'Consultation with minorities should take place before pursuing any activity that may result in negative impacts on minorities and their environments or create community tensions'.
[125] Das and Grant, 'Land Grabbing, Sustainable Development and Human Rights', 290.

are informed throughout the consultation process.[126] This especially applies to development projects with potential long-term environmental impacts and health risks.[127] Third, the consultation must be conducted in good faith. This includes providing affected communities with 'a full and fair opportunity to be heard and to genuinely influence the decision before them',[128] 'under conditions of equality',[129] and 'with the objective of reaching an agreement'.[130] And finally, the methodology of the consultation must be 'appropriate and accessible'.[131] This includes translation of documents into indigenous languages and/or overcoming further communication issues such as illiteracy.[132] It also requires that consultation take place 'in conformity with [the groups'] customs and traditions' and in accordance with 'the traditional decision-making practices of the people or community'.[133] The court has also emphasised that the obligation 'to prove that all aspects of the right to prior consultation were effectively guaranteed' rests with the state, and not with the affected group.[134]

In the case of indigenous peoples, especially when their interests in their territory are at stake due to large-scale development projects, the duty to obtain free, prior, and informed consent beyond mere consultation has been asserted frequently in the case law and international

---

[126] *Maya Indigenous Communities of the Toledo District* v. *Belize*, Inter-American Court of Human Rights, Report No. 40/04, Case 12.053 (12 October 2004), para. 3; *Sarayaku* v. *Ecuador*, paras. 126 and 178.
[127] *Saramaka* v. *Suriname*, para. 133; *Maya* v. *Belize*, para. 3.
[128] *Maya* v. *Belize*, para. 56.
[129] Ibid., para. 117.
[130] *Saramaka* v. *Suriname*, para. 133; *Sarayaku* v. *Ecuador*, paras. 177–178, 185, cited Article 6 (3) of the ILO Convention 169. In the latter case, the court also indicated situations that would fall short of acting in good faith. Examples include: 'attempts to undermine the social cohesion of the affected communities, either by bribing community leaders or by establishing parallel leaders, or by negotiating with individual members of the community' (para. 186); the militarisation of a territory (para. 190); offering money or economic benefits in place of consultation (para. 194); 'a clear determination to seek consensus, which encourages situations of tension and dispute' including delegation of the obligation to consult to the private company concerned (paras. 198–199).
[131] *Sarayaku* v. *Ecuador*, para. 178.
[132] *Centre for Minority Rights Development and Minority Rights Group International and Centre on Housing Rights and Evictions (on behalf of Endorois Welfare Council)* v. *Kenya* (*Endorois* case), African Commission on Human and Peoples' Rights, Comm. 276/2003, 46th Ordinary Session (11–25 November 2009), para. 292.
[133] *Saramaka* v. *Suriname*, paras. 129, 133, 177.
[134] *Sarayaku* v. *Ecuador*, para. 179

instruments on indigenous rights.[135] In contrast, in applying Article 27 of the ICCPR, the Human Rights Committee had historically implied that mere consultation was sufficient for constituting effective participation.[136] This was so until the case of *Ángela Poma Poma* v. *Peru*, in which it was concluded that 'participation in the decision-making process must be effective, which requires not mere consultation but the free, prior and informed consent of the members of the community'.[137] However, this judgment also made explicit references to the indigenous character of the complainant. Therefore, whilst the right to consent may be persuasively argued in the case of indigenous peoples, international law jurisprudence offers little support for the requirement of such a right in the case of minority groups.

While underscoring the importance of effective minority participation in the decision-making process within the normative framework of 'deliberative democracy' for ethnic accommodation, Steven Wheatley nevertheless acknowledges the real-life limitations of minorities' right to effective participation. He thus concludes:

> [T]he deliberative model does not recognize any right of veto for minorities. The value of a deliberative understanding of democracy for minorities is not that it necessarily affords minorities a share of political power, but that it requires that individuals belonging to minority groups are recognized as equal, albeit culturally distinct, members of the polity with a right to be included in the decision-making process. As a minimum, this will allow members of ethno-cultural groups to bring issues onto the political agenda, correct

---

[135] See Articles 10, 11, 19, 28, 29, and 32 (2) of the United Nations Declaration on the Rights of Indigenous Peoples (2007); *Maya* v. *Belize,* para. 117; *Saramaka* v. *Suriname*, para. 134.

[136] *Lansman et al.* v. *Finland (No. 2)*, HRC, Communication No. 671/1995 (22 November 1996), UN Doc CCPR/C/58/D/671/1995, para. 6.12, cited General Comment No. 23 on Article 27 and para. 10.5 where the Committee concluded that 'that this consultation process was unsatisfactory to the authors and was capable of greater interaction does not alter the Committee's assessment. It transpired that the State party's authorities did go through the process of weighing the authors' interests and the general economic interests in the area specified in the complaint when deciding on the most appropriate measures of forestry management'. Pentassuglia suggests that in the *Lansman* or *Apriana Mahuika* cases 'the HRC is concerned with the fairness and effectiveness of the participatory process while leaving the specific contours and content of the arrangement to direct state-group negotiations'. See Gaetano Pentassuglia, 'Evolving Protection of Minority Groups: Global Challenges and the Role of International Jurisprudence', *International Community Law Review* 11(2009), 185, 201.

[137] *Ángela Poma Poma* v. *Peru*, HRC, Communication No. 1457/2006 (26 March 2009), UN Doc CCPR/C/95/D/1457/2006, para. 7.6.

factual errors and ensure that their interests and perspectives are recognized in the process.[138]

With such a minimalist approach, the deliberative model of minority participation in policymaking is at best a useful tool for minorities to express their concerns, and for sympathetic governments to do something about those concerns. But it has hardly any significance in cases where the state itself is oppressive, while in a worst-case scenario, such an ornamental engagement with minorities in development decision-making can potentially generate a wrong indication of minority consent. As the case study on the CHT will demonstrate, various development actors are rather more interested in this sort of token participation of minorities in relation to important development projects. It cannot be argued, however, that minority inclusion in any form whatsoever will automatically render the adopted policy lawful and legitimate.[139]

Another area of complexity, as has already been noted, is that all cases in which the Human Rights Committee applied Article 27 of the ICCPR underscoring the importance of effective participation of affected groups involve indigenous peoples, not minority groups.[140] The Committee frequently relied on minority rights provisions in Article 27 to offer remedies to persons belonging to indigenous communities within the individualist framework of the ICCPR. The question arises as to whether the more robust international legal regime of rights for indigenous peoples under the ILO Convention 169 (1989) or the United Nations Declaration on the Rights of Indigenous Peoples (UNDRIP, 2007) applies equally to minority groups.[141]

These two instruments offer a wide range of protections to indigenous peoples, especially against developmental atrocities affecting their lands and livelihood. For example, the ILO Convention stipulates that special

---

[138] Steven Wheatley, 'Deliberative Democracy and Minorities', *European Journal of International Law* 14, no. 3 (2003), 527.
[139] Ibid., 524.
[140] See, for example, *Lansman et al. v. Finland*, para. 10.5; *Mahuika et al. v. New Zealand*, HRC, Communication No. 547/1993 (15 November 2000), UN Doc CCPR/C/70/D/547/1993, para. 9.6; *Hopu and Bessert v. France*, HRC, Communication No. 549/1993 (9 December 1997), UN Doc CCPR/C/60/D/549/1993/Rev. 1, para. 10.3; *Ángela Poma Poma v. Peru*, para. 7.6.
[141] Article 1 (b) of the ILO Convention 169 defines indigenous peoples as those 'peoples in independent countries who are regarded as indigenous on account of their descent from the populations which inhabited the country, or a geographical region to which the country belongs, at the time of conquest or colonisation or the establishment of present State boundaries and who, irrespective of their legal status, retain some or all of their own social, economic, cultural and political institutions'.

measures should be taken ensuring: the safeguard of the persons, institutions, property, labour, cultures, and environment of indigenous and tribal peoples;[142] the right to decide their own priorities for the development process;[143] and the right to retain their own customs and institutions.[144] Part II of the Convention includes a wide range of rights in relation to lands and the use, management, and conservation of natural resources pertaining to their lands.[145] Likewise, the UNDRIP expanded the legal protection and safeguards for indigenous peoples by recognising their right to self-determination, which in practice implies an extensive right to autonomy.[146] Article 32 substantiates this by declaring that indigenous peoples have the right to determine and develop priorities and strategies for the development or use of their lands, territories, and other resources.

While these protections can hardly eradicate the marginalisation and disenfranchisement of indigenous peoples within the pervasive neoliberal framework of the global economy, the focus of the international legal regime for indigenous peoples has undoubtedly, albeit gradually, shifted from 'development' as a mode of modernisation and assimilation to the notion of 'self-determined development'.[147] Therefore, an extension of these rights to minority groups would potentially bring the latter under a much better *legal* protection in the face of harmful development projects.

Responding to the question about applying rights for indigenous peoples to minority groups, Eide unequivocally asserts that special rights designed for persons belonging to national or ethnic, linguistic, or religious minorities can also be claimed by persons belonging to indigenous peoples. But the rights of indigenous peoples under ILO Convention 169 or the UNDRIP can only be asserted by persons belonging to indigenous peoples or their representatives; members of non-indigenous minorities cannot assert the rights contained in that Convention.[148] This is because,

---

[142] Article 4 of the ILO Convention No. 169 (1989).
[143] Article 7.
[144] Article 8.
[145] Articles 13–19. Compared to the ILO Convention No. 107 (1957), the new Convention provides a more robust and comprehensive protection to indigenous peoples and breaks with the old perceptions of indigenous peoples as primitive and, hence, in need of modernisation.
[146] See Articles 3 and 4 of UNDRIP.
[147] For an in-depth analysis, see Cathal Doyle and Jérémie Gilbert, 'Indigenous Peoples and Globalisation: From "Development Aggression" to "Self-Determined Development"', in *European Yearbook on Minority Issues*, 67–117.
[148] Asbjørn Eide, 'An Overview of the UN Declaration and Major Issues Involved', in *The United Nations Declaration on Minorities*, 82–83.

Eide argues, the specific rights of indigenous peoples contained in the above instruments are significantly different from those in the Minority Rights Declaration (1992):

> Whereas the Minority Declaration and other instruments concerning persons belonging to minorities aim at ensuring a space for pluralism in togetherness, while ensuring equality and non-discrimination in the common domain, the instruments concerning indigenous peoples are intended to allow for a high degree of autonomous development. Whereas the Minority Declaration places considerable emphasis on effective participation in the larger society of which the minority is a part [...], the provisions regarding indigenous peoples seek to allocate authority to these peoples so that they can make their own decisions.[149]

It needs to be noted, however, that universal human rights norms – as the general premise of both minority rights and the rights of indigenous peoples – are equally applicable to both groups. Therefore, it might be worth exploring the extent to which the 'human rights' language, adopted by regional human rights courts in their legal reasoning in litigations involving land rights and protection against development-induced displacement of indigenous peoples, could be expanded to encompass minority groups in general. For example, the jurisprudence of both the African Commission on Human and Peoples' Rights (African Commission), along with the African Court on Human and Peoples' Rights (ACtHPR), and the Inter-American Court of Human Rights have repeatedly recognised indigenous customary systems of tenure over ancestral lands, alongside the common law and statutory framework governing land law.[150] As a result, the state is obliged to recognise and protect indigenous land via delimitation, demarcation, and titling.[151] A failure to do so was considered a violation of the right to non-discrimination in *Sawhoyamaxa Indigenous Community* v. *Paraguay*.[152] Similarly, in *Maya* v. *Belize*, it was noted that 'one of the greatest manifestations' of racial discrimination against indigenous peoples was found in 'the failure of state authorities to recognize indigenous customary forms of possession and use of lands'.[153] While one could argue then that based on the universal principles of

---

[149] Ibid., 82.
[150] *Mayagna (Sumo) Awas Tingni Community* v. *Nicaragua*, Inter-American Court of Human Rights, Series C, No. 79 (2001), para. 148.
[151] *Saramaka* v. *Suriname*, para. 115; *Maya* v. *Belize*, paras. 5–6 and 152; *Awas Tigni* case, paras. 127 and 151; *Endorois* case, para. 196; *Sarayaku* v. *Ecuador*, para. 171.
[152] *Sawhoyamaxa Indigenous Community* v. *Paraguay*, Inter-American Court of Human Rights, Series C, No. 146 (2006), para. 120.
[153] *Maya* v. *Belize*, para. 167.

equality and non-discrimination the recognition of customary law should be extended to other groups, including minorities, who own or use lands in the same way,[154] such an argument is limited in two ways. First, in the legal reasoning of this case, specific references have been made to instruments concerning the rights of indigenous peoples, namely Article 26 of UN Declaration on the Rights of Indigenous Peoples and Article 14 (1) of the ILO Convention 169.[155] Second, the decision is driven by specific concerns for *indigenous* custom, tradition, and survival – particularly seeking to ensure 'that colonial title to land ownership, and its ensuing postcolonial legacy, have not "extinguished" indigenous peoples' land rights'.[156]

It cannot be concluded that other groups do not equally rely on customary systems of land tenure that deserve protection. It is especially relevant to groups that rely on publicly owned lands and forests used by communities for different purposes, such as gathering or cultivation of food, grazing, transit routes, and so on. Individual titling may fail to adequately protect those whose livelihoods depend on communal natural resources.[157] In many countries, indigenous peoples and minority groups share the system of governance, management, and customary land-use practices.[158] The Human Rights Council has acknowledged that 'systems of shared or collective land rights and customary land tenure and property rights', in the context of minorities, should also be subject to strategies of protection.[159] Furthermore, a tendency towards an expansive interpretation of customary forms of tenure is implicit in a number of court decisions. In *Saramaka v. Suriname*, the court highlighted that 'it is a well-established principle of international law that unequal treatment towards persons in unequal situations does not necessarily amount to impermissible discrimination'; thus,

---

[154] See, for example, Lucy Claridge, *Victory for Kenya's Ogiek as African Court Sets Major Precedent for Indigenous Peoples' Land Rights* (London: Minority Rights Group International, 2017), 8.

[155] *Maya v. Belize*, para. 49. See also *African Commission on Human and Peoples' Rights v. Republic of Kenya* (*Ogiek* case), African Court of Human and Peoples' Rights, Application No. 006/2012 (2017), paras. 125–128.

[156] Jérémie Gilbert, 'Litigating Indigenous Peoples' Rights in Africa: Potentials, Challenges and Limitations', *International and Comparative Law Quarterly* 66, no. 3 (2017), 666. See also *Maya v. Belize*, para. 117; *Saramaka v. Suriname*, para. 103.

[157] De Schutter, 'The Green Rush', 504, 533–534.

[158] Sub-committee on Human Rights of the European Parliament, *Land grabbing and human rights: The involvement of European corporate and financial entities in land grabbing outside the European Union* (May 2016), EP/EXPO/B/DROI/2015/02, 8, 35.

[159] UNCHR, *Recommendations of the Forum on Minority Issues at its third session, on minorities and effective participation in economic life*, UN Doc A/HRC/16/46 (January 2011), para. 25.

the recognition of a different form of ownership for indigenous peoples is justified.[160] If other groups are in the same 'unequal situation', it seems only logical and fair that they receive the same recognition of their customary land rights. Indeed, in *Moiwana v. Suriname*, the occupation and possession of lands in a customary manner was recognised as a right of a community of descendants of African slaves who had resided on the territory since the nineteenth century.[161]

Similarly, the issue of forced eviction has been identified as a violation of 'the full-spectrum' of human rights.[162] In the African human rights mechanism, the prohibition on forced evictions has been creatively applied. For example, in *SERAC and CESR v. Nigeria*, a 'massive violation of the right to shelter' was found, despite no right to shelter being provided for in the African Charter, via a violation of the right to health (Article 16), the right to property (Article 14), and the right to family (Article 18).[163] In this case, the government had destroyed indigenous Ogoni villages, and then 'its security forces obstructed, harassed, beat and, in some cases, shot and killed innocent citizens who had attempted to return to rebuild their ruined homes' – all in an attempt to grant oil concessions to foreign corporations.[164] Interestingly, in its decision the African Commission did not refer to the indigenous status of the Ogoni people; instead, the Commission cited paragraph 8 (1) of General Comment No. 4, emphasising that '*all persons* should possess a degree of security of tenure, which guarantees legal protection against forced eviction, harassment and other threats'. Likewise, in *COHRE v. Sudan*, the Commission had to decide whether the forced eviction and displacement of non-indigenous groups violated Article 14 of the Charter. The Commission concluded that it did, arguing that 'the fact that the victims cannot derive their livelihood from what they possessed for generations

---

[160] *Saramaka v. Suriname*, para. 103.
[161] *Moiwana Community v. Suriname*, Inter-American Court of Human Rights, Series C, No. 124 (2005), para. 133.
[162] UNHCR, *Forced evictions: Fact Sheet No. 25/Rev.1* (2014). See also UN Committee on Economic, Social and Cultural Rights (UNCESCR), *General Comment No. 7: The Right to Adequate Housing (Art. 11 (1) of the Covenant): Forced Eviction* (1997), UN Doc E/1998/22; UNCESCR, *General Comment No. 4: The Right to Adequate Housing (Article 11 (1) of the Covenant)* (1991), UN Doc E/1992/23.
[163] *Social and Economic Rights Action Centre (SERAC) and the Centre for Economic and Social Rights (CESR) v. Nigeria*, African Commission on Human and Peoples' Rights, Communication No. 370/09 (2008), paras. 60–63.
[164] *Centre on Housing Rights and Evictions (COHRE) v. Sudan*, African Commission on Human and Peoples' Rights, Communication No. 296/2005 (2009), paras. 60–62.

means they have been deprived of the use of their property under conditions which are not permitted by Article 14'.[165] Whilst armed conflict was the cause of the displacement in this case, the reasoning could equally be applied to development-induced displacement. Finally, the prohibition on forced evictions in relation to Article 14 was highlighted in the *Endorois* case, where paragraph 18 of General Comment No. 4 was again referred to, confirming that only 'in the most exceptional circumstances and in accordance with the relevant principles of international law' would forced evictions be justified.[166] The issue of the 'objective of the displacement' was also considered in the *Endorois* case in relation to the 'public interest' test.[167] The African Commission noted that where indigenous land is concerned, the threshold is much higher than a case regarding a private property.[168] Whether the land used and owned by minority groups would be considered to be on that spectrum is unclear. Overall, the prohibition on forced eviction in the African system may be applied as an alternative methodology for minorities elsewhere to claim the right to property.

While relevant human rights provisions can potentially be interpreted in such ways to offer better protection to minority groups, the individualist premise of those rights – at the cost of group identity – is omnipresent. This diffusion of groups into individual right-holders also undermines the capacity of minorities to engage with and effectively participate in development decision-making *as groups*. Unlike indigenous peoples, whose group identity is recognised and protected under corresponding international instruments, minorities do not enjoy such recognition or protection. Thus, even if relevant human rights provisions are interpreted with the best of intentions, certain key challenges will persist due to the inherent limitations of the liberal-individualist human rights regime in dealing with group identities. Pentassuglia, however, optimistically suggests that 'international jurisprudence holds the promise of a wide and deeper (re-)assessment of minority issues within the human rights canon'.[169] Whether or not this suggestion has the potential to materialise can be deduced to some extent by the reasoning in the existing jurisprudence on indigenous peoples but ultimately will require

---

[165] Ibid., para. 205.
[166] *Endorois* case, para. 200.
[167] Ibid., para. 212.
[168] Ibid. Cf. *Yordanova and Others v. Bulgaria*, European Court of Human Rights, Application no. 25446/06 (2012), para. 144.
[169] Pentassuglia, 'Evolving Protection of Minority Groups', 185.

a purposively positive interpretation of the relevant instruments. At the practical level, the prospect of the universal application of the African and Inter-American jurisprudence is also limited.

Beyond the muddling of fact and fiction, intent and interpretation, the UN Forum on Minority Issues has more recently taken up the issue of development-related vulnerabilities of minorities. The Forum has taken note of the 'negative outcomes' of 'large-scale economic development projects or commercial activities carried out on the lands and territories where minorities live', such as 'forced displacement, the perpetuation of poverty and, in some cases, violence, including sexual violence'.[170] Otherwise, the international legal regime designed for minorities appears largely ambivalent to the atrocities arising from development projects. This explains why many postcolonial states are keen to impose 'ethnic minority' identity on groups that are traditionally known and self-defined as 'indigenous peoples' and, thereby, to downgrade these groups' legal status and deprive them of a more robust international legal regime of protection.

The hill people of the CHT in Bangladesh would be a pertinent example here. Briefing foreign diplomats and UN agencies in Dhaka on 26 July 2011, the then Foreign Minister of Bangladesh expressed concerns over attempts from some quarters at home and abroad to identify the ethnic minority groups in the CHT region as indigenous people. In her effort to clarify some 'recent misconceptions' about the identity of the people in the CHT, she claimed that people in the CHT were 'ethnic minorities' and should not be called 'indigenous'.[171] As we shall see in the case study on the CHT, the denial of the status of an indigenous people and the resulting lack of protection of land rights have heightened the degree of development-led suffering of the CHT hill people. I also noted

---

[170] UNCHR, *Recommendations of the Forum on Minority Issues at its third session, on minorities and effective participation in economic life* (2011), paras. 6, 24–26; also see UNCHR, *Recommendations of the Forum on Minority Issues at its seventh session: Preventing and addressing violence and atrocity crimes targeted against minorities* (2014), para. 34. It states: 'Non-State actors and business enterprises should, in line with the Guiding Principles on Business and Human Rights [...] promote and respect human rights wherever they operate and refrain from any actions which may create tensions between groups or directly or indirectly lead to violence targeted against minority groups, for example regarding land and access to resources or national development projects. Consultation with minorities should take place before pursuing any activity that may result in negative impacts on minorities and their environments or create community tensions'.

[171] Reported on *The Daily Star*, 27 July 2011, available at www.thedailystar.net/news-detail-195963.

earlier that the Rohingya in Myanmar are not even allowed to use the word 'Rohingya', as a step towards suppressing any claim to indigeneity. Ironically, the Rohingya have also lost the legal status of an ethnic minority; instead, they are depicted by the state as illegal Bangalee immigrants.

In the preceding sections, to substantiate my argument that international law plays a key role in the ideological function of the postcolonial 'developmental' state, I have explained how the development discourse in international law ignores minority concerns and focuses almost exclusively on states and individuals. The resulting ethnic tension is often dealt with through 'development' prescribed as a policy response towards peacebuilding. In this section, we have seen how the international legal regime on minorities also fails to offer minority groups adequate protection against land-grabbing or forced eviction. Within the individualist human rights framework of minority protection, the right to participation in development decision-making is not effective either. Collectively, international legal regimes on development and minorities then create and sustain a condition in which minorities suffer disproportionately as the ideology of the postcolonial 'developmental' state legitimises, dissimulates, and reifies developmental violence. The following case studies illustrate this assertion.

5.4 The Case of the Rohingya in Myanmar

By the old Moulmein Pagoda, lookin' lazy at the sea,
There's a Burma girl a-settin', and I know she thinks o' me;
For the wind is in the palm-trees, and the temple-bells they say:
'Come you back, you British soldier; come you back to Mandalay!'[172]

During his official visit to Myanmar in January 2017, the then British Foreign Secretary Boris Johnson was accused of 'incredible insensitivity', for while in the Shwedagon Pagoda he suddenly started reciting this opening verse from Kipling's colonial-era poem 'Mandalay' in front of local dignitaries. The accompanying tense British High Commissioner had to stop him by reminding him that reciting this poem was '[p]robably not a good idea'.[173] Not unlike in many postcolonial states, a bitter feeling about British colonialism is still fresh in the collective social psyche in

---

[172] Rudyard Kipling, 'Mandalay' (1890), in *Barrack-Room Ballads and Other Verses* (London: Methuen, 1892).
[173] Robert Booth, 'Boris Johnson Caught on Camera Reciting Kipling in Myanmar Temple', *The Guardian*, 30 September 2017, available at www.theguardian.com.

Myanmar, and it is rather a conventional wisdom to blame colonial rule for ethnic troubles in the country.

Johnson was visiting Myanmar in the aftermath of the country's apparent transition to democracy beginning in 2011 after decades of military rule and of self-imposed isolation from global politics and economy. Following the country's opening-up and democratic elections in 2015, Suu Kyi, Myanmar's de facto leader, invited foreign investment with open arms. Investment-led economic growth is seen as the key to the country's economic development and ethnic peace, which would ultimately help achieve the long-cherished goal of stability and national unity. Paradoxically, the moment of transition to democracy and market liberalisation was also marked by fresh major waves of ethnic violence against the Rohingya minority – first in 2012, with many dead and nearly 150,000 displaced,[174] and again in 2017, genocidal in nature and turning an additional 750,000 Rohingyas, including 400,000 children, into refugees in neighbouring Bangladesh.[175]

It is, therefore, no surprise that the development discourse in Myanmar is closely linked to ethnic insurgency and peacebuilding. On the one hand, ethnic tensions and separatist tendencies among various ethnic groups are seen as a major impediment to Myanmar's economic growth since independence. On the other hand, 'development' is considered an effective remedy for and a policy response to protracted ethnic conflicts in the country. The recently formulated Myanmar Sustainable Development Plan (2018–2030) recognises this mutual relationship between peace and development. Designating 'peace and stability' as one of its three pillars, the Plan requires that all development initiatives 'are designed, implemented, managed and monitored with the participation of all stakeholders in a conflict-sensitive manner'.[176]

Similarly, the Annan Commission approached the Rohingya crisis in Myanmar through the optics of three crises – of 'development', 'human rights', and 'security'.[177] International business firms, too, adopt the language of peace and development to wrap their penetration into the lucrative Myanmar market in humanist fervour. For example, in his

---

[174] Ian Holliday, 'Addressing Myanmar's Citizenship Crisis', *Journal of Contemporary Asia* 44, no. 3 (2014), 409.
[175] UN Office for the Coordination of Humanitarian Affairs. See www.unocha.org/rohingya-refugee-crisis.
[176] Ministry of Planning & Finance, Government of Myanmar, *Myanmar Sustainable Development Plan (2018–2030)*, 3 August 2018, available at www.mopf.gov.mm/en.
[177] *Final Report of the Advisory Commission*, 9.

keynote speech before the Oslo Business for Peace Foundation, the Myanmar head of the Norwegian mobile firm Telenor claimed that the company's work in building mobile towers in remote parts of the country and negotiating with rebels in this regard was contributing to nation-building and should be celebrated as such.[178] However, as we shall see, the very pursuit by successive colonial and postcolonial regimes of development and economic growth in Myanmar has heightened, rather than abated, ethnic strife. At the same time, the propagation of 'development' as a solution to ethnic problems often performs the ideological function of obscuring structural injustice vis-à-vis minorities. The case of the Rohingya offers the most pertinent example in this regard. In order to understand the political economy of violence against the Rohingya and the invocation of the developmental ideology to address the problem, we first need to return to the colonial capitalist mode of resource exploitation and its impacts on inter-ethnic relations in colonial Burma.

5.4.1 Colonial Capitalism, Mass Migration, and Inter-ethnic Relations

After the British victory in the first Anglo-Burma War in 1826, the East India Company annexed Arakan and subsequently incorporated it into colonial Bengal.[179] The Bengal Council in Calcutta soon appointed a four-member Commission for the administration of Arakan.[180] In line with the Company policy elsewhere, the priority of the colonial administration was to generate revenue from occupied territories by exploiting and exporting raw materials and natural resources.[181]

As a result, Arakan – and gradually the entire Lower Burma – became a vital source of rice exports for the global market. Burma had a negligible rice trade before the British conquest of Arakan, but by 1845 its rice

---

[178] Petter Furberg, 'Keynote Presentation', Oslo Business for Peace Foundation event, 7 May 2016, cited in Jason Miklian, 'Contextualising and Theorising Economic Development, Local Business and Ethnic Cleansing in Myanmar', *Conflict, Security, and Development* 19, no. 1 (2019), 57.

[179] In 1886, all of Burma formally became a province of British India.

[180] The Commission consisted of Major General Sir Archibald Campbell, Thomas Robertson, John Crawford, and Ross Mangles. See John L. Christian, *Modern Burma: A Survey of Political and Economic Development* (Berkeley, CA: University of California, 1942), 57.

[181] See generally John V. Levin, *The Export Economies* (Cambridge, MA: Harvard University Press, 1960). For an account of colonial capitalism and the political economy of raw material extraction in the Burmese context, see Hans O. Schmitt, 'Decolonisation and Development in Burma', *Journal of Development Studies* 4, no. 1 (1967), 97–109.

exports exceeded 74,000 tons and by 1861 exports had risen to 160,000 tons, most of which went to India.[182] The exponential growth in rice production and exports within a relatively short period of time was largely due to the fact that following the second Anglo-Burma War in 1852, Britain had annexed the entire Lower Burma and all Maritime Provinces. As one author writes to emphasise the importance of the region to the rice economy, 'Lower Burma has never known a crop failure or a famine. It is, in fact, one of the most constantly productive agricultural areas in the world'.[183] One impetus for the intensive rice production was the American Civil War, which cut off Britain's regular supply arrangements with the Carolinas.[184] Following the opening of the Suez Canal in 1869, Burma's rice exports grew to 500,000 tons a year, the lion's share of which went to European markets.[185] In the 1933–1934 season alone, Burma's rice exports amounted to an impressive 3,779,000 tons.[186]

The large-scale rice production was absolutely dependent on intensive human labour and in turn necessitated a policy of encouraging mass migration of impoverished Indians into Burma. In Arakan, the ever-increasing need for agricultural workers was largely filled by landless Muslim peasants from Bengal, mainly from the adjoining district of Chittagong. Many of these workers came on a seasonal basis but some settled down permanently, thereby altering the ethnic and religious composition of the region.[187] Thus, as a direct result of the colonial mass migration policy to boost revenue generation, the preexisting Muslim community in Arakan expanded significantly, combining the historical Rohingya community with the newly arrived Bangalee Muslim agricultural workers. The 1882 census indicates that between the 1880s and the 1930s, the size of the Muslim community in Arakan had doubled, increasing from about 13 to 25 per cent of Arakan's total population.[188] However, to get a better sense of how the colonial open-door immigration policy engendered a strong countrywide anti-Indian sentiment during British rule that in turn shaped the postcolonial Burma's response to Bangalee Muslims in general and the Rohingya in particular, one needs to look beyond Arakan.

[182] F. B. Leach, 'The Rice Industry of Burma', *Journal of the Burma Research Society* 27, no. 1 (1937), 61–73.
[183] Christian, *Modern Burma*, 106.
[184] Ibid., 105.
[185] Ibid.
[186] Ibid.
[187] *Final Report of the Advisory Commission*, 18.
[188] Report on the Census of British Burma, Part I: The Enumeration and Compilation of Results, 1881; Census of India 1931, vol. XI: Burma, Part I: Report, 1933.

Following the second Anglo-Burma War, Lower Burma around the Irrawaddy Delta became a lucrative source of large-scale rice cultivation. Commercial logging of teak and oil and mineral mining expanded considerably at the same time. With the rapid consolidation of power, deepening of colonial control, and the arrival of colonial capitalism, railways were constructed and river steamer services increased markedly. Following the third Anglo-Burma War in 1885 and the ensuing colonisation of all of Burma, substantial irrigation projects were launched, the post and telegraph system was overhauled, and a modern system of currency and banking was established.[189] Although the booming rice economy of Lower Burma (outside Arakan) attracted a significant number of workers from Upper Burma, it also gave a large number of Indians – primarily from neighbouring Bengal and coastal areas of southern India – impetus to immigrate.[190] There have always been Indian settlements in Burma, but the scale of Indian influx was unprecedented. Geographical proximity and existing sea routes between coastal areas of India and Burma played a key role in this regard. The Chief Commissioner Arthur Phayre's preference for encouraging Chinese immigrants, on the grounds that the Burmese have more in common with the Chinese than with Indians, did not work out well for this reason. The fact that Burma was officially a province of British India also favoured Indian immigrants.[191] On the part of the immigrants, chronic poverty, landlessness, the lower-caste status of many of the Hindus, and entrepreneurial zeal (especially in the case of the Chettiars of southern India), on top of the prospect of a better life in Burma, offered the necessary incentive for migration.

While there were approximately 37,500 Indians in Lower Burma in 1872, the number exponentially rose to over 297,000 – constituting 7 per cent of the population – by 1901.[192] According to one estimate, between 1852 and 1937, nearly 2,600,000 Indians migrated to Burma.[193] Most Indian migrants lived in Rangoon (now known as Yangon) and

---

[189] Roman David and Ian Holliday, *Liberalism and Democracy in Myanmar* (Oxford: Oxford University Press, 2018), 15.
[190] For a detailed account of Indian labour immigration to Lower Burma and the ensuing socio-political impacts, see Michael Adas, *The Burma Delta: Economic Development and Social Change on an Asian Rice Frontier, 1852–1941* (Madison, WI: University of Wisconsin Press, 2011), 83–102, 154–181.
[191] Ibid., 83.
[192] Ibid., 85.
[193] Kingsley Davis, *The Population of India and Pakistan* (Princeton, NJ: Princeton University Press, 1951), 101.

other large cities. While Indians (both Hindus and Muslims) constituted 26.5 per cent of the population of Rangoon in 1872, the percentage went up to 51 in 1901, making it an 'Indian city'.[194] Starting in agricultural work, this staggering number of Indian immigrants, as well as the Chinese and Europeans, soon took control of a large portion of the Burmese economy encompassing a wide range of sectors, including rice processing, moneylending, landholding, trade, and transportation. Since Rangoon was the administrative, mercantile, and industrial centre of Burma, upper-class Indian immigrants along with the Europeans monopolised bureaucratic, professional, and commercial positions.[195]

Largely due to economic hardships in colonial India, the rate of Indian migration to Lower Burma continued to rise in the first three decades of the twentieth century despite a simultaneous sharp decline in migration from Upper Burma.[196] Between 1911 and 1931, the population of Lower Burma increased by 1,333,000.[197] But at the same time, the Burmese rice economy started showing signs of slowing down after decades of boom, and the economy was no longer capable of supporting the ever-increasing population. In this classic situation of a gap between the supply of and the demand for workers, competition intensified. As Michael Adas notes, in homogenous agrarian societies worsening economic conditions have historically resulted in struggles between the classes that engage in production and the classes that control the means of production, but in plural societies such divisions have primarily been along ethno-cultural lines.[198] Consequently,

> [a]s competition for control of the common institutions of [Lower Burma] became more pronounced, the members of each of the cultural segments which composed it grew more and more conscious of the differences which distinguished their group from the others. The cleavages between cultural groups hardened, and their interaction was increasingly hostile. The divisions which separated them were further emphasized by the growth of nationalism in India, China, and Burma. Even as it matured, the plural society of Burma began to break down.[199]

In general, a sense of hierarchy, dominance, and deprivation in colonial Burma's public administration, commerce, and industry came to be

---

[194] Burma Census Reports, 1901, 26. See also Adas, *The Burma Delta*, 99.
[195] Ibid., 90, 99.
[196] For an explanation of this rise and fall in migration, see ibid., 154–163.
[197] The Burma Census Reports, 1931, 2 and 6. See also Adas, *The Burma Delta*, 165.
[198] Adas, *The Burma Delta*, 166, 180–181.
[199] Ibid., 166.

depicted along racial lines – with Europeans at the top, Indians and Chinese in the middle, and the Burmese at the bottom.[200]

In particular, the Burmese apprehension of a complete Indian takeover of the economy can be substantiated by the fact that an official survey in 1921 found that in all industrial establishments in Burma employing more than ten persons, Indians made up 55 per cent of the skilled and 73 per cent of the unskilled workforce, in contrast to the Burmese who constituted only 37 and 23 per cent, respectively.[201] Another survey, in 1934, specifically on the rice-processing sector – the leading industry in Burma at the time – revealed that 74.4 per cent of skilled and 80.9 per cent of unskilled rice-mill workers in Burma were Indians.[202] It is claimed that almost half of the total cultivated area of the country came under the ownership of non-Burmese absentee landlords.[203] The sheer extent of Indian control over the Burmese economy also appears, albeit paradoxically, in the statement of the Indian representative during the British Parliamentary Round Table Conference (1931–1932). The Conference was convened in London to discuss constitutional arrangements for separating Burma from British India. To underscore the contributions that Indian immigrants had made to the Burmese economy, the statement highlighted that most of the properties in Rangoon were owned by Indians, who paid more than 60 per cent of the city's total municipal tax collected; the banking business of Burma was mainly, if not entirely, Indian; and had it not been for the enterprise of the Chettiar moneylenders, Burma's rice economy could not have flourished.[204]

It is in the context of the disproportionate dominance of the Indians in Burmese economy that the political demand that Burma be separated from the administration of British India intensified. During the Round Table, the statement of delegates representing the majority interests of Burma unambiguously identified Indian immigration as the root cause behind the suffering of the majority. The statement argued that Burma's status as a statutory part of India allowed all measures to be considered from the point of view of India as a whole and to the detriment of

---

[200] Myat Thein, *Economic Development of Myanmar* (Singapore: Institute of Southeast Asian Studies, 2004), 14.
[201] Benninson, *Report on Rangoon Working Class*, 91, cited in Adas, *The Burma Delta*, 178.
[202] Baxter, *Indian Immigration*, 64–66, cited in Adas, *The Burma Delta*, 179.
[203] Thein, *Economic Development of Myanmar*, 14.
[204] Statement read by N. M. Cowasjee. See House of Commons Parliamentary Papers, *Proceedings of the Burma Round Table Conference, 27 November 1931 to 12 January 1932* (London: His Majesty's Stationery Office, 1932), 278.

Burmese interests. The policy of unregulated immigration to Burma was one of the deplorable outcomes. 'The labour immigrants had a lower standard of living than ourselves, and in consequence drove us out of the labour market. Other immigrants arrived with capital and trading experience, and, having the lead of us, were able to establish themselves to our detriment. The economic equilibrium of Burmese society was destroyed.'[205] The statement thus concluded that the 'diseased condition' of Burmese society created by uncontrolled immigration could be cured only by severing ties with the Indian administration and offering the Burmese the right to self-government.[206]

Burma was finally separated from British India in 1937 under the Government of Burma Act (1935) to become a Crown Colony. The Government of Burma was, however, legally prohibited from enacting any discriminatory legislation that would jeopardise the interests of any individual or corporation of the United Kingdom or British India. The Act also specifically stipulated that no one domiciled in Burma was ineligible only on grounds of religion, place of birth, descent, or colour to hold any public office nor prohibited by any law from acquiring, holding, or disposing of property or carrying on any occupation, trade, business, or profession in Burma.[207] But in reality, these provisions could not prevent the waves of anti-Indian riots. Although such riots and calls for boycotting Indian shops took place in May and June 1930, provoking a significant number of Indians to leave Burma, these events intensified in the immediate aftermath of the separation and under the conditions of the global economic depression.[208] A comparison of the 1931 and 1941 censuses indicates a 10 per cent decline in the Indian population in Burma.[209] The Japanese invasion of Burma during WWII also forced many Indians to leave; many of them did not return to Burma following the independence of the country.[210] Those who decided to remain in the face of violence would experience even worse in postcolonial Burma.

---

[205] Statement read by U Ba Pe. See *Proceedings of the Burma Round Table Conference*, 263.
[206] Ibid., 264.
[207] See Section 462 of the Government of Burma Act, *Government of Burma Gazette*, 30 March 1936.
[208] Nyi Nyi Kyaw, 'Islamophobia in Buddhist Myanmar: The 969 Movement and Anti-Muslim Violence', in *Islam and the State in Myanmar: Muslim–Buddhist Relations and the Politics of Belonging*, ed. Melissa Crouch (Delhi: Oxford University Press, 2016), 192.
[209] David and Holliday, *Liberalism and Democracy in Myanmar*, 30.
[210] Nalini Ranjan Chakravarti, *The Indian Minority in Burma: The Rise and Decline of an Immigrant Community* (Oxford: Oxford University Press, 1971), 170–171.

5.4.2 Economic Competition and Ethnic Backlash in Postcolonial Burma

By the time Burma achieved independence in 1948, 'development' had become the norm of the day. In line with India and many other postcolonial states of the time, Burma was quick to announce its national economic plan that came to be known as the Two-Year Plan, in April 1948. Burma's economic planning was driven by two key considerations. First, to legitimise their power, the ruling elites of the postcolonial Burmese state had to crush the non-Burmese dominance over almost all sectors of the economy. And second, the transition from a colonial to a postcolonial economy did not immediately produce a Burmese bourgeois class, which would be needed to take over the means of production – developed under colonial capitalism and thitherto dominated by the Europeans, Chinese, and especially Indians. The nationalisation of the economy was, therefore, the natural preference to address both concerns.[211] In this sense, nationalisation was in fact a mode of 'Burmanisation' of the economy.[212] As Myat Thein notes, soon after independence, the government nationalised all agricultural land under the Land Nationalisation Act (1948), took control of the rice trade, nationalised the timber and mineral extraction industries, brought shipping companies under state control, and reorganised the Burma Oil Company into joint ventures.[213]

Also, within the common framework of economic development of the time, industrialisation became the centrepiece of national economic planning. The Eight-Year Plan that Burma adopted in 1952 was based on the report of a team of American engineers and economists from the American consultancy firm Knappen Tippetts Engineering Co. (KTA). The KTA Plan had the ambitious target of doubling the GDP within its lifespan.[214] The Plan ultimately failed due to a number of factors, including the worsening law and order situation in the country, secessionist demands by a number of ethnic minority groups across the country, and a shortage of skilled workers.[215] The contemporary Burmese economist Mali argued that the sudden shift in priority from

---

[211] For a general discussion on why most postcolonial states follow the same path in the transitional phase, see Schmitt, 'Decolonisation and Development in Burma', 97–109.
[212] Ibid., 97.
[213] Thein, *Economic Development of Myanmar*, 15.
[214] Ibid., 16.
[215] Ibid., 20–21.

agriculture to industrialisation was also to blame, in that actual expenditures in agricultural and other primary resource sectors were only 35 per cent of what they were originally allocated while the actual expenditures for industries exceeded their allocation.[216] The KTA Plan was ultimately abandoned in 1955, leading to the First Four-Year Plan with less ambitious targets and goals.[217]

The combined effect of a worsening economy and nationwide minority insurgency, the latter being officially described as the crucial factor behind the economic downfall, served as an excuse for the armed forces to take power in a coup d'état in 1962. At the political level, the new Prime Minister General Ne Win opted for a unitary state with centralised power, and in the economic domain, he launched a new policy – the 'Burmese Way to Socialism'. Under the new economic policy, many Indian-owned properties were confiscated in the name of nationalisation. Renaud Egreteau notes that years of 'Burmanisation' processes turned the age-old anti-Indian sentiments into Islamophobic tendencies, explicitly targeting the Muslim communities of Indian origin.[218] In Arakan, most businesses were owned by Muslims from Chittagong and North India, who had to abandon their businesses and properties and return to their countries of origin in tens of thousands.[219] Arakanese Muslims, in particular, came under serious attack as they continued to immigrate to commercially vital areas such as Mandalay and Pegu.[220]

The Ne Win government prohibited Muslims from travelling east of the Akyab District near the Bangladesh border and between villages and, to make the situation even worse, entrusted the local Rakhine Buddhists with enforcing the travel embargo.[221] Under the new regime, all Muslim organisations were banned, religious schools closed, and the construction of new mosques stopped.[222] The most visible demonstration of Burmese

---

[216] K. S. Mali, *Fiscal Aspects of Development Planning in Burma, 1950–1960* (Rangoon: University of Rangoon, 1962), 85.
[217] Thein, *Economic Development of Myanmar*, 22.
[218] Renaud Egreteau, 'Burmese Indians in Contemporary Burma: Heritage, Influence and Perceptions since 1988', *Asian Ethnicity* 12, no. 1 (2011), 33–54. Kyaw, however, argues that in today's Myanmar, Islamophobia is directed towards all Muslims, not just those of Indian origin. See Kyaw, 'Islamophobia in Buddhist Myanmar', 193.
[219] Md. Mahbubul Haque, 'Rohingya Ethnic Muslim Minority and the 1982 Citizenship Law in Burma', *Journal of Muslim Minority Affairs* 37, no. 4 (2017), 456.
[220] Patrick Hein, 'The Re-ethnicisation of Politics in Myanmar and the Making of the Rohingya Ethnicity Paradox', *Indian Quarterly* 74, no. 4 (2018), 368.
[221] Alistair D. B. Cook, 'The Global and Regional Dynamics of Human Aid in Rakhine State', in *Islam and the State in Myanmar*, 263.
[222] Hein, 'The Re-ethnicisation of Politics in Myanmar', 368.

xenophobia was in the policy of almost total obstruction of Muslims from entering the public sector.[223] The situation worsened as the Bangladesh War of Independence in 1971 forced a significant number of people to migrate to Burma, leading to further agitation against Muslims in Burma. The resulting *Nagamin* (Dragon King) operation forced nearly 200,000 Muslims to enter Bangladesh.[224] It was indeed a process of wholesale Burmanisation and the exclusion of the Muslim 'other'.

This is the politico-economic backdrop against which the nationwide resentment and animosity towards Indian migrants in general and Rohingya and Bangalee Muslims in particular can be explained. The depiction of the Rohingya as illegal Bangalee immigrants fits squarely into the dominant political narrative of historical injustice against the Burmese majority, and serves to reignite the same nationalist sentiment that led to the country's independence. As a scholar has recently argued, the Burmese nationalist movement originated in 'Indophobia'.[225] In this historical continuum, it appears that despite the prevalence of minority problems on other frontiers and the chronic crises of governance all over, the countrywide popular zeal for the suppression of any political and economic aspiration the Rohingya may have, if necessary by brutal means, has offered today's Myanmar a national purpose.

Since Myanmar's transition to so-called democracy, anti-Muslim sentiment has only deepened. A survey conducted by Roman David and Ian Holliday in 2014 in the Yangon and Mandalay regions and the Kachin, Kayin, and Shan States reveals that the Rohingya are the most disliked group in Myanmar; only 5–7 per cent of the respondents supported Rohingyas' right to live in Myanmar and enjoy civil and political rights.[226] The survey records that 72 per cent of respondents did not wish to have a Muslim neighbour; the figure increased to 82 per cent in a similar survey conducted in 2017.[227]

In 2012, a group of Buddhist monks launched the 969 Movement, calling for all business transactions with Muslims to be boycotted. The political economy of the anti-Muslim rhetoric appears vividly in the words of the leading figure of the movement, Ashin Wirathu: 'Over the past 50 years, we have shopped at Muslim shops and then they became richer and wealthier than us and can buy and marry our girls. In this way,

[223] Kyaw, 'Islamophobia in Buddhist Myanmar', 193–194.
[224] David and Holliday, *Liberalism and Democracy in Myanmar*, 32.
[225] Kyaw, 'Islamophobia in Buddhist Myanmar', 192.
[226] David and Holliday, *Liberalism and Democracy in Myanmar*, 130.
[227] Ibid., 114.

they have destroyed and penetrated not only our nation but also our religion.'[228] Elsewhere, he writes: 'With money, they become rich and marry Buddhist Burmese women who convert to Islam, sparing their religion. Their business become bigger and they buy more land and houses, and that means fewer Buddhist shrines.'[229] In this way, Wirathu combines competing economic interests with a sense of 'majoritarian vulnerability' to depict a constant threat to the Burmese-Buddhist national identity. The depiction of Burmese women as the biological career of the Burmese-Buddhist nation and the need for their bodies to be protected by Burmese men can hardly be ignored in his writing.

The unofficial but extremely popular 969 Movement is taking place at a time when various official measures from the previous military regime that systematically deprive the Rohingya of their livelihood are still in place. Preexisting policies of travel restrictions hinder employment and educational opportunities, making the community economically vulnerable. Also, the on-going practice of forced labour for government agencies takes Rohingya men away from their work opportunities, thereby depriving their families of the main source of income.[230] This in turn results in increased child labour to meet family needs. These policies also have serious implications for food security. A study conducted by the UN Food and Agriculture Organization (FAO) and the World Food Programme (WFP) found that restricted mobility, inadequate access to land, and lack of casual labour opportunities have contributed to grave food insecurity in the Rohingya community.[231]

Another important aspect of the ideology of the postcolonial 'developmental' state and the political economy of violence against minorities is the way ethnic violence then hinders the desired objective of development and economic growth. In the context of the violence against the Rohingya since 2012, the Annan Commission report highlights this aspect and asserts that the violence had a damaging impact on inter-communal trade and commerce as well as cross-border trade with Bangladesh, thereby hindering the rapid economic development of the region.[232] As noted at the beginning of

---

[228] Quoted in Kyaw, 'Islamophobia in Buddhist Myanmar', 202.
[229] Quoted in ibid.
[230] Tamara Nair, 'The Rohingya of Myanmar and the Biopolitics of Hunger', *Journal of Agriculture, Food Systems, and Community Development* 5, no. 4 (2015), 145.
[231] Food and Agriculture Organization (FAO) and the World Food Programme (WFP), *Special Report: FAO/WFP Crop and Food Security Assessment Mission to Myanmar* (Rome: Authors, 2009).
[232] *Final Report of the Advisory Commission*, 20–21.

this section, the current development discourse in Myanmar is therefore intrinsically connected to the notion of peacebuilding. However, as we shall see later, like in the previous 'developmental' moments under successive regimes in postcolonial Myanmar, the developmental ideology in reality serves as a tool for further marginalisation of the Rohingya in the form of land-grabbing and securitisation but at the same time attempts to obscure and gloss over such marginalisation.

5.4.3 *'Development' as a Peace Strategy and Rohingya Marginalisation*

In her seminal work *Expulsions*, Saskia Sassen argues that in the new global order since the 1980s, economic policies and programmatic interventions of international financial and regulatory institutions, such as the IMF, World Bank, and WTO, have facilitated the 'systemic deepening of advanced capitalism' with a view to keeping 'the increasingly privatized and corporatized economy going'.[233] As a result, any competing interest in the way of corporate profit-making is quickly, and often brutally, expelled from the system. These expulsions are made possible with the help of a wide range of instruments, from 'elementary policies to complex institutions, systems, and techniques that require specialized knowledge and intricate organizational formats'.[234] Especially, international and national legal instruments often enable foreign governments and corporations to acquire vast stretches of land in developing countries, destroying the rural economies that are there. In this regard, she argues, the neoliberal policy directives of the IMF and World Bank and the stipulations of the WTO often prepare the ground for land grabs by weakening developing economies and making their governments willing to 'sell vast amounts of land and expel whole villages from their land to do so'.[235] In this process, the global economy has been critically restructured to 'reposition developing countries as suppliers of land, mineral and water resources to foreign capital, leading to massive surges in land grabs across the world'.[236] Since 2006, foreign governments and investors have

---

[233] Saskia Sassen, *Expulsions: Brutality and Complexity in the Global Economy* (Cambridge, MA: Harvard University Press, 2014), 41. See also pp. 86, 214.
[234] Ibid., 2.
[235] Ibid., 86–87.
[236] Shapan Adnan, 'Book Review: Expulsions: Brutality and Complexity in the Global Economy', *The Journal of Peasant Studies* 43, no. 5 (2016), 1096.

THE CASE OF THE ROHINGYA IN MYANMAR   253

acquired 220 million hectares (over 540 million acres) of land in developing countries, causing the eviction of millions of small farmers.[237] In addition to foreign governments and corporations, domestic agencies, including the state, private corporations, interest groups, and criminal organisations, are also involved in large-scale land grabs.

Specifically in the case of Rakhine State, large-scale development projects primarily target the agricultural land and households of the Rohingya, making them internally displaced, although the Rakhine communities have also been affected by such developmental displacements.[238] The Kaladan Multi-Modal Transit Transport Project is one such major project that is nearly completed. This USD 484 million project, jointly carried out by India and Myanmar, aims to connect the eastern Indian seaport of Kolkata to the conflict-prone Mizoram state in northeast India through Rakhine State and Chin State in Myanmar. The project, connecting Kolkata with Sittwe seaport in Rakhine State, is expected to improve Rakhine's access to Indian markets. Due to concerns about the impact of the project on the environment and the livelihood of local communities, military groups of both the Rohingya and Rakhine communities – the Arakan Rohingya Salvation Army (ARSA) and Arakan Army (AA), respectively – have mounted armed resistance to the project but could not stop it.

Alongside India, Myanmar's largest development partner and strongest political ally, China, is also active in Rakhine State with large development projects. The Chinese state-owned investment company China International Trust Investment Corporation (CITIC) is providing 85 per cent of the funding for a USD 7.3 billion deep-sea port project in Kyaukpyu in Rakhine State with a capacity of 7.8 million tons of cargo bulk. CITIC is also investing another USD 3.2 billion to develop the Kyaukpyu Special Economic Zone project on Ramree Island.[239] Under the revised Myanmar Special Economic Zone Law (2014), investors will enjoy income tax holidays for up to seven years, followed by a 50 per cent exemption for another ten years if profits are reinvested. Custom duties

---

[237] Sassen, *Expulsions*, 3.
[238] This phenomenon is not unique to the Rohingya. Development activities in the ethnic states of Shan and Karen in the north-eastern and eastern parts of Myanmar have also brought disaster to local communities and fuelled armed insurgency.
[239] Achmad Ismail, 'Motives and Rivalry of Superpower Countries: The United States and China in Rohingya Humanitarian Crisis', *Jurnal Hubungan Internasional* 7, no. 1 (2018), 112.

and related taxes for imported raw materials and machinery are also exempted.[240] More importantly, to address a major concern of investors regarding access to lands, provisions for 50-year leases have been introduced under the new law.[241] CITIC has also acquired the rights to operate the Kyaukpyu port for 50 years with the prospect of extending for another 25 years.[242] The port will offer China a much-needed foothold to extend its influence to the Bay of Bengal and the Indian Ocean and keep its strategic rival India in check. These projects are also important links to China's ambitious Belt and Road Initiative.

Arakan in general and Kyaukpyu development projects in particular are also important for meeting China's energy needs. Arakan is believed to have an offshore oil reserve of 11 trillion cubic feet and a gas reserve of 23 trillion cubic feet.[243] In 2004, the Korean company Daewoo discovered the Shwe gas field in Sittwe, northern Rakhine. Since 2013, oil and gas have been exported to Kunming in southern China's Yunnan province via the 771-km-long Shwe pipeline. Once completed, the Kyaukpyu port will allow China to transport its oil imports from the Middle East to Yunnan through the Shwe pipeline, avoiding the busy Malacca Strait.[244]

The Annan Commission has expressed serious concerns over potential negative consequences of these projects, in that local communities have not been consulted, paid adequate compensation for the loss of their land, or employed in jobs created by these projects. The Commission also notes environmental risks associated with these projects and local communities' concerns about this.[245] The new Special Economic Zone Law violates a number of international human rights law provisions by not including mandatory provisions for consultations or information sharing with local communities.[246] The law also does not guarantee affected communities any protection from land confiscation and arbitrary displacement, or adequate compensation for such displacement.[247] Importantly,

---

[240] Josh Wood, 'Special Economic Zones: Gateway or Roadblock to Reform', in *The Business of Transition: Law Reform, Development, and Economics in Myanmar*, ed. Melissa Crouch (Cambridge: Cambridge University Press, 2017), 181.
[241] Ibid.
[242] Ismail, 'Motives and Rivalry of Superpower Countries', 112.
[243] Ibid., 115.
[244] Wood, 'Special Economic Zones', 187–188.
[245] *Final Report of the Advisory Commission*, 22–23.
[246] See Lauren Nishimura, 'Facing the Concentrated Burden of Development: Local Responses to Myanmar's Special Economic Zones', in *The Business of Transition*, 202–208.
[247] Ibid.

development-driven economic disparity can potentially aggravate existing communal tensions. During the communal violence of 2012, the Kyaukpyu Islamic quarter was burnt to the ground, forcing thousands of Muslim residents to move into military-protected camps on the outskirts of the town.[248]

To facilitate various investment and rural development projects and in line with its security agenda, the Myanmar government has acquired a significant amount of land in Rakhine State. While 17,000 acres of land in Rakhine was allocated in the national list of land allocation for economic development in 2012 when Myanmar opened up its economy, the figure rose to a staggering 3.1 million acres in 2016.[249] This rise in the grabbing of Rohingya land correlates directly with foreign investment as developmentalism. A number of changes in laws governing land ownership were also introduced in 2012 to attract investors: the 1963 Peasant Law was annulled, and the Farmland Law and the Vacant Land Law were amended to make large corporate acquisition easier. These changes allowed 100 per cent foreign capital and lease periods of up to 70 years.[250] The new Foreign Investment Law (2012) allows foreign firms to invest in all sectors of the economy and offers them greater certainty over land use.[251] As a whole, Myanmar is losing more than a million acres of forest a year in the name of development.[252] The expulsion of minorities like the Rohingya from their homeland is a direct consequence of the ever-increasing craving for more land and water for development activities. On the other hand, the unceasing marginalisation of minorities is set to deteriorate ethnic relations and lead to more violence. Thus, the neoliberal model of developmentalism as a peacebuilding tool is counterproductive, as we discussed earlier.

Nevertheless, more investment and more development are being advocated by the Suu Kyi government as a strategy for bringing peace to Rakhine State. A committee called the Union Enterprise for Humanitarian Assistance, Resettlement and Development in Rakhine (UEHRD) was created in October 2017 under Suu Kyi's chairpersonship

---

[248] Wood, 'Special Economic Zones', 190.
[249] Saskia Sassen, 'The Assault on the Rohingya is Not Only About Religion – It's Also About Land', *Huffpost*, 15 September 2017, available at www.huffpost.com.
[250] See Saskia Sassen, 'Is Rohingya Persecution Cause by Business Interests Rather than Religion?' *The Guardian*, 4 January 2017, available at www.theguardian.com.
[251] See Wood, 'Special Economic Zones', 181.
[252] See Kevin Woods, *Commercial Agriculture Expansion in Myanmar: Links to Deforestation, Conversion Timber and Land Disputes* (Washington, DC: Forest Trends, 2015), iii.

to lead rebuilding efforts. The government is encouraging Burmese business tycoons, many of whom were formerly under US sanctions, to invest in development projects in Rakhine. David Mathieson, a Yangon-based independent analyst, asserts that 'the UEHRD was formed to divert attention from violent ethnic cleansing. Tasking cronies to construct [...] villages won't wash away the stain of mass crimes.'[253] In the aftermath of the genocidal crackdown on the Rohingya in August 2017 and fierce international criticism of her government, Suu Kyi convened an international investment fair on 22 February 2019 to address the problem of ethnic tension in Rakhine State. To make the point clearer, she chose southern Rakhine's Ngapali Beach Resort as the venue for the event. In her opening remarks, Suu Kyi expressed her frustration that '[f]or too long, the international community's attention has been focused narrowly on negative aspects related to problems in North Rakhine, rather than on the panoramic picture that shows the immense potential of this state for peace and prosperity'.[254]

What Suu Kyi referred to as 'problems in North Rakhine' was in fact described by the UN Human Rights Council as ethnic cleansing and genocide against the Rohingya Muslim minority. The dark image of northern Rakhine is then contrasted with the picturesque southern region where the Rakhine Buddhists live and where the investment forum was convened. In fact, due to the Rohingya's statelessness and travel restrictions on them, Rakhine Buddhists are likely to benefit from most development projects in the region. However, a recent empirical study notes that local Rakhine Buddhist communities – who are also a minority vis-à-vis the dominant Burmese – often complain that the benefits of development do not reach them either; instead, the government's development initiatives are meant to benefit Burmese elites and foreign investors.[255] In this sense, Suu Kyi's opening remarks symbolise the essence of the ideology of the postcolonial 'developmental' state that the regime is propagating to legitimise, obscure, and gloss over decades of economic marginalisation and political persecution of the Rohingya in particular, and all other communities in Rakhine, in general.

---

[253] Quoted in Timothy McLaughlin, 'Burma Is Pumping Millions into Rebuilding Rakhine. But Is It for the Rohingya?' *The Washington Post*, 14 March 2018, available at www.pulitzercenter.org.
[254] The text of the full speech is available at www.statecounsellor.gov.mm/en/node/2351. North Rakhine State typically refers to Maungdaw and Buthidaung townships, which collectively comprise Maungdaw District.
[255] See generally Miklian, 'Contextualising and Theorising Economic Development', 60–65.

It therefore makes complete sense, from Myanmar's point of view, to bulldoze burned Rohingya houses and in some cases entire villages that the Rohingya had to leave behind in the wake of the 2017 violence. Given the official ban on access to these sites, Amnesty International has analysed satellite imagery, photographs, videos, and victim testimonies and determined that since October 2017 the government has started a major operation to clear burned villages and build new homes, security force bases, and infrastructure in the region. Such wiping out of Rohingya villages also helps destroy evidence of the genocide committed by the Myanmar army and local Rakhine Buddhists. There is notable international pressure to bring the perpetrators before international criminal justice.

Alarmingly, the new houses and villages are being built on bulldozed Rohingya land only to bring non-Rohingya, and in some cases even non-Rakhine, settlers into the area.[256] Amnesty International also found that the rapid development and expansion of mining fields is taking place in northern Rakhine as well as in Rathedaung Township in Sittwe District. Also, a new road to a recently expanded mine has been built right across a now-depopulated Rohingya village in Rathedaung.[257] Clearly, the already vulnerable Rohingya minority are shouldering the heavy cost of 'economic development' imposed as a peace strategy. These so-called development projects in northern Rakhine also undercut the prospect of the voluntary, safe, and dignified repatriation – as per international refugee law norms – of more than a million Rohingya refugees, who are currently living in miserable conditions in refugee camps in Bangladesh.[258] As a whole, this experience exposes the fallacy of the neoliberal market-democracy model as a peacebuilding strategy. The head of a Rohingya NGO makes the point succinctly:

> Economic growth due to development works and peace processes with armed groups in Myanmar are different issues. These issues are separate and not related at all. Ethnic minorities are not getting the rights of their natural resources in their own home territory. They are not in the

---

[256] See generally Amnesty International, *Remaking Rakhine State* (London: Amnesty International, 2017).
[257] Ibid., 18–21.
[258] Although the Bangladesh government and policymakers of relevant international organisations frequently reiterate the legal requirement for Rohingya repatriation to their place of origin, my findings during my fieldwork in Cox's Bazar reveal that Bangladesh government officials and international organisations dealing with the Rohingya refugees on the ground are not confident about the prospect of such repatriation. For a critical normative perspective on repatriation under international refugee law, see Chimni, 'Refugees, Return and the Reconstruction of "Post-Conflict" Societies', 163–180.

decision-making processes of the political arena. Ethnic Burmese are penetrating in every section of the state [...] to meet only Burmese interests. They (ignore) the rights of ethnic minorities residing in the frontier of Myanmar.[259]

5.4.4 Developmentalism and International Organisations

The UN's handling of Rohingya human rights issues, when they are challenged by developmental priorities, shows that international organisations are in no mood to learn from past mistakes either. Soon after the genocidal atrocities of 2017, reports emerged that in the four years prior to these horrific events, the Resident Coordinator of the UN Country Team (UNCT), Renata Lok-Dessallien, 'tried to stop human rights activists travelling to Rohingya areas, attempted to shut down public advocacy on the subject, and isolated staff who tried to warn that ethnic cleansing might be on the way'.[260] This is because a decision had been made to prioritise long-term development in Rakhine in the hope that development would eventually lead to ethnic peace. As a result, UN staff concerned about the Rohingya issues were hushed up and sidelined. As early as 2015, the UN commissioned a report to examine UN priorities in Myanmar. The confidential report, entitled 'Slippery Slope: Helping Victims or Supporting Systems of Abuse', gave a damning verdict on UNCT's approach to the Rohingya crisis: 'The UNCT strategy with respect to human rights focuses too heavily on the over-simplified hope that development investment itself will reduce tensions, failing to take into account that investing in a discriminatory structure run by discriminatory state actors is more likely to reinforce discrimination than change it.'[261]

The violence of 2017, however, prompted another independent inquiry into the UN's involvement in Myanmar from 2010 to 2018, the report of which was published in May 2019. Its author, the veteran Guatemalan diplomat Gert Rosenthal, notes that although several attempts were made to reconcile UN priorities on development, peace, security, and human rights, those efforts remained inconclusive. The

---

[259] Comments made during an interview in Rakhine in June 2016 as part of an empirical study conducted by Miklian. See Miklian, 'Contextualising and Theorising Economic Development', 65.

[260] BBC report based on sources within the UN and the aid community both inside and outside Myanmar. See Jonah Fisher, 'Rohingya Muslims Fear the UN Failed Them', *BBC News*, 28 September 2017, available at www.bbc.co.uk/news/world-asia-41420973.

[261] The report was leaked to BBC and quoted in ibid.

report repeatedly refers to the UN's failings in similar situations in Sri Lanka in 2012 during the country's wholesale war on Tamil insurgency, highlighting that lessons have not been learned. While analysing dysfunctional actions of the UNCT in Myanmar, Rosenthal specifically notes that the placement of the UN Resident Coordinator under the supervision of the UN Development Programme (UNDP) helped further shift UNCT's priorities towards development. The UNDP had prioritised development objectives over human rights and was keen on building a relation of trust and predictability with the host government.[262]

To make it even worse, to achieve development goals the Resident Coordinator had to partner with other multilateral organisations such as ASEAN, the World Bank, and the local diplomatic community of bilateral donors – human rights was not surely on the top of their priority lists.[263] It is worth noting here that while the BBC was investigating the UNCT's problematic role in the Rohingya crisis, ten ambassadors, including ones from the United Kingdom and the United States, sent unsolicited emails to the BBC unsurprisingly expressing their support for the Resident Coordinator.[264] The Myanmar government officially protested when the UN finally decided to remove the controversial Resident Coordinator from the country. This is a classic example of what happens to vulnerable minorities when priorities and vested interests of hawkish capitalists, spineless-by-design international institutions, and hegemonic-majoritarian postcolonial states converge under the common ideology of development.

Yet, the issue is far from being straightforward. International organisations with the responsibility of offering human rights and humanitarian protection sometimes need to rely on IFIs to discharge their mandate. Especially in cases where host states refrain from ratifying relevant international human rights conventions and manage to keep themselves outside the formal legal mechanisms under the treaty regime, international human rights organisations often count on their partnership with financial institutions and development agencies to put pressure on host states.[265] The use of human rights protection as 'conditionality' for

---

[262] Gert Rosenthal, *A Brief and Independent Inquiry into the Involvement of the United Nations in Myanmar from 2010 to 2018* (29 May 2019), 22, available at www.un.org.sg /files.
[263] Ibid.
[264] Fisher, 'Rohingya Muslims Fear the UN Failed Them'.
[265] This has certainly been the case in securing Bangladesh's commitment to the protection of Rohingya refugees, as I found during the fieldwork.

IFI-funded development projects in the host state in turn paves the way for 'development' to encroach on the human rights agenda.

In the midst of global criticism of the UN's failure, Rohingyas' ongoing struggle for bare survival in make-shift refugee camps in Bangladesh, and Myanmar's bulldozing of Rohingya villages to free up land for economic development, in May 2019 the World Bank announced a new USD 100 million project for Rakhine Recovery and Development Support.[266] Building on recommendations in Annan Commission reports and the Myanmar Sustainable Development Plan (MSDP), the project aims to achieve 'productive inclusion' by generating short- and long-term income, and 'improved livelihood' for all communities by supporting the growth and development of SMEs.[267] The Project Information Document itself acknowledges that with Rohingya statelessness and mobility restrictions still in place, the project might be less beneficial to the Rohingya community and so increase inter-communal economic disparity and discrimination.[268] More than a dozen international NGOs in Myanmar have written a letter to the World Bank warning that the proposed project could worsen the situation in Rakhine State. The Bank's statement on 17 May 2019 reveals that the proposed project is a response to Suu Kyi's call to the Bank to use its expertise to help create a 'peace dividend' by creating economic opportunities for diverse communities across Myanmar.[269]

Even the Rosenthal Inquiry Report on UN involvement in the Rohingya crisis did not fail to identify positive trends in Myanmar's economy: 'a more open, market-oriented economy', 'a rapid influx of foreign investment', 'an important expansion in infrastructure', and 'increasing numbers of white-collar and blue-collar jobs'.[270] His regret – that despite this progress, preexisting ethnic tension persists – completely failed to appreciate that it is *because of* such 'progress' that minorities have become more vulnerable and conflicts have intensified. Thus, it is more or less clear that the neoliberal model of developmentalism will continue to dominate peacebuilding strategies in Myanmar in coming years and simultaneously perform the ideological function of 'legitimising' and 'dissimulating' the economic vulnerability, political persecution, and cultural extinction of the Rohingya minority.

---

[266] Details are available at www.projects.worldbank.org.
[267] See Project Information Document (PID), 5–6.
[268] Ibid., 6.
[269] Simon Lewis and Poppy McPherson, 'World Bank under Fire for Development Plan in Myanmar's Divided Rakhine', *Reuters*, 17 May 2019, available at www.reuters.com.
[270] Rosenthal, *A Brief and Independent Inquiry*, 6.

5.5 The Case of the CHT Hill People in Bangladesh

Compared to the 'national' and 'liberal' ideologies, the 'developmental' ideology of the postcolonial state affected the hill people of the CHT in a more disastrous manner. Economic exploitation of the CHT by Pakistan and, later, Bangladesh often followed the colonial framework, but it did not limit itself to that framework in seeking more efficient and direct, albeit brutal, means of economic gain. Dominating the colonial discourse on the hill tribes was the idea that backward communities cannot survive and progress towards modernity without the helping hand of colonial rule. Thus, most British colonial policies governing hill communities in India were presented in protectionist terms, although often they were, in reality, driven by British political, economic, and strategic interests.[271] The colonial governance in the CHT was depicted as a necessary mode of protecting hill peoples in part from the exploitation of 'cunning' Bangalees.[272] Colonial officers' narratives frequently juxtaposed the simple mindedness of hill people with the shrewdness of Bangalees, who frequently exploited the hill people with their trickery.[273] While such exploitation of hill people by Bangalees in privileged positions is not uncommon even today, it has to be noted that the Bangalee petty bourgeoisie acquired asymmetric power positions vis-à-vis hill peoples primarily through various colonial policy interventions.

5.5.1 Colonial Exploitation, Protectionist Rhetoric, and Inter-ethnic Relations

As noted in Chapter 3, the Chakma armed resistance to the East India Company's ever-increasing tax ended with a truce in 1787, in which the Chakma chief had to agree to pay cotton tribute to the Company on a regular basis in exchange for trading rights between the hills and the

---

[271] However, Damodaran contends that despite the dominance of evolutionary ideas, nineteenth-century British attitudes towards indigenous peoples in India were not 'homogeneous or unchanging'. She depicts at least some British protectionist policies as informed by an emerging sense of genuine humanitarianism towards indigenous peoples and their futures, and she evidently found in the writings of Hunter '[a] vision of partnership between the colonial state and non-Aryan groups'. Vinita Damodaran, 'Indigenous Agency: Customary Rights and Tribal Protection in Eastern India, 1830–1930', *History Workshop Journal* 76, no. 1 (2013), 85–89.
[272] Other protective rhetoric included protection from invading tribes and oppressive tribal chiefs. See Shahabuddin, 'The Myth of Colonial "Protection" of Indigenous Peoples', 210–235.
[273] Lewin, *The Hill Tracts of Chittagong and Dwellers Therein*, 25–33.

plains.[274] However, only two years later, in 1789, the colonial administration modified this arrangement egregiously by changing the form of the tribute from kind to cash. This introduction of a money economy into the CHT made the hill people even more vulnerable; they faced renewed exploitation at the hands of powerful Bangalees. To pay taxes in cash, they had to rely upon Bangalee traders paying for their products. These traders controlled and manipulated the market, and hill peoples had to sell their products at a greatly reduced price.[275] Short of cash, the hill peoples were then forced to borrow money from Bangalee *mahajans* (money lenders), who charged exorbitant interest rates, sometimes as much as 600 per cent.[276] These colonial economic policy interventions fundamentally changed the indigenous economic system of the hill people. As Mohsin notes, colonial policy challenged and ultimately displaced the hill people's age-old understanding of material ownership, economic exchange, and sharing.[277] 'At a more fundamental level it alienated the Hill people from their means of production and turned them into a dependent and marginalised population.'[278] Thus, instead of protecting 'innocent' hill people from 'crafty' Bangalees, as the colonial protectionist rhetoric suggests, the colonial policy interventions further empowered profit-seeking Bangalee *mahajans* and traders and, ironically, pushed hill people even deeper into economic vulnerability.

Also, behind the protectionist rhetoric remained the colonial policy of natural resource exploitation and marketisation. Following the imposition of direct British rule over India in the aftermath of the Sepoy Revolt (1857) and the creation of the hill district of the CHT, the British colonial state claimed ownership of all lands in the hills in 1868. Although the tribal chiefs claimed to be proprietors of the land, the British government categorically stated that '[t]he chiefs of the CHT have no title to the ownership of the land which is vested exclusively in the Crown: they exercise only the delegated right of collecting taxes and rents on behalf of government'.[279] The Deputy Commissioner was given absolute powers over land matters.

---

[274] Raja Devasish Roy, 'The Erosion of Legal and Constitutional Safeguards of the Hill Peoples of the CHT in Bangladesh: An Historical Account', unpublished paper (1992).
[275] Mohsin, *The Politics of Nationalism*, 80.
[276] Wolfgang Mey, *Genocide in the Chittagong Hill Tracts, Bangladesh*, International Working Group for Indigenous Affairs (IWGIA) Document No. 51 (Copenhagen: IWGIA, 1984), 79.
[277] Mohsin, *The Politics of Nationalism*, 77.
[278] Ibid.
[279] Government of Bengal, *Proceedings of the Government of Bengal in the Political Department, June 1918*, Bengal, 32, cited in ibid., 87.

Another notorious technique of land-grabbing targeted forest lands. Forests constituted about 82 per cent of the total area of the CHT.[280] The hill people had traditionally been dependant on forests not only for the traditional joom cultivation but also for other domestic purposes. With the introduction of commercial forestry (replacing social/communal forestry), the colonial administration collected a large sum of annual revenue from the tolls levied on all forest products brought down by water and river routes to the Chittagong port.[281] In 1865, the Indian Forest Reserve Act was passed – ostensibly in an attempt to 'protect' the forest resources – restricting the local people's access to and use of the resources of the hills. In reality, the rhetoric of protecting forest sources facilitated a wholesale plunder of forestry for the benefit of the colonial administration: the timber from Indian forests was required by the Royal Navy for the construction of its ships and by the Indian Railway for its railway sleepers; forests were also cleared for agricultural purposes in order to raise revenues.[282] As Captain Lewin admitted: 'Throughout the whole [CHT] district are found large tracts of valuable forest trees [...]. A large trade in railway-sleepers has lately sprung up from the port of Chittagong; the Port Conservator estimates that upwards of 30,000 sleepers have been exported during the last two years.'[283]

More and more forest areas continued to fall under the rubric of the reserved forests. By February 1871, an area of 5,670 square miles out of 6,882 was declared to be Government Reserve Forest.[284] The local hill peoples were allowed to use forest produce only for domestic purposes.[285] Further restrictions on forest use were introduced in 1875 through the creation of District Forests (now known as 'Unclassed State Forest'). While joom cultivation and any other use of forest products were totally prohibited in the reserved forests, the use of forests for domestic consumption only was allowed in district forests, subject to restrictions the Deputy Commissioner could impose from time to time.[286] As a consequence,

---

[280] William W. Hunter, *The Annals of Rural Bengal* (Calcutta: Indian Studies Past and Present, 1876), 29.
[281] Lewin, *The Hill Tracts of Chittagong and Dwellers Therein*, 27.
[282] Mohsin, *The Politics of Nationalism*, 90.
[283] Lewin, *The Hill Tracts of Chittagong and Dwellers Therein*, 25.
[284] J. M. Cowan, *Working Plan for the Forests of Chittagong Hill Tracts Division* (Calcutta: Bengal Government Press, 1923), 14.
[285] Mohsin, *The Politics of Nationalism*, 91.
[286] Government of Bengal, *Selections from the Correspondence on the Revenue Administration of the Chittagong Hill Tracts, 1862–1927* (Calcutta: Government of Bengal Press, 1929), 202–204.

the areas available for joom were reduced to one-third of what they were, and by the end of the twentieth century, the alienation of the hill people from their land and forest was near-total.[287] The colonial policy of encouraging plough cultivation, as opposed to the traditional joom cultivation, with a view to ensuring stable revenue generation further exacerbated the economic plight of the hill people by making them dependent upon not only the colonial state but also the profit-seeking Bangalees.[288]

5.5.2 The CHT and the Postcolonial 'Developmental' State

The protectionist rhetoric of the colonial administration to exploit land and natural resources in the CHT was translated into the ideology of the postcolonial 'developmental' states of Pakistan and Bangladesh. As explained in Chapter 1, the partition of India was largely a result of the conflict of interests between the Hindu and Muslim petty bourgeois classes. In independent Pakistan, a small but dominant bourgeois class flourished under the military dictator Ayub Khan, who sought the legitimacy of his power in the very idea of 'economic development'. Under his watch, an industrialist class, essentially based in West Pakistan, quickly established a monopoly over the national economy under the direct patronage of the state.[289] The rapid concentration of wealth in the hands of a small class was enabled by the surplus extraction and resource transfer from the then East Pakistan (currently Bangladesh), including the CHT, to West Pakistan. By the mid-1960s, only forty-three West Pakistan-based families held more than 72 per cent of the fixed assets in the modern private manufacturing sector and 45 per cent of the total assets of all privately controlled firms in East Pakistan.[290] Like the British, the new industrialist class of Pakistan and the patron postcolonial state saw the CHT as a rich resource base for fuelling the engine of economic development. The government even declared the CHT a tax-free or concession area, apparently to accelerate economic development in the

---

[287] Ibid., 91–92.
[288] Ibid., 93.
[289] See Talukder Maniruzzaman, *The Politics of Development: The Case of Pakistan 1947–1958* (Dhaka: Green Book House, 1971); G. F. Papanek, *Pakistan's Development – Social Goals and Private Incentives* (Cambridge, MA: Harvard University Press, 1966); L. J. White, *Industrial Concentration and Economic Power in Pakistan* (Princeton, NJ: Princeton University Press, 1974).
[290] Rehman Sobhan and Muzaffar Ahmad, *Public Enterprise in an Intermediate Regime: A Study in the Political Economy of Bangladesh* (Dhaka: Bangladesh Institute of Development Studies, 1980), 60.

region. Government encouragement to both public and private sectors to undertake industrial ventures based on the resources of the area resulted in mega-development projects in the CHT.

The first large-scale industrial development project in the CHT was the Karnaphuli Paper Mill, established in 1954 by the Pakistan Industrial Development Corporation. This project, costing USD 13 million, was funded by external resources including a World Bank loan of USD 4.2 million.[291] The whole idea behind selecting the CHT as the project site was to have access to 'limitless quantities of fibrous raw materials'; accordingly, the mill was given rights for 99 years to extract its raw materials from forest areas.[292] The paper mill, seen as an icon of the economic development of Pakistan, turned into a source of environmental catastrophes. The mill was ultimately sold to the Dawood Group – one of the West Pakistan-based industrialist families – at a much lower price that did not even cover the cost of land and transport or other infrastructure development.[293]

Also, to meet the ever-increasing demand for commercial energy necessary for rapid industrialisation and therefore 'development', in 1963 a hydro-electricity project was constructed on the Karnaphuli River in the CHT at the cost of USD 100 million with funds from USAID. The Karnaphuli hydro-electricity project has been the most devastating development project for the hill peoples in the CHT. A 250-square-mile upstream reservoir created by the project submerged 25 per cent of human settlement and 40 per cent of the best arable land. Around 100,000 hill peoples, along with a small number of Bangalee settlers, were uprooted and rendered homeless and landless.[294] Ironically, the hydro-electricity project produces only a negligible share of the total energy supply and the commercial energy of the country.[295]

It needs to be noted that the local hill communities that suffered the most due to these development projects in the CHT hardly benefited from them. Although the hydro-electricity project was justified as an

---

[291] Jenneke Arens, 'Winning Hearts and Minds: Foreign Aid and Militarization in the Chittagong Hill Tracts', *Economic and Political Weekly* 32, no. 29 (1997), 1812.
[292] Philip Gain, 'Life and Nature at Risk', in *The Chittagong Hill Tracts: Life and Nature at Risk*, ed. Philip Gain (Dhaka: Society for Environment and Human Development, 2000), 32–33.
[293] Sobhan and Ahmad, *Public Enterprise in an Intermediate Regime*, 37–38.
[294] Gain, 'Life and Nature at Risk', 33.
[295] M. G. Sarwar, *Global Energy Crisis and Bangladesh* (Dhaka: External Relations Division, Government of Bangladesh, 1980), 27.

essential move towards rapid development of the country and the region, less than 1 per cent of the total area of the CHT was actually covered by electricity generated by the project.[296] Most jobs created by this megaproject went to Bangalees; that also meant another wave of Bangalee settlement in the area. The resettlement and compensation scheme for the displaced hill people utterly failed to provide a sustainable livelihood for the vast majority of them, and many ultimately became refugees in neighbouring India. The anger and resentment caused by the project subsequently contributed to the protracted civil war in the region. Similarly, the construction of the Karnaphuli Paper Mill created 10,000 jobs but the hill people got only around 5 per cent of them – mainly in lower ranks.[297] The situation was the same in the case of the Karnaphuli Ryon Mill, established in 1966 with foreign funds. To make things even worse, soon after the completion of the hydro-electricity project, the special status of the CHT, along with the ban on the entry, settlement, and acquisition of land in the CHT by outsiders, was removed. This change threw open the CHT to Pakistani bourgeois and petty bourgeois classes for land-grabbing and extraction of natural resources.

The situation only deteriorated in independent Bangladesh. As we saw in the preceding chapters, the ideology of the postcolonial 'national' and 'liberal' state left no room for ethnic accommodation. The exploitation of land and natural resources in the CHT increased exponentially, given the complete absence of any constitutional safeguard for the region and under the pretext of security concerns in the face of armed resistance by the hill people. Direct state patronage was also provided to the relatively underdeveloped Bangalee bourgeois class to exploit resources in the CHT. 'Development' soon became the umbrella term to address multifaceted concerns of security, resource management, nation-building, and economic prosperity. As a result, the hill people of the CHT became rather the easy victims of the ideology of developmentalism, as they have never been the primary focus of development in the region.

For example, the claim that the problems of the CHT emanated from the root cause of underdevelopment led to the establishment in 1976 of the CHT Development Board, whose official purpose was 'accelerating development' of the area, and thereby solving the problem of ethnic

---

[296] Unknown, 'Revolt in Chittagong Hill Tracts', *Economic and Political Weekly* 13, no. 17 (1978), 726.
[297] Arens, 'Winning Hearts and Minds', 1812.

tension.[298] However, the counter-insurgency focus of the Board became clear when the General Commanding Officer (GOC) of the 24th Infantry Division (Chittagong) of the Bangladesh Army was appointed as its ex-officio chairman in 1982.[299] It was only after the Peace Accord in 1997 that an elected local representative assumed the chairmanship of the Board. All major development interventions in the region are designed, managed, and overseen by the Board. During the years of insurgency, most development projects undertaken by the Board were directed towards building necessary infrastructure for expanding the domain of military influence or bribing local hill elites and bringing them into confidence to subvert popular resistance.[300] Projects that indeed involved any intention of 'economic development' of hill peoples were, however, directed towards integrating hill communities into the market economy. For instance, the Board's flagship programme on *Joutha Khamar* (collective farm) targeted the resettlement of landless hill peoples and provided them with land and cash to produce vegetables, fruits, and plants for commercial purposes.[301] Given that the communities in these collective farms were not allowed to grow rice and other staple food, they became permanently dependent on the market – for selling their commercial produce in order to buy staple foods. This was also a perfect avenue for the Bangalee middlemen to exploit the vulnerability of the hill people.[302]

The colonial rhetoric of 'reserved forests', too, continues to be a dominant language of 'development' in the CHT, causing immense misery for the hill people. As we saw earlier, the colonial Forest Act of 1865, along with the subsequent legislations of 1873 and 1927, purportedly enacted for conserving forest resources, performed as an effective tool for the exploitation of resources in the CHT. In the independent states of Pakistan and then Bangladesh, the Forest Department further advanced this mode of land-grabbing and resource exploitation. Even though existing reserved forests had already covered nearly 25 per cent of the CHT, the Forest Department continued to expand such areas from the late 1980s, reducing the size of Unclassed State Forest (USF) and

---

[298] Ibid., 1814.
[299] Gain, 'Life and Nature at Risk', 34.
[300] See Arens, 'Winning Hearts and Minds', 1813–1815.
[301] Muhammad Mufazzalul Huq, 'Government Institutions and Underdevelopment: A Study of the Tribal Peoples of Chittagong Hill Tracts, Bangladesh', unpublished MSS Thesis, University of Birmingham (1982), 115–123.
[302] Ibid.

leaving local hill people with only limited access to forest resources.[303] Since 1989, the cumulative total of USF lands in the CHT targeted for acquisition by the Forest Department has amounted to a staggering 218,000 acres, and from 2009 attempts have been renewed to acquire customary lands of hill communities to set up new reserved forests.[304]

While such expansions of reserved forests in the name of natural conservation limit the livelihood of hill peoples, who heavily rely on forest resources, facilitating illegal logging in reserved forests has been a lucrative source of income for corrupt personnel of the Forest Department and military and other law enforcement agencies. Also, vast areas of forests are frequently leased out for private commercial plantations in order to generate revenue and economic growth. Back in the Pakistan period, the government engaged the Canadian consultant Forestal Inc. to develop a 'master plan for the integrated development of the area' based on optimum land-use possibilities. Although Forestal's report found that under optimum conditions traditional jooming was highly sustainable, it nonetheless recommended gradual phasing out of jooming and concluded that industrial development in the vicinity of the dam and fruit production elsewhere would be the best way to maximise the region's resource potential.[305]

In independent Bangladesh too, forests of the CHT have been a unique source of patronising and grooming Bangalee bourgeois and petty bourgeois classes. From 1979 onwards, the government leased out large consolidated tracts to private entrepreneurs for rubber and other commercial plantations.[306] It is reported that even the Dunlop Company expressed interest in setting up a rubber plantation covering an area of 32,000 acres in the CHT; however, the government preferred Bangalee entrepreneurs in this role.[307] In 1980, the government allocated 550 plots of 25 acres each to Bangalee businessmen on a trial basis; given increasing demand the size of allocation ultimately went up to 1,000 acres and then 5,000 acres each.[308] The areas leased out were mostly taken from the common lands of the hill people in the USF areas that they had

---

[303] Shapan Adnan and Ranjit Dastidar, *Alienation of the Lands of Indigenous Peoples in the Chittagong Hill Tracts of Bangladesh* (Dhaka and Copenhagen: Chittagong Hill Tracts Commission and International Work Group for Indigenous Affairs, 2011), 48.
[304] Ibid., 49.
[305] See Mark Levene, 'The Chittagong Hill Tracts: A Case Study in the Political Economy of "Creeping" Genocide', *Third World Quarterly* 20, no. 2 (1999), 351.
[306] Ibid., 77–78.
[307] Huq, 'Government Institutions and Underdevelopment', 65.
[308] Ibid., 66.

traditionally used for joom cultivation, grazing, and other purposes. An official review of the status of leased plantations in the CHT, undertaken in 2009 to provide information required by the Parliamentary Standing Committee for the Ministry of CHT Affairs, found that many leased plots had not yet been utilised for plantations and some plots had been sublet in violation of the lease contract. Some members of the Committee also noted that powerful land grabbers were using these lease documents to evict local hill peoples from their land.[309]

Thus, seen through the Gramscian optic of the passive revolution of capital, the postcolonial states of Pakistan and Bangladesh hardly deviated from the colonial economic structure within which exploitation of the CHT was made possible. As the current titular Raja of the Chakma Circle in the CHT, Devasish Roy, succinctly notes,

> [d]espite various legal amendments to the land laws of the region starting from the period of British rule, through to the Pakistani period and after Bangladesh's independence in 1971, the pattern of land and forest management in the CHT has essentially remained somewhat "colonialist", in the sense that the major policy benefits have accrued not to the local population, but to the state.[310]

The new postcolonial states had to rely on bourgeois and petty bourgeois classes in the process of consolidating political power, especially when the very legitimacy of states was challenged by the hill communities of the CHT. Here, the notions of nation-building, security, and development all come together, and the ideology of the postcolonial 'developmental' state legitimises and dissimulates exploitation of the hill people.

It is hardly surprising that the most devastating policy of settling hundreds of thousands of Bangalees from the rest of the country into

---

[309] In line with the corresponding provision of the CHT Peace Accord, the Parliamentary Standing Committee gave the directive to cancel the leases of unproductive and idle plantation lands. However, it transpired that many leaseholders who had neglected their plantations suddenly became active after the directive to cancel unproductive leases was announced. It was reported that lorry-loads of eucalyptus, acacia, and other seedlings were brought in by these leaseholders immediately after the cancellation order to 'create' plantations overnight on plots that had remained undeveloped for years. Furthermore, even though the leases of many plantation plots were initially cancelled, most of these were re-issued within a few months. See Adnan and Dastidar, *Alienation of the Lands of Indigenous Peoples*, 80–85.

[310] Raja Devasish Roy, 'Challenges for Juridical Pluralism and Customary Laws of Indigenous Peoples: The Case of the Chittagong Hill Tracts, Bangladesh', *Arizona Journal of International & Comparative Law* 21, no. 1 (2004), 150.

the CHT – largely to change the demographic composition of the region and subvert separatist activities – was also initially justified using the language of 'development'. Since the CHT comprises a vast territory of 'underused' land and the hill people do not or cannot cultivate it, the argument went, in the interests of productivity and development 'new productive hands are to be exported there'.[311] This Lockean argument for utilitarianism was well reflected in the First Five Year Plan of Bangladesh, which underscored the urgent need to use the CHT land for the sake of the national economy.[312] Government-sponsored reports in the 1990s suggested that the CHT was geopolitically vital, with its forest and mineral resources and its 147 inhabitants per square mile – compared with 1,567 per square mile in the rest of the country – underscoring that the future of the CHT 'should be viewed from a total national perspective'.[313] This utilitarian argument in the context of the CHT also reflects the logic of native development under the Mandate System, as discussed earlier.

5.5.3 International Development Agencies and Peacebuilding

Unsurprisingly, IFIs and donor agencies have historically been an integral part of developmentalism in the CHT, and gross violations of human rights in the CHT by successive military regimes had little effect on international financial support for development in the region. As noted earlier, two of the most damaging development projects in the CHT under Pakistan rule were funded by the World Bank and USAID. The involvement of IFIs and donor agencies in various development projects in the CHT remained unabated in independent Bangladesh. The Multi-sectoral Programme in Khagrachari district, one of the major programmes in the CHT, was started in 1979 at the cost of USD 41.8 million, of which USD 28.5 million was provided by the Asian Development Bank (ADB) as a loan and 0.4 million as a grant; the UNDP provided USD 0.7 million.[314] Additional funds were made available for this programme by these two institutions to extend the programme until 1993. The Upland Settlement Scheme (USS) to settle joom cultivators was one of the key components of the Multi-Sectoral

---

[311] Huq, 'Government Institutions and Underdevelopment', 64.
[312] See Government of Bangladesh, *The First Five Year Plan of Bangladesh, 1973–78* (Dhaka: Planning Commission, 1973), section on Forestry.
[313] See Levene, 'The Chittagong Hill Tracts', 348.
[314] Arens, 'Winning Hearts and Minds', 1815.

THE CASE OF THE CHT HILL PEOPLE IN BANGLADESH   271

Programme. Under the scheme, a total of 8,000 acres of rubber and 4,000 acres of horticulture were to be planted.[315] In general, major forestry initiatives in the CHT, including the National Forestry Policy of 1979 and the Forestry Master Plan of 1994, have been undertaken with the assistance of ADB.[316] Many of these policies and projects have 'systematically promoted industrial forestry by expanding rubber and timber plantations' to the detriment of hill peoples.[317] As Shapan Adnan and Ranjit Dastidar note, '[f]orest-dwelling [hill] communities have been involved in such projects merely as providers of cheap labour. Even though formally designated as "beneficiaries" or "participants", they have never been allowed to have any meaningful decision-making roles in these forestry projects.'[318]

Various other Western countries also mobilised their development agencies or private corporations to secure their shares of the lucrative resource exploitation opportunities in the CHT. In 1981, the petroleum giant Shell, jointly with the Petro-Bangla (a government agency), secured concession for oil exploration in the CHT for 25 years, although Shell had to abandon the project following the abduction of four of its employees by the Shanti Bahini – the then armed wing of the PCJSS.[319] The Australian Development Assistance Bureau (currently known as Australian Aid) committed USD 11 million to a road construction project allegedly to secure access to oil prospects, but it ultimately pulled out for security reasons.[320] Likewise, until 1981, the Swedish government aid agency SIDA was involved in a USD 10 million afforestation programme and other large-scale commercial forestry programmes that threatened the livelihood of hill peoples in significant ways. Sweden had to finally withdraw from this venture in the face of harsh criticism in the Swedish press.[321] The notorious resettlement project under which hundreds of thousands Bangalees from various parts of the country were settled in the CHT was largely funded by the ADB, USAID, WHO, and UNICEF.[322]

In the aftermath of the Peace Accord and in the context of post-conflict peacebuilding in the CHT, international development agencies are more

---

[315] Ibid.
[316] Adnan and Dastidar, *Alienation of the Lands of Indigenous Peoples*, 48.
[317] Ibid.
[318] Ibid.
[319] Arens, 'Winning Hearts and Minds', 1815.
[320] Ibid., 1816; Levene, 'The Chittagong Hill Tracts', 355.
[321] Arens, 'Winning Hearts and Minds', 1816.
[322] Levene, 'The Chittagong Hill Tracts', 355–356.

active than ever before. The United Nations Development Programme Chittagong Hill Tracts Development Facility (UNDP-CHTDF) is the largest post-conflict reconstruction project undertaken by international stakeholders with a total of USD 156 million in funding.[323] While the European Union is the single largest contributor (59.4 per cent) to this fund, other contributors include UNDP (12 per cent) and state development agencies of the United States, Canada, Denmark, Norway, Sweden, Australia, and Japan.[324] The multi-dimensional project has the official agenda of capacity-building for key local CHT institutions, community empowerment, delivery of essential services, and the implementation of the CHT Accord.[325] The availability of sizable international funding has led to an exponential growth of NGOs operating in the region. Numerous local, national, and international NGOs as well as Christian missionaries are active in various 'development' projects in the CHT.

However, in reality, local NGOs work only towards delivering goods to their international donors as the development agenda is heavily donor driven. A recent empirical study reveals that grassroots organisations that indeed have a better idea about local needs do not have any control in development agenda setting.[326] As one local NGO representative is reported to have said:

> We are bound to work on the project of violence against women if donors want to work on it. Now we are working on village common forests with donors, but I am surprised when I think why this project is important in the CHT since we have already a culture that emphasizes [sic] the preservation of village common forests.[327]

Although most international development agencies have elaborate procedures for ensuring local participation in need assessments and decision-making, the aforementioned empirical study finds that those procedures are not actually followed in the CHT:

---

[323] Anurug Chakma, 'The Peacebuilding of the Chittagong Hill Tracts (CHT), Bangladesh: Donor-Driven or Demand-Driven?' *Asian Journal of Peacebuilding* 5, no. 2 (2017), 224. See also Ashok Kumar Chakma, *An Assessment of the UNDP-CHTDF Project on Promotion of Development and Confidence Building in the Chittagong Hill Tracts Relating to the Implementation of the CHT Accord 1997* (Rangamati: Maleya Foundation, 2013).
[324] Official website of the UNDP available at www.bd.undp.org.
[325] Ibid.
[326] See generally Chakma, 'The Peacebuilding of the Chittagong Hill Tracts (CHT), Bangladesh', 223–242.
[327] Ibid., 236.

[I]nternational stakeholders have consulted with the community on very few projects, and local participation was absolutely ignored in the majority of the post-conflict reconstruction projects. An international staff member of a donor organization also reports that international organizations basically design peacebuilding interventions for the CHT based on the availability of funds with a special focus on the interests and priorities of donors.[328]

Also, the government and security agencies have significant influence and control on the activities of local NGOs: they need to get their projects approved by the Ministry of CHT Affairs and the NGO Bureau and cleared by intelligence units, the Deputy Commissioner of the concerned district, and the CHT Regional Council. Thus, the cumulative result of government surveillance, donor heavy-handedness, and a top-down approach to development has been the further disenfranchisement of hill peoples in development decision-making.

More importantly, in line with the policy of market liberalisation as a standard international response to peacebuilding as we have seen earlier, the UNDP-CHTDF project too has adopted the policy of 'marketisation' as a peace strategy. The project's annual report of 2014 describes in a self-congratulatory fashion how the project contributed to increased productivity and efficiency of hill farmers in the CHT:

> The Facility continues to support value chain enhancement of Hill Tracts agro-products, facilitating a shift from subsistence-based agriculture towards a more market-driven approach, finding linkages with economic activity and capturing the benefits of local economic development. The formulation of a marketing intervention strategy for the region's agro-products, developed in 2014, is an example of our commitment to helping local farmer's [sic] access economic growth opportunity.[329]

With the overarching objective of connecting the CHT with the larger national and regional market economy, in 2014 the World Bank initiated the Bangladesh Trade and Transport Facilitation Studies (RETF Project) under the theme of 'trade facilitation and market access, rural services and infrastructure'.[330] Under this USD 5 million project, relevant ministries of the Bangladesh government conducted feasibility studies on multiple infrastructure development projects, including the Chittagong-Thegamukh Connectivity Project in the CHT. The main purpose of the

---

[328] Ibid., 232.
[329] Chittagong Hill Tracts Development Facility, *Promotion of Development and Confidence Building in the Chittagong Hill Tracts* (Annual Report) (Dhaka: UNDP, 2014), 25.
[330] See the World Bank project website at www.projects.worldbank.org/P148881.

project is for the World Bank to support the Bangladesh government to connect the remote Thegamukh area in east-central CHT, bordering Mizoram State in India and currently inaccessible by road, with the Chittagong sea port, through Rangamati town and sub-district centres within the Rangamati district of the CHT.[331]

Although the project was earmarked for full environmental assessment (category A), local hill communities allege that the study was completed without any consultation with local communities or their elected representatives. In a formal Request for Inspection dated 31 August 2016, hill communities and civil society organisations complained that the proposed connectivity route passes through reserved forests and several settlements of hill peoples along with privately titled lands and customarily owned and used lands of both hill and settler-Bangalee communities in the CHT. It is to be noted that many of these hill communities in the project area were in fact re-settled here after being initially displaced due to the Karnaphuli hydro-electricity project.

Yet, the government and its private consultants completed the study without any meaningful consultation with hill peoples or their representatives – undermining the Bank's own official guidelines on 'free, prior and informed consultation'.[332] The complaint also noted that the study failed to assess and address crucial issues, such as land and resource rights, benefit sharing, sacred sites, and cultural impacts, seen from the perspectives of indigenous hill communities.[333] It is only after the local resistance that the Bank decided not to fund the CHT connectivity component of the RETF project. 'Development' therefore remains an incessant threat to the life, livelihood, and natural environment of hill peoples and requires their constant vigilance against incessant reckless interventions.

In this sense, recent development initiatives in the CHT funded by international agencies are hardly any deviation from what the colonial administration and subsequently the postcolonial states of Pakistan and Bangladesh pursued as a policy goal in the name of 'protection' or 'development': making the CHT economically profitable, if necessary at considerable socio-cultural cost to the hill people. Thus, as Prashanta Tripura notes, for the hill peoples of the CHT 'development' has always

---

[331] See *Project Information Document*, Report No. 84373, available at ibid.

[332] See The World Bank Project Inspection Panel, *Memorandum to the Executive Directors, International Development Association* (IPN Request RQ 16/06), 18 October 2016, Annex I.

[333] Ibid.

meant dislocation, disruption, and destruction, and development agents have always failed to grasp alternative visions of development in the plurality of lived experiences in the CHT itself, going beyond a monolithic, pre-determined conception.[334]

The foregoing analysis of developmentalism in the CHT underscores the general phenomenon that the discourse on 'development' and the governing international legal regime readily sacrifices legitimate interests of minorities, precisely because they are 'minorities' with little or no ownership in postcolonial states *as* minorities. This phenomenon feeds into the ideology of the postcolonial 'developmental' state, which legitimises and glosses over violence towards and marginalisation of already vulnerable minorities to safeguard majoritarian bourgeois interests, the latter being increasingly and more closely tied up with neoliberal modes of exploitation and accumulation at the global stage.

5.6 Conclusion

The preceding case studies on the Rohingya in Myanmar and the CHT hill people in Bangladesh demonstrate how the postcolonial 'developmental' state operates as an ideology. First, it organises the economic life of the state in a way that further marginalises politically suppressed minorities. And then, it justifies the marginalisation in the name of national economic growth and development. Throughout this chapter, I have argued that international law plays a key role in the ideological operation of the postcolonial 'developmental' state. I have substantiated this argument with an in-depth and multi-layered analysis of the complex interrelationship between minorities, postcolonial states, and neoliberal international actors with reference to 'development', minority rights, and international law.

My analysis has exposed the way the postcolonial state, on the one hand, and liberal individuals, on the other, remain at the centre of the developmental discourse in international law. In this regard, I have highlighted the implications of such an approach to economic development for minorities. Then, shifting my focus from international law of development to the minority rights regime, I have also demonstrated how international law discourse on minority and group rights fails to

---

[334] Prashanta Tripura, 'Culture, Identity and Development', in *The Chittagong Hill Tracts: Life and Nature at Risk*, 97–105. For an account of the indigenous paradigm of development in the CHT, see Nasir Uddin, 'Paradigm of "Better Life": "Development" among the Khumi in the Chittagong Hill Tracts', *Asian Ethnicity* 15, no. 1 (2014), 62–77.

offer necessary protection to minorities against developmental violence in the form of land-grabbing and forced displacement. Thus, it transpires in both cases that international law maintains a framework within which international actors and postcolonial states suppress minority interests in the name of national (read majoritarian) economic development, whereas politically marginalised minorities suffer the most due to such development activities.

In this way, international law advances the ideology of the postcolonial 'developmental' state through the ideological mode of operation of legitimation. Such legitimation of minority oppression in the name of economic development glosses over the existing structural power imbalance between the minority and the dominant majority in both the political and the socio-economic domain. Therefore, dissimulation as a mode of ideological operation also comes into play. Since the very notion of development is conceived as an integral part of the transition narrative of modernity, international law at the same time reifies the centrality of 'development' in the making of the postcolonial state – undermining minority rights concerns. And, finally, given their common liberal-individualist ideological premise, the merger of the discourse on development with that of human rights – as expressed in the right to development – diffuses minority groups into individuals through fragmentation as the ideological mode of operation.

In the foregoing three chapters in Part II, I have dealt with the third building block of this book, namely, a critical examination of the role that international law plays in the ideological function of the postcolonial state. We are therefore left with the fourth and the final key question that this book is designed to address: as the postcolonial state operates as an ideology to create and sustain asymmetric power relations vis-à-vis the minority, and international law plays a central role in this ideological function of the postcolonial state, what is the way forward? What future awaits minorities in postcolonial states while the future of the postcolonial state itself is in doubt in an increasingly complex and multi-faceted transformation of the existing global order? The conclusion of the book sheds light on some forward looking aspects of the historical relationship between minorities, postcolonial states, and international law.

Conclusion

The postcolonial state operates as an ideology to create and sustain asymmetric power relations vis-à-vis minorities. The ideological function of the postcolonial state takes three different yet interconnected forms: the postcolonial 'national' state, the postcolonial 'liberal' state, and the postcolonial 'developmental' state. As ideologies, the three visions of the postcolonial state inflict various forms of marginalisation on minorities but simultaneously justify the oppression in the name of national unity, liberal principles of equality and non-discrimination, and economic development. International law plays a central role in this ideological function of the postcolonial state and contributes to the marginalisation of minorities. It does so by playing a key role in the ideological making of the postcolonial national, liberal, and developmental states through legitimation, dissimulation, unification, fragmentation, and reification as ideological modes of operation.

First, the ideology of the postcolonial 'national' state is intrinsically connected to the process by which homogeneous national states are made within the confines of colonial boundaries. The making of the postcolonial 'national' state leads to the marginalisation of various minority groups, for these minorities often find themselves on the wrong side of state boundaries and under the jurisdiction of hostile new states. International law unequivocally facilitates the ideological function of the postcolonial national state by prescribing the continuity of colonial boundaries, which were drawn arbitrarily without any regard to the ethnic makeup of the population. As a result, minorities are denied the legitimate right to self-determination. Minority oppression in the hands of hostile national states and the ensuing ethnic conflicts are direct results of this. With the reification of the nation-state form at the core of the international legal imagination and as the building block of the international order, international law legitimises the marginalisation of minorities as the leftover of the state-making process. International law, at the same time, dissimulates the vulnerabilities of ethnic minorities in the name of national unification. In this way, international law advances the ideology of the postcolonial 'national' state through a number of general modes of ideological operation.

Second, given the dominance of liberal universalism in the aftermath of WWII, the ideology of the postcolonial 'liberal' state promises a post-ethnic world order and offers the template for the internal organisation of ethnic relations in postcolonial states. International law with its liberal underpinning feeds into the vision of the postcolonial 'liberal' state, which is then translated into an ideology to marginalise ethnic minorities within the liberal framework of equality and non-discrimination. Liberal individualism in international law continues to shrink the scope of external and internal self-determination, thereby perpetuating the vulnerability of minority groups. Also, within the individualist human rights framework, the international law of minority protection, offered as a fall-back position to groups that have been denied the right to self-determination, fails to adequately protect minorities. Taking these methods together, international law facilitates the ideology of the postcolonial 'liberal' state with fragmentation and legitimation as its ideological modes of operation. Working through these modes, international law diffuses minority groups into individual subjects of human rights, and legitimises the denial of minority *group* protection within the constitutional architecture of the postcolonial 'liberal' state. In this sense, the diffusion of minority groups into individual citizens, followed by their subjection to a human rights regime that maintains formal equality among citizens, is seen as the very precondition of the postcolonial 'national' state.

Third, the ideology of the postcolonial 'developmental' state, operating along the line of the same liberal ideological vision, puts forward the agenda for the postcolonial state's internal and external organisation of economic affairs. The developmental ideology not only results in the marginalisation of minorities but also serves to legitimise and gloss over asymmetric power relations that produce such marginalisation. Development projects disproportionately target minority lands and forests, with long-term devastating effects on the cultures and the very existence of minorities. International law provides a framework within which international actors and postcolonial states suppress minority interests in the name of economic development, whereas minorities – being politically marginalised – suffer the most due to such development activities. In this way, international law advances the ideology of the postcolonial 'developmental' state through legitimation as its ideological mode of operation. Such legitimation of minority oppression in the name of economic development glosses over the existing structural power imbalance between the minority and the dominant majority in the political as well as the socio-economic domain. Thus, dissimulation as a mode of ideological operation also comes into play. Since the very notion of development is conceived as an integral part of the transition narrative of modernity, international law at the same time reifies the centrality of 'development' in the making of the postcolonial state, undermining minority rights concerns. And finally, given their common liberal-individualist ideological premise, the merger of the discourse on development with that on human rights – as expressed in the right to development – diffuses minority groups into individuals, with fragmentation as the ideological mode of operation. In this sense, the ideologies of the postcolonial 'national', 'liberal', and 'developmental' state are interconnected and depend on each other for fruition.

What to do with the disturbing relationship between the postcolonial state and international law, then? This relationship evolved in a historical process and any attempt to mend it will entail unsettling various established international legal norms. Some of the ideological tensions that the book grasps and that are reiterated here – for example, between territorial integrity and remedial secession, sovereignty and humanitarian intervention, individualism and group rights, and so on – are not easily reconcilable, so any such attempt is likely to be marked with ambivalence at best, and hollowness at worst. Given the gravity of human sufferings that the ideological function of the postcolonial state inflicts on minorities, the status quo and inaction is not a viable option either. As Chimni passionately argues, 'while contemporary international law is imperial in character the possibility and benefits of reform should not be ruled out through the struggles of subaltern groups, peoples and nations'.[1]

In what follows, I critically examine a wide range of possible ways out and reform agendas to propose a more humane interrelationship between minorities, postcolonial states, and international law. My reflections here should be seen as potential approaches to redefining international legal architectures to the advantage of minority groups, rather than as a set of ready-made solutions. These reflections cover a wide range of avenues, from revisiting colonial boundaries in principled ways to accommodating more robust protection for minorities within existing state structures, to radically reconceptualising the state itself through feminist and historiographic revision. The issues covered in the following section are, however, far from exhaustive.

---

[1] Chimni, *International Law and World Order*, 476–477.

Conclusion

Towards an Alternative Future for Minorities

Beyond Colonial Boundaries

The idea of revising colonial boundaries was raised by Makau Mutua, in the context of ethnic tensions in postcolonial African states, nearly three decades ago. Being concerned with the stability as well as the ultimate viability of postcolonial states in Africa and apprehensive about Western 'recolonisation' in subtle forms, he argued that these states were doomed as, not reflecting pre-colonial ethnic representation, they lacked moral legitimacy.[2] At the moment of decolonisation, the right to self-determination was exercised not by the 'victims of colonization' but their 'victimizers, i.e. the elites who control the international state system'.[3] Mutua argues that this fundamental moral and structural illegitimacy is the reason that various attempts to manage ethnic relations, such as federalism and power-sharing within the inherited structure of colonial states, failed in postcolonial Africa.[4]

Thus, he proposes that 'pre-colonial entities within the post-colonial order be allowed to exercise their right to self-determination'.[5] For him, a dual but simultaneous process of 'new map-making together with norm re-examination and reformulation' can finally address the protracted legitimacy crisis of African states and reconnect the continent to pre-colonial ideals of community and social organisation as well as democratisation.[6] But, to that end, 'Africa's political map must first be unscrambled and the post-colonial state disassembled before the continent can move forward', and '[o]nly this radical but necessary step can legitimize the African state and avoid its demise'.[7]

Soon after the end of the Cold War, when violent ethnic conflicts erupted across the world, Mutua was not alone in arguing for decolonising the colonial boundaries of postcolonial states. He in fact referred to the African scholar Ali Mazrui, who predicted in a 1993 article that in the course of the twenty-first century the outlines of most of the African states at the time would change in at least one of two main ways: ethnic self-determination, which would create smaller states; and regional integration, making larger political communities and economic

---

[2] Mutua, 'Why Redraw the Map of Africa', 1116 and 1166.
[3] Ibid., 1118.
[4] Ibid., 1151–1160.
[5] Ibid., 1118.
[6] Ibid., 1162.
[7] Ibid., 1162 and 1118.

unions.[8] The secession of Eritrea from Ethiopia in 1993 might have prompted his first prediction. In defiance of his second prediction, between then and now, neither the political nor the economic integration in Africa has progressed enough to pose any real challenge to the conventional notion of statehood. The political integration project of the European Union, seen for some time as a model for a wider political union in Africa, has taken rather a U-turn in recent years. However, in the face of armed struggles for ethnic self-determination, the existing territorial boundaries have already been revised in Sudan to create the new state of South Sudan in 2011. This example alone cannot be seen as even an early sign of the collapse of the African state system as a whole. The important point to note here is that for Mutua, such an alteration of colonial boundaries to accommodate the right to self-determination of pre-colonial ethnic groups is not merely a pragmatic choice for peace but a moral imperative. Inspired by Mutua, more recently Okafor too called for the peaceful reconfiguration of African states under the auspices of his proposed African Union Special Commission on National Minorities.[9]

The role of colonial boundaries in facilitating ethnic conflicts in postcolonial states is undeniable. As discussed in relation to case studies on the Rohingya and the CHT hill people, the international law principle of the continuity of colonial boundaries in postcolonial states (*uti possidetis*) denies minority groups their legitimate right to self-determination and puts them in vulnerable positions vis-à-vis dominant and often hostile majority groups. Given international law's strong preference for territorial integrity and for maintaining the existing international order based on sovereign states, any revision of existing territorial boundaries, except by mutual consent, in order to grant pre-colonial ethnic groups the right to self-determination is quite unlikely. The principle of *uti possidetis* itself is an epitome of this dominant normative position on territorial integrity.

However, highlighting the limits of the traditional understanding of *uti possidetis*, Ratner proposes four guidelines for formulating a normative basis for an alternative to the principle. First, as a point of departure, decision makers need to appreciate the original Roman-law purpose of *uti possidetis*, that is, to preserve the *status quo* only until states can resolve their competing claims, and thereby, move beyond the

---

[8] See also Ali Mazrui, 'The Bondage of Boundaries', *The Economist*, 11 September 1993, 28.
[9] Okafor, '"Righting", Restructuring, and Rejuvenating the Postcolonial African State', 43–64.

automatic application of colonial boundaries between postcolonial states. An acknowledgment of the provisional status of the colonial boundaries this principle creates will put a burden on decision makers to consider other possibilities for potential boundaries.[10] Second, any such process of alternative border-drawing must take place only through peaceful means under international law.[11] Third, in line with the preceding principles, decision makers should then closely scrutinise existing administrative boundaries to determine whether a substantially better alternative is available before drawing a final line. In this regard, they should consider the age of the existing administrative line, the process by which the line was drawn, and its functional suitability as an international frontier.[12] And finally, meaningful efforts should be made towards some form of consultation, including plebiscites where possible, with the populace of a disputed territory on its future.[13]

Similarly, the political theorist David Miller proposes a combination of 'pragmatic', 'political', and 'homeland' approaches to boundary-drawing with a view to developing a principled position on this vital subject. The pragmatic approach to boundaries seeks to create political units that are viable in terms of size and essential resources, and fit for performing economic and defence functions expected of a modern state.[14] The political approach asks for the legitimacy of the territorial unit, especially its democratic nature. Inhabitants of a given unit need to be convinced that the political regime that is exercising sovereign powers over them within that territory is indeed a legitimate authority.[15] And finally, the homeland approach requires attention to the preexisting territorial claims of nations and other groups. Premised upon such groups' perspectives and priorities, this approach to boundaries seeks to create an area of jurisdiction wherein these groups can control the territory in question, preserving and/or developing it according to their needs and aspirations.[16] Although these approaches have their own limits, as both Miller and Ratner acknowledge, there is certainly some virtue in engaging with these concepts as an

---

[10] Ratner, 'Drawing a Better Line', 617–619.
[11] Ibid., 619–620.
[12] Ibid., 620–621.
[13] Ibid., 622–623.
[14] David Miller, 'Boundaries, Democracy, and Territory', *The American Journal of Jurisprudence* 61, no. 1 (2016), 37–40.
[15] Ibid., 40–44.
[16] Ibid., 44–47.

alternative to the existing international law obsession with territorial integrity and maintenance of colonial borders.

Another factor that occasionally challenges the dominance of territorial integrity is gross violations of human rights. While Mutua and Okafor rely on such actual and potential humanitarian catastrophes to advance their argument for a preemptive redrawing of maps and an orderly restructuring of postcolonial states, international law traditionally responds to such catastrophes within the framework of exceptionalism. The issue of remedial secession that I discussed earlier would be a pertinent example here. The issue becomes even more complicated as already vulnerable minorities often do not have the necessary means to fight back the oppressor majoritarian state to materialise their right to self-determination in the form of remedial secession. The protection of such minorities, then, often depends on the goodwill as well as the political, economic, and strategic interests of powerful nations in the West. Compared to their role in the Balkans, for example, these powerful states are traditionally less inclined to shoulder the costs of military interventions in the Global South out of humanitarian concerns alone. The genocide committed against the Rohingya minority in 2017 failed to mobilise any such support from the leading powers, especially because these countries prioritised maintaining good relationships with the Myanmar regime to safeguard their vested interests.

At the normative level, as we have also seen, the development of the Responsibility to Protect (R2P) principle has been marred by uncertainty and lack of clarity on objective criteria, as well as by subjective considerations on who should get to decide where and when to intervene. These ambiguities make the entire project tenuous, and it is hardly surprising that many postcolonial states look at the R2P project with suspicion. The hard-earned sovereignty of the postcolonial state is also a protective shield under which minority oppression is possible. While minorities in postcolonial states are stuck in this sovereignty dilemma, Third World international lawyers unfailingly side with the supremacy of state sovereignty in international law. As Chimni approvingly notes, '[t]he TWAIL view is that "rule of law" should be valued even as third world nations and peoples contest, resist and reform particular legal regimes. Any other view facilitates the rule of the strong over the weak.'[17]

It is therefore unlikely that an alternative future for the Rohingya or the CHT hill people, envisioned outside the territorial framework of their

---

[17] Chimni, *International Law and World Order*, 347. Footnotes omitted.

respective states, will gain ground any time soon. Especially in the case of the Rohingya, despite adequate documentation of genocidal violence committed against them, the issue of remedial secession never became part of the international policy discourse. An individual proposal of a US Congressman to cede north Rakhine to Bangladesh, as noted earlier, was quickly labelled by the international community – including Bangladesh – as bizarre and immoral. Nevertheless, the option of remedial secession of north Rakhine by the Rohingya should be part of any future peace negotiation with Myanmar. It is worth remembering that arguments for remedial secession paved Bangladesh's way to statehood in 1971 and finally brought an end to the indiscriminate brutality of the Pakistan army against Bangalees in the then East Pakistan. The creation of South Sudan is a more recent example.

At the same time, it also needs to be acknowledged that creating a new state by breaking with the oppressive state does not always solve minority problems, in that the new state is unlikely to be ethnically homogeneous. Therefore, problems inherent to the very ideology of the postcolonial state will multiply and continue in new forms to marginalise minorities in the new state, especially in the absence of strong representative institutions.[18] Again, the creation of Bangladesh and the country's treatment of its own ethnic minorities make the point clear. While the need for remedial secession cannot be denied as the last resort in extreme cases, such as the Rohingya, other viable alternatives need to be explored within the territorial confines of the postcolonial 'national' state or, more radically, outside the tired category of the nation-state altogether.

Beyond Liberal Individualism

While international law is vigorously opposed to the revision of external boundaries, it is worth examining what alternative future for minorities is possible *within* the existing framework of territorial sovereignty. In recent years successful experiments have been made in internal reorganisation of nation-states to accommodate ethnic diversity beyond the individualist human rights framework. As discussed earlier, the human

---

[18] Chandhoke makes the argument especially in relation to Jammu and Kashmir in India. See generally Neera Chandhoke, *Contested Secessions: Rights, Self-determination, Democracy, and Kashmir* (New Delhi: Oxford University Press, 2012). Mullerson makes the same argument in the context of Eastern Europe and the former USSR. See Rein Mullerson, 'Minorities in Eastern Europe and the Former USSR: Problems, Tendencies and Protection', *Modern Law Review* 56 (1993), 801–802.

rights approach to minorities, within the framework of liberal individualism, does not offer minorities adequate protection against the majoritarian hegemony and dominance.

In contrast, when oppressed ethnic minorities have recourse to violence with a view to redressing historical injustice against them, the solutions to such armed conflicts often involve ethnic-group-oriented arrangements, such as autonomy and power-sharing, going beyond the standard individualist human rights framework. However, in many cases, such pragmatic measures to secure peace stand in normative inconsistency with the liberal constitutional architecture of the postcolonial state. I discussed this phenomenon in detail in relation to the CHT Peace Accord. Many peace treaties, designed to address pragmatic needs in peace negotiations, operate within a quasi-legal domain, largely due to the liberal-individualist constitutional framework of equality and non-discrimination that nullifies special privileges for any particular ethnic group.

To mitigate this problem, it is imperative that postcolonial states break with the ideology of the homogeneous 'national' state and recognise the special status of contesting ethnic groups in the constitution. As the experience with the CHT Peace Accord reveals, a constitutional recognition of the special status of the CHT hill people could address the concerns emanating from the conflicting provisions on equality and non-discrimination. This bold move will eventually help the state itself to reimagine its own postcolonial identity beyond the template of post-WWII liberal universalism. The longstanding minority problem in many postcolonial states in turn is a necessary reminder of the deeper crises of postcolonial statehood itself and hegemonic nation-building projects that these states embody.

Not all minority groups have the means to mount armed resistance against the powerful state, draw international attention and sympathy – thereby internationalising the otherwise internal conflict – and ultimately secure a peace deal involving special group measures. It is also not in the best interest of the postcolonial state to follow the path of violent conflicts while the possibility of peace is real. Ethnic federalism, regional autonomy, consociational democracy, and other power-sharing models can pre-emptively reduce the risk of ethnic conflicts. While these arrangements cannot completely erase ethnic tensions within a state, they are very much capable of channelling such tensions into constructive debates and amicable outcomes. For example, federalism helped Nigeria convert inter-ethnic conflicts into intra-ethnic conflicts, thereby reducing ethnic tensions to some extent. Consociational arrangements aided Lebanese efforts to reach a constitutional solution, albeit temporary, to the civil war. In other cases, such measures, while not yet implemented, have at least been recognised by progressive political parties as a potential way forward.[19] As we have already seen, the dominance of liberal individualism as the universal norm that reduces all alternative possibilities of ethnic relations to pragmatic exceptionalism is not very helpful in this regard. Normative individualism, the foundation of the liberal international legal architecture, is often seen as incompatible with the notion of the centrality of ethnicity in identity formation, as in ethnic minorities, and therefore inconsistent with any ethnic group measure. In this sense, a reimagination of liberalism itself is also warranted.

I have argued elsewhere that while such revisionist projects have already been undertaken by leading liberal scholars who attempted to accommodate group differentiated measures within a reinterpreted framework of liberalism, such moves did not go far. This is because 'liberal' attempts to accommodate ethnicity within liberalism have also been viciously attacked by fellow liberals on the grounds that such measures are counterproductive to the core liberal values of individual freedom and equality.[20] Condemning such so-called liberal attempts, one author even emphatically argued that '[a] theory that has the implication that nationalities (whether they control a state or a sub-state polity) have a fundamental right to violate liberal principles is not a liberal theory of group rights. It is an *illiberal theory* with a bit of liberal hand-writing thrown in as an optional extra.'[21]

Liberal or not, the relevance of group differentiated measures remains unabated in a world that is so hostile to minorities. As a matter of fact, the purported universality of liberalism and the role it has assumed as the yardstick of legitimacy is increasingly challenged. So far as the postcolonial states are concerned, the ideology of the 'liberal' state has caused more harm than good, as I have demonstrated throughout this book. Therefore, normative inconsistencies with liberalism cannot be a legitimate excuse to undermine the conflict evading potential of group differentiated measures to safeguard minority interests in an otherwise majoritarian state.

---

[19] See, for example, Section 1 (kha) of the Declaration and Programme of the Communist Party of Bangladesh (adopted in March 1999, last updated in October 2016), available at www.cpbbd.org/?page=details&serial=287, and Section 6:3 (II) of the Programme of the Communist Party of India (Marxist) (adopted in November 1964, last updated in October 2000), available at www.cpim.org/party-programme.

[20] See Shahabuddin, *Ethnicity and International Law*, 221–227.

[21] Brian Barry, *Culture and Equality* (Cambridge: Polity Press, 2001), 140. Emphasis added.

Specifically, in the case of the CHT, the Constitution of Bangladesh needs to recognise the special status of the hill people and pave the way for the full implementation of the CHT Peace Accord, including elements of regional autonomy. The constitutional recognition of the CHT hill people as an indigenous people and the ratification of the ILO Convention 169 (1989) will bring the community under more robust international protection. As we discussed in the preceding chapter, state parties to the Convention must ensure the safeguard of the persons, institutions, property, labour, culture, and environment of indigenous and tribal peoples.[22] Such recognition of special status of the hill people will then reconcile the normative inconsistency pertaining to the accommodation of group rights within the liberal-individualist constitutional architecture of rights. In the case of the Rohingya minority, Myanmar must recognise them as one of the country's original ethnic groups, guarantee them the rights that are enjoyed by all citizens, and provide for additional measures in the form of regional autonomy in north Rakhine so that the Rohingya can enjoy, protect, and nurture their distinct cultural and religious identity without the fear of further persecution. However, as a precondition and against all odds, drastic measures need to be taken first to ensure voluntary, safe, and dignified repatriation of more than a million Rohingya refugees to their places of origin in Rakhine State. On this score, it is also worth reiterating that the formal categories of 'ethnic minorities' and 'indigenous peoples' in international law, premised upon uniquely European experience, appear to be less definitive and more ambiguous in Asia and Africa due to these continents' very different experience of colonial encounter and postcolonial state-making.

Beyond 'Developmentalism' and Neoliberal Economic Growth

Minorities are routinely the foremost victims of development activities, even as various atrocities against minorities are justified in the name of economic growth. Because, WWII the developmental ideology has found its breeding ground in the postcolonial national state. In their resistance to the hegemony of former colonial powers and equally notorious international financial institutions, both nationalist elites and international lawyers in postcolonial states focused exclusively on the state. Their activism for 'permanent sovereignty over natural resources' and a 'new

---

[22] Articles 4, 8, and 13–19 of the ILO Convention No. 169 (1989).

international economic order' did not go beyond state centrism. The formal merger in the 1980s of the development discourse with human rights, in the form of the right to development, put the liberal individual at the centre of the development discourse, while postcolonial international lawyers continued to argue for and maintain the centrality of the state. In this dichotomy of the state and the individual, however, minorities and their sufferings – due to development and also to the lack of it – never drew adequate attention from national and international development actors. As a result, minorities and their life, culture, and livelihood are frequently sacrificed at the altar of economic growth.

In the current era of neoliberal economy, the situation of minorities and other vulnerable groups has only worsened. International law has created and sustained an environment of legitimacy in the domain of economy, as much as in the sphere of politics, that has made such minority oppression possible. In this sense, development-induced persecutions of the minority cannot be fully addressed in isolation from the existing hegemonic neoliberal economic structure at the global scale. As the examples of the CHT hill people and the Rohingya exposed, gross violations of human rights and the destruction of life and nature took place in the name of market liberalisation, privatisation of lands, increased connectivity with regional and global markets, and the promotion of foreign direct investment. The incessant demand for more lands and natural resources to feed the neoliberal economic needs resulted in the development-led forced displacement of the Rohingya and the CHT hill people from their ancestral lands. These minorities are not unique in this regard; such violent expulsions are a global phenomenon. Unless something is done soon, a vast number of minorities and indigenous peoples – along with their cultures and traditions – will be wiped off the planet. Therefore, global action and solidarity is required to put the brakes on this monstrous neoliberal invasion.[23] As part of this project, it is also essential to problematise and challenge the dominant idea of 'development' as the teleological end of human progress, to counterbalance its

---

[23] However, such global actions and solidarity beyond the network of empathetic vulnerable groups appear to be a big ask in the current environment of what Chimni calls 'global imperialism' sustained by 'global imperial international law'. He regrets that global imperialism has caused a strong sense among many human beings of alienation from their nature, from their own productive activity, from their 'species being', and from each other. As a result, '[w]e live in a world that is increasingly devoid of sentiments of solidarity with the deprived and oppressed'. See Chimni, *International Law and World Order*, 515–516. For the concept of 'alienation', Chimni relied on Mészáros's take on Marx's theory of alienation in *Economic and Philosophic Manuscripts*. See Istvan Mészáros, *Marx's Theory of Alienation*, 3rd ed. (London: Merlin Press, 1972).

tendency to commodify, and to expose its capacity to articulate state power in terms of economic growth rather than welfare.

Pushed to the edge, some of the deprived and oppressed communities disappear; others have recourse to resistance. Large development projects in postcolonial states, often funded by international financial institutions and development agencies of industrialised nations of the Global North, face armed resistance that ultimately results in protracted violent conflicts. Ironically, as we have seen, it is the 'neoliberal development plus democracy' model that is invariably imposed on postcolonial states as the post-conflict peacebuilding strategy. In many cases, such a strategy causes further ethnic tension and violence. Therefore, the free-market democracy model of peacebuilding and its underlying neoliberal ideological premise need to be revisited. Specifically in the cases of the Rohingya and the CHT hill people, the free-market economy model of development as a peace strategy is making these groups even more vulnerable vis-à-vis dominant majority groups, while simultaneously glossing over that vulnerability. The development strategy in post-conflict situations should be subject to serious scrutiny from the minority perspective, as opposed to the dominant national perspective.

I have also noted that unlike the international legal regime on indigenous peoples, the international law of minority protection is rather underdeveloped when it comes to the protection of vulnerable minorities against land-grabbing and development-induced displacement. Within the individualist framework of human rights, the right to participation is also less effective in dealing with transnational corporations, which are in many cases more powerful than the postcolonial states in question. The idea that minorities can be displaced from their ancestral territories, or that their lands can be allocated to predatory corporations for national economic development, and that in such cases, minorities cannot have the final say on the development decision-making, operates within the colonial framework of power relations and economic exploitation. As I have demonstrated in my case studies, the majoritarian postcolonial states have indeed reinforced the colonial relations of economy and power vis-à-vis their minorities, creating some forms of internal colonisation within postcolonial states. Therefore, rather than paving the way for assimilation into the host state, the international legal regime on minority rights must go beyond the liberal-individualist framework of human rights if it is genuinely interested in the *protection* of minorities. What I call for is the decolonisation of minority rights, and of international law in general, from liberal ideological hegemony.

Beyond Masculinity

The UN Independent International Fact-Finding Mission on Myanmar has identified sexual violence as one of the hallmarks of military operations conducted by the Myanmar Army (Tatmadaw). During one of Tatmadaw's 'clearance operations' in the Rohingya village of Tula Toli (Min Gyi) on 30 August 2017, after indiscriminately shooting and killing villagers, the soldiers took surviving women and girls in groups of between five and seven to some larger houses in the village. 'Women and girls were taken into rooms where their jewellery and money was taken from them. They were beaten, brutally raped and frequently stabbed. Children or infants who were with them in the room were also killed or severely injured, often by stabbing. The houses were then locked and set on fire.'[24] This is just one of numerous examples over a long period of time of horrific sexual violence against Rohingya women that the Mission's report documents. Sexual violence, to varied degrees, is a common feature of almost all organised and state-sponsored marginalisation of minorities. The sufferings of hill women at the hands of law enforcement agencies in the CHT, especially during the years of insurgency, are now well known, although not yet officially acknowledged.[25]

Rape as a war strategy, along with other forms of sexual violence against women (in some cases, also men), is indeed a global phenomenon. This is largely due to the embedding of masculinity in the notion of nation-state, operating in two different yet interconnected ways. As feminist scholars have demonstrated, women are often conceived of as the biological carriers of the nation – by both the in-group and the out-group. In that role, women have the politically and socially assigned task of giving birth to (preferably male) children with in-group males. Until recently, laws of many countries denied citizenship rights to offspring born in mixed marriages involving foreigner fathers. In contrast, male members are assigned the role of the protector of the nation and its

---

[24] UN Doc A/HRC/39/CRP.2 (2018), para. 772.
[25] See, for example, Meghna Guhathakurta, 'Women's Survival and Resistance', in *The Chittagong Hill Tracts: Life and Nature at Risk*, ed. Philip Gain (Dhaka: Society for Environment and Human Development, 2000), 79–95; Meghna Guhathakurta, 'The Chittagong Hill Tracts (CHT) Accord and After: Gendered Dimensions of Peace', in *Gendered Peace: Women's Struggles for Post-War Justice and Reconciliation*, ed. Donna Pankhurst (London: Routledge, 2008), 187–204; Meghna Guhathakurta, 'Minorities, Women and Peace: A South Asian Perspective', in *Women in Peace Politics*, ed. Paula Banerjee (London: Sage South Asian Peace Studies, vol. 3, 2008), 218–231.

women and children.[26] From the masculine perspective, even if various forms of violence against women are socially and legally approved within the framework of gender-differentiated roles within the nation, violence against their women by out-group members is perceived as a stain on the nation's dignity as well as on their masculine pride. Veena Das articulated this point beautifully in her seminal work on the issue of abducted women and the recovery of them in the course of the partition of the Punjab in 1947 and its aftermath.[27]

This is for precisely the same reason that in a conflict situation, out-group members target women of the rival group to 'violate' the entire nation by raping them and fathering their children, often dubbed 'war children'. As is now well known, during the conflicts in the Balkans, widespread rape and forced impregnation of Bosnian women by the Serbian paramilitary was an official policy and specifically driven by the Serbian masculine-nationalist ideology imposed on the Bosnian nation.[28] 'Serbian children', given birth to by Bosnian women, symbolised indignity and shame for the Bosnian nation. During Bangladesh's War of Independence in 1971, the Pakistani army used rape as a war strategy. Around 200,000 Bangalee women were raped during the nine months of war and thousands of war children were born as a result. These children came to be seen as 'Pakistani children'; many of them were later placed for adoption abroad due to the prevalent social taboo and a sense of shame and indignity. Many rape victims committed suicide.[29] In cases like this, the perception of women as the biological carriers of the nation

---

[26] See J. Ann Tickner, 'Inadequate Providers? A Gendered Analysis of State and Security', in *The State in Transition*, eds. J. Camilleri, A. Jervis, and A. Paolini (Boulder, CO: Lynne Rienner Publishers, 1995), 129.

[27] See Das, *Life and Words*, 18–37. See also Urvashi Butalia, *The Other Side of Silence: Voices from the Partition of India* (New Delhi: Penguin Books, 1998).

[28] Wendy Bracewell, 'Rape in Kosovo: Masculinity and Serbian Nationalism', *Nations and Nationalism* 6, no. 4 (2000), 563–590; Beverly Allen, *Rape Warfare: The Hidden Genocide in Bosnia-Herzegovina and Croatia* (Minneapolis, MN: University of Minnesota Press, 1996); Tatjana Takševa, 'Genocidal Rape, Enforced Impregnation, and the Discourse of Serbian National Identity', *CLCWeb: Comparative Literature and Culture* 17, no. 3 (2015), available at www.doi.org/10.7771/1481-4374.2638. For an account of the legacy of rape and other sexual violence against women and men of all communities in Bosnia and Herzegovina from transitional justice perspectives, see Janine N. Clark, *Rape, Sexual Violence and Transitional Justice Challenges: Lessons from Bosnia Herzegovina* (Abingdon: Routledge, 2017).

[29] Bina D'Costa has written extensively on this issue. See, for example, Bina D'Costa, *Nationbuilding, Gender and War Crimes in South Asia* (New York: Routledge, 2011); Bina D'Costa, 'Women, War, and the Making of Bangladesh: Remembering 1971', *Journal of Genocide Research* 14, no. 1 (2012), 110–114; Bina D'Costa, 'Birangona:

is shared equally by the masculine psyche in the in-group and the out-group. Interestingly, based on a recent empirical study on Rohingya rape victims, Mohsin notes that Rohingya women, otherwise quite conservative in their social outlook, are surprisingly open about sharing their traumatic experience. Unlike the victims in the events of the Partition and the liberation war of Bangladesh, wherein rape of women amounted to shame and dishonour for the nation-state, Mohsin argues, the Rohingya women do not have a 'nation-state' to glorify; '[t]hey are not only victims of a nation-state but also humans with tales of horrors and violations'.[30] This makes a difference.

Thus, once it is considered beyond the framework of vulnerability, sexual violence during ethnic conflicts exposes the very masculine construction of the nation-state, which has a lot to do with oppression of minorities in general. With reference to the celebration of the *uti possidetis* principle in international law, Hilary Charlesworth and Christine Chinkin argue that 'the rhetoric of territorial integrity in international law rests on a particular view of male body and the nature of its sexual intercourse with female body' and 'an account of the state as a bounded entity assumes that state will be worse off if any aspect of their territorial sovereignty is sublimed'.[31] Such a rhetoric in turn undermines the legitimate claims to self-determination of other non-state groups. Similarly, the masculine notion of organised and effective government as another important criterion of statehood 'enables the state to be seen as a competent, coherent, bounded entity that speaks with one voice' and in the process suppresses the diversity of voices within the state.[32] The masculinity of the state is also reflected in the right to self-determination – in the idea that there is only one homogeneous 'self'. The state as the only self-determining unit subsumes all other individual and group aspirations and goals within its priorities.[33] Taken together, many of the international law provisions that help marginalise minority groups within the state are the products of masculinity embedded within the architecture of the nation-state itself. Aoife O'Donoghue traces the origin of this masculinity

---

Bearing Witness in War and "Peace"', in *Of the Nation Born*, eds. Hameeda Hossain and Amena Mohsin (New Delhi: Zubaan, 2016), 68–112.

[30] Amena Mohsin, 'Caught between the Nation and the State: Voices of Rohingya Refugee Women in Bangladesh', *Asian Journal of Comparative Politics* 20, no. 10 (2019), 9.

[31] Hilary Charlesworth and Christine Chinkin, *The Boundaries of International Law: A Feminist Analysis* (Manchester: Manchester University Press, 2000), 131.

[32] Ibid., 133.

[33] Ibid., 151–164.

to the gendered personification of the state in the writings of white, male, and often racist international lawyers of the nineteenth century, such as Bluntschli and Westlake. Although explicitly gendered language of the nineteenth century is no longer used in present international law, she argues, the terms of statehood remain sexed.[34]

If the persecution of minorities is an outcome of the masculine construction of the nation-state, then what can a feminist revision offer towards an alternative future for the minority?[35] While the masculine construction of the state persists, feminist international lawyers have in fact offered alternative visions of statehood in international law that have bearing for minorities. Going beyond the essentialisation of women in power as more kind, accommodative, considerate, and peace-loving than their male counterparts – a proposition that in turn reinforces the conventional gender stereotypes – it is necessary to focus instead on how feminist approaches can help to restructure the international order.[36] To begin with, feminist scholars have called for moving beyond the idea of state as a homogeneous entity with a single centre of power and, instead, appreciating the state as a complex network of interrelated but distinct institutions, relations, hierarchies, discourses, interests, and players. This will then enable us to closely study the particular mechanisms of power within the state.[37] In this connection, Charlesworth and Chinkin hope that '[t]he methodology of challenging gendered dichotomies classifying the world according to male perspectives and priorities could be used to scrutinise established dichotomies', for example, of state/non-state actors.[38]

---

[34] Aoife O'Donoghue, '"The Admixture of Feminine Weakness and Susceptibility": Gendered Personifications of the State in International Law', *Melbourne Journal of International Law* 19, no. 1 (2018), 227–258.

[35] It is important to note here that feminism is by no means a monolithic idea. Influential strands of feminism include liberal feminism, radical feminism, critical legal feminism – including the idea of governance feminism – postcolonial and Third World feminism, poststructuralist feminism, and socialist feminism. For a survey and critique of various approaches to feminism, see Ratna Kapur and Brenda Cossman, *Subversive Sites: Feminist Engagement with Law in India* (London: Sage Publications, 1996), 21–38; Chimni, *International Law and World Order*, 370–409.

[36] Charlesworth and Chinkin, *The Boundaries of International Law*, 168; Kapur, *Gender, Alterity and Human Rights*, 101.

[37] See Wendy Brown, *States of Injury* (Princeton, NJ: Princeton University Press, 1995), 179; Judith Allen, 'Does Feminism Need a Theory of "The State"?' in *Playing the State: Australian Feminist Intervention*, ed. Sophie Watson (Sydney: Allen & Unwin, 1990), 21–38; Rosemary Pringle and Sophie Watson, 'Fathers, Brothers, Mates: The Fraternal State in Australia', in *Playing the State: Australian Feminist Intervention*, 229–243.

[38] Charlesworth and Chinkin, *The Boundaries of International Law*, 167.

In this regard, Karen Knop in particular has emphasised the need for going beyond the assumed centrality of statehood and sovereignty in the international legal order and exploring possibilities of its reconstruction by understanding the relationship between the state and civil society.[39] Knop focused primarily on how the existence of a robust civil society at the international level and more active participation of women therein can challenge the asymmetric power relations in both the state system and the civil society, thereby making the global decision-making more responsive to women's interest. The same argument can be made about more visibility of minority groups in international decision-making. On the other hand, Ruth Houghton and Aoife O'Donoghue bring feminist insights into the discourse on global constitutionalism and its utopian vision of international law.[40] Critically engaging with feminist utopias in science fiction, they demonstrate how such utopias help understand ways of dismantling hierarchical structures and of devising non-patriarchal approaches to governance. Such insights, in turn, facilitate the reimagining of global constitutionalism by problematising the relationship between constituent power holders and the constituent moment, thereby 'offering new points of departure for global constitutionalist debates'.[41] Their feminist approach to global constitutionalism also dismantles the homogeneous concept of 'global community' by highlighting alternative ways of constructing communities. Such a feminist revision allows for an 'alternative basis for understanding global community and its relationship with constituent and constituted power'.[42] Any project on reconceptualising the minority as an organising element of the global order, as discussed later, has a lot to benefit from feminist approaches to global constitutionalism.

In the context of the post-conflict peacebuilding, Madeleine Rees and Christine Chinkin find the traditional transitional justice model utterly broken, and call for a transformative justice that has gender relations at its centre. They argue that considering the gender dimension of

---

[39] Karen Knop, 'Re/statements: Feminism and State Sovereignty in International Law', *Transnational Law and Contemporary Problems* 3 (1993), 293–344; Karen Knop, 'Why Rethinking the Sovereign State is Important for Women's Human Rights Law', in *Human Rights of Women: National and International Perspectives*, ed. R. Cook (Philadelphia, PA: University of Pennsylvania Press, 1994), 153–164.

[40] Routh Houghton and Aoife O'Donoghue, '"Ourworld": A Feminist Approach to Global Constitutionalism', *Global Constitutionalism* 9, no. 1 (2020), 38–75. They define global constitutionalism as 'theories of constitutionalism for global governance'.

[41] Ibid., 48.

[42] Ibid., 61.

peacebuilding helps understand how the nexus between political economy and gender relations leads to violent conflicts in the first place.[43] Since men control the means of production in a given society, they get to dominate power structures. In most conflicts, only a small group of men support and propagate violence, but they manage to silence most of the members – both women and men – in the respective group and co-opt some of the latter into the violent campaign.[44] Thus, what is at the core of the problem, they argue, is 'patriarchy', understood as 'a political system that upholds and perpetuates artificially constructed "masculine" values'.[45] This patriarchy enables a relatively small number of men to use privilege and power to exert authority over less privileged and less powerful members of their respective groups, including non-violent men and women, minorities, and other vulnerable peoples. Ironically, the participation of these non-dominant peoples in the peace-making process, while essential for the legitimacy of the process, is routinely undermined. Peace negotiations, more often than not, are ways for conflicting masculinities to show off. As Bell's extensive research on this subject indicates, a feminist approach to peacebuilding can thus address concerns of underprivileged sections within the state as well as the minority group in question.[46]

However, with reference to post-conflict international peacebuilding in Sri Lanka, Nesiah also reminds us how the international community's narrow neoliberal gender focus has given rise to a particular form of 'governance feminism', what she calls 'international conflict feminism'.[47]

---

[43] See generally Madeleine Rees and Christine Chinkin, 'Exposing the Gendered Myth of Post Conflict Transition: The Transformative Power of Economic and Social Rights', *New York University Journal of International Law and Politics* 48 (2016), 1211–1226.

[44] Ibid., 1216.

[45] Ibid.

[46] See Bell, 'Power-Sharing, Conflict Resolution, and Women', 13–32; Christine Bell, 'Women, Peace Negotiations, and Peace Agreements: Opportunities and Challenges', in *The Oxford Handbook of Gender and Conflict*, eds. Fionnuala Ní Aoláin, Naomi Cahn, Dina Francesca Haynes, and Nahla Valji (Oxford: Oxford University Press, 2017), 417–429; Laura Wise, Robert Forster, and Christine Bell, *Local Peace Processes: Opportunities and Challenges for Women's Engagement* (Edinburgh: Global Justice Academy, University of Edinburgh, 2019).

[47] For a detailed discussion on governance feminism, see Janet Halley, Prabha Kotiswaran, Rachel Rebouché, and Hila Shamir, *Governance Feminism: An Introduction* (Minneapolis, MN: University of Minnesota Press, 2018); Janet Halley, Prabha Kotiswaran, and Hila Shamir, 'From the International to the Local in Feminist Legal Responses to Rape, Prostitution/ Sex Work, and Sex Trafficking: Four Studies in Contemporary Governance Feminism', *Harvard Journal of Law & Gender* 29 (2006), 335–423.

This Sri Lankan story is part of a general pattern. Nesiah argues that this model of feminism in post-conflict societies has become yet another vehicle for advancing problematic 'good governance' and 'rule of law' agendas with a view to promoting neoliberal economic goals.[48] As we have seen, the neoliberal development model is prone to engendering more conflicts than it curtails.

Governance feminism is ironically counterproductive to gender equality as well. Dianne Otto depicts the institutional reception and management of feminist ideas, and the way those ideas are divested of their emancipatory content in the process, as 'cooption' (rather than governance feminism) to underscore that the result is intentional.[49] Critically engaging with Security Council Resolutions 1325 (2000) and 1820 (2008) on women, peace and security, Otto demonstrates that despite the gender mainstreaming agenda of these resolutions, the Security Council ultimately reasserted its role as a 'protector' of women, thereby undermining feminist goals of women's emancipation.[50] The protective representation of vulnerable and sexualised women's bodies serves institutional purposes of the Security Council by reinvigorating a narrative of gender that supports militarism and justifies the hegemonic use of power in a crisis.[51] In her more recent work, Karen Engle also demonstrates how mainstream feminists' near-total emphasis on sexual violence in conflicts not only deprioritises but also undermines critiques of economic maldistribution, imperialism, and cultural essentialism by feminists from the Global South.[52]

Similarly, Kapur argues that international peacebuilding within the liberal governance framework often paves the way for a wholesale reinstatement of normative gender and familial arrangements based on privileged hegemonic masculinities.[53] Thus, '[w]hile "doing gender"

---

[48] See generally Vasuki Nesiah, 'Uncomfortable Alliances: Women, Peace, and Security in Sri Lanka', in *South Asian Feminisms*, eds. Ania Loomba and Ritty A. Lukose (Durham, NC: Duke University Press, 2012), 139–161. Cf. Anne Orford, *Reading Humanitarian Intervention: Human Rights and the Use of Force in International Law* (Cambridge: Cambridge University Press, 2003), 126–157.

[49] Dianne Otto, 'The Exile of Inclusion: Reflections on Gender Issues in International Law over the Last Decade', *Melbourne Journal of International Law* 10 (2009), 13.

[50] See United Nations, Official Records of the Security Council (2000), UN Doc S/RES/1325; United Nations, Official Records of the Security Council (2008), UN Doc S/RES/1820.

[51] Otto, 'The Exile of Inclusion', 11–26. See also Dianne Otto, 'Power and Danger: Feminist Engagement with International Law through the UN Security Council', *Australian Feminist Law Journal* 32 (2010), 97–121.

[52] Karen Engle, *The Grip of Sexual Violence in Conflict: Feminist Interventions in International Law* (Stanford, CA: Stanford University Press, 2020).

[53] Kapur, *Gender, Alterity and Human Rights*, 101.

enhances the "progressive" credentials of states and non-state actors', she argues, governance feminism finds 'literal manifestation in the international legal regime, where gender is regulated, disciplined and managed in ways that do *not* necessarily emancipate women'.[54] Instead, it advances a new colonialism that celebrates global hegemony in the form of free markets, human rights, and democracy. 'It is a humanitarian vision of empire, where rule of law rationales become part of a technocratic enterprise that incorporates gender/gender activism and women's rights in thorough accordance with the diktat of neoliberal governmentality.'[55] In the post-9/11 context, Cyra Chowdhury demonstrates how liberal feminists, within the same imperialist framework, engage with the issue of violence against Muslim women by constructing a homogeneous category of 'Muslim men' as 'wife-beating husbands', 'honour-killing fathers', 'jihadist terrorists', and so on. Specifically relying on religion and culture as the determinants of violence, such liberal feminist projects on emancipating vulnerable Muslim women in many postcolonial states in turn serve to justify Western imperialism in the form of the 'War on Terror', thereby creating a feminist-imperialist alliance.[56] Thus, in devising a feminist approach to minority protection under international law – beyond the vulnerability framework and against the backdrop of neoliberalism and imperialism – it is imperative that these critical and TWAIL feminist perspectives are considered seriously.

Beyond 'the State'?

And finally, the future direction of minority rights and the position of minorities within postcolonial states largely depend on the future of the state itself. The idea of the state is at the centre of the dominant legal imagination of the world order. But James Scott, in his influential work *The Art of Not Being Governed,* reminds us that until 'not so long ago' the great majority of humankind remained self-governing outside the now-conventional framework of the nation-state. Since WWII, with the exponential increase in the state's capacity to intervene in the remotest corners of the world, it has brought all but some tribal communities under its rubric.[57] The all-pervasiveness of the state has suffered a setback only recently.

[54] Ibid., 104.
[55] Ibid., 103.
[56] Chowdhury, 'Beyond Culture', 244–250.
[57] James C. Scott, *The Art of Not Being Governed: An Anarchist History of Upland Southeast Asia* (New Haven, CT: Yale University Press, 2009).

In an increasingly complex, rapid, and multi-faceted transformation of the existing global order, for which 'globalisation' has become the shorthand, the future of the state is now heavily debated. Especially in the immediate aftermath of the collapse of the Soviet Union and the apparent landslide of liberal values, the Kantian worldview and the notion of global Republicanism enjoyed prominence. At that watershed moment of the ambitious liberal project of reimagining and reconstructing the world order, the future of the nation-state was indeed a central concern for scholars to grapple with.

In his article 'The Future of Statehood', published in 1991, Martti Koskenniemi predicts the continued survival of the state as the second-best choice in the absence of any universal understanding and agreement on a better life beyond the state. Lacking such an agreement, he argues, the three dominant challenges to statehood, namely, human rights, national self-determination, and global order, failed in the past.[58] Moreover, each of these normative positions posits an ideal of authenticity and superiority that in turn leads to a malign form of ideological authoritarianism. Paradoxically, for Koskenniemi, the state itself then remains the useful check against such authoritarianism. He, thus, concludes that statehood 'should continue to survive for the foreseeable future because its formal-bureaucratic rationality provides safeguard against the totalitarianism inherent in a commitment to substantive values, which forces those values on people not sharing them'.[59]

Three decades on, Koskenniemi's prediction, if not its rationale, stands correct. Interestingly, writing in 1986, Karl Deutsch puts a date – until about 2200 AD – on the survival of the state, so far as its enforcement characteristics, such as enforcement mechanisms, decision-making, and administration and coordination, are concerned.[60] As of now, states do indeed remain the core of the international system and there is no sign of their demise anytime soon. However, one needs to concede that the role of the state has changed significantly since then. In his 1996 work 'The Future of the State', Eric Hobsbawm acknowledges that after more than two centuries of unbroken advancement in state development, the state entered an era of uncertainty or even retreat. He identifies three major

---

[58] Martti Koskenniemi, 'The Future of Statehood', *Harvard International Law Journal* 32, no. 2 (1991), 397–404.
[59] Ibid., 407.
[60] Karl W. Deutsch, 'Functions and the Future of the State', *International Political Science Review* 7, no. 2 (1986), 221.

ways in which supranational forces have weakened the state: the growth of the transnational economy restricting the state's capacity to direct national economies; the rise of regional and global institutions to which individual states defer; and the technological revolution in transport and communications that has significantly reduced the relevance of territorial borders.[61] Hobsbawm, however, notes that the real weakness of the state arises when it is no longer identified with a common public good, or when only individual advantage and not common interest is recognised.[62] It is for this reason that he rejects both the free-market model of ultra-liberalism and the notion of decentralisation – breaking up existing states into smaller units – as viable alternatives to statehood. For, the neoliberal economic growth is set to allow a smaller proportion of the total population to generate and accumulate wealth, necessitating more state interventions than ever towards economic redistribution.[63]

This is also why the self-congratulatory liberal celebration of liberalising the international system and downsizing the state did not excite minorities for long. States being the traditional oppressor of minorities, there was ostensibly a hope that the weakening of states would open new avenues for minorities to assert influence in the functioning of the state. In reality, whatever vacuum in the sovereign domain was created in the process of the state submission to the neoliberal economy was quickly filled by transnational actors. In fact, the neoliberal economic system itself was designed to make this happen. Minorities are now in a precarious position where for survival they need to simultaneously resist the state and the corporations, who have converging vested interests vis-à-vis minority lands and resources.

The dominant discourse on the future direction of minority rights in international law largely revolves around the integration of minorities within the state they live in.[64] At the same time, the majoritarian suspicion about the minority's allegiance to the state remains unabated, as minorities keep challenging the legitimacy of the existing territorial, political, and

---

[61] Eric J. Hobsbawm, 'The Future of the State', *Development and Change* 27 (1996), 272.
[62] Ibid., 273.
[63] Ibid., 274–276.
[64] The UN Declaration on Minorities epitomises a strong focus on minorities' inclusion in the national society, in the sense of 'no segregation, no emergence of parallel society'. Although the Declaration rules out forced assimilation and approves integration that allows the minority's distinct identity to be retained, the underlying philosophy remains state-centric: 'when minorities feel that their separate identity, their concerns and their rights are taken seriously, this is bound to increase their feeling of belonging, and thus also their identificational integration'. See Kristin Henrard, 'The UN Declaration on Minorities' Vision of "Integration"', in *The United Nations Declaration on Minorities*, 191.

economic structures of the state. In this regard, re-historicising the state itself essentially from minority perspectives would demystify many of the suspicions around the special status of minorities within a state and make political and economic concessions to them more palatable to the broader society. A key part of this historical project should be to clearly demonstrate how the process of state-making and border drawing left minorities behind and denied them their legitimate right to self-determination.

Since the birth of modern statehood in Westphalia, whenever states have been re-organised, the minority question re-appeared in relation to the very political organisation of the state: how to deal with the leftover population (minorities), who have been denied their own 'state'? This underscores the sui generis nature of minorities, compared to other vulnerable social groups – based on gender, sex, or age – that too routinely face discrimination but generally do not question the legitimacy of the state itself. Within the traditional vulnerability framework minorities are generally understood as mere subjects of oppression; this in turn makes them the individual objects of international human rights discourse along with other oppressed social group members. While this traditional framework will continue to have its relevance, it is far from adequate to fully grasp the peculiarities of minority groups as political entities and their particular needs within the state they find themselves in. This project of re-telling the history of the state from minority perspectives is especially relevant to postcolonial states wherein state-making has been a hasty and messy affair.

In other words, a normative argument for a more effective regime for minority protection under international law must go beyond the vulnerability framework and re-conceptualise the minority. Therefore, this book calls for a new vision of minority groups as an organising element of the state as well as of the global order. In this regard, the book also calls for an international legal regime of minority rights that is fit for purpose and responsive to subaltern voices, so that the international legal system actually works for minorities by fixing the problem of democratic deficit in international law. As a Rohingya community leader succinctly makes the point before the Human Rights Council:

> Today, when this meeting is over, everybody will go back home. I have no home to go back to. When I leave Geneva, I return to the refugee camp in Cox's Bazar. I go to my shelter made of tarpaulin and bamboo. I invite you to come and visit me in my shelter. Come and visit the one million

Rohingya refugees like me. Come and explain to us about the discussions you are having about us. Or, *include us and listen to us.*[65]

*****

Minorities and the Making of Postcolonial States in International Law is an attempt to explain how the postcolonial state operates as an ideology and what happens to minorities as a result. In this connection, it also explores the role of international law in the ideological operation of postcolonial states and offers insights on possible ways forward for an alternative future for minorities. My investigation into these crucial issues was triggered by the genocidal persecution of the Rohingya in the horrific weeks of August 2017. News of indiscriminate murder, rape, torture, and other inhuman treatment of the Rohingya shook global public morale but failed to generate any decisive political action at the international level. During my field visits to Bangladesh in 2019 and 2020, it clearly appeared that after the initial phase of shock and desperation, various international agencies have now come to terms with the challenging situation and are getting used to it. But the same cannot and should not be expected of more than one million Rohingya refugees. During an interview in Bangladesh, responding to my question about the future of this crisis ten years down the line, a senior official of an influential international organisation candidly expressed their utter frustration: 'The refugees will still be here. Have we managed to solve any problem anywhere in the world?' There was a brief moment of awkward silence before they said: 'The world will soon forget the Rohingya.'

That is generally the case, indeed. Following the initial humanitarian impulse, the host state Bangladesh, now more worried about 'security concerns' emanating from this vast number of refugees, is trying its best on its own to put diplomatic pressure on Myanmar and keep the issue alive on the international stage. Unfortunately, there is no shortage of competing humanitarian crises, often involving minorities, that demand global attention too. China's ruthless treatment of its Uighur Muslim population has attracted considerable media attention in the West. Also, during the time I have been writing this book, the Kashmir issue – as a constant reminder of the chaotic decolonisation process in India – has resurfaced and deserves some elaboration here.

---

[65] UN Human Rights Council, Oral Statement for the Interactive Dialogue with the Special Rapporteur on the Situation of Human Rights in Myanmar, 11 March 2019. Statement made by Muhib Ullah, representing Arakan Rohingya Society for Peace and Human Rights. Available at www.fidh.org. Emphasis added.

In August 2019, India stripped Jammu and Kashmir, the only Muslim majority state in India, of the special autonomous status guaranteed under Article 370 of the Indian constitution. The autonomy that Kashmiris enjoyed under this constitutional provision was one of the main reasons that the Muslim-majority state decided to join India, instead of Pakistan, following the Partition of 1947.[66] By abolishing the special status, the government of Narendra Modi with its vicious Hindutva ideology has opened up new avenues for further marginalising the already vulnerable Muslim population in the region, while justifying the move as a way of ensuring economic development for the people of Kashmir. For the last many decades, Kashmir has already been the most militarised region in the world, and human rights violations by security forces there are rampant. The first-ever UN Human Rights Report on Kashmir (2018) called for an international inquiry into multiple violations committed between June 2016 and April 2018.[67] The new Kashmir policy is set to make the situation even worse. However, Modi's Hindu-nationalist popular support base welcomed the policy as a useful means of grabbing land; some even celebrated the decision as an opportunity for marrying 'white Kashmiri girls'.[68] To suppress any Kashmiri resistance to this policy, the Indian government put the region under complete lockdown for months, isolating more than eight million people from the rest of the world. Whatever reporting was possible by international media outlets within their restrictions records brutality and torture against Kashmiri youths by the military and other law enforcement agencies.

As part of the attempt to re-Hinduise the country, India also passed the Citizenship (Amendment) Act (CAA) in 2019, which allows the possibility of citizenship to the Hindu and other non-Muslim minorities from Afghanistan, Bangladesh, and Pakistan. The move sparked fierce criticism and nationwide protest as the law is both discriminatory against Muslims and a deviation from the 'secular' spirit of Indian constitution. However, the CAA is in fact far more noxious for the Muslim minority in India when operating in conjunction with the ongoing National Register

---

[66] For a brief modern political history of Kashmir, see Sumantra Bose, *Kashmir: Roots of Conflict, Paths to Peace* (Cambridge, MA: Harvard University Press, 2003); Chandhoke, *Contested Secessions*, 16–32.

[67] The Office of the UN High Commissioner for Human Rights, *Report on the Situation of Human Rights in Kashmir: Developments in the Indian State of Jammu and Kashmir from June 2016 to April 2018, and General Human Rights Concerns in Azad Jammu and Kashmir and Gilgit-Baltistan* (14 June 2018), available at www.ohchr.org.

[68] See Zeba Siddiqui, 'Indian men who see new policy as chance to marry Kashmiri women accused of chauvinism', *Reuters*, 8 August 2019, available at www.reuters.com.

of Citizenship (NRC) campaign, which requires proof of citizenship entitlements for registration as a citizen. While there are a vast number of Indians who will find it impossible to prove their citizenship – simply because they have never had to document their citizenship rights before – the CAA offers a pathway to naturalise all *non-Muslims* who would fail to prove their Indian citizenship. Thus, the combined effect of the CAA and the NRC means that of the Indian Muslims, the subset who would fail to prove their citizenship would become stateless. As a matter of fact, the NRC campaign is designed mainly to target Muslims as part of the Hindutva project that the ruling BJP regime has imposed on India. The enforcement of the NRC in the state of Assam has seen millions of ethnic Bangalees, mainly Muslims, stripped of Indian citizenship.

On 1 March 2020, BJP goons with the active support of the local police attacked anti-CAA protesters in Delhi. That initially led to a Hindu–Muslim riot but ultimately to an indiscriminate massacre of Muslims. As of 3 March, forty-six people – mostly Muslims – were reported dead.[69] Many places of Muslim worship, along with houses and businesses, have also been burned or destroyed. The NRC is set to be implemented in the rest of India, despite a good number of Indian states vowing to resist the NRC within their jurisdictions. The controversial move is going to ignite yet another terrible refugee crisis for neighbouring Bangladesh.

Conversely, as the case study on the hill people of the CHT demonstrates, Bangladesh itself has an awful record of state hegemony vis-à-vis minorities. Persecution of religious minorities there draws on the 'Muslim' identity of the country based on the constitutional recognition of Islam as the state religion.[70] In Pakistan, brutality against religious minorities is common, under the heinous blasphemy law. The country's response to separatist movements in the province of Balochistan also relies heavily on gross violations of human rights. Sri Lanka committed war crimes with impunity in the final phase of its war on Tamil insurgency in 2009. The country's post–civil war national reconciliation is yet to see fruition, while religious hatred and bigotry have been renewed following the dreadful terrorist attacks on churches during Easter Sunday prayers in 2019 by a group of followers of the so-called Islamic State (IS).

Beyond South Asia, Turkey invaded the Kurdish autonomous region in north Syria in October 2019 to create a 20-mile-deep buffer zone inside the

---

[69] 'Death toll in Delhi violence mounts to 46', *India Today*, 2 March 2020, available at www.indiatoday.in.

[70] See Tapas Baul and Priyanka Bose Kanta, 'Religious Minorities', in *Bangladesh and International Law*, ed. Mohammad Shahabuddin (London: Routledge, 2021).

Syrian border. This is an attempt to change the demography of the region by re-settling non-Kurdish Syrian refugees in the occupied territory and, thereby, to contain the risk of what Turkey calls 'Kurdish terrorist activities' from Syria. It needs to be noted here that following the Great War, the borders of modern Turkey, Iraq, and Syria were defined by Allied powers under the Treaty of Lausanne in 1923. The Treaty denied the Kurds independent statehood, leaving them as minorities in those three countries. The Kurds have been fighting since then for their right to unify as a nation and exercise the right to self-determination to form a new independent state. The Republic of Ararat, a self-proclaimed Kurdish state, was in place for some time, but Britain and France as the Mandate Powers under the League imposed restrictions on the activities of the central party in the Republic between 1927 and 1930. The Republic was defeated by the Turkish military in 1930. In the aftermath of the Arab Spring and the ensuing Syrian civil war beginning in 2011, the Kurds gained considerable territory and power in Iraq and Syria and established an autonomous region with the help of their Western allies, especially the United States, in the war against IS terrorists. However, the sudden withdrawal of the US support from the Kurds in October 2019 paved the way for the latest Turkish invasion. The political future of the Kurds remains in limbo while their desperate struggles for the right to self-determination continue.

Similarly, Christian and Yazidi minorities in the Middle East suffered immensely during the brutal reign of IS in the last few years. Palestinians' struggle for self-determination and independent statehood and the Israeli state violence that they have been enduring in the process remain as one of the most protracted, visible, and high-profile cases yet without any solution. The list can easily get longer with reference to other regions of the world.

Despite the unique nature of each conflict, what is common in all these cases of violence against minorities and international legal responses to them is a precariousness in the process of the making of postcolonial states within the mould of international law's problematic colonial legacies and neo-imperial ambitions. If this book has managed to expose the way in which international law advances the ideological making of the postcolonial state vis-à-vis minorities, then this normative argument can also be replicated in cases beyond the Rohingya and the CHT hill people. I conclude this book with the sincerest hope that something meaningful for minorities in general will come out of this humble intellectual endeavour.

BIBLIOGRAPHY

Abi-Saab, Georges. 'Permanent Sovereignty over Natural Resources and Economic Activities' in *International Law: Achievements and Prospects*, ed. Mohammed Bedjaoui (Paris: UNESCO, 1991), 597–617.

Abraham, Itty. *How India Became Territorial: Foreign Policy, Diaspora, Geopolitics* (Palo Alto, CA: Stanford University Press, 2014).

Adas, Michael. *The Burma Delta: Economic Development and Social Change on an Asian Rice Frontier, 1852–1941* (Madison, WI: University of Wisconsin Press, 2011).

Adnan, Shapan. 'Book Review: Expulsions: Brutality and Complexity in the Global Economy'. *The Journal of Peasant Studies* 43, no. 5 (2016), 1095–1100.

Adnan, Shapan and Ranjit Dastidar. *Alienation of the Lands of Indigenous Peoples in the Chittagong Hill Tracts of Bangladesh* (Dhaka and Copenhagen: Chittagong Hill Tracts Commission and International Work Group for Indigenous Affairs, 2011).

Advisory Commission on Rakhine State. *Towards a Peaceful, Fair and Prosperous Future for the People of Rakhine* (August 2017), available at www.rakhinecommission.org.

African Commission on Human and Peoples' Rights. Advisory Opinion of the African Commission on Human and Peoples' Rights on the United Nations Declaration on the Rights of Indigenous Peoples (41st Session, Accra, 2007).

Ahmed, Dirdeiry M. *Boundaries and Secession in Africa and International Law: Challenging Uti Possidetis* (Cambridge: Cambridge University Press, 2015).

Akins, Harrison. 'The Two Faces of Democratisation in Myanmar: A Case Study of the Rohingya and Burmese Nationalism'. *Journal of Muslim Minority Affairs* 38, no. 2 (2018), 229–245.

Alam, Mohammed Ashraf. *Marginalization of the Rohingya in Arakan State of Western Burma* (Chittagong: Kaladan Press, 2011).

Alexandrowicz, Charles H. *The Law of Nations in Global History*, eds. David Armitage and Jennifer Pitts (Oxford: Oxford University Press, 2017).

Alfredsson, Gudmundur. 'Minority Rights and the United Nations' in *The United Nations Declaration on Minorities: An Academic Account on the Occasion of Its*

20th Anniversary (1992–2012), eds. Ugo Caruso and Rainer Hofmann (Leiden: BRILL, 2015), 19–45.

Ali, S. Mahmud. *The Fearful State: Power, People and Internal War in South Asia* (London: Zed Books, 1993).

Allen, Beverly. *Rape Warfare: The Hidden Genocide in Bosnia-Herzegovina and Croatia* (Minneapolis, MN: University of Minnesota Press, 1996).

Allen, Judith. 'Does Feminism Need a Theory of "The State"?' in *Playing the State: Australian Feminist Intervention*, ed. Sophie Watson (Sydney: Allen & Unwin, 1990), 21–38.

Ambedkar, B. R. *States and Minorities: What are Their Rights and How to Secure them in the Constitution of Free India* (1947), Memorandum on the Safeguards for the Scheduled Castes submitted to the Constituent Assembly on behalf of the All India Scheduled Castes Federation, available at www.cadindia.clpr.org.in.

Amnesty International. *'My World is Finished': Rohingya Targeted in Crimes against Humanity in Myanmar* (London: Amnesty International, 2017).

Amnesty International. *Remaking Rakhine State* (London: Amnesty International, 2017).

Anand, Ram P. 'Attitude of the Asian-African States Towards Certain Problems of International Law' (1962) in *Third World Attitudes Toward International Law: An Introduction*, eds. F. Snyder and Surakiart Sathirathai (Boston, MA: Martinus Nijhoff, 1987), 5–22.

Anghie, Antony. 'Bandung and the Origins of Third World Sovereignty' in *Bandung, Global History, and International Law: Critical Pasts and Pending Futures*, eds. Luis Eslava, Michael Fakhri, and Vasuki Nesiah (Cambridge: Cambridge University Press, 2017), 535–551.

Anghie, Antony. 'Colonialism and the Birth of International Institutions: Sovereignty, Economy, and the Mandate System of the League of Nations'. *New York University Journal of International Law and Politics* 34 (2001–2002), 513–633.

Anghie, Antony. 'Human Rights and Cultural Identity: New Hope for Ethnic Peace'. *Harvard International Law Journal* 33 (1992), 341–352.

Anghie, Antony. 'The Heart of My Home: Colonialism, Environmental Damage, and the Nauru Case'. *Harvard International Law Journal* 34, no. 2 (1993), 445–506.

Anghie, Antony. *Imperialism, Sovereignty and the Making of International Law* (Cambridge: Cambridge University Press, 2005).

Anghie, Antony. 'TWAIL: Past and Future'. *International Communities Law Review* 10, no. 4 (2008), 479–481.

Arendt, Hannah. *The Origins of Totalitarianism* (London: Allen and Unwin, 1967).

Arens, Jenneke. 'Winning Hearts and Minds: Foreign Aid and Militarization in the Chittagong Hill Tracts'. *Economic and Political Weekly* 32, no. 29 (1997), 1811–1819.

Ashraf, K. M. 'Muslim Revivalists and the Revolt of 1857' in *Rebellion, 1857*, ed. Puran C. Joshi (Delhi: People's Publication House, 1957), 71–102.

Asthana, Pratima. *Women's Movement in India* (New Delhi: Vikas Publishing House, 1974).
Atrey, Shreya. *Intersectional Discrimination* (Oxford: Oxford University Press, 2019).
Austin, Dennis. *Democracy and Violence in India and Sri Lanka* (London: Royal Institute of International Affairs, 1994).
Bajpai, Rochana. 'Minority Rights in the Indian Constituent Assembly Debates, 1946-1950'. Queen Elizabeth House Working Paper Series, University of Oxford 30 (2002).
Banerjee, Sikata. 'Gender and Nationalism: The Masculinisation of Hinduism and Female Political Participation in India'. *Women's Studies International Forum* 26, no. 2 (2003), 167-179.
Bangladesh Bureau of Statistics. *Statistical Pocket Book Bangladesh 2012* (Dhaka: Bangladesh Bureau of Statistics, 2013).
Barros, James. *The Aland Islands Question: Its Settlement by the League of Nations* (New Haven, CT: Yale University Press, 1968).
Barry, Brian. *Culture and Equality* (Cambridge: Polity Press 2001).
Barten, Ulrike. 'Article 27 of ICCPR: A First Point of Reference' in *The United Nations Declaration on Minorities: An Academic Account on the Occasion of Its 20th Anniversary (1992-2012)*, eds. Ugo Caruso and Rainer Hofmann (Leiden: BRILL, 2015), 46-65.
Basu, Baman Das. *Consolidation of the Christian Power in India* (Calcutta: R. Chatterjee, 1927).
Baul, Tapas K. and Priyanka B. Kanta. 'Religious Minorities' in *Bangladesh and International Law*, ed. Mohammad Shahabuddin (London: Routledge, 2021).
Baxi, Upendra. 'What May the "Third World" Expect from International Law?'. *Third World Quarterly* 27, no. 5 (2006), 713-725.
Bedjaoui, Mohammed. 'The Right to Development' in *International Law: Achievements and Prospects*, ed. Mohammed Bedjaoui (Paris: UNESCO, 1991), 1177-1203.
Bedjaoui, Mohammed. *Towards a New International Economic Order* (Paris: UNESCO, 1979).
Bell, Christine. *Peace Agreements and Human Rights* (Oxford: Oxford University Press, 2004).
Bell, Christine. 'Peace Settlements and Human Rights: A Post-Cold War Circular History'. *Journal of Human Rights Practice* 9, no. 3 (2017), 358-378.
Bell, Christine. 'Women, Peace Negotiations, and Peace Agreements: Opportunities and Challenges' in *The Oxford Handbook of Gender and Conflict*, eds. Fionnuala Ní Aoláin, Naomi Cahn, Dina Francesca Haynes, and Nahla Valji (Oxford: Oxford University Press, 2017), 417-429.
Bell, Christine. 'Power-Sharing, Conflict Resolution, and Women: A Global Reappraisal'. *Nationalism and Ethnic Politics* 24, no. 1 (2018), 13-32.

Benedikter, Thomas. 'The South Asian Regional Charter on Minority and Group Rights: A Proposal for Soft Law at Its Softest' in *European Yearbook on Minority Issues* (special issue on South Asia), eds. Arie Bloed, et al. (Bolzano: EURAC, 2010), 119-124.

Bennouna, Mohamed. 'International Law and Development' in *International Law: Achievements and Prospects*, ed. Mohammed Bedjaoui (Paris: UNESCO, 1991), 619-631.

Berberoglu, Berch. *Nationalism and Ethnic Conflict: Class, State, and Nation in the Age of Globalization* (Lanham, MD: Rowman and Littlefield, 2004).

Bereketeab, Redie (ed.). *Self-determination and Secession in Africa: The Postcolonial State* (London: Routledge, 2015).

Berlie, J. A. *The Burmanization of Myanmar's Muslims* (Bangkok: White Lotus Press, 2008).

Berlin, Isaiah. *Two Concepts of Liberty* (Oxford: Clarendon Press, 1958).

Berman, Nathaniel. 'A Perilous Ambivalence: Nationalist Desire, Legal Autonomy, and the Limits of the Interwar Framework'. *Harvard International Law Journal* 33, no. 2 (1992), 353-380.

Berman, Nathaniel. '"But the Alternative Is Despair": European Nationalism and the Modernist Renewal of International Law'. *Harvard Law Review* 106, no. 8 (1993), 1792-1904.

Berman, Nathaniel. 'International Law of Nationalism: Group Identity and Legal History' in *International Law and Ethnic Conflict*, ed. David Wippman (Ithaca, NY: Cornell University Press, 1998), 25-57.

Bernier, François. *Travels in the Mogul Empire, 1656-1668* (*Histoire de la dernière révolution des états du Grand Mogol*, 1671), trans. Irving Brock, rev. ed. Archibald Constable (Westminster: Archibald Constable and Company, 1891).

Berry, David S. 'Conflicts Between Minority Women and Traditional Structures: International Law, Rights and Culture'. *Social and Legal Studies* 7, no. 1 (1998), 55-75.

Bessaignet, Pierre. *Tribesmen of Chittagong Hill Tracts* (1958), trans. Sufia Khan (Dhaka: Bangla Academy, 1997).

Bishui, Kalpana. 'The Origin and Evolution of the Scheme for the First Partition of Bengal (1905)'. *Quarterly Review of Historical Studies* 5, no. 2 (1965-6), 76-96.

Bloed, Arie and Nicole Girard. 'ASEAN: Background and Human Rights Mechanisms' in *The United Nations Declaration on Minorities: An Academic Account on the Occasion of Its 20th Anniversary (1992-2012)*, eds. Ugo Caruso and Rainer Hofmann (Leiden: BRILL, 2015), 306-318.

Bose, Sumantra. *Bosnia after Dayton: Nationalist Partition and International Intervention* (London: Hurst and Company, 2002).

Bose, Sumantra. *Kashmir: Roots of Conflict, Paths to Peace* (Cambridge, MA: Harvard University Press, 2003).

Boutros-Ghali, Boutros. *The Addis Ababa Charter* (New York: Carnegie Endowment for International Peace, 1964).
Bracewell, Wendy. 'Rape in Kosovo: Masculinity and Serbian Nationalism'. *Nations and Nationalism* 6, no. 4 (2000), 563–590.
Brown, Wendy. *States of Injury* (Princeton, NJ: Princeton University Press, 1995).
Brownlie, Ian (ed.). *Basic Documents on African Affairs* (Oxford: Oxford University Press, 1971).
Buchan, John. *Lord Minto: A Memoir* (London: Thomas Nelson and Sons Ltd., 1924).
Buchanan, Allan. 'Democracy and Secession' in *National-Self-determination and Secession*, ed. M. Moor (Oxford: Oxford University Press, 1998), 14–33.
Buci-Glucksmann, Christine. 'State, Transition and Passive Revolution' in *Gramsci and Social Theory*, ed. Chantal Mouffe (London: Routledge, 1979), 113–167.
Buci-Glucksmann, Christine. *Gramsci and the State*, trans. David Fernbach (London: Lawrence and Wishart, 1980).
Bussmann, Margit, Gerald Schneider, and Nina Wiesehomeier. 'Foreign Economic Liberalization & Peace: The Case of Sub-Saharan Africa'. *European Journal of International Relations* 11, no. 4 (2005), 551–579.
Butalia, Urvashi. *The Other Side of Silence: Voices from the Partition of India* (New Delhi: Penguin Books, 1998).
Capotorti, Francesco. *Study on the Rights of Persons Belonging to Ethnic, Religious or Linguistic Minorities* (20 May 1977). UN Doc E/CN.4/Sub.2/384/Rev.1.
Carbonnier, Gilles. 'The Competing Agendas of Economic Reform and Peace Process: A Politico-Economic Model Applied to Guatemala'. *World Development* 30, no. 8 (2002), 1323–1339.
Caselli, Francesco and Wilbur J. Coleman II. 'On the Theory of Ethnic Conflict'. *Journal of the European Economic Association* 11, no. 1 (2013), 161–192.
Castellino, Joshua and Elvira Domínguez-Redondo. 'The Declaration and Its Guidance: A View from South Asia' in *The United Nations Declaration on Minorities: An Academic Account on the Occasion of Its 20th Anniversary (1992-2012)*, eds. Ugo Caruso and Rainer Hofmann (Leiden: BRILL, 2015), 283–305.
Castellino, Joshua. 'The Secession of Bangladesh in International Law: Setting New Standards?'. *Asian Yearbook of International Law* 7 (1997), 83–104.
Chakma, Ananda Bikash. 'Partition of India, Incorporation of Chittagong Hill Tracts into Pakistan and the Politics of Chakmas: A Review'. *Journal of the Pakistan Historical Society* 63, no. 2 (2015), 7–32.
Chakma, Anurug. 'The Peacebuilding of the Chittagong Hill Tracts (CHT), Bangladesh: Donor-Driven or Demand-Driven?'. *Asian Journal of Peacebuilding* 5, no. 2 (2017), 223–242.
Chakma, Ashok Kumar. *An Assessment of the UNDP-CHTDF Project on Promotion of Development and Confidence Building in the Chittagong Hill*

Tracts Relating to the Implementation of the CHT Accord 1997 (Rangamati: Maleya Foundation, 2013).

Chakma, D. K. (ed.). *The Partition and the Chakmas and other Writings of Sneha Kumar Chakma* (unknown place, India: published by the author, 2013).

Chakrabarty, Dipesh. *Provincializing Europe – Postcolonial Thought and Historical Difference* (Princeton, NJ: Princeton University Press, 2000).

Chakraborty, R. L. 'Chakma Resistance to Early British Rule'. *Bangladesh Historical Studies* 2 (1977), 133–156.

Chakravarti, Nalini Ranjan. *The Indian Minority in Burma: The Rise and Decline of an Immigrant Community* (Oxford: Oxford University Press, 1971).

Chakravartty, Renu. *Communists in Indian Women's Movement* (New Delhi: People's Publishing House, 1980).

Chandhoke, Neera. *Contested Secessions: Rights, Self-determination, Democracy, and Kashmir* (New Delhi: Oxford University Press, 2012).

Charlesworth, Hilary and Christine Chinkin. *The Boundaries of International Law: A Feminist Analysis* (Manchester: Manchester University Press, 2000).

Charlesworth, Hilary. 'Martha Nussbaum's Feminist Internationalism'. *Ethics* 111, no. 1 (2000), 64–78.

Charney, Michael W. *Where Jambudipa and Islamdom Converged: Religious Change and the Emergence of Buddhist Communalism in Early Modern Arakan (Fifteenth to Nineteenth Centuries)*. Unpublished PhD dissertation, University of Michigan (1999).

Chatterjee, Partha. *Nationalist Thought and the Colonial World* (London: Zed Books for the United Nations University, 1986).

Chatterjee, Partha. *The Nation and Its Fragments* (Princeton, NJ: Princeton University Press, 1993).

Chatterji, Joya. 'The Fashioning of a Frontier: The Radcliffe Line and Bengal's Border Landscape, 1947-52'. *Modern Asian Studies* 33, no. 1 (1999), 185–242.

Chatterji, Joya. *Bengal Divided: Hindu Communalism and Partition, 1932-1947* (Cambridge: Cambridge University Press, 1994).

Chimni, B. S. 'International Institutions Today: An Imperial Global State in the Making'. *European Journal of International Law* 15, no. 1 (2004), 1–37.

Chimni, B. S. 'Refugees, Return and Reconstruction of "Post-conflict" Societies: A Critical Perspective'. *International Peacekeeping* 9, no. 2 (2002), 163–180.

Chimni, B. S. 'The Past, Present and Future of International Law: A Critical Third World Approach'. *Melbourne Journal of International Law* 8, no. 2 (2007), 499–515.

Chimni, B. S. *International Law and World Order: A Critique of Contemporary Approaches*, 2nd ed. (Cambridge: Cambridge University Press, 2017).

Chowdhury, Cyra Akila. 'From Bandung 1955 to Bangladesh 1971: Postcolonial Self-determination and Third World Failure in South Asia' in *Bandung, Global*

History, and International Law, eds. Luis Eslava, Michael Fakhri, and Vasuki Nesiah (Cambridge: Cambridge University Press, 2017), 322–336.

Choudhury, Cyra Akila. 'Beyond Culture: Human Rights Universalisms Versus Religious and Cultural Relativism in the Activism for Gender Justice'. *Berkeley Journal of Gender, Law & Justice* 30 (2015), 226–266.

Chowdhury, Subrata Roy. 'Legal Status of the Charter of Economic Rights and Duties of States' in *Legal Aspects of the New International Economic Order*, ed. Kamal Hossain (London: Frances Pinter Publishers Ltd., 1980), 79–94.

Christian, John L. *Modern Burma: A Survey of Political and Economic Development* (Berkeley, CA: University of California, 1942).

Christie, Clive. *A Modern History of Southeast Asia: Decolonisation, Nationalism, and Separatism* (London: I. B. Tauris, 1998).

Chua, Amy. *World on Fire: How Exporting Free Market Democracy Breeds Ethnic Hatred and Global Instability* (New York: Doubleday, 2003).

Chukwurah, A. O. 'The Organisation of African Unity and African Territorial and Boundary Problems: 1963–1973'. *Indian Journal of International Law* 13, no. 2 (1973), 176–206.

Claridge, Lucy. *Moving towards a Right to Land: The Committee on Economic, Social and Cultural Rights' Treatment of Land Rights as Human Rights* (London: Minority Rights Group International, 2015).

Claridge, Lucy. *Victory for Kenya's Ogiek as African Court Sets Major Precedent for Indigenous Peoples' Land Rights* (London: Minority Rights Group International, 2017).

Clark, Janine N. *Rape, Sexual Violence and Transitional Justice Challenges: Lessons from Bosnia Herzegovina* (Abingdon: Routledge, 2017).

Cohen, Roberta and Francis M. Deng. *Masses in Flight: The Global Crisis of Internal Displacement* (Washington, DC: Brookings Institution Press, 1998).

Cohen, Roberta. 'Humanitarian Imperatives are Transforming Sovereignty'. *Northwestern Journal of International Affairs* 9 (Winter 2008), 2–13.

Cook, Alistair D. B. 'The Global and Regional Dynamics of Human Aid in Rakhine State' in *Islam and the State in Myanmar: Muslim–Buddhist Relations and the Politics of Belonging*, ed. Melissa Crouch (Delhi: Oxford University Press, 2016), 258–278.

Coomaraswamy, Radhika. 'Identity Within: Cultural Relativism, Minority Rights, and the Empowerment of Women'. *George Washington International Law Review* 34, no. 3 (2002), 483–514.

Coomaraswamy, Radhika. 'To Bellow Like a Cow: Women, Ethnicity, and the Discourse of Rights' in *Human Rights of Women: National and International Perspectives*, ed. Rebecca J. Cook (Philadelphia, PA: University of Pennsylvania Press, 1994), 39–57.

Cowan, J. M. *Working Plan for the Forests of Chittagong Hill Tracts Division* (Calcutta: Bengal Government Press, 1923).

Craven, Matthew. *The Decolonisation of International Law* (Oxford: Oxford University Press, 2007).
Crawford, James. *The Creation of States in International Law*, 2nd ed. (Oxford: Oxford University Press, 2007).
Crenshaw, Kimberlé W. 'Demarginalizing the Intersection of Race and Sex: A Black Feminist Critique of Antidiscrimination Doctrine, Feminist Theory and Antiracist Politics'. *University of Chicago Legal Forum* (1989), 139–167.
D'Costa, Bina. 'Birangona: Bearing Witness in War and "Peace"' in *Of the Nation Born*, eds. Hameeda Hossain and Amena Mohsin (New Delhi: Zubaan, 2016), 68–112.
D'Costa, Bina. 'Women, War, and the Making of Bangladesh: Remembering 1971'. *Journal of Genocide Research* 14, no. 1 (2012), 110–114.
D'Costa, Bina. *Nationbuilding, Gender and War Crimes in South Asia* (New York: Routledge, 2011).
Dahl, Robert A. *Democracy, Liberty, and Equality* (Oslo: Norwegian University Press, 1986).
Dalberg-Acton, John E. *The History of Freedom and Other Essays*, eds. John N. Figgis and Reginald V. Laurence (London: Macmillan & Co. Ltd., 1907).
Damodaran, Vinita. 'Indigenous Agency: Customary Rights and Tribal Protection in Eastern India, 1830-1930'. *History Workshop Journal* 76, no.1 (2013), 85–110.
Das, Veena. *Life and Words: Violence and the Descent into the Ordinary* (Berkeley, CA: University of California, 2006).
David, Roman and Ian Holliday. *Liberalism and Democracy in Myanmar* (Oxford: Oxford University Press, 2018).
Davis, Horace B. *Towards a Marxist Theory of Nationalism* (New York: Monthly Review Press, 1978).
Davis, Kingsley. *The Population of India and Pakistan* (Princeton, NJ: Princeton University Press, 1951).
Davitti, Daria. *Investment and Human Rights in Armed Conflicts: Charting an Elusive Intersection* (Oxford: Hart Publishing, 2019).
De Mello-Franco, Afranio. 'Report of the Council Meeting of 9 December 1925'. *League of Nations Official Journal* 7, no. 2 (1926), 138–144.
De Schutter, Olivier. 'The Green Rush: The Global Race for Farmland and the Rights of Land Users'. *Harvard International Law Journal* 52, no. 2 (2011), 504–559.
Dersoo, Solomon A. 'The 1992 UN Declaration on Minorities and the African Human Rights System' in *The United Nations Declaration on Minorities: An Academic Account on the Occasion of Its 20th Anniversary (1992–2012)*, eds. Ugo Caruso and Rainer Hofmann (Leiden: BRILL, 2015), 253–282.
Deutsch, Karl W. 'Functions and the Future of the State'. *International Political Science Review* 7, no. 2 (1986), 209–222.

Dewan, Biraj Mohan. *The Chronicle of the Chakma Nation* (1969) (in Bangla, *Chakma Jatir Itibritto*) (Rangamati: Uday Shankar Dewan, 2005).

Dickens, Peter. *Social Darwinism* (Buckingham: Open University Press, 2000).

Dirar, Luwam. 'Rethinking the Concept of Colonialism in Bandung and Its African Union Aftermath' in *Bandung, Global History, and International Law*, eds. Luis Eslava, Michael Fakhri, and Vasuki Nesiah (Cambridge: Cambridge University Press, 2017), 355–366.

Douglas, Ian Henderson. *Abul Kalam Azad: An Intellectual and Religious Biography*, eds. Gail Minault and Christian W. Troll (New Delhi: Oxford University Press, 1988).

Doyle, Cathal and Jérémie Gilbert. 'Indigenous Peoples and Globalisation: From "Development Aggression" to "Self-Determined Development"' in *European Yearbook on Minority Issues* (special issue on South Asia), ed. Arie Bloed, et al. (Bolzano: EURAC, 2010), 67–117.

Dutt, Rajani Palme. *India To-day* (1940), 10th ed. (New Delhi: People's Publishing House Ltd., 2008).

Eagleton, Terry. *Ideology* (Essex: Pearson Education Ltd., 1994).

Edwards, Alice. 'The Meaning of Nationality in International Law in an Era of Human Rights: Procedural and Substantive Aspects' in *Nationality and Statelessness under International Law*, eds. Alice Edwards and Laura van Waas (Cambridge: Cambridge University Press, 2014), 11–43.

Egreteau, Renaud. 'Burmese Indians in Contemporary Burma: Heritage, Influence and Perceptions since 1988'. *Asian Ethnicity* 12, no. 1 (2011), 33–54.

Eide, Asbjørn. 'An Overview of the UN Declaration and Major Issues Involved' in *The United Nations Declaration on Minorities: An Academic Account on the Occasion of Its 20th Anniversary (1992–2012)*, eds. Ugo Caruso and Rainer Hofmann (Leiden: BRILL, 2015), 66–86.

Eide, Asbjørn. *Final Text of the Commentary to the Declaration on the Rights of National or Ethnic, Religious and Linguistic Minorities*. Sub-Commission on Promotion and Protection of Human Rights (2 April 2001). UN Doc E/CN4/Sub2/AC5/2001/2.

Engle, Karen. *The Grip of Sexual Violence in Conflict: Feminist Interventions in International Law* (Stanford, CA: Stanford University Press, 2020).

Eslava, Luis. *Local Space, Global Life: The Everyday Operation of International Law and Development* (Cambridge: Cambridge University Press, 2015).

European Community. *Declaration on the Guidelines on the Recognition of New States in Eastern Europe and in the Soviet Union* (16 December 1991). *European Journal of International Law* 3 (1993), 72.

European Community. *Declaration on Yugoslavia*. Extraordinary EPC Ministerial Meeting, Brussels (16 December 1991). *European Journal of International Law* 3 (1993), 73.

European Parliament, Sub-committee on Human Rights. *Land Grabbing and Human Rights: The involvement of European corporate and financial entities in land grabbing outside the European Union* (May 2016). EP/EXPO/B/DROI/2015/02.

Evans, Gareth. *The Responsibility to Protect: Ending Mass Atrocity Crimes Once and For All* (Washington, DC: Brookings Institution Press, 2008).

Farid, Cynthia. 'Legal Scholactivists in the Third World: Between Ambition, Altruism and Access'. *Winsor Yearbook of Access to Justice* 33 (2016), 57–86.

Farzana, Kazi Fahmida. 'Music and Artistic Artefacts: Symbols of Rohingya Identity and Everyday Resistance in Borderlands'. *Austrian Journal of South-East Asian Studies* 4, no. 2 (2011), 215–236.

Fichte, Johanne Gottlieb. 'Addresses to the German Nation – Thirteenth Address' (1808) in *The Political Thought of the German Romantics*, eds. H. S. Reiss and P. Brown (Oxford: Basil Blackwell, 1955), 102–118.

Fichte, Johanne Gottlieb. 'An Outline of International and Cosmopolitan Law' (1796–97) in *The Political Thought of the German Romantics*, eds. H. S. Reiss and P. Brown (Oxford: Basil Blackwell, 1955), 73–85.

Food and Agriculture Organization (FAO) and the World Food Programme (WFP). *Special Report: FAO/WFP Crop and Food Security Assessment Mission to Myanmar* (Rome: Authors, 2009).

Forchhammer, Emanuel. *Report on the Antiquities of Arakan* (Rangoon: Government Printing and Stationary, 1891).

Foreign Relations of the United States (FRUS). *Papers Relating to the Foreign Relations of the United States 1913–1921: Paris Peace Conference 1919*, vols. I–VI (Washington: Government Printing Press, 1942).

Franck, Thomas M. *Fairness in International Law and Institutions* (Oxford: Oxford University Press, 1995).

Franck, Thomas. 'Postmodern Tribalism and the Right to Secession' in *Peoples and Minorities in International Law*, eds. Catherine Brölmann, René Lefeber, and Marjoleine Zieck (Dordrecht: Martinus Nijhoff, 1993), 3–27.

Franck, Thomas. 'The Emerging Right to Democratic Governance'. *American Journal of International Law* 86 (1992), 46–91.

Franck, Thomas. *Nation Against Nation* (New York: Oxford University Press, 1985).

Franklin, John Hope (ed.). *Colour and Race* (Boston, MA: Houghton Mifflin Co., 1968).

French, Duncan (ed.). *Statehood and Self-determination: Reconciling Tradition and Modernity in International Law* (Cambridge: Cambridge University Press, 2013).

Fukurai, Hiroshi. 'Fourth World Approaches to International Law (FWAIL) and Asia's Indigenous Struggles and Quests for Recognition under International Law'. *Asian Journal of Law and Society* 5 (2018), 221–231.

Fukuyama, Francis. 'The End of History?'. *The National Interest* 16 (1989), 3–18.

Gain, Philip. 'Life and Nature at Risk' in *The Chittagong Hill Tracts: Life and Nature at Risk*, ed. Philip Gain (Dhaka: Society for Environment and Human Development, 2000), 1–41.

Gandhi, Mohandas K. 'Hindu Muslim Unity' in *Young India (1924–1926)*, ed. Mahatma Gandhi (Madras: S. Ganesan, 1927), 73–76.

Gathii, James T. 'TWAIL: A Brief History of Its Origins, Its Decentralized Network, and a Tentative Bibliography'. *Trade, Law and Development* 3, no. 1 (2011), 26–64.

Geertz, Clifford. *Old Societies and New States* (NY: Free Press, 1963).

Geertz, Clifford. *The Interpretation of Cultures* (1973) (New York: Basic Books, 2000).

Ghosh, Snehasish. *Political Separation in the Chittagong Hill Tracts of Bangladesh with Special Reference to the Chakma Issue*. Unpublished PhD Thesis, Jadavpur University, Calcutta (1996).

Gibney, Matthew. 'Statelessness and Citizenship in Ethical and Political Perspectives' in *Nationality and Statelessness under International Law*, eds. Alice Edwards and Laura van Waas (Cambridge: Cambridge University Press, 2014), 4–63.

Gilbert, Jérémie. 'Land Grabbing, Investors, and Indigenous Peoples: New Legal Strategies for an Old Practice?'. *Community Development Journal* 51, no. 3 (2015), 350–366.

Gilbert, Jérémie. 'Litigating Indigenous Peoples' Rights in Africa: Potentials, Challenges and Limitations'. *International and Comparative Law Quarterly* 66, no. 3 (2017), 657–686.

Gordon, Leonard A. 'Divided Bengal: Problems of Nationalism and Identity in the 1947 Partition' in *India's Partition: Process, Strategy and Mobilisation* (2001), ed. Mushirul Hasan (New Delhi: Oxford University Press, 2013), 279–321.

Government of Bangladesh, Special Affairs Division. *A Report on the Problems of Chittagong Hill Tracts and Bangladesh: Responses for their Solution* (Dhaka: Government of Bangladesh, 1993).

Government of Bangladesh. *Debates of the Constituent Assembly of Bangladesh*, vol. II (12 October 1972–15 December 1972) (Dhaka: Parliament Secretariat, 1973).

Government of Bangladesh. *The First Five Year Plan of Bangladesh, 1973–78* (Dhaka: Planning Commission, 1973).

Government of Bengal. *Selections from the Correspondence on the Revenue Administration of the Chittagong Hill Tracts, 1862–1927* (Calcutta: Government of Bengal Press, 1929).

Government of India, *Constituent Assembly Debates: Official Report*, vols. I–XII (Delhi: Lok Sabha Secretariat, 1946–1950).

Graham, G. F. I. *The Life and Works of Sir Syed Ahmed* (1885) (Calcutta: Thacker, Spink & Co., 1909).

Gramsci, Antonio. *Selections from the Prison Notebooks*, trans. Q. Hoare and G. Nowell Smith (New York: International Publishers, 1971).
Grant, Evande and Onita Das. 'Land Grabbing, Sustainable Development and Human Rights'. *Transnational Environmental Law* 4, no. 2 (2015), 289–317.
Griffiths, Ieuan Ll. *The Atlas of African Affairs* (1984), 2nd ed. (London: Routledge, 1995).
Guha, Ranajit. *Dominance without Hegemony: History and Power in Colonial India* (Cambridge, MA: Harvard University Press, 1998).
Guha, Ranajit. *Elementary Aspects of Peasant Insurgency in Colonial India* (Delhi: Oxford University Press, 1983).
Guha, Ranajit. *History at the Limit of World-History* (New York: Columbia University Press, 2002).
Guha-Roy, S. N. 'Is the Law of Responsibility of States for Injuries to Aliens a Part of Universal International Law?'. *American Journal of International Law* 55, no. 4 (1961), 863–891.
Guhathakurta, Meghna. 'Minorities, Women and Peace: A South Asian Perspective' in *Women in Peace Politics*, ed. Paula Banerjee (London: Sage South Asian Peace Studies, vol. 3, 2008), 218–231.
Guhathakurta, Meghna. 'Overcoming Otherness and Building Trust: The Kalpana Chakma Case' in *Living on the Edge: Essays on the Chittagong Hill Tracts*, eds. Subir Bhaumik, et al. (Kathmandu: SAFHR, 1997), 109–126.
Guhathakurta, Meghna. 'The Chittagong Hill Tracts (CHT) Accord and After: Gendered Dimensions of Peace' in *Gendered Peace: Women's Struggles for Post-War Justice and Reconciliation*, ed. Donna Pankhurst (London: Routledge, 2008), 187–204.
Guhathakurta, Meghna. 'Women's Survival and Resistance' in *The Chittagong Hill Tracts: Life and Nature at Risk*, ed. Philip Gain (Dhaka: Society for Environment and Human Development, 2000), 79–95.
Gupta, Priya S. 'From Statesmen to Technocrats to Financiers: Development Agents in the Third World' in *Bandung, Global History, and International Law*, eds. Luis Eslava, Michael Fakhri, and Vasuki Nesiah (Cambridge: Cambridge University Press, 2017), 481–497.
Güzel, Mehmet Şükrü. *Solving Statelessness in Myanmar* (Ankara: Sonçağ Matbaacilik Ltd., 2018).
Halley, Janet, Prabha Kotiswaran, and Hila Shamir. 'From the International to the Local in Feminist Legal Responses to Rape, Prostitution/ Sex Work, and Sex Trafficking: Four Studies in Contemporary Governance Feminism'. *Harvard Journal of Law & Gender* 29 (2006), 335–423.
Halley, Janet, Prabha Kotiswaran, Rachel Rebouché, and Hila Shamir. *Governance Feminism: An Introduction* (Minneapolis, MN: University of Minnesota Press, 2018).

Hancock, Ange-Marie. *An Intellectual History of Intersectionality* (Oxford: Oxford University Press, 2016).

Haque, Md. Mahbubul. 'Rohingya Ethnic Muslim Minority and the 1982 Citizenship Law in Burma'. *Journal of Muslim Minority Affairs* 37, no. 4 (2017), 454–469.

Harvey, David. *The New Imperialism* (New York: Oxford University Press, 2003).

Hasan, Mushirul. *Nationalist Conscience: M. A. Ansari, the Congress and the Raj* (New Delhi: Manohar, 1987).

Hegel, George W. F. *Lectures on the Philosophy of World History* (1837), ed. D. Forbes, trans. H.B. Nisbet (Cambridge: Cambridge University Press, 1975).

Hein, Patrick. 'The Re-ethnicisation of Politics in Myanmar and the Making of the Rohingya Ethnicity Paradox'. *Indian Quarterly* 74, no. 4 (2018), 361–382.

Henrard, Kristin and Robert Dunbar. *Synergies in Minority Protection* (Cambridge: Cambridge University Press, 2009).

Henrard, Kristin. *Devising an Adequate System of Minority Protection* (The Hague: Martinus Nijhoff Publishers, 2000).

Henrard, Kristin. 'The UN Declaration on Minorities' Vision of "Integration"' in *The United Nations Declaration on Minorities: An Academic Account on the Occasion of Its 20th Anniversary (1992-2012)*, eds. Ugo Caruso and Rainer Hofmann (The Hague: BRILL, 2015), 156–191.

Higgins, Rosalyn. 'Postmodern Tribalism and the Right to Secession: Comments' in *Peoples and Minorities in International Law*, eds. Catherine Brölmann, René Lefeber, and Marjoleine Zieck (Dordrecht: Martinus Nijhoff, 1993), 29–35.

Higgins, Rosalyn. *Problems and Process: International Law and How We Use It* (Oxford: Oxford University Press, 1994).

Hobsbawm, Eric J. 'The Future of the State'. *Development and Change* 27 (1996), 267–278.

Holliday, Ian. 'Addressing Myanmar's Citizenship Crisis'. *Journal of Contemporary Asia* 44, no. 3 (2014), 404–421.

Hoque, Mofidul (ed.). *The Rohingya Genocide: Compilation and Analysis of Survivors' Testimonies* (Dhaka: Center for the Study of Genocide and Justice, 2018).

Horowitz, Donald. *Ethnic Groups in Conflict* (1985) (Berkeley, CA: University of California Press, 2000).

Hossain, Kamal. 'Introduction' in *Legal Aspects of the New International Economic Order*, ed. Kamal Hossain (London: Frances Pinter Publishers Ltd., 1980), 1–8, 33–43.

Hossain, Kamal. 'Introduction' in *Permanent Sovereignty over Natural Resources in International Law: Principle and Practice*, eds. Kamal Hossain and Subrata Roy Chowdhury (London: Frances Pinter, 1984), ix–xx.

Houghton, Routh and Aoife O'Donoghue. '"Ourworld": A Feminist Approach to Global Constitutionalism'. *Global Constitutionalism* 9, no. 1 (2020), 38–75.

House of Commons Parliamentary Papers. *Proceedings of the Burma Round Table Conference, 27 November 1931 to 12 January 1932* (London: His Majesty's Stationery Office, 1932), 233–281.

Htin, Kyaw Minn. 'The Marma from Bangladesh: A "De-Arakanized" Community in Chittagong Hill Tracts'. *Suvannabhumi* 7, no. 2 (2015), 133–153.

Hughes, Alexandra. *PRSPs, Minorities and Indigenous Peoples – An Issue Paper* (London: Minority Rights Group International, 2005).

Humphrey, John P. 'The United Nations Sub-Commission on the Prevention of Discrimination and the Protection of Minorities'. *American Journal of International Law* 62 (1968), 869–888.

Hunter, William W. *The Annals of Rural Bengal* (Calcutta: Indian Studies Past and Present, 1876).

Hunter, William W. *The Indian Musalmans* (London: Williams and Norgate, 1871).

Hunter, William W. *The Indian Musalmans*, 3rd ed. (London: Trubner and Company, 1876).

Huntington, Samuel P. 'Democracy for the Long Haul'. *Journal of Democracy* 7, no. 2 (1996), 3–13.

Huq, M. Mufazzalul. 'Changing Nature of Dominant Social Forces and Interventions in the Chittagong Hill Tracts'. *The Journal of Social Studies* 56 (1992), 71–85.

Huq, Muhammad Mufazzalul. 'Government Institutions and Underdevelopment: A Study of the Tribal Peoples of Chittagong Hill Tracts, Bangladesh'. Unpublished MSS Thesis, University of Birmingham (1982).

Hussain, Saiyyad Abid. *The Destiny of Indian Muslims* (Bombay: Asia, 1965).

Hutchinson, Sneyd. *An Account of the Chittagong Hill Tracts* (Calcutta: The Bengal Secretariat Book Depot, 1906).

Hutchinson, Sneyd. *Eastern Bengal and Assam District Gazetteers: Chittagong Hill Tracts* (Allahabad: Pioneer Press, 1909).

India Home Rule League of America. *Self-Determination for India* (New York: India Home Rule League of America, 1919).

India Office Records and Private Papers. *Burma Office Minute Paper (B/C 1235/47)*. IOR/M/4/2503, 10–11.

India Office Records and Private Papers. *Confidential Report for Secretary of State for Commonwealth Relations on the Events in India and Pakistan* (15–20 August 1947). IOR, L/I/1/42/12.

India Office Records and Private Papers. *Extract Military Letter from Bengal* (31 December 1827). IOR/F/4/1050/28956.

India Office Records and Private Papers. *Law and Order: Arakan* (12 April -1 December 1947). IOR/M/4/2503.

India Office Records and Private Papers. *Letter from U Hla Tun Pru, Chairn, All Arakan Representative Working Committee to the Secretary of State for Burma* (21 June 1947). IOR/M/4/2503, 18–19.

India Office Records and Private Papers. *Papers Regarding the Colony of Arakan Emigrants in Chittagong District.* IOR/F/4/99/2029.
India Office Records and Private Papers. *Viceroys Personal Report No. 17 (Appendix III: Letter to Lord Mountbatten from Vallabhbhai Patel regarding Chittagong Hill Tracts).* IOR/L/PO/6/123.
Indian Statutory Commission. *Report of the Indian Statutory Commission* (Simon Commission Report), 17 vols. (London: H. M. Stationery Office, 1930).
International Commission on Intervention and State Responsibility. *The Responsibility to Protect* (Ottawa: International Development Research Centre, 2001).
Isakovic, Zlatko. 'Democracy, Human Rights and Ethnic Conflicts in the Globalised World'. *East European Human Rights Review* 8, no. 2 (2002), 199–236.
Ishaq, M. (ed.). *Bangladesh District Gazetteers: Chittagong Hill Tracts* (Dhaka: Ministry of Cabinet Affairs, Government of Bangladesh, 1971).
Islam, M. Rafiqul. 'Secessionist Self-Determination: Some Lessons from Katanga, Biafra and Bangladesh'. *Journal of Peace Research* 22, no. 3 (1985), 211–221.
Islam, S. (ed.). *Bangladesh District Records: Chittagong*, vol. I (1760–1787) (Dhaka: University of Dacca Press, 1978).
Ismail, Achmad. 'Motives and Rivalry of Superpower Countries: The United States and China in Rohingya Humanitarian Crisis'. *Jurnal Hubungan Internasional* 7, no. 1 (2018), 102–117.
Jain, Pratibha. 'Balancing Minority Rights and Gender Justice: The Impact on Protecting Multiculturalism on Women's Rights in India'. *Berkeley Journal of International Law* 23, no. 1 (2005), 201–222.
Jayawardena, Kumari. *Feminism and Nationalism in the Third World* (1982) (London: Verso Books, 2016).
Jones, Peter. 'Collective and Group-Specific: Can the Rights of Ethno-Cultural Minorities Be Human Rights?' in *Ethno-Cultural Diversity and Human Rights*, ed. Gaetano Pentassuglia (Leiden: Brill-Nijhoff, 2018), 27–58.
Jones, Peter. 'Human Rights, Group Rights and Peoples' Rights'. *Human Rights Quarterly* 21 (1999), 80–107.
Kadir, Muhammad Y. Aiyub and Alexander Murray. 'Resource Nationalism in the Law and Policies of Indonesia: A Contest of State, Foreign Investors, and Indigenous Peoples'. *Asian Journal of International Law* 9, no. 2 (2019), 298–333.
Kakuzo, Okakura. *The Awakening of Japan* (London: John Murray, 1905).
Kakuzo, Okakura. *The Book of Tea* (1906) (New York: Dover, 1964).
Kant, Immanuel. 'Perpetual Peace: A Philosophical Sketch' (1795) in *Kant: Political Writings*, ed. H. S. Reiss, trans. H. B. Nisbet (New York: Cambridge University Press, 1970), 93–130.
Kant, Immanuel. 'The Metaphysics of Morals' (1797) in *Kant: Political Writings*, ed. H. S. Reiss, trans. H. B. Nisbet (New York: Cambridge University Press, 1970), 164–173.

Kapur, Ratna and Brenda Cossman. '*Subversive Sites* 20 Years Later: Rethinking Feminist Engagements with Law'. *Australian Feminist Law Journal* 44, no. 2 (2018), 265-287.

Kapur, Ratna and Brenda Cossman. *Subversive Sites: Feminist Engagement with Law in India* (London: Sage Publications, 1996).

Kapur, Ratna. 'Human Rights in the 21st Century: Take a Walk on the Dark Side'. *Sydney Law Review* 28, no. 4 (2006), 665-688.

Kapur, Ratna. *Gender, Alterity and Human Rights: Freedom in a Fishbowl* (Gloucestershire: Edward Elgar, 2018).

Kaur, Manmohan. *Women in India's Freedom Struggle* (New Delhi: Sterling Publishers Private Ltd., 1985).

Keane, David. 'Draft South Asian Regional Charter on Minority and Group Rights: Comparative Regional Analysis' in *European Yearbook on Minority Issues* (special issue on South Asia), ed. Arie Bloed, et al. (Bolzano: EURAC, 2010), 125-158.

Kennedy, David. 'International Human Rights Movement: Part of the Problem?'. *Harvard Human Rights Journal* 14 (2002), 101-126.

Kennedy, David. *A World of Struggle: How Power, Law, and Expertise Shape Global Political Economy* (Princeton, NJ: Princeton University Press, 2016).

Kennedy, David. *Dark Sides of Virtue: Reassessing International Humanitarianism* (Princeton, NJ: Princeton University Press, 2004).

Kennedy, David. *Of War and Law* (Princeton, NJ: Princeton University Press, 2006).

Kesby, Alison. *The Right to Have Rights: Citizenship, Humanity, and International Law* (Oxford: Oxford University Press, 2012).

Khan, Borhan Uddin and Mahbubur Rahman. *Protection of Minorities: Regimes, Norms, and Issues in South Asia* (Newcastle: Cambridge Scholars Publishing, 2012).

Khan, Mohammad Tanzimuddin and Saima Ahmed. 'Dealing with the Rohingya Crisis: The Relevance of the General Assembly and R2P'. *Asian Journal of Comparative Politics* 20 (2019), 1-23.

Khisha, Mukur K. *Time and Again* (New Delhi: Macmillan India Ltd., 2004).

Kingston, Lindsey N. 'Protecting the World's Most Persecuted: The Responsibility to Protect and Burma's Rohingya Minority'. *The International Journal of Human Rights* 19, no. 8 (2015), 1163-1175.

Kingston, Lindsey. '"A Forgotten Human Rights Crisis": Statelessness and Issue (Non)Emergence'. *Human Rights Review* 14, no. 2 (2013), 73-87.

Kipling, Rudyard. 'Mandalay' (1890) in *Barrack-Room Ballads and Other Verses* (London: Methuen, 1892).

Knop, Karen. 'Re/statements: Feminism and State Sovereignty in International Law'. *Transnational Law and Contemporary Problems* 3 (1993), 293-344.

Knop, Karen. 'Why Rethinking the Sovereign State is Important for Women's Human Rights Law' in *Human Rights of Women: National and International*

Perspectives, ed. R. Cook (Philadelphia, PA: University of Pennsylvania Press, 1994), 153–164.

Kohen, Marcelo G. (ed.). *Secession: International Law Perspectives* (Cambridge: Cambridge University Press, 2006).

Koskenniemi, Martti. 'National Self-determination Today: Problems of Legal Theory and Practice'. *International and Comparative Law Quarterly* 43, no. 1 (1994), 241–269.

Koskenniemi, Martti. 'The Future of Statehood'. *Harvard International Law Journal* 32, no. 2 (1991), 397–410.

Kukathas, Chandran. *The Liberal Archipelago* (Oxford: Oxford University Press 2003).

Kundu, Tridibsantapa. 'The Partition (1947) and the Chakmas of Chittagong Hill Tracts'. *Partition Studies* (18 June 2006), available at www.bengalpartitionstudies.blogspot.com.

Kunz, Joseph L. 'The Present Status of the International Law for the Protection of Minorities'. *American Journal of International Law* 48 (1954), 282–287.

Kuper, Adam. *Culture: The Anthropologists' Account* (Cambridge, MA: Harvard University Press, 1999).

Kyaw, Nyi Nyi. 'Islamophobia in Buddhist Myanmar: The 969 Movement and Anti-Muslim Violence' in *Islam and the State in Myanmar: Muslim–Buddhist Relations and the Politics of Belonging*, ed. Melissa Crouch (Delhi: Oxford University Press, 2016), 183–210.

Lalonde, Suzanne. *Determining Boundaries in a Conflicted World: The Role of* Uti Possidetis (Montreal: McGill-Queen's University Press, 2002).

Lansing, Robert. *The Peace Negotiations: A Personal Narrative* (Boston, MA: Houghton Mifflin Company, 1921).

Leach, F. B. 'The Rice Industry of Burma'. *Journal of the Burma Research Society* 27, no. 1 (1937), 61–73.

Lerner, Natan. *Group Rights and Discrimination in International Law*, 2nd ed. (The Hague: Martinus Nijhoff, 2003).

Levene, Mark. 'The Chittagong Hill Tracts: A Case Study in the Political Economy of "Creeping" Genocide'. *Third World Quarterly* 20, no. 2 (1999), 339–369.

Levin, John V. *The Export Economies* (Cambridge, MA: Harvard University Press, 1960).

Lewin, T. H. *The Hill Tracts of Chittagong and Dwellers Therein with Comparative Vocabularies of the Hill Dialect* (Calcutta: Bengal Printing Company Ltd., 1869).

Lijphart, Arend. *Democracy in Plural Societies* (New Haven, CT: Yale University Press, 1977).

Lorca, Arnulf Becker. 'Petitioning the International: A 'Pre-history' of Self-determination'. *European Journal of International Law* 25, no. 2 (2014), 497–523.

Lugard, Lord. *The Dual Mandate in British Tropical Africa* (1922) (Hamden, CT: Archon Books, 1965).

Lukacs, Georg. *History and Class Consciousness* (1923) (Cambridge, MA: MIT Press, 1971).
Luther, Timothy C. *Hegel's Critique of Modernity – Reconciling Individual Freedom and the Community* (New York: Lexington Books 2009).
Macfarlane, Charles. *A History of British India, from the Earliest English Intercourse to the Present Time* (London: George Routledge & Co., 1853).
Mackenzie, A. *History of the Relations of the Government with the Hill Tribes of the North-East Frontier of Bengal* (Calcutta: Home Office Department Press, 1884).
Mahalanobis, P. C. 'Distribution of Muslims in the Population of India: 1941'. *Sankhyā: The Indian Journal of Statistics (1933–1960)* 7, no. 4 (1946), 429–434.
Maitra, Jayanti. *Muslim Politics in Bengal 1855–1906* (Calcutta: K. P. Bagchi & Company, 1984).
Mali, K. S. *Fiscal Aspects of Development Planning in Burma, 1950–1960* (Rangoon: University of Rangoon, 1962).
Maniruzzaman, Talukder. *The Politics of Development: The Case of Pakistan 1947–1958* (Dhaka: Green Book House, 1971).
Mannheim, Karl. *Ideology and Utopia* (London: Routledge, 1936).
Mansergh, Nicholas. *Documents and Speeches on British Commonwealth Affairs 1931–1952*, vol. II (Oxford: Oxford University Press, 1953).
Marks, Susan. *The Riddle of All Constitutions* (Oxford: Oxford University Press, 2000).
Marx, Karl and Friedrich Engels, *Selected Works* (London: Lawrence and Wishart, 1968).
Marx, Karl and Friedrich Engels. *Selected Works*, vol. I (Moscow: Progress Publishers, 1969).
Marx, Karl and Friedrich Engels. *The German Ideology* (1846), ed. C. J. Arthur (New York: International Publishers, 1986).
Mazumdar, Vina. 'The Social Reform Movement in India from Ranade to Nehru' in *Indian Women: From Purdah to Modernity*, ed. Bal Ram Nanda (New Delhi: Radiant Publishers, 1976), 41–66.
McGregor, Katharine and Vannessa Hearman. 'Challenging the Lifeline of Imperialism: Reassessing Afro-Asian Solidarity and Related Activism in the Decade 1955-1965' in *Bandung, Global History, and International Law*, eds. Luis Eslava, Michael Fakhri, and Vasuki Nesiah (Cambridge: Cambridge University Press, 2017), 161–176.
Mehta, A. and A. Patwardhan. *The Communal Triangle in India* (Allahabad: Kitabistan, 1942).
Mészáros, Istvan. *Marx's Theory of Alienation*, 3rd ed. (London: Merlin Press, 1972).
Metcalf, T. R. *The Aftermath of Revolt: India 1857–1870* (Princeton, NJ: Princeton University Press, 1965).

Mey, Wolfgang. *Genocide in the Chittagong Hill Tracts, Bangladesh*. International Working Group for Indigenous Affairs (IWGIA) Document No. 51 (Copenhagen: IWGIA, 1984).

Mickelson, Karin. 'Taking Stock of TWAIL Histories'. *International Community Law Review* 10, no. 4 (2008), 355–362.

Miklian, Jason. 'Contextualising and Theorising Economic Development, Local Business and Ethnic Cleansing in Myanmar'. *Conflict, Security, and Development* 19, no. 1 (2019), 55–78.

Mill, John Stuart. *Three Essays on Liberty, Representative Government, and the Subjugation of Women* (London: Pelican Classics, 1975).

Miller, David H. *The Drafting of the Covenant*, vol. II (New York: G. P. Putnam's Sons, 1928).

Miller, David. 'Boundaries, Democracy, and Territory'. *The American Journal of Jurisprudence* 61, no. 1 (2016), 33–49.

Ministry of Foreign Affairs, Republic of Indonesia (ed.). 'Final Communiqué of the Asian-African Conference of Bandung (24 April 1955)' in *Asia-Africa Speak from Bandung* (Djakarta: Ministry of Foreign Affairs, 1955), 161–169.

Mohsin, Amena. 'Caught between the Nation and the State: Voices of Rohingya Refugee Women in Bangladesh'. *Asian Journal of Comparative Politics* 20, no. 10 (2019), 1–14.

Mohsin, Amena. *The Politics of Nationalism: The Case of the Chittagong Hill Tracts, Bangladesh* (1997) (Dhaka: University Press Ltd., 2002).

Morawa, Alexander H. E. 'The United Nations Treaty Monitoring Bodies and Minority Rights, with particular Emphasis on the Human Rights Committee' in *Mechanisms for the Implementation of Minority Rights*, eds. M. Weller and A. H. E. Morawa (Strasbourg: Council of Europe Publishing, 2004), 29–53.

Mufti, Aamir. *Enlightenment in the Colony: The Jewish Question and the Crisis of Postcolonial Culture* (Princeton, NJ: Princeton University Press, 2007).

Mukherji, P. *All About Partition* (Calcutta: 2 Sreenath Das's Lane, 1905).

Mullerson, Rein. 'Minorities in Eastern Europe and the Former USSR: Problems, Tendencies and Protection'. *Modern Law Review* 56 (1993), 793–811.

Musgrave, Thomas D. *Self-Determination and National Minorities* (Oxford: Clarendon Press, 1997).

Mutua, Makau and Antony Anghie. 'What is TWAIL?'. *Proceedings of the Annual Meeting (American Society of International Law)* 94 (2000), 31–40.

Mutua, Makau. 'Savages, Victims, and Saviors: The Metaphor of Human Rights'. *Harvard International Law Journal* 42, no. 1 (2001), 201–245.

Mutua, Makau. 'Why Redraw the Map of Africa: A Moral and Legal Inquiry'. *Michigan Journal of International Law* 16, no. 4 (1995), 1113–1176.

Myint-U, Thant. *The Making of Modern Burma* (Cambridge: Cambridge University Press, 2001).

Nair, Tamara. 'The Rohingya of Myanmar and the Biopolitics of Hunger'. *Journal of Agriculture, Food Systems, and Community Development* 5, no. 4 (2015), 143–147.
Nanda, Ved P. 'Self-Determination in International Law: The Tragic Tale of Two Cities – Islamabad (West Pakistan) and Dacca (East Pakistan)'. *American Journal of International Law* 66, no. 2 (1972), 321–336.
Nandy, Ashis. 'State' in *The Development Dictionary: A Guide to Knowledge as Power*, ed. Wolfgang Sachs (London: Zed Books, 1992), 264–274.
Natesan, G. A. *Eminent Mussalmans* (Madras: G. A. Natesan & Co., 1926).
Nehru, Jawaharlal. *An Autobiography* (1936) (New Delhi: Oxford University Press, 2002).
Nehru, Jawaharlal. *The Discovery of India* (1946), 3rd ed. (New Delhi: Oxford University Press, 1999).
Nesiah, Vasuki. 'Priorities of Feminist Legal Research: A Sketch, A Draft Agenda, A Hint of an Outline...'. *feminists@law* 1, no. 1 (2011), 1–4.
Nesiah, Vasuki. 'Uncomfortable Alliances: Women, Peace, and Security in Sri Lanka' in *South Asian Feminisms*, eds. Ania Loomba and Ritty A. Lukose (Durham, NC: Duke University Press, 2012), 139–161.
Newman, Dwight. 'Why Majority Rights Matter in the Context of Ethno-Cultural Diversity: The Interlinkage of Minority Rights, Indigenous Rights, and Majority Rights' in *Ethno-Cultural Diversity and Human Rights*, ed. Gaetano Pentassuglia (Leiden: Brill-Nijhoff, 2018), 59–89.
Newman, Edward, Roland Paris, and Oliver P. Richmond. *New Perspectives on Liberal Peacebuilding* (Tokyo: United Nations University Press, 2009).
Nishimura, Lauren. 'Facing the Concentrated Burden of Development: Local Responses to Myanmar's Special Economic Zones' in *The Business of Transition: Law Reform, Development, and Economics in Myanmar*, ed. Melissa Crouch (Cambridge: Cambridge University Press, 2017), 176–197.
Noel, Sid (ed.). *From Power Sharing to Democracy* (Montreal: McGill-Queen's University Press, 2005).
Nu, U. *Burma Looks Ahead. Translation of selected speeches by the Honorable PM of the Union of Burma, delivered on various occasions from 19th July 1951 to 4th August 1952* (Rangoon: The Ministry of Information, Government of Burma, 1952).
O'Donoghue, Aoife. '"The Admixture of Feminine Weakness and Susceptibility": Gendered Personifications of the State in International Law'. *Melbourne Journal of International Law* 19, no. 1 (2018), 227–258.
Okafor, Obiora C. 'Critical Third World Approaches to International Law (TWAIL): Theory, Methodology, or Both?'. *International Community Law Review* 10, no. 4 (2008), 371–378.
Okafor, Obiora Chinedu. '"Righting", Restructuring, and Rejuvenating the Postcolonial African State: The Case for the Establishment of an AU Special

Commission on National Minorities'. *African Yearbook of International Law* (2006), 43–64.

Okafor, Obiora Chinedu. 'After Martyrdom: International Law, Sub-State Groups, and the Construction of Legitimate Statehood in Africa'. *Harvard International Law Journal* 41 (2000), 503–528.

Orford, Anne. 'Feminism, Imperialism and the Mission of International Law'. *Nordic Journal of International Law* 71 (2002), 275–296.

Orford, Anne. *International Authority and the Responsibility to Protect* (Cambridge: Cambridge University Press, 2011).

Orford, Anne. *Reading Humanitarian Intervention: Human Rights and the Use of Force in International Law* (Cambridge: Cambridge University Press, 2003).

Osaghae, Eghosa E. 'Human Rights and Ethnic Conflict Management: The Case of Nigeria'. *Journal of Peace Research* 33, no. 2 (1996), 171–188.

Otto, Dianne. 'The Exile of Inclusion: Reflections on Gender Issues in International Law over the Last Decade'. *Melbourne Journal of International Law* 10 (2009), 11–26.

Otto, Dianne. 'Power and Danger: Feminist Engagement with International Law through the UN Security Council'. *Australian Feminist Law Journal* 32 (2010), 97–121.

Özsu, Umut. '"In the Interests of Mankind as a Whole": Mohammed Bedjaoui's New International Economic Order'. *Humanity: An International Journal of Human Rights, Humanitarianism, and Development* 6, no. 1 (2015), 129–143.

Özsu, Umut. 'Grabbing Land Legally: A Marxist Analysis'. *Leiden Journal of International Law* 32, no. 2 (2019), 215–233.

Packer, John. 'Problems in Defining Minorities' in *Minority and Group Rights in the New Millennium*, eds. Deirdre Fottrell and Bill Bowring (Leiden: Brill, 1999), 223–273.

Pahuja, Sundhya and Luis Eslava. 'The State and International Law: A Reading from the Global South?'. *Humanity: An International Journal of Human Rights, Humanitarianism and Development* 11, no. 1 (2020), 118–138.

Pahuja, Sundhya. 'Rights as Regulation: The Integration of Development and Human Rights' in *The Intersection of Rights and Regulation: New Directions in Socio-Legal Scholarship*, ed. B. Moran (Surrey: Ashgate, 2007), 167–191.

Pahuja, Sundhya. *Decolonising International Law: Development, Economic Growth, and the Politics of Universality* (Cambridge: Cambridge University Press, 2011).

Papanek, G. F. *Pakistan's Development – Social Goals and Private Incentives* (Cambridge, MA: Harvard University Press, 1966).

Parashar, Archana and Jobair Alam. 'The National Laws of Myanmar: Making of Statelessness for the Rohingya'. *International Migration* 57, no. 1 (2019), 94–108.

Paris, Roland. 'International Peacebuilding and the *Mission Civilisatrice*'. *Review of International Studies* 28, no. 4 (2002), 637–656.
Paris, Roland. 'Peacebuilding and the Limits of Liberal Internationalism'. *International Security* 22, no. 2 (1997), 54–89.
Paris, Roland. 'Saving Liberal Peacebuilding'. *Review of International Studies* 36 (2010), 337–365.
Paris, Roland. *At War's End: Building Peace after Civil Conflict* (Cambridge: Cambridge University Press, 2004).
Parsons, Talcott. *Societies: Evolutionary and Comparative Perspectives* (New York: Prentice Hall, 1966).
Partition Proceedings, vols. I-VI (Alipore: West Bengal Government Press, 1950).
Payero-López, Lucia and Ephraim Nimni. 'The Liberal Democratic Deficit in Minority Representation: The Case of Spain' in *Ethno-Cultural Diversity and Human Rights*, ed. Gaetano Pentassuglia (Leiden: Brill-Nijhoff, 2018), 90–121.
Pellet, Alain. 'The Opinions of the Badinter Arbitration Committee: A Second Breath for the Self-Determination of Peoples'. *European Journal of International Law* 3 (1992), 178–185.
Pentassuglia, Gaetano. 'Do Human Rights Have Anything to Say about Group Autonomy?' in *Ethno-Cultural Diversity and Human Rights*, ed. Gaetano Pentassuglia (Leiden: Brill-Nijhoff, 2018), 125–167.
Pentassuglia, Gaetano. 'Introduction: The Unpacking of Ethno-Cultural Diversity' in *Ethno-Cultural Diversity and Human Rights*, ed. Gaetano Pentassuglia (Leiden: Brill-Nijhoff, 2018), 1–24.
Pentassuglia, Gaetano. *Minority Groups and Judicial Discourse in International Law* (The Hague: Martinus Nijhoff Publishers, 2009).
Phayre, Arthur P. *History of Burma* (London: Trubner & Co., 1883).
Phillips, Alan. 'Historical Background on the Declaration' in *The United Nations Declaration on Minorities: An Academic Account on the Occasion of Its 20th Anniversary (1992–2012)*, eds. Ugo Caruso and Rainer Hofmann (Leiden: BRILL, 2015), 3–18.
Piang, L. Lam Khan. 'Overlapping Territorial Claims and Ethnic Conflict in Manipur'. *South Asia Research* 35, no. 2 (2015), 158–176.
Pittaway, E. 'The Rohingya Refugees in Bangladesh: A Failure of the International Protection Regime' in *Protracted Displacement in Asia: No Place to Call Home*, ed. H. Adelman (Surrey: Ashgate, 2008), 83–106.
Pomerance, Michla. 'Methods of Self-Determination and the Argument of "Primitiveness"'. *Canadian Yearbook of International Law* 12 (1974), 38–66.
Poulantzas, Nicos. *Political Power and Social Classes* (London: New Left Books, 1973).
Preece, Jennifer. 'Minority Rights in Europe: From Westphalia to Helsinki'. *Review of International Studies* 23 (1997), 75–92.

Preece, Jennifer. 'National Minorities and International System'. *Politics* 18 (1998), 17–23.
Pringle, Rosemary and Sophie Watson. 'Fathers, Brothers, Mates: The Fraternal State in Australia' in *Playing the State: Australian Feminist Intervention*, ed. Sophie Watson (Sydney: Allen & Unwin, 1990), 229–243.
Puri, Jyoti. *Encountering Nationalism* (Hoboken, NJ: Wiley, 2004).
Rabushka, Alvin and Kenneth A. Shepsle. *Politics in Plural Societies: A Theory of Democratic Instability* (Columbus, OH: Charles E. Merrill, 1972).
Radan, Peter. 'Post-secession International Borders: A Critical Analysis of the Opinions of the Badinter Arbitration Commission'. *Melbourne University Law Review* 24 (2000), 50–76.
Radhakrishna, Meena. 'Of Apes and Ancestors: Evolutionary Science and Colonial Ethnography' in *Adivasis in Colonial India: Survivals, Resistance and Negotiation*, ed. Biswamoy Pati (New Delhi: Orient Blackswan Private Ltd., 2011), 31–54.
Rahman, Mizanur and Tanim H. Shawon (eds.). *Tying the Knot: Community Law Reform and Confidence Building in the CHT* (Dhaka: ELCOP, 2001).
Rajagopal, Balakrishnan. *International Law from Below: Development, Social Movement and Third World Resistance* (Cambridge: Cambridge University Press, 2003).
Ratner, Steven R. 'Drawing a Better Line: Uti Possidetis and the Borders of New States'. *American Journal of International Law* 90, no. 4 (1996), 590–624.
Ravnbøl, Camilla Ida. 'The Human Rights of Minority Women: Romani Women's Rights from a Perspective on International Human Rights Law and Politics'. *International Journal on Minority and Group Rights* 17, no. 1 (2010), 1–45.
Rees, Madeleine and Christine Chinkin. 'Exposing the Gendered Myth of Post-Conflict Transition: The Transformative Power of Economic and Social Rights'. *New York University Journal of International Law and Politics* 48 (2016), 1211–1226.
Research in International Law of the Harvard Law School. 'The Law of Nationality'. *American Journal of International Law* 23 no. 1 (1929), 21–79.
Robert Birsel and Thu Thu Aung, 'Myanmar army chief says Rohingya Muslims "not natives", numbers fleeing exaggerated', *Reuters*, 12 October 2017.
Robert Booth, 'Boris Johnson Caught on Camera Reciting Kipling in Myanmar Temple', *The Guardian*, 30 September 2017, available at www.theguardian.com.
Robinson, Francis. 'Review: Congress Muslims and Indian Nationalism'. *Modern Asian Studies* 23, no. 3 (1989), 609–619.
Rostow, Walt W. *The Stages of Economic Growth: A Non-Communist Manifesto* (Cambridge: Cambridge University Press, 1960).
Roucek, Joseph S. *The Working of the Minorities System under the League of Nations* (Prague: Orbis Publishing, 1929).
Roy, Raja Devasish. 'The Discordant Accord: Challenges in the Implementation of the Chittagong Hill Tracts Accord of 1997' in *Implementing Negotiated*

Agreements: The Real Challenge to Intrastate Peace, ed. M. Boltjes (The Hague: TMC Asser Press, 2007), 115–146.
Roy, Raja Devasish. 'Administration' in *The Chittagong Hill Tracts: Life and Nature at Risk*, ed. Philip Gain (Dhaka: Society for Environment and Human Development, 2000), 43–57.
Roy, Raja Devasish. 'Challenges for Juridical Pluralism and Customary Laws of Indigenous Peoples: The Case of the Chittagong Hill Tracts, Bangladesh'. *Arizona Journal of International & Comparative Law* 21, no. 1 (2004), 113–182.
Roy, Raja Tridiv. *The Departed Melody* (Islamabad: PPA Publications, 2003).
Salée, Daniel. 'Quebec Sovereignty and the Challenge of Linguistic and Ethnocultural Minorities: Identity, Difference, and the Politics of Ressentiment' in *Contemporary Quebec: Selected Readings and Commentaries*, eds. M. D. Behiels and M. Hayday (Montreal: McGill-Queen's University Press, 2011), 472–493.
Sandbrook, Richard. 'Transitions Without Consolidation: Democratization in Six African Cases'. *Third World Quarterly* 17, no. 1 (1996), 69–87.
Sarkar, Sumit. *Modern India 1885–1947* (New Delhi: Macmillan, 1983).
Sarkar, Sumit. *The Swadeshi Movement in Bengal 1903–1908* (1973), 2nd ed. (Ranikhet: Permanent Black, 2010).
Sarkar, Tanika. *Hindu Wife and Hindu Nation* (Ranikhet: Permanent Black, 2003).
Sarwar, M. G. *Global Energy Crisis and Bangladesh* (Dhaka: External Relations Division, Government of Bangladesh, 1980).
Sassen, Saskia. *Expulsions: Brutality and Complexity in the Global Economy* (Cambridge, MA: Harvard University Press, 2014).
Sassoon, Anne S. 'Passive Revolution and the Politics of Reform' in *Approaches to Gramsci*, ed. Anne S. Sassoon (London: Writers and Readers, 1982), 127–148.
Schmitt, Hans O. 'Decolonisation and Development in Burma'. *Journal of Development Studies* 4, no. 1 (1967), 97–108.
Schrijver, Nico. *Permanent Sovereignty over Natural Resources* (Cambridge: Cambridge University Press, 1997).
Scott, James C. *The Art of Not Being Governed: An Anarchist History of Upland Southeast Asia* (New Heaven, CT: Yale University Press, 2009).
Seervai, H. M. *Partition of India: Legend and Reality* (Bombay: Emmenem Publications Pvt. Ltd., 1990).
Senaratne, Kalana. 'Internal Self-Determination: A Critical Third World Perspective'. *Asian Journal of International Law* 3, no. 2 (2013), 305–339.
Serajuddin, A. M. 'The Chakma Tribe of the Chittagong Hill Tracts in the 18th Century'. *Journal of the Royal Asiatic Society of Great Britain and Ireland* 1 (1971), 90–98.
Shahabuddin, Mohammad. '"Ethnicity" in the International Law of Minority Protection: The Post–Cold War Context in Perspective'. *Leiden Journal of International Law* 25, no. 4 (2012), 885–907.

Shahabuddin, Mohammad. 'Ethnicity' in *Concepts for International Law: Contributions to Disciplinary Thoughts*, eds. Jean d'Aspremont and Sahib Singh (Gloucestershire: Edward Elgar, 2019), 279–293.
Shahabuddin, Mohammad. 'The Myth of Colonial Protection of Indigenous Peoples: The Case of the Chittagong Hill Tracts under British Rule'. *International Journal on Minority and Group Rights* 25, no. 2 (2018), 210–235.
Shahabuddin, Mohammad. *Ethnicity and International Law: Histories, Politics and Practices* (Cambridge: Cambridge University Press, 2016).
Shaw, Malcolm N. 'Peoples, Territorialism and Boundaries'. *European Journal of International Law* 3 (1997), 478–507.
Shils, Edward. 'Colour, the Universal Intellectual Community, and the Afro-Asian Intellectual'. *Daedalus* 96, no. 2 (Colour and Race) (1967), 279–295.
Shils, Edward. 'Political Development in the New States'. *Comparative Studies in Society and History* 2, no. 3 (1960), 265–292.
Shils, Edward. 'Primordial, Personal, Sacred, and Civil Ties'. *British Journal of Sociology* 8, no. 2 (1957), 130–145.
Siddiqi, Dina M. 'Secular Quests, National Others: Revisiting Bangladesh's Constituent Assembly Debates'. *Asian Affairs* 49, no. 2 (2018), 238–258.
Singh, Jaswant. *Jinnah: India-Partition-Independence* (New Delhi: Rupa Co., 2009).
Sinha, Pradip. *Nineteenth Century Bengal: Aspects of Social History* (Calcutta: Firma K. L. Mukhopadhyay, 1965).
Sloane, Robert D. 'Breaking the Genuine Link: The Contemporary International Legal Regulation of Nationality'. *Harvard International Law Review* 50, no. 1 (2009), 1–60.
Smart, R. B. *Burma Gazetteer* (Rangoon: Government Printing and Stationary, 1917).
Smith, Martin. *Burma: Insurgency and the Politics of Ethnicity* (London: Zed Books, 1991).
Sobhan, Rehman and Muzaffar Ahmad. *Public Enterprise in an Intermediate Regime: A Study in the Political Economy of Bangladesh* (Dhaka: Bangladesh Institute of Development Studies, 1980).
Sopher, David E. 'The Swidden/Wet Rice Transition in the Chittagong Hill'. *Annals of the Association of American Geographers* 54, no. 1 (1964), 107–126.
Sorens, Jason and William Ruger. 'Globalisation and Intrastate Conflict: An Empirical Analysis'. *Civil Wars* 14, no. 4 (2015), 381–401.
Southwick, Katherine. 'Preventing Mass Atrocities against the Stateless Rohingya in Myanmar: A Call for Solutions'. *Journal of International Affairs* 68, no. 2 (2015), 137–156.
Steiner, Henry J. 'Ideals and Counter-Ideals in the Struggle over Autonomy Regimes for Minorities'. *Notre Dame Law Review* 66 (1991), 1539–1560.
Strachey, John. *India* (London: Kegan Paul & Co., 1888).
Strachey, John. *India*, rev. ed. (London: Kegan Paul & Co., 1894).

Suriano, Gregory R. (ed.). *Great American Speeches* (New York: Gramercy Books, 1993).

Tadjbaksh, Shahrbanou. 'Conflicted Outcomes and Values: (Neo)Liberal Peace in Central Asia and Afghanistan'. *International Peacekeeping* 16, no. 5 (2009), 635-651.

Taha, Mai. 'Reimagining Bandung for Women at Work in Egypt: Law and the Woman between the Factory and the "Social Factory"' in *Bandung, Global History, and International Law*, eds. Luis Eslava, Michael Fakhri, and Vasuki Nesiah (Cambridge: Cambridge University Press, 2017), 337-354.

Takševa, Tatjana. 'Genocidal Rape, Enforced Impregnation, and the Discourse of Serbian National Identity'. *CLCWeb: Comparative Literature and Culture* 17, no. 3 (2015), available at www.doi.org/10.7771/1481-4374.2638.

Tan, Celine. *Governance through Development: Poverty Reduction Strategies, International Law and the Disciplining of Third World States* (London: Routledge, 2011).

Tesón, Fernando. 'Ethnicity, Human Rights, and Self-Determination' in *International Law and Ethnic Conflict*, ed. David Wippman (Ithaca, NY: Cornell University Press, 1998), 86-111.

Tesón, Fernando. 'The Kantian Theory of International Law'. *Columbia Law Review* 92 (1992), 53-102.

Than, Kyaw Mra. *The Extraction of Rakhine Divisional Establishment Gazetteers* (Dhaka: Type-script Manuscript, 1993).

The CHT Commission. *"Life is Not Ours": Land and Human in the Chittagong Hill Tracts, Bangladesh* (Dhaka: The CHT Commission, 1991).

Thein, Myat. *Economic Development of Myanmar* (Singapore: Institute of Southeast Asian Studies, 2004).

Thompson, John B. *Ideology and Modern Culture: Critical Social Theory in the Era of Mass Communication* (Cambridge: Polity Press, 1990).

Thompson, Richard H. *Theories of Ethnicity - A Critical Appraisal* (London: Greenwood Press, 1989).

Thornberry, Patrick. *International Law and the Rights of Minorities* (Oxford: Clarendon Press, 1991).

Tickner, J. Ann. 'Inadequate Providers? A Gendered Analysis of State and Security' in *The State in Transition: Reimagining Political Space*, eds. J. Camilleri, A. Jervis, and A. Paolini (Boulder, CO: Lynne Rienner Publishers, 1995), 125-137.

Tinker, Hugh. 'Pressure, Persuasion, Decision: Factors in the Partition of the Punjab, 15 August 1947'. *The Journal of Asian Studies* 36, no. 4 (1977), 695-704.

Trinidad, Jamie. *Self-Determination in Disputed Colonial Territories* (Cambridge: Cambridge University Press, 2018).

Tripura, Prashanta. 'Culture, Identity and Development' in *The Chittagong Hill Tracts: Life and Nature at Risk*, ed. Philip Gain (Dhaka: Society for Environment and Human Development, 2000), 97–105.

Tucker, R. (ed.). *The Marx and Engels Reader*, 2nd ed. (New York: Norton, 1978).

Tun, Than (ed.). *The Royal Orders of Burma, AD 1598–1885*, vol. IV & VII (1782–1787) (Kyoto: Kyoto University Centre for Southeast Asian Studies, 1988).

Tun, Than. 'Paya Lanma – Lord's Highway, over the Yoma – Yakhine Range'. *Journal of Asian and African Studies* 25 (1983), 233–241.

Tzouvala, Ntina. 'A False-Promise? Regulating Land-grabbing and the Post-colonial State'. *Leiden Journal of International Law* 32, no. 2 (2019), 235–253.

Uddin, Nasir. 'Paradigm of "Better Life": "Development" among the Khumi in the Chittagong Hill Tracts'. *Asian Ethnicity* 15, no. 1 (2014), 62–77.

Ullah, A. K. M. Ahsan. 'Rohingya Refugees to Bangladesh: Historical Exclusions and Contemporary Marginalisation'. *Journal of Immigrant & Refugee Studies* 9, no. 2 (2011), 139–161.

UNCHR, *Report of the United Nations High Commissioner for Human Rights, Economic and Social Council* (2014), UN Doc E/2014/86, para. 5.

UNCHR, *Report of the Special Rapporteur on the Right to Food: 'Large-scale Acquisitions and Leases: A Set of Minimum Principles and Measures to Address the Human Rights Challenge'* (2009), UN Doc A/HRC/13/33/Add.2, p. 1.

United Nations Commission on Human Rights. *Drafting Committee Reports on International Bill of Rights* (11 June 1947). UN Doc E/CN.4/AC.1/3/Add.1.

United Nations Commission on Human Rights. *Report of the 10th Session, 23 February–16 April 1954* (April 1954). UN Doc E/2573.

United Nations Commission on Human Rights. *Report of the Drafting Committee (1st session) on an International Bill of Rights* (1 July 1947). UN Doc E/CN.4/21.

United Nations Commission on Human Rights. *Report of the Third Session of the Sub-Commission on the Prevention of Discrimination and the Protection of Minorities to the Commission on Human Rights* (30 January 1950). UN Doc E/CN.4/358.

United Nations Economic and Social Council. *General United States Approach: Contribution by Professor Peter L. Berger, United States Expert* (26 November 1981). UN Doc E/CN. 4/ AC. 34/ WP. 13.

United Nations Economic and Social Council. *Report of the Secretary-General on the International Dimensions of the Right to Development as a Human Right* (2 January 1979). UN Doc E/CN. 4/1334.

United Nations Economic and Social Council. *Report of the Working Group of Governmental Experts on the Right to Development* (11 February 1982). UN Doc E/CN. 4/1489.

United Nations General Assembly. *2005 World Summit Outcome.* UNGA Resolution 60/1 (24 October 2005). UN Doc A/RES/60/1.

United Nations General Assembly. *Declaration on Principles of International Law concerning Friendly Relations and Cooperation among States in accordance with the Charter of the United Nations* (24 October 1970). UNGA Resolution 2625 (XXV). UN Doc A/RES/2625 (XXV).

United Nations General Assembly. *Declaration on the Establishment of a New International Economic Order* (1 May 1974). UNGA Resolution 3201 (S-VI). UN Doc A/RES/3201(S-VI).

United Nations General Assembly. *Declaration on the Granting of Independence to the Colonial Countries and Peoples* (14 December 1960). UNGA Resolution 1514 (XV). UN Doc A/RES/1514(XV).

United Nations General Assembly. *Declaration on the Right to Development* (4 December 1986). UNGA Resolution No. 41/128. UN Doc A/RES/41/128.

United Nations General Assembly. *Declaration on the Rights of Persons Belonging to National or Ethnic, Religious and Linguistic Minorities* (18 December 1992). UNGA Resolution 47/135. UN Doc A/RES/47/135.

United Nations General Assembly. *Draft International Covenants on Human Rights: Report of the Third Committee* (5 December 1951). UN Doc A/5000.

United Nations General Assembly. *Integrated Economic Development and Commercial Agreements* (12 January 1952). UNGA Resolution 523 (VI). UN Doc A/RES/523(VI).

United Nations General Assembly. *Principles which should Guide Members in Determining whether or not an Obligation Exists to Transmit the Information Called for under Article 73 e of the Charter* (15 December 1960). UNGA Resolution 1541. UN Doc A/RES/1541.

United Nations General Assembly. *Programme of Action on the Establishment of a New International Economic Order* (1 May 1974). UNGA Resolution 3202 (S-VI). UN Doc A/RES/3202(S-VI).

United Nations General Assembly. *Report of the Secretary General Concerning the Act of Self-Determination in West Irian* (6 November 1969). UN Doc A/7723.

United Nations General Assembly. *Report of the Special Rapporteur on the Situation of Human Rights in Myanmar 2016* (29 August 2016). UN Doc A/71/361.

United Nations General Assembly. *Report of the Special Rapporteur on the Situation of Human Rights in Myanmar 2018* (20 August 2018). UN Doc A/73/332.

United Nations General Assembly. *Right to Exploit Freely Natural Wealth and Resources* (21 December 1952). UNGA Resolution 626 (VIII). UN Doc A/RES/626(VIII).

United Nations General Assembly. *Right to Exploit Freely Natural Wealth and Resources* (21 December 1952). UNGA Resolution 626 (VII). UN Doc A/RES/626(VII).

United Nations General Assembly. *Declaration on the Right to Development* (4 December 1986). UNGA Resolution 41/128. UN Doc A/RES/41/128.

United Nations General Assembly. *Permanent Sovereignty over Natural Resources* (19 December 1961). UNGA Resolution 1803 (XVII). UN Doc A/RES/1720.

United Nations Human Rights Council. *Recommendations of the Forum on Minority Issues at its seventh session: Preventing and addressing violence and atrocity crimes targeted against minorities* (January 2014). UN Doc A/HRC/28/77.

United Nations Human Rights Council. *Recommendations of the Forum on Minority Issues at its third session, on minorities and effective participation in economic life* (January 2011). UN Doc A/HRC/16/46.

United Nations Human Rights Council. *Report of the Detailed Findings of the Independent International Fact-Finding Mission on Myanmar* (17 September 2018). UN Doc A/HRC/39/CRP2.

United Nations Secretary-General. *Implementing the Responsibility to Protect: Report of the Secretary-General* (12 January 2009). UN Doc A/63/677.

United Nations. *Revue des Nations Unies* 6, no. 2 (1957).

Unknown. 'Revolt in Chittagong Hill Tracts'. *Economic and Political Weekly* 13, no. 17 (1978), 76.

Van Panhuys, Haro. *The Role of Nationality in International Law: An Outline* (Leyden: A. W. Sythoff, 1959).

Van Schendal, Willem. 'The Invention of "Jumma": State Formation and Ethnicity in Southeastern Bangladesh'. *Modern Asian Studies* 26, no. 1 (1992), 95–128.

Van Schendel, Willem. *The Bengal Borderland: Beyond State and Nation in South Asia* (London: Anthem Press, 2004).

Von Frenz, Christian Raitz. *A Lesson Forgotten – Minority Protection under the League of Nations. The Case of the German Minority in Poland, 1920–1934* (New York: St. Martin's Press, 1999).

Von Herder, Johann Gottfried. 'Ideas towards a Philosophy of the History of Mankind' (1785) in *Modern Political Doctrines*, ed. Alfred Zimmern (Oxford: Oxford University Press, 1939), 164–167.

Von Herder, Johann Gottfried. 'Reflections on the Philosophy of the History of Mankind' (1791) in *The Nationalism Reader*, eds. Omar Dahbour and Micheline R. Ishay (Atlantic Highlands, NJ: Humanities Press, 1995), 48–57.

Von Ranke, Leopold. 'The Great Powers' (1833) in *The Nationalism Reader*, eds. Omar Dahbour and Micheline R. Ishay (Atlantic Highlands, NJ: Humanities Press, 1995), 156–159.

Weber, Max. *Economy and Society: An Outline of Imperative Sociology*, ed. Guenther Roth and Claus Wittich (Berkeley, CA: University of California Press, 1978).

Weissbrodt, David and Clay Collins. 'The Human Rights of Stateless Persons'. *Human Rights Quarterly* 28, no. 1 (2006), 245–276.
Wheatley, Steven. 'Deliberative Democracy and Minorities'. *European Journal of International Law* 14, no. 3 (2003), 507–527.
Wheatley, Steven. *Democracy, Minorities and International Law* (Cambridge: Cambridge University Press, 2005).
White, L. J. *Industrial Concentration and Economic Power in Pakistan* (Princeton, NJ: Princeton University Press, 1974).
Wilson, Horace H. *Narrative of the Burmese War, 1824–1826* (London: W. H. Allen and Co,. 1852).
Wilson, S. G. *Modern Movement among Moslems* (New York: Fleming H. Revell, 1916).
Wing, Adrien K. (ed.). *Critical Race Feminism: A Reader*, 2nd ed. (New York: New York University Press, 2003).
Wippman, David. 'Practical and Legal Constraints on Internal Power Sharing' in *International Law and Ethnic Conflict*, ed. David Wippman (Ithaca, NY: Cornell University Press, 1998), 211–241.
Wise, Laura, Robert Forster, and Christine Bell. *Local Peace Processes: Opportunities and Challenges for Women's Engagement* (Edinburgh: Global Justice Academy, University of Edinburgh, 2019).
Wood, Alexi Nicole. 'A Cultural Rite of Passage, or a Form of Torture: Female Genital Mutilation from an International Law Perspective'. *Hastings Women's Law Journal* 12, no. 2 (2001), 347–386.
Wood, Josh. 'Special Economic Zones: Gateway or Roadblock to Reform' in *The Business of Transition: Law Reform, Development, and Economics in Myanmar*, ed. Melissa Crouch (Cambridge: Cambridge University Press, 2017), 148–175.
Woods, Kevin. *Commercial Agriculture Expansion in Myanmar: Links to Deforestation, Conversion Timber and Land Disputes* (Washington, DC: Forest Trends, 2015).
Yegar, Moshe. *The Muslims of Burma: A Study of a Minority Group* (Wiesbaden: Otto Harrassowitz, 1972).
Yuval-Davis, Nira. *Gender and Nation* (London: Sage Publications, 1997).
Zaidi, A. Moin and Shaheda G. Zaidi (eds.). *The Encyclopaedia of the Indian National Congress*, vol. XXII (New Delhi: S. Chand & Co., 1981).
Zaidi, Z. H. 'The Political Motive in the Partition of Bengal'. *Journal of the Pakistan Historical Society* 12 (1964), 113–149.
Zakariya, Hasan S. 'Sovereignty over Natural Resources and the Search for a New International Economic Order' in *Legal Aspects of the New International Economic Order*, ed. Kamal Hossain (London: Frances Pinter Publishers Ltd., 1980), 208–219.

INDEX

969 Movement, 250, 251

Aaland Islands, 98, 99, 104
Abi-Saab, G., 209, 212
Åbo, 98, 99
ADB, 270, 271
Administrative services
　in British India, 45
Advisory Commission on Rakhine
　　State, 175, 176, 241, 251, 254
Advisory Committee
　of the Indian Constituent Assembly
　　minority protection, 64–82
Afghanistan, 226, 302
AFPFL, 177, 179
Africa, 13, 19, 35, 92, 94, 95, 99, 100,
　　118, 147, 206, 226, 280, 281, 287
　decolonisation, 101
　ethnic conflicts in, 5
　nation-building in, 5
　postcolonial boundaries, 90–105
　postcolonial states in, 4
　uti possidetis, 90–105
African Charter on Human and
　　Peoples' Rights, 150, 237
African Commission on Human and
　　Peoples' Rights, 13, 150, 151,
　　235, 237, 238
African Court on Human and Peoples'
　　Rights, 235
African Union, 99
Ahmed, S., 53
Ali, S. A., 52
Aligarh College, 51, 52, 53
Ambedkar, B. R., 64–82
Amnesty International, 257
Anghie, A., 5, 95, 203, 212
Anglo-Burma Wars, 11, 106, 113–116,
　　117, 242, 243, 244

Anglo-Indian communities, 43, 64–82
Anjumans, 52
Annan, K., 175, 241, 251, 254
Ansari, M. A., 53
Anticolonial ethno-nationalism, 17, 27,
　　35–36
　in India, 32–54
Arab, 108
Arab Spring, 304
Arakan, 10–14, 105–123, 177, 179,
　　242–247, 249, *See* Rakhine State
Arakan Army, 253
Arakanese Buddhists, 179
Arendt, H., 171–174
ARSA, 120, 253
Arya Samaj, 49
ASEAN, 11, 170, 171, 259
Asia, 13, 35, 92, 94, 95, 118, 147,
　　206, 287
Asian Relations Conference, 92
Assam, 43, 303
Assimilation, 65, 66, 83, 84,
　　139–175
Australian Aid, 271
Authoritarianism, 298
Ava, Kingdom of, 109–112, 113, 117
Awami League, 136
Azad, A. K., 40, 53

Badinter Commission, 102–104
Balkans, 283
Balochistan, 303
Bandarban, 133, 136
Bandung Conference, 92, 93, 206
Bangalee, 121–137, 148, 175–196,
　　284, 303
　exploitation of hill peoples by,
　　261–275
　immigrants, 242–247

335

INDEX

Bangladesh, 3, 8, 10–14, 18, 120, 121–137, 184, 186–196, 249, 250, 251, 257, 260, 261–275, 284, 292, 301, 303
   international organisations in, 18
   Rohingya refugees in, 1, 301
   war of independence, 291
Bangladesh Army, 15
Bankim, 36, 49
Base and superstructure, 59
Battle of Plassey, 109
BBC, 259
Bedjaoui, M., 214, 216
Belgium, 94
Belt and Road Initiative, 254
Bengal, 40–54, 55, 108, 109, 111, 113–116, 127–134
Bengal Provincial National Assembly, 127
Berlin Conference, 100
BJP, 303
Bolshevik Revolution, 98
Bombay, 45
Bosnia and Herzegovina, 102–104, 291
Boundaries
   of Arakan, 105–121
Boundary Commission, 127–134
Bourgeois class, 32–40, 266, 268, See Bourgeoisie
Bretton Woods Institutions, 207
British Government, 40–54
British imperialism, 40
British India, 11, 242–247
British Indian Ocean Territory, 96
British policy, 40–54, 66, 68
British rule, 11, 32–54, 109–112, 116, 121–137
Buddhism, 11, 107, 110, 183
Burkina Faso, 100
Burma, 10–14, 105–121, 175–186, 240–260
Burma Office, 118

CAA, 302, 303
Cabinet Mission Plan, 65, 66
Calcutta, 44, 45, 52, 242
Capitalism, 7–8, 32–40, 54–55, 82
Capotorti, F., 159

Catalonia, 192
CEDAW, 16
Central planning, 37–38, 77–82, See Economic planning
Chagos Archipelago, 96
Chakma, 121–137, 186–191, 261–264, 269
Chatterjee, P., 32–40, 77, 80
Chimni, B. S., 8, 18, 224, 225, 279, 283
China, 117
Chinese
   immigrants, 244, 245, 246
Chittagong, 108, 109–112, 121–137, 243, 249, 263, 274
CHT, 3, 10–14, 19, 111, 121–137, 186–196, 287, 290, 303
   economic development, 261–275
   hill women, 15
CHT Development Board, 266, 267
CHT Hill District Council, 191–196
CHT hill people, 8, 10–14, 121–137, 186–196, 281, 283, 285, 287, 288, 289
   economic development, 261–275
CHT Peace Accord, 137, 191–196, 198, 267, 272, 285, 287
CHT Regional Council, 191–196
CHT Regulation, 135, 186–191
CITIC, 253, 254
Citizen Scrutiny Cards, 181
Citizenship, 14, 37, 71–77, 119, 120, 171–174, 197, 290, 303
   of CHT hill people, 186–196
   of Rogingyas, 175–186
Citizenship (Amendment) Act, 302, See CAA
Citizenship Law, 180, 181
Civic state, 25–28
Civil society, 294
Civilisation, 24, 30, 95, 143, 202–206
Civilised, 141–144
Civilising mission, 203, 206
Class, 59, 60, 78, 79
   bourgeois and petty bourgeois, 32–40
Class interest, 32
Cold War, 4, 280
Collective rights, 139–175, 215–221

Colonial administration, 29, 36, 40–54, 83, 118, 124, 125, 242
Colonial borders, 94, *See* Colonial boundaries
Colonial boundaries, 2, 3, 6, 90–105, 137, 280–284
   international law, 9
   of Arakan, 105–121
   of Burma, 105–121
Colonial capitalism, 23, 32–40, 55, 242–247, 248
Colonial Declaration, 93, 94, 95, 96
Colonial peoples, 147
Colonial policies, 28–32, 36, 40–54, 129, 262
   India, 54–55
   of divide and rule, 27
Colonial rule, 23, 24, 28–32, 77, 241, 242–247, *See* Colonialism
   economic exploitation of CHT, 261–264
Colonial state, 37
Colonialism, 5, 7–8, 27, 36, 38–40, 44, 77, 82, 202–206, *See* Colonial rule
   of India, 54–55
Commercial forestry, 261–275
Communal organisations, 49
Communalism, 37, 38–54
Confederation, 153
Conflict studies, 24
Congo, 94
Congress Muslims, 53
Consciousness
   ideological, 58
Consociationalism, 156–159, 284–287
Constituent Assembly debates
   of Bangladesh, 186–191
   of India, 8, 55, 57, 64–82
Constitution of Bangladesh, 137, 186–196, 287
Constitution of India, 40, 66, 73, 76, 302
Constitution of Myanmar, 175–186, 189, 190
Constitution of Pakistan, 134–137
Cow protection, 74, 75, 76
Cow slaughter, 52
Cox's Bazar, 15, 107, 300

Crawford, J., 3
Croatia, 102–104
Cultural identity, 35
Cultural synthesis, 36
Culture, 202–206
Curzon, Lord, 43

Darwinism, 30, *See* Social Darwinism
Decentralisation, 299
Declaration on Friendly Relations, 151
Declaration on Minority Rights, 159–175, 229, 230, 235
Decolonisation, 3, 4, 5, 8, 84, 90–105, 137, 202, 206–215, 280
   of India, 8, 37
Delhi, 44, 50, 92, 130, 303
Deliberative democracy, 232
Democracy, 64, 152–153, 195, 205, 297
   post-conflict peacebuilding, 221–227
Democratic entitlement, 152–153, 183
Deoband, 53
Depressed community, 43, 64–82
Development, 14, 37–38, 77–82, 84, *See* Economic development
Developmentalism, 2, 6, 7–8, 10, 77–82, 200–240, *See* Economic development
   in Rakhine State, 252–258
   in the CHT, 261–275
   marginalisation of CHT hill people, 261–275
   marginalisation of minorities, 289
   peacebuilding in the CHT, 270–275
   post-conflict peacebuilding, 221–227
Dhaka, 43, 44, 108
Differential treatment
   of ethnic groups. *See* Group differentiation
Dissimulation, 70, 72, 82, 201, 227, 260, 276, 277–279
   ideological mode of operation, 61–64
Divide and rule, 27, 29, 31, 40–54, 63
   of India, 54–55
Divide et impera, 41, *See* Divide and rule
Domestic violence
   against women, 15

East Bengal, 40–54, 127–137
East India Company, 45, 109, 112, 122, 123–127, 242, 261
East Pakistan, 10, 127–137, 148, 264–270, 284
Eastern and Central Europe, 144–147
Economic development, 3, 10, 17, 37, 77–82, 84, 200–240, 277–279
  in minority rights discourse, 227–240
  marginalisation of Rohingya, 240–260
Economic imperialism, 84
Economic planning, 37–38
Elite-constructivism, 24, 25, 78
Elites
  dominant minority, 14
Engels, F., 58, 59
English education, 45, 48, 51
Enlightenment, 35–36, 141
Equality, 3, 120, 139–175, 177, 183, 189, 191–196, 198, 219, 277–279, 284–287
  Indian Constituent Assembly debates, 71–77
erga omnes, 147
Eritrea, 281
Ethiopia, 281
Ethnic attachments, 24, *See* Ethnicity
Ethnic cleansing, 1, 171, 258
Ethnic conflicts, 24, 174, 198, 221, 227, 285, 289
Ethnic entitlements, 36, 39
Ethnic federalism, 156–159
  in CHT, 191–196
Ethnic group comparison, 28–32
Ethnic identity, 25
Ethnic minorities, 13, 30, 196
  economic development, 227–240
Ethnic relations, 28–32
Ethnic tension, 5, 28–32, 78, 267, 285
Ethnic violence, 4, 23–25, *See* Ethnic tension
Ethnicity, 5, 24, 78
Ethno-national politics, 23–25, 28–32
Ethno-nationalism, 1, 23–25, 54–55, 56, 78, 82, 105
  geneses of, 7–8
  in India, 54–55
  in Indian nationalist movement, 40–54
  in postcolonial states, 5, 7–8, 25–28
Ethno-nationalist movements, 225
Ethno-religious, 54
Europe, 13, 35
European Framework Convention, 169
European Union, 281
Evolutionary progress, 30

Fact-Finding Mission on Myanmar, 1, 176, 183, 290
FAO, 251
Faraizi
  in Bengal, 46, 51
Federalism, 156–159, 280, 284–287
  in CHT, 191–196
Feminism, 290–297, *See* Feminist approaches
Feminist
  international lawyers, 290–297
  nationalist movements in India, 40
Feminist approaches, 16
  to statehood, 290–297
Finland, 98
Forced displacement, 227–240, 288
  of Rohingya, 252–258
Foreign investment, 211, 226, 252–258
Foreigners Act, 177, 178
Forum on Minority, 165, 239
Fragmentation, 72, 82, 159, 174, 196, 220, 276, 277–279
  ideological mode of operation, 61–64
France, 96
Free market economy, 288, 297
  peacebuilding in CHT, 270–275
  post-conflict peacebuilding, 221–227
FWAIL, 6

Gambia, 1
Ganapati festival, 52
Gandhi, M., 36–37, 50, 132
Geertz, C., 25–28, 38–40, 54, 61
Gender, 17, 290–297
Gender equality, 16
Genocide, 171
  against the Rohingya, 1

Genocide Convention, 1
German ideology, 58, 59, 143
Global constitutionalism, 294
Globalisation, 85, 203, 225, 226, 297–301
Governance feminism, 295, 296
Government of Burma Act, 247
Government of India Act, 43, 126, 129, 133, 134, 136
Gramsci, A., 32–40
Great War, 90
Group differentiation
   colonial policy of, 28–32
Group identity, 72
Group rights, 9–10, 84, 139–175, 191–196, 198, 284–287
   economic development, 215–221

Hegel, G. W. F., 58, 141, 142
Hindu bourgeoisie, 40–55
Hindu communalism, 52
Hindu landlord, 45
Hindu Mahasabha, 129
Hindu Raj, 50
Hindu reform, 49
Hindu revivalism, 49, 52
Hinduism, 40–54
Hindu-Muslim, 36–37, 38–55, 127–134, 303
Hindus, 40–54, 64–82, 127–134
Hindutva, 76, 303
Horowitz, D., 28–32, 38–40, 44, 54
Hossain, K., 208
Human rights, 3, 65, 83, 84, 139–175, 196, 197, 199, 206, 207, 210, 211, 212, 213, 215–221, 238, 258–260, 284–287, 297
   approach to minority protection, 9–10
   of women, 16
Human Rights Commission, 170, 210, 213, 218, 219, 256, See Human Rights Council
Human Rights Committee, 159–175, 232
Human Rights Council, 1, 171, 176, 236, 300

Humanitarian intervention, 184
Hunter Commission Report, 45

ICCPR, 157, 158, 159–175, 213, 218, 232, 233
ICESCR, 192
ICJ, 1, 96, 99, 100, 148
Ideology, 61–64
   international law
   postcolonial states and minority, 8–10
   marginalisation of minorities, 3–5, 7–8
   meaning of, 57–61
   of postcolonial India
   religious minorities, 64–82
   of the postcolonial state, 3–5, 6, 7–8, 55
Ideology of developmental state
India
   Constituent Assembly debates, 77–82
   international law, 200–240
Ideology of liberal state
India
   Constituent Assembly debates, 71–77
   international law, 139–175
Ideology of national state
India, 64–71
   international law, 90–105
Ideology of the postcolonial state, 277–279
IFIs, 224, 225, 260, 287
ILO Convention, 13, 233, 234, 236, 287
IMF, 223, 252
India, 8, 10–14, 91, 112, 114, 116, 121–137
   anticolonial ethno-nationalism, 32–40
   anticolonial nationalist movement, 32–54
   Constituent Assembly debates, 64–82
   ideology of the developmental state, 77–82
   ideology of the liberal state, 71–77
   ideology of the national state, 64–71

India (cont.)
nationalist movements in, 3, 8
partition of, 25
social Darwinism in, 30
Indian community
in Burma, 116
Indian Home Rule League, 90
Indian Independence Act, 134
Indian National Congress, 39, 40–54, 64–82, 127–134
Indian-Christians, 43
Indigenous peoples, 39, 221, 227–240, 287
in Asia, 6
under international law, 10–14
Individualism, 139–175, 202–215
right to development, 215–221
Indonesia, 94, 95
Industrialisation, 206–215, 249
Instrumentalism, 24, 25, 78
Inter-American Court of Human Rights, 230, 235
International conflict feminism, 295
International institutions, 84, 203, 207, 258–260, 301
peacebuilding in CHT, 270–275
International law, 3, 137
colonial boundaries, 9
creation of postcolonial states, 5
creation of states, 3–5
development
minority protection, 200–240
economic development and developmentalsim, 200–240
ethnicity in, 24
ideological making of postcolonial states, 6
ideology of developmental state, 200–240
ideology of liberal state, 139–175
ideology of national state, 90–105
ideology of the postcolonial state, 3–5, 8–10, 82–85, 277–279
individual and group rights, 16
marginalisation of minorities, 3–5, 8–10
postcolonial boundaries, 90–105, 280–284

postcolonial developmental state, 10, 82–85
postcolonial liberal state, 9–10, 82–85
postcolonial national state, 9, 82–85
uti possidetis, 90–105
IS, 303, 304
Islam, 107, 183
Islamic tradition, 50
Israel, 304

Jammu and Kashmir, 302
Jihad, 51
Jinnah, M. A., 53, 119
Johnson, B., 240, 241
Joom cultivation, 123, 261–275
jus cogens, 84

Kaladan Project, 253
Kant, I., 141, 152, 154, 298
Kaptai dam, 264–270, 274
Karnaphuli Paper Mill, 265, 266
Katanga, 94, 99, 150, 151
Khagrachari, 136
Khan, Nawab Salimullah, 44
Khan, S. A., 51
Kosovo, 149, 150
Kurdish minority, 303, 304
Kyaukpyu projects, 253, 254, 255

Land grabbing, 227–240
against Rohingya, 252–258
in the CHT, 261–275
Land rights, 227–240
Latif, A., 51
Latin America, 19, 97, 99, 100, 101
uti possidetis, 90–105
League of Nations, 144–147, 197
Commission of Jurists, 98
Commission of Rapporteurs, 98
Mandate System, 202–206
Lebanon, 286
Legitimation, 70, 72, 82, 196, 201, 227, 260, 275, 276, 277–279
ideological mode of operation, 61–64
Lewin, T. H., 111, 121, 134, 263
Liberal constitutionalism, 37, 38, 71–77, 196, 284–287

INDEX

Liberal democracy, 152–153, 224
Liberal feminism, 296, 297
Liberal individualism, 3, 6, 9–10, 17, 83, 139–175, 193, 196, 197, 284–287, 288, 289, *See* Liberalism
  Indian Constituent Assembly debates, 71–77
Liberal tradition, 24, 160
  of the 19th century, 141–144
Liberal universalism, 190, 285
Liberalism, 7–8, 48, 139–175, 191–196, 213, 299
Liberation war
  of Bangladesh, 11, 15
Lok-Dessallien, R., 258
Lower Burma, 242–247

Madras, 45
Mahamuni, 110
Majoritarian, 65, 72, 83, 175, 197, 259, 276
Mali, 100
Mandalay, 109, 240, 249
Mandate System, 202–206
Marks, S., 17, 57–61, 63, 64
Marx, K., 57–61
Marxism, 32–40
Masculinity, 290–297
Mass mobilisation, 32, 36, 48, 49, 50
Material condition, 58
  of capitalism, 33
Mauritius, 96
Middle East, 108, 304
Migration, 29, 68, 122, 250
  to Burma, 242–247
Militant nationalists
  of India, 49
Minorities, 55, 57, 82–85, 90–105, 139–175, 284–287, *See* Minority groups
  definition of, 159, 160
  feminist approach to, 17
  future of statehood, 297–301
  global order, 297–301
  in Indian Constitution, 8
  India
    marginalisation of, 64–82

  marginalisation of, 3
  international law and ideology, 8–10
  oppression of, 1
  postcolonial boundaries, 90–105
Minority groups, 23–25
  marginalisation of, 6
Minority protection, 3, 4, 65, 67, 69, 138, 139–175, *See* Minority rights
  economic development, 200–240
  feminist approaches to, 290–297
Minority protection mechanism
  under the League of Nations, 144–147
Minority rights, 2, 4, 5, 10, 65, 72
  under international law, 6, 10–14
Minority treaties, 144–147
Minority women, 15
Modern state, 38–40
  of India, 54–55
Modernist, 25, 48, 54, 55
  response to primordial attachments, 25–28
Modernity, 24, 35–36, 37–40, 48, 201, 204, 207, 221, 276
Modi, N., 76, 302
Mohammedans, 40–54, 107
Molecular transformation, 34
  passive revolution, 33
Moment of Arrival, 37–38
Moment of Departure, 36
Moment of Manoeuvre, 36–37, 48
Mountbatten, Lord, 131, 132
Mughals, 107, 108, 123–127, 261–264
Mughs, 111, 112, 121
Muhammadan Literary Society, 52
Multiculturalism, 143
Muslim aristocracy
  of north India, 45
Muslim bourgeoisie, 40–55
Muslim League, 39, 40–54, 64–82, 127–134
Muslim peasantry, 45
Muslim revivalism, 52
Muslim rule, 49
Muslim upper class. *See* Muslim bourgeoisie

Muslims, 11, 35–36, 38–54, 64–82, 127–134, 303
Mussulmans, 40–54, *See* Mohammedans
Myanmar, 1, 3, 8, 10–14, 15, 18, 105–121, 131, 171, 175–186, 190, 240–260, 287
Myanmar Army, 1, 176, 290
Myanmar Sustainable Development Plan, 241

Nation, 5, 91
National ethnic races of Myanmar, 181
National identity, 65
National Planning Committee of Indian National Congress, 80, 81
National Register of Citizenship, 303, *See* NRC
National state, 37–38, 77, 79
National unity, 3, 7–8, 27, 79
   Constituent Assembly debates, 64–71
Nationalisation
   of Burmese economy, 248, 249
Nationalism, 23, 27, 48, 196, 197
   in non-Western world, 32
Nationalist consciousness, 35–36
Nationalist elites, 3, 48, 55, 64, 68, 92, 93, 287
Nationalist movements, 79
   in India, 36–37, 54
Nationalist politics, 36
Nationalist thought, 32–40
Nationality, 171–174
Nation-building, 5, 7–8, 25–28, 38–40, 64–71, 82, 139, 183, 190, 211, 221, 266, 285
Nation-state, 5, 13, 92, 137, 202, 284
NATO, 185
Natural resources, 200–240, 288
Nazi, 147
Nehru, J., 37–38, 40, 41, 64–82, 130, 131, 134
Neoliberal developmentalism, 200–240, 270–275
Neoliberal economy, 299
   post-conflict peacebuilding, 221–227

New Guinea, 94
NGOs, 261–275
NIEO, 84, 206–215, 216, 222, 288
Nigeria, 198, 285
Non-cooperation movement, 50
Non-discrimination, 3, 120, 139–175, 176, 177, 183, 189, 191–196, 198, 219, 277–279, 284–287
   Indian Constituent Assembly debates, 71–77
Non-interference, 83
Non-self-governing territories, 96, 97, 148, 161
North India, 49
NRC, 303

opinio juris, 100
Organisation of African Unity, 99, 100
   Charter of, 99
Orthodox Hinduism, 49
Orthodox Islam, 50
Otherness
   ethnicity as, 24

Pakistan, 11, 54, 64–82, 119, 121, 134–137, 186–191, 264–270, 274, 291, 302, 303
Palestine, 304
Paris Peace Conference, 90, 144–147
Partition
   of Bengal, 43, 47
   of India, 8, 10–14, 44, 54–55, 64–82, 127–134, 170, 264, 302
Partition Plan, 127–134
Passive Revolution, 55
   of capital, 32–40
Patel, S., 64–82, 130, 134
Patriarchy, 295
PCIJ, 146, 173
PCJS, 130
PCJSS, 190, 191, 271
Peacebuilding, 221–227, 260
   feminist approaches to, 294, 295
   in Rakhine State, 252–258
   in the CHT, 270–275
Peasantry, 36–37, 39, 51
Peoples, 84, 91, 206–215
Permanent Settlement, 45

Petty bourgeois class, 32–40, 54, 268
Polish Minority Treaty, 145, 146
Portuguese, 108
Postcolonial boundaries, 17, 83, 90–105, 277–279, 280–284
  of Burma, 105–121
Postcolonial developmental state, 3, 6, 7–8, 57, 277–279
  international law, 3, 10, 82–85, 200–240
  marginalisation of minorities, 200–240
Postcolonial liberal state, 3, 6, 7–8, 57, 139–175, 196, 199, 277–279
  international law, 3, 9–10, 82–85
Postcolonial national state, 3, 6, 7–8, 57, 89, 90–105, 137, 190, 212, 277–279
  India
    Constituent Assembly debates, 64–71
  international law, 3, 9, 82–85, 90–105
Postcolonial states, 3, 5, 17, 23–25, 54–55, 137
  ethnic violence in, 3
  ethno-nationalism in, 25–28, 56
  ethno-nationalist politics in, 28–32
  making of, 4, 6
  minority protection in, 4
Poulantzas, N., 58, 59
Power-sharing, 151, 156–159, 280, 284–287
  in CHT, 191–196
Preferential treatment
  of ethnic groups, 54
Primordial attachments, 28, 36, 37, 38–40
Primordialism, 24, 25–28, 54
Progress, 37–38, 202, 204, 207, 288
PSNR, 84, 206–215, 216, 222, 287
Public employment, 46
Punjab, 55, 127, 132

Qu'ran, 50
Québec, 148, 153

R2P, 184, 185, 283, *See* Responsibility to protect
Radcliffe, C., 128, 132
Rakhine Buddhists, 15, 105–121, 122, 181, 182, 240–260
Rakhine State, 1, 10–14, 105–121, 171, 175–186, 284, 287, *See* Arakan
Rangamati, 133, 136
Rangoon, 117, 244
Rape, 15, 290–297
Recognition
  of states, 5
Refugees, 301, 303
  Rohingya refugees, 1, 301
Regional autonomy, 151, 156–159, 198, 284–287
  in CHT, 186–196
Regionalism
  in CHT, 191–196
Reification, 82, 201, 276, 277–279
  ideological mode of operation, 61–64
Relations of production, 59
Relative group entitlement, 28–32, 44
Relative group legitimacy, 28–32, 39
Relative group worth, 28–32, 39
Religion, 10–14, 64–82
Religious communalism, 36–37
Religious obscurantism, 37
Religious reforms, 35, 48
Religious revivalism, 36–37
Religious violence, 47
Remedial self-determination, 183
Reorganisation
  of economic structures, 37–38
Reserved forests, 261–275
Resident Coordinator
  of UN Country Team in Myanmar, 258–260
Resistance, 14
Responsibility to protect, 3, 184, 185, 283, *See* R2P
Resurgence, Italian, 32, 33
RETF project, 273, 274
Rice economy, 242–247
Right to development, 213, 215–221, 222

INDEX

Right to participation
  in development policy-making, 227–240
  of CHT hill people, 270–275
Rohingya, 2, 8, 10–14, 15, 19, 131, 171, 175–186, 240–260, 281, 283, 284, 287, 288, 289, 290, 300
  Rohingya women, 290–297
Rohingya Muslims, 105–121, 133, 175–186, 240–260
Rohingya refugees, 15, 18, 184, 301
Roman law, 97, 281
Royal Order of Burma, 109–112, 114
Russia, 98
Rwandan genocide, 15

Secession, 94, 178, 183, 248, 279, 280–284
Secular
  India, 53
Secular nationalism, 52
Secular state, 69
  Indian Constituent Assembly debates, 71–77
Secularism, 71–77
Self-determination, 2, 3, 4, 5, 9–10, 79, 84, 90–105, 118, 137, 138, 139–175, 183, 184, 197, 206–215, 219, 280–287, 298, 300
  of CHT hill people, 191–196
Separate electorate, 40–54
Separate representation, 40–54, See Separate electorate
Separatism, 118
Sepoy Revolt, 41, 46, 51, 125, 262
Serbia, 102–104, 291
Settlement of Bangalees, 190
Sexual violence, 290–297
SFRY, 102–104, 162
Shanti Bahini, 271
SIDA, 271
Sikhs, 43, 64–82
Social conservatism, 49
Social Darwinism, 204
  monogenic and polygenic, 30
Social justice, 37–38
Social reforms, 48
South Asia, 11, 18, 120, 169, 170, 303

South Asian Regional Charter, 169, 170
South Sudan, 281, 284
Southeast Asia, 11
Sovereign equality, 9, 83
Sovereignty, 5, 209, 215, 219
Spain, 100
Spiritual, 48, 49
Sri Lanka, 195, 198, 226, 259, 295, 303
State
  nascent postcolonial state, 37–38
Statehood, 3, 5, 64, 84, 91, 151
  feminist approaches to, 17, 290–297
  future of, 297–301
  in international law, 6
Statelessness, 2, 171–174
  of Rogingyas, 175–186
Structural Adjustment Programmes, 224
Subaltern historiography, 39
Subaltern politics, 38
Sudan, 281
Sultanate of Bengal, 106, 107
Sunnah, 50
Supranational, 299
Supreme Court of Bangladesh, 191–196
Suu Kyi, A. S., 175, 241, 255, 256, 260
Sweden, 98

Tahzibul Akhlaq, 52
Tamil insurgency, 303
Tatmadaw, 1, 176, 290, See Myanmar Army
Territorial integrity, 9, 83, 90–105, 192, 215, 219, 279, 280–284
  Constituent Assembly debates, 64–71
Territory, 5, 90–105
Third World, 186, 206–215, 216, 283
Thompson, J., 7, 56, 58, 61–64
Totalitarianism, 298
Transitional justice
  feminist approaches to, 294
Tribal, 137, 154, 191
Tribal community, 64–82
Turkey, 303, 304
TWAIL, 5, 6, 18, 283, 297
TWAIL feminism, 297
Two nations theory, 55, 127

UDHR, 157, 159–175
UEHRD, 255, 256
Uighur Muslims, 301
UK, 96
UN Charter, 91, 93, 211, 222
UN General Assembly, 92, 94, 96, 184, 206–215, 222
UN Secretary-General, 218
UN Security Council, 185, 186, 207, 296
UN Special Rapporteurs, 176, 177
UNDP, 259
UNDP-CHTDF, 272, 273
UNDRIP, 13, 233, 234, 236
UNICEF, 271
Unification, 70, 82, 277–279
  ideological mode of operation, 61–64
Union Citizenship (Election) Act, 179
Union Citizenship Act, 179
Unitary state, 194, 195
United Nations, 1, 90–105, 133, 197
  in Myanmar, 258–260
United Nations Country Team
  in Myanmar, 258–260
Universalism, 141–144, 206
UPDF, 191
Upper Burma, 242–247
Urdu-Nagri controversy, 52
US State Department, 120
USA, 96
USAID, 265, 270, 271

USSR, 162
uti possidetis, 2, 9, 83, 90–105, 137, 147, 280–284, 292

Vulnerability, 14
  framework of minority protection, 297–301
  of minorities, 16, 289
  of minority women, 16

Wahabism
  in Bengal, 46, 50
War crimes, 303
War of position, 34
War on Terror, 297
West Bengal, 43, 127–134
West Irian, 94, 95
West Pakistan, 148, 264–270
Western democracies, 23
Western education, 53, *See* English education
Westphalia, 300
WFP, 251
WHO, 271
Wilson, W., 90, 91, 144–147
Women, 15, 290–297
Working class, 32, *See* Class
World Bank, 223, 224, 252, 259, 260, 265, 270, 273, 274
WTO, 252

Yazidi, 304

Zaminders, 51

CAMBRIDGE STUDIES IN INTERNATIONAL AND
COMPARATIVE LAW

Books in the Series

154 *Minorities and the Making of Postcolonial States in International Law*
Mohammad Shahabuddin

153 *Preclassical Conflict of Laws*
Nikitas E. Hatzimihail

152 *International Law and History: Modern Interfaces*
Ignacio de la Rasilla del Moral

151 *Marketing Global Justice: The Political Economy of International Criminal Law*
Christine Schwöbel-Patel

150 *International Status in the Shadow of Empire*
Cait Storr

149 *Treaties in Motion: The Evolution of Treaties from Formation to Termination*
Edited by Malgosia Fitzmaurice and Panos Merkouris

148 *Humanitarian Disarmament: An Historical Enquiry*
Treasa Dunworth

147 *Complementarity, Catalysts, Compliance: The International Criminal Court in Uganda, Kenya, and the Democratic Republic of Congo*
Christian M. De Vos

146 *Cyber Operations and International Law*
François Delerue

145 *Comparative Reasoning in International Courts and Tribunals*
Daniel Peat

144 *Maritime Delimitation as a Judicial Process*
Massimo Lando

143 *Prosecuting Sexual and Gender-Based Crimes at the International Criminal Court: Practice, Progress and Potential*
Rosemary Grey

142 *Capitalism as Civilisation: A History of International Law*
Ntina Tzouvala

141 *Sovereignty in China: A Genealogy of a Concept Since 1840*
Adele Carrai

140 *Narratives of Hunger in International Law: Feeding the World in Times of Climate Change*
Anne Saab

139 *Victim Reparation under the Ius Post Bellum: An Historical and Normative Perspective*
Shavana Musa

138 *The Analogy between States and International Organizations*
Fernando Lusa Bordin

137 *The Process of International Legal Reproduction: Inequality, Historiography, Resistance*
Rose Parfitt

136 *State Responsibility for Breaches of Investment Contracts*
Jean Ho

135 *Coalitions of the Willing and International Law: The Interplay between Formality and Informality*
Alejandro Rodiles

134 *Self-Determination in Disputed Colonial Territories*
Jamie Trinidad

133 *International Law as a Belief System*
Jean d'Aspremont

132 *Legal Consequences of Peremptory Norms in International Law*
Daniel Costelloe

131 *Third-Party Countermeasures in International Law*
Martin Dawidowicz

130 *Justification and Excuse in International Law: Concept and Theory of General Defences*
Federica Paddeu

129 *Exclusion from Public Space: A Comparative Constitutional Analysis*
Daniel Moeckli

128 *Provisional Measures before International Courts and Tribunals*
Cameron A. Miles

127 *Humanity at Sea: Maritime Migration and the Foundations of International Law*
Itamar Mann

126 *Beyond Human Rights: The Legal Status of the Individual in International Law*
Anne Peters

125 *The Doctrine of Odious Debt in International Law: A Restatement*
Jeff King

124 *Static and Evolutive Treaty Interpretation: A Functional Reconstruction*
Christian Djeffal

123 *Civil Liability in Europe for Terrorism-Related Risk*
Lucas Bergkamp, Michael Faure, Monika Hinteregger and Niels Philipsen

122 *Proportionality and Deference in Investor-State Arbitration: Balancing Investment Protection and Regulatory Autonomy*
Caroline Henckels

121 *International Law and Governance of Natural Resources in Conflict and Post-Conflict Situations*
Daniëlla Dam-de Jong

120 *Proof of Causation in Tort Law*
Sandy Steel

119 *The Formation and Identification of Rules of Customary International Law in International Investment Law*
Patrick Dumberry

118 *Religious Hatred and International Law: The Prohibition of Incitement to Violence or Discrimination*
Jeroen Temperman

117 *Taking Economic, Social and Cultural Rights Seriously in International Criminal Law*
Evelyne Schmid

116 *Climate Change Litigation: Regulatory Pathways to Cleaner Energy*
Jacqueline Peel and Hari M. Osofsky

115 *Mestizo International Law: A Global Intellectual History 1842–1933*
Arnulf Becker Lorca

114 *Sugar and the Making of International Trade Law*
Michael Fakhri

113 *Strategically Created Treaty Conflicts and the Politics of International Law*
Surabhi Ranganathan

112 *Investment Treaty Arbitration As Public International Law: Procedural Aspects and Implications*
Eric De Brabandere

111 *The New Entrants Problem in International Fisheries Law*
Andrew Serdy

110 *Substantive Protection under Investment Treaties: A Legal and Economic Analysis*
Jonathan Bonnitcha

109 *Popular Governance of Post-Conflict Reconstruction: The Role of International Law*
Matthew Saul

108 *Evolution of International Environmental Regimes: The Case of Climate Change*
Simone Schiele

107 *Judges, Law and War: The Judicial Development of International Humanitarian Law*
Shane Darcy

106 *Religious Offence and Human Rights: The Implications of Defamation of Religions*
Lorenz Langer

105 *Forum Shopping in International Adjudication: The Role of Preliminary Objections*
Luiz Eduardo Salles

104 *Domestic Politics and International Human Rights Tribunals: The Problem of Compliance*
Courtney Hillebrecht

103 *International Law and the Arctic*
Michael Byers

102 *Cooperation in the Law of Transboundary Water Resources*
Christina Leb

101 *Underwater Cultural Heritage and International Law*
Sarah Dromgoole

100 *State Responsibility: The General Part*
James Crawford

99 *The Origins of International Investment Law: Empire, Environment and the Safeguarding of Capital*
Kate Miles

98 *The Crime of Aggression under the Rome Statute of the International Criminal Court*
Carrie McDougall

97 *'Crimes against Peace' and International Law*
Kirsten Sellars

96 *Non-Legality in International Law: Unruly Law*
Fleur Johns

95 *Armed Conflict and Displacement: The Protection of Refugees and Displaced Persons under International Humanitarian Law*
Mélanie Jacques

94 *Foreign Investment and the Environment in International Law*
Jorge E. Viñuales

93 *The Human Rights Treaty Obligations of Peacekeepers*
Kjetil Mujezinović Larsen

92 *Cyber Warfare and the Laws of War*
Heather Harrison Dinniss

91 *The Right to Reparation in International Law for Victims of Armed Conflict*
Christine Evans

90 *Global Public Interest in International Investment Law*
Andreas Kulick

89 *State Immunity in International Law*
Xiaodong Yang

88 *Reparations and Victim Support in the International Criminal Court*
Conor McCarthy

87 *Reducing Genocide to Law: Definition, Meaning, and the Ultimate Crime*
Payam Akhavan

86 *Decolonising International Law: Development, Economic Growth and the Politics of Universality*
Sundhya Pahuja

85 *Complicity and the Law of State Responsibility*
Helmut Philipp Aust

84 *State Control over Private Military and Security Companies in Armed Conflict*
Hannah Tonkin

83 *'Fair and Equitable Treatment' in International Investment Law*
Roland Kläger

82 *The UN and Human Rights: Who Guards the Guardians?*
Guglielmo Verdirame

81 *Sovereign Defaults before International Courts and Tribunals*
Michael Waibel

80 *Making the Law of the Sea: A Study in the Development of International Law*
James Harrison

79 *Science and the Precautionary Principle in International Courts and Tribunals: Expert Evidence, Burden of Proof and Finality*
Caroline E. Foster

78 *Transition from Illegal Regimes under International Law*
Yaël Ronen

77 *Access to Asylum: International Refugee Law and the Globalisation of Migration Control*
Thomas Gammeltoft-Hansen

76 *Trading Fish, Saving Fish: The Interaction between Regimes in International Law*
Margaret A. Young

75 *The Individual in the International Legal System: Continuity and Change in International Law*
Kate Parlett

74 *'Armed Attack' and Article 51 of the UN Charter: Evolutions in Customary Law and Practice*
Tom Ruys

73 *Theatre of the Rule of Law: Transnational Legal Intervention in Theory and Practice*
Stephen Humphreys

72 *Science and Risk Regulation in International Law*
Jacqueline Peel

71 *The Participation of States in International Organisations: The Role of Human Rights and Democracy*
Alison Duxbury

70 *Legal Personality in International Law*
Roland Portmann

69 *Vicarious Liability in Tort: A Comparative Perspective*
Paula Giliker

68 *The Public International Law Theory of Hans Kelsen: Believing in Universal Law*
Jochen von Bernstorff

67 *Legitimacy and Legality in International Law: An Interactional Account*
Jutta Brunnée and Stephen J. Toope

66 *The Concept of Non-International Armed Conflict in International Humanitarian Law*
Anthony Cullen

65 *The Principle of Legality in International and Comparative Criminal Law*
Kenneth S. Gallant

64 *The Challenge of Child Labour in International Law*
Franziska Humbert

63 *Shipping Interdiction and the Law of the Sea*
Douglas Guilfoyle

62 *International Courts and Environmental Protection*
Tim Stephens

61 *Legal Principles in WTO Disputes*
Andrew D. Mitchell

60 *War Crimes in Internal Armed Conflicts*
Eve La Haye

59 *Humanitarian Occupation*
Gregory H. Fox

58 *The International Law of Environmental Impact Assessment: Process, Substance and Integration*
Neil Craik

57 *The Law and Practice of International Territorial Administration: Versailles to Iraq and Beyond*
Carsten Stahn

56 *United Nations Sanctions and the Rule of Law*
Jeremy Matam Farrall

55 *National Law in WTO Law: Effectiveness and Good Governance in the World Trading System*
Sharif Bhuiyan

54 *Cultural Products and the World Trade Organization*
Tania Voon

53 *The Threat of Force in International Law*
Nikolas Stürchler

52 *Indigenous Rights and United Nations Standards: Self-Determination, Culture and Land*
Alexandra Xanthaki

51 *International Refugee Law and Socio-Economic Rights: Refuge from Deprivation*
Michelle Foster

50 *The Protection of Cultural Property in Armed Conflict*
Roger O'Keefe

49 *Interpretation and Revision of International Boundary Decisions*
Kaiyan Homi Kaikobad

48 *Multinationals and Corporate Social Responsibility: Limitations and Opportunities in International Law*
Jennifer A. Zerk

47 *Judiciaries within Europe: A Comparative Review*
John Bell

46 *Law in Times of Crisis: Emergency Powers in Theory and Practice*
Oren Gross and Fionnuala Ní Aoláin

45 *Vessel-Source Marine Pollution: The Law and Politics of International Regulation*
Alan Khee-Jin Tan

44 *Enforcing Obligations* Erga Omnes *in International Law*
Christian J. Tams

43 *Non-Governmental Organisations in International Law*
Anna-Karin Lindblom

42   *Democracy, Minorities and International Law*
Steven Wheatley

41   *Prosecuting International Crimes: Selectivity and the International Criminal Law Regime*
Robert Cryer

40   *Compensation for Personal Injury in English, German and Italian Law: A Comparative Outline*
Basil Markesinis, Michael Coester, Guido Alpa and Augustus Ullstein

39   *Dispute Settlement in the UN Convention on the Law of the Sea*
Natalie Klein

38   *The International Protection of Internally Displaced Persons*
Catherine Phuong

37   *Imperialism, Sovereignty and the Making of International Law*
Antony Anghie

35   *Necessity, Proportionality and the Use of Force by States*
Judith Gardam

34   *International Legal Argument in the Permanent Court of International Justice: The Rise of the International Judiciary*
Ole Spiermann

32   *Great Powers and Outlaw States: Unequal Sovereigns in the International Legal Order* Gerry Simpson

31   *Local Remedies in International Law*
(second edition) Chittharanjan Felix Amerasinghe

30   *Reading Humanitarian Intervention: Human Rights and the Use of Force in International Law*
Anne Orford

29   *Conflict of Norms in Public International Law: How WTO Law Relates to Other Rules of International Law*
Joost Pauwelyn

27   *Transboundary Damage in International Law*
Hanqin Xue

25   *European Criminal Procedures*
Edited by Mireille Delmas-Marty and J. R. Spencer

24   *Accountability of Armed Opposition Groups in International Law*
Liesbeth Zegveld

23   *Sharing Transboundary Resources: International Law and Optimal Resource Use*
Eyal Benvenisti

22   *International Human Rights and Humanitarian Law*
René Provost

21   *Remedies against International Organisations*
Karel Wellens

20   *Diversity and Self-Determination in International Law*
Karen Knop

19 *The Law of Internal Armed Conflict*
Lindsay Moir

18 *International Commercial Arbitration and African States: Practice, Participation and Institutional Development*
Amazu A. Asouzu

17 *The Enforceability of Promises in European Contract Law*
James Gordley

16 *International Law in Antiquity*
David J. Bederman

15 *Money Laundering: A New International Law Enforcement Model*
Guy Stessens

14 *Good Faith in European Contract Law*
Reinhard Zimmermann and Simon Whittaker

13 *On Civil Procedure*
J. A. Jolowicz

12 *Trusts: A Comparative Study*
Maurizio Lupoi and Simon Dix

11 *The Right to Property in Commonwealth Constitutions*
Tom Allen

10 *International Organizations before National Courts*
August Reinisch

9 *The Changing International Law of High Seas Fisheries*
Francisco Orrego Vicuña

8 *Trade and the Environment: A Comparative Study of EC and US Law*
Damien Geradin

7 *Unjust Enrichment: A Study of Private Law and Public Values*
Hanoch Dagan

6 *Religious Liberty and International Law in Europe*
Malcolm D. Evans

5 *Ethics and Authority in International Law*
Alfred P. Rubin

4 *Sovereignty over Natural Resources: Balancing Rights and Duties*
Nico Schrijver

3 *The Polar Regions and the Development of International Law*
Donald R. Rothwell

2 *Fragmentation and the International Relations of Micro-States: Self-Determination and Statehood*
Jorri C. Duursma

1 *Principles of the Institutional Law of International Organizations*
C. F. Amerasinghe

CPSIA information can be obtained
at www.ICGtesting.com
Printed in the USA
LVHW011048030821
694401LV00005B/355